SUBSISTENCE AND SOCIETY IN PREHISTORY

Since the last few years of the 20th century, new scientific techniques have revolutionized our understanding of prehistoric economies. They enable a sound comprehension of human diet and subsistence in different environments, which is an essential framework for appreciating the rich tapestry of past human cultural variation. This volume first considers the origins of economic approaches in archaeology and the theoretical debates surrounding issues such as 'environmental determinism'. Using globally diverse examples, Alan K. Outram and Amy Bogaard critically investigate the best way to integrate newer lines of evidence such as ancient genetics, stable isotope analysis, organic residue chemistry and starch and phytolith studies with long-established forms of archaeobotanical and zooarchaeological data. Two case study chapters, on early Neolithic farming in central Europe, and the origins of domestic horses and pastoralism in central Asia, illustrate the benefit of a multi-proxy approach and how economic considerations feed into broader social and cultural questions.

Alan K. Outram is Professor of Archaeological Science at the University of Exeter. A zooarchaeolgist who specializes in the domestication of the horse, he has conducted extensive archaeological fieldwork in Europe, central Asia and North America. The former editor of *World Archaeology* and current editor of *Science and Technology of Archaeological Research*, he has published several ground-breaking publications in *Science* and *Nature*.

Amy Bogaard is Professor of Neolithic and Bronze Age at the University of Oxford. She is a botanically inclined archaeologist who specializes in the study of ancient agroecology and its social ramifications by conducting archaeological fieldwork alongside the study of present-day farming systems. She is the current executive editor of *World Archaeology*.

Subsistence and Society in Prehistory

New Directions in Economic Archaeology

ALAN K. OUTRAM

University of Exeter

AMY BOGAARD

University of Oxford

CAMBRIDGE
UNIVERSITY PRESS

CAMBRIDGE
UNIVERSITY PRESS

University Printing House, Cambridge CB2 8BS, United Kingdom

One Liberty Plaza, 20th Floor, New York, NY 10006, USA

477 Williamstown Road, Port Melbourne, VIC 3207, Australia

314-321, 3rd Floor, Plot 3, Splendor Forum, Jasola District Centre, New Delhi - 110025, India

103 Penang Road, #05-06/07, Visioncrest Commercial, Singapore 238467

Cambridge University Press is part of the University of Cambridge.

It furthers the University's mission by disseminating knowledge in the pursuit of education, learning and research at the highest international levels of excellence.

www.cambridge.org
Information on this title: www.cambridge.org/9781107128774
DOI : 10.1017/9781316415177

First published 2019

A catalogue record for this publication is available from the British Library

ISBN 978-1-107-12877-4 Hardback

In loving memory of Helen Outram

and

for Mike

Contents

Figures

Table

Preface

The 'palaeoeconomy' school of thought developed in Cambridge after the Second World War under the influence of Graham Clark and Eric Higgs. Whether meant as a term of endearment or disparagement, those who were taught by Higgs became known by some as 'Higglets'. Both of us, therefore, can be regarded as second generation Higglets. We were educated in this field during the 1990s, when many of the newer techniques discussed in this book were still in their infancy, largely by tutors who came out of the Cambridge palaeoeconomy stable. Both of us are products of the same year group who studied for an MSc in environmental archaeology and palaeoeconomy at Sheffield and whilst Amy stayed in Sheffield to undertake a PhD under Glynis Jones specializing in archaeobotany, Alan returned to Durham to do a zooarchaeology PhD supervised by Peter Rowley-Conwy, another Higglet. Since then we have worked extensively with a range of scientists specialized in residue chemistry, stable isotope analysis, genetics, plant ecology and a range of new morphometric and microscopic techniques. The time seemed right for us to recombine our efforts to produce a second generation Higglets' eye view of the field.

The 1990s was an interesting time to be studying environmental and economic approaches as such work was under attack from proponents of post-processual archaeology who rejected much of our type of work as 'determinist'. However, simultaneously, very powerful new scientific techniques for investigating diet and economy were coming into play within archaeological research, but often based in hard science departments or undertaken by people trained in chemistry or genetics rather than archaeology. The palaeoeconomy school, and processual archaeology in general, had developed a considerable theoretical framework, including Binfordian middle range theory, but was under attack from post-processualists whilst much of the new science was being undertaken outside any such framework.

None of this prevented much excellent work being undertaken, but what this book attempts to do is to address the post-processual criticism, take the best theoretical aspects of palaeoeconomy forward and integrate some of the key techniques that have become available since the school of thought was originally developed. A key aim of the book is to assess critically the inferences that can be made from these newer lines of evidence and how they differ and complement older techniques. In general we find that no single approach really replaces another, and none are 'silver bullets'. Multi-proxy approaches within a sound theoretical framework seem the best way forward. We have also attempted a little future-scoping for the key up-and-coming techniques and some of the challenges facing archaeology as it tries to keep pace with the financial and technical requirements of such science.

We would firstly like to thank all the people who taught us and inspired our approach to researching prehistoric subsistence and society in prehistory, including Paul Buckland, Mike Charles, Kevin Edwards, Paul Halstead, Glynis Jones, Peter Rowley-Conwy and Marek Zvelebil. We are also most grateful to our key research collaborators from whom we have learnt much about a wide range of techniques over the years. In this regard, special thanks go from both of us to Richard Evershed, but also to Robin Bendrey, Ian Bull, Lucy Cramp, Roz Gillis, Anthony Harding, John Hodgson, Martin Jones, Landon Karr, Christopher Knüsel, Sandra Olsen, Ludovic Orlando, Mélanie Roffet-Salque, Amy Styring, Adrian Timpson, Mark Thomas and Eske Willerslev. All of our colleagues and students, past and present, deserve our gratitude, but within this field of research particular thanks go to Robin Dennell, Laura Evis, José Iriarte, Emily Johnson, Greger Larson, Julia Lee-Thorp, Catriona McKenzie, Pip Parmenter, Alex Pryor, Rick Schulting and Naomi Sykes. We are indebted to both Paul Halstead and Richard Evershed for their valuable comments on an earlier version of this book.

Alan would like additionally to thank all the people he has worked with in Kazakhstan, including the many students who have helped him in the field. Special thanks are owed to Sandra Olsen, Victor Zaibert, Victor Varfolomeev, Emma Usmanova, Victor Mertz, Ilya Mertz, Sergey Babich, Sergey Sazhin, Nurbol Baimukhan, Elina Ananyevskaya, Aleksei Kasparov, Irina Shevina, Andre Logvin, Victor Logvin, Elena Isayev, Natalie Stear, Ivy Owens and Louise Anning. Seán Goddard and Emily Johnson have provided valuable assistance with illustrations and Sarah Barakat, Hannah Britton and Tereza Nesnidalova kindly helped set up cover image shots in our laboratories. Thanks also for the friendship and support of Bruce

Bradley, Oliver Creighton, Adrien Hannus, Linda Hurcombe and Stephen Rippon, and for constant encouragement from my parents, Helen and Derek, and brother, John.

Amy would like additionally to thank all of the people who opened doors into central European Neolithic research. Special thanks go to Peter Bogucki, Stefi Jacomet, Rüdiger Krause, Angela Kreuz, Jens Lüning, Ursula Maier, Manfred Rösch, Jörg Schibler, Helmut Schlichtherle, Hans-Christoph Strien and Alasdair Whittle. Thanks also to friends and family, near and far, for unfailing support.

Whilst not directly funding this book, we are exceedingly grateful to all the funding bodies who have supported our research in both the laboratory and the field, including the Natural Environment Research Council (UK), Arts and Humanities Research Council (UK), British Academy, National Science Foundation (US), European Research Council (EU), University of Exeter Archaeology Exploration Fund and Leverhulme Trust. Alan is also grateful to the University of Exeter for its general support and for a period of research leave to progress this volume.

CHAPTER 1

Introduction

> *"…ultimately all human culture and society is based upon and only made possible by biological and economic viability…"*
>
> Higgs and Jarman 1975: 2

In 1975 Eric Higgs and Michael Jarman laid out their manifesto for 'palaeoeconomy' as a specific approach to archaeological research. They were cognizant that the fully integrated study of social, demographic, ecological, technological and economic aspects of human communities was the ideal way to proceed, but argued that, in order to comprehend human cultural 'peculiarities', it was necessary to have a sound understanding of biological and economic influences. They also pressed the point that advances in science, in conjunction with a ubiquity of appropriate evidence, allowed for the very effective study of environment and economy, whilst archaeological methods dealt 'ineffectively or not at all' with many other aspects of human behaviour. They aimed to concentrate on 'predictable laws of human behaviour' (Higgs and Jarman 1975). This school of thought became intertwined with the 'New Archaeology', developed on both sides of the Atlantic by scholars such as Kent Flannery, David Clarke, Lewis Binford and Colin Renfrew (Trigger 1989; Johnson 1999), but it really had separate and earlier origins in Graham Clark's focus on 'the economic basis' for prehistoric life, which began prior to the Second World War (Fagan 2001). This book aims to examine the development of economic archaeology, its major achievements, the views of its critics and its legacy, but above all it aims to take the best elements from that approach and update them in the light of new techniques and theoretical perspectives.

Authors of textbooks on archaeological theory (e.g. Trigger 1989; Johnson 1999; Renfrew and Bahn 2012) almost inevitably, given the format of a book, outline theoretical paradigms sequentially; they describe the transition from antiquarianism to culture history and, post-war, the rise of functionalism, the New Archaeology and processual approaches, followed by post-processual and relativist ways of thinking. Our basic teaching of undergraduate archaeological theory largely follows the same pattern and it is all too easy to over-simplify that history as being a sequence of replacements. Of course, the real situation is much more complex and all of those approaches are still actively applied within modern archaeological research. The prevalence of different theoretical perspectives certainly varies geographically, but all are still practised, hopefully in dialogue with each other, but often also in unreconciled parallel. The heyday of the Cambridge-based palaeoeconomy school of thought generated many influential environmental archaeologists and their international diaspora has resulted in further generations of influential scholars still heavily influenced by foundations laid by Clark and Higgs.

The 1980s and 1990s saw considerable criticism of over-reliance upon universal, deterministic laws of behaviour that denied individual agency and the role of cultures (e.g. Hodder 1986; Thomas 1991). Few economic or environmental archaeologists, however, 'converted' to post-processualism, but they did take to heart some of the criticism. What resulted, in many cases, was research that attempted to 'move beyond protein and calories' (Russell 2012: 1) to deal with 'social' aspects of food procurement and consumption (e.g. Palmer and van der Veen 2002; O'Day, van Neer and Ervynck 2004; Overton and Hamilakis 2013). This line of research is a welcome addition to the practice of environmental archaeology. However, this book is not simply concerned with moving beyond matters of subsistence and economy, but in reconsidering the value of economic archaeology and the powerful role it can still play in interpreting past human behaviour. It is not the case that the economic basis for past human societies has already been fully understood and, given that any strict dichotomy between environment/economy and culture is fallacious, it remains as important as ever to gain a full understanding of it. There is bountiful evidence for the economic archaeologist to work with and its potential increases as scientific techniques develop. Subsistence needs to be put back into the study of past societies, but within a new, and more integrated, theoretical framework. There are exciting case studies of this kind of work, such as Marciniak's (2005) *Placing Animals in the Neolithic*, Halstead's (2014) *Two Oxen Ahead* or Sykes's (2014) *Beastly Questions*, which achieve an impressive balance of social, economic and scientific factors. This book aims to retain the significant achievements of the palaeoeconomy school, whilst revising aspects of its theoretical outlook and integrating new methodologies.

A plethora of significant new techniques have emerged since the 1970s, most of which relate to either biomolecular or microscopic evidence. In relation to biomolecular evidence, the extraction of ancient DNA (aDNA) first became possible in the early 1980s and by the middle of that decade it could be sequenced (Pääbo 1989). The first examples were based upon aDNA extracted from soft tissues, such as from museum specimens of the extinct quagga (Higuchi et al. 1984) and, of direct relevance to archaeology, an Egyptian mummy (Pääbo 1985). Extraction from bone started in the late 1980s, but robust precautions against contamination had really only developed by the late 1990s (Brown 2001). The field is, therefore, very young, but is now having massive impact on our understanding of domestication and colonization events, as well as population dynamics and the origins of particular phenotypes. Early archaeological use of stable isotope evidence to reconstruct aspects of human diet, initially levels of consumption of C_4 plants like maize, began in the late 1970s (e.g. Vogel and Van der Merwe 1977; Van der Merwe and Vogel 1978), but the field expanded massively from the 1990s to address much more complex questions of dietary reconstruction as well as issues such as origins and movement patterns of humans, plants and animals (Sealy 2001; Bogaard and Outram 2013). Isotopes have also played a key role in the development of lipid residue analysis. Whilst the molecular identification of certain organic residues in archaeological ceramics dates back to the 1970s (e.g. Condamin et al. 1976), the method was revolutionized in the 1990s by the introduction of carbon isotope ratio mass spectrometry (Evershed et al. 1994), which allowed more accurate origins of residues to be determined, eventually including important commodities like milk (Dudd and Evershed 1998). Since then, determination of hydrogen isotope ratios (e.g. Outram et al. 2009) has facilitated consideration of climatic and seasonal signals. Protein residue analysis techniques, initially based upon immunoassay, also developed during this same period (Gernaey et al. 2001; Smith and Wilson 2001), at first suffering, like early aDNA work, from issues of contamination and diagenesis, but also from cross-reactivity. The momentum in protein analysis now seems to have shifted towards mass spectrometry-based analyses such as ZooMS that allows for species recognition from collagen peptide 'fingerprinting' or 'barcoding' (Buckley et al. 2010, 2014; Collins et al. 2010).

The analysis of microscopic evidence, such as pollen, was already a long-established technique when the palaeoeconomic approach developed, but, of course, such methods have continued to be refined. However, there are also new classes of microscopic remains of economic significance now being routinely researched, such as phytoliths and starch grains. Whilst phytoliths were known about as far back as 1900, their regular study in American archaeological contexts did not take off until the late 1970s (Pearsall 2000). Starch grains have also been known about since the early 20th century, but their regular study in archaeobotany commenced in the 1980s (Piperno and Holst 1998). The great significance of these two new lines of evidence is that they open up to study a vast range of economically significant plants that otherwise happen not to produce macrofossils likely to preserve well through charring or desiccation, such a tubers (Iriarte 2007). They have had a revolutionary effect upon our understanding of past plant use and domestication in the Americas and tropical regions, but remain, perhaps, under-utilized in Europe.

Whilst the study of phytoliths and starch grains developed largely within the discipline of archaeology, the same is not true for the biomolecular techniques. Early practitioners of these techniques tended to be based in either biology or chemistry departments; indeed, many leading research groups in these fields still are. Of course, excellent research is continually being produced through appropriate multi-disciplinary collaborations and many archaeology departments have brought biomolecular specialists into their fold. However, many biomolecular methods were developed outside the discipline and, in some cases, technical capabilities have forged ahead more quickly than appropriate interpretative frameworks. This book aims not only to update the canon of techniques available to palaeoeconomic research, but also to provide appropriate theoretical frameworks for their application alongside established techniques. This involves comparing and contrasting the site formation processes, taphonomy and quantification of each type of evidence, as well as highlighting the interpretative assumptions being made. Fortunately, weaknesses in one type of evidence are frequently strengths in others, offering fruitful ways forward.

The Origins and Development of Economic Prehistory

Grahame Clark was awarded his doctorate, entitled 'The Mesolithic, Neolithic, and Early Metal Age Industries of Britain' in 1934, and his many references to the work of pollen specialist Harry Godwin (Fagan 2001) already displayed an increasing awareness of environmental context. It was also in 1934 that geographer, ethnologist and sometime archaeologist, C. Daryll Forde published his highly influential volume *Habitat, Economy and Society* (Forde 1934). The vast majority of Forde's volume is dedicated to summarizing ethnological research regarding a series of pre-industrial peoples from around the world, but what is interesting is that

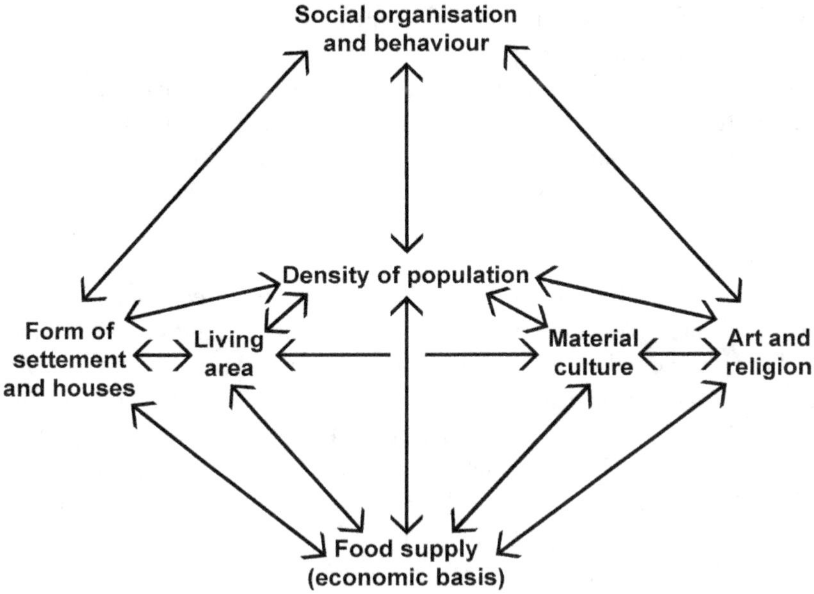

FIGURE 1.1 Clark's 1939 model from *Archaeology and Society* depicting the relationship between economic basis and other key factors of past society (after Clark 1939: 152).

they are divided into groups according to their mode of subsistence and there is a keen interest in their ecological setting. The volume concludes with generalized discussion of hunter-gatherers, pre-industrial farmers, pastoralists and the origins of domestic plants and animals. This discussion pays some considerable attention, in theoretical terms, to the relationship between environmental context, mode of subsistence and their interplay with human cultural agency. Forde is not often cited directly by Clark, but his work contributed significantly to the academic zeitgeist at a time when scientific approaches to archaeology were increasing.

By 1939, Clark had published the methodological work *Archaeology and Society: Reconstructing the Prehistoric Past,* which specifically considered food supply and the 'economic basis' of prehistoric peoples (Clark 1939: 152) and included a diagram modelling the interrelationships between economy, demographics, social organization, settlement and material culture (Fig. 1.1). This is an interesting emerging line of thought within the volume, but not a particular focus, as the book broadly covers other aspects of archaeological method in much more detail. Only later, revised editions of the volume contain a full chapter dedicated to economic reconstruction, based upon archaeological evidence, ethnographic parallels and palaeoenvironmental context (Clark 1957). It was in the post-war years that Clark more particularly focused upon economy and, after writing a series of subsistence-related papers (e.g. Clark 1942, 1947a, 1947b), he published *Prehistoric Europe: The Economic Basis* (Clark 1952) in the same year that he was appointed to the Disney Chair at Cambridge (Fagan 2001). This survey of prehistoric subsistence evidence in Europe expanded considerably upon earlier economic works, but also added the notion of progressive 'economic stages' (Clark 1952: 7) and the proposition that significant adjustments, indeed advancements, in economic systems occurred at times of environmental 'disequilibrium'. In this way, economic and environmental approaches to archaeology were presented as capable of considerable explanatory power. The following year, in addressing the British Academy, Clark outlined a specific 'economic approach to prehistory' (Clark 1953) which, by way of conclusion, he recognized was only one of many potential approaches, and not one that provided answers to all questions, but he noted that 'the influence of economic factors permeates all levels of social life'. The Star Carr excavation report, an exemplar case study of such an approach, followed the next year (Clark 1954).

Perhaps not everybody recognizes 'palaeoeconomy' as a major, independent school of archaeological thought, but there is a strong argument that by the 1970s, that is what it had become. Clark certainly did not limit himself to economic approaches alone and addressed a very wide range of prehistoric research questions; by the 1960s he was championing 'world prehistory' (Clark 1961). However, the concept of economic prehistory was being adopted by others and there was the start of a diaspora of Cambridge alumni to other regions of the world, who were schooled in that way of thinking (e.g. Nenquin 1961). The apex of the palaeoeconomy school within Cambridge, however, centred around the granting of a British Academy Major Research Project entitled 'The Early History of Agriculture' in 1966 (Clark 1972a). To direct this project, Clark and his management committee turned to Eric Higgs. Higgs was an experienced hill-farmer who had worked as a research assistant in Cambridge since 1956. He had a keen interest in human–animal interactions in prehistory and had field experience in the UK (Hurst Fen), Greece (Nea Nikomedia) and the Middle East (Cyrenaica, Iran) and led the project from its start until his death in 1976 (Clark 1989). Higgs, perhaps more than anybody, is associated with palaeoeconomy as a specific movement within archaeology and the group of researchers and students who surrounded him, during the heyday of the Early History of Agriculture project, generated a rich vein of new methodologies and evidence that created a step change in the field.

Whilst the diaspora of economic prehistorians had begun under Clark, the spread of this project's associates to teaching positions around the UK and internationally had a dramatic effect upon archaeological science and the way it interacted with environmental sciences and anthropology.

Michael Jarman was appointed as assistant director of the project (Clark 1989), whilst Heather Jarman was its secretary and Sebastian Payne an associated British Academy Fellow (Higgs 1972). From the start, the project involved research associates and collaborators at a number of other institutions, such as Claudio Vita-Finzi at University College London, Jane Renfrew at the University of Sheffield, Derek Webley at the Agricultural Development and Advisory Service in Cardiff (Clark 1989) and Gordon Hillman at the University of Reading (Higgs 1972). Within Cambridge, the post-graduates associated with Higg's group included names that would later prove very influential, such as Robin Dennell, Tony Legge, Derek Sturdy, Paul Wilkinson (Clark 1989) and Geoff Bailey (Jarman et al. 1982). Some other key figures at Cambridge to be heavily influenced by the palaeoeconomy school were Andrew Sherratt, Clive Gamble, Paul Halstead and Peter Rowley-Conwy, who were undergraduates at the height of the project, and John O'Shea, Glynis Jones and Marek Zvelebil who came to Cambridge as doctoral students.

The impact of the project and 'palaeoeconomy' went far and wide beyond Cambridge, and by the 1980s, it is arguable that the source of academic momentum for palaeoeconomy had shifted to the Department of Archaeology and Prehistory at the University of Sheffield. During that period Sheffield was home to Graeme Barker, Robin Dennell, Paul Halstead, Glynis Jones and Marek Zvelebil. With that skills base it obviously followed that the Department would become a centre for education relating to environment and economy in prehistory. The MSc in 'environmental archaeology and palaeoeconomy' was born and still runs. Particularly through the late 1980s and 1990s it trained a hugely significant proportion of currently active environmental archaeologists, including the authors of this book. Below, the major academic achievements of the palaeoeconomy school are outlined, but that movement's effects on the education of environmental archaeologists and bioarchaeologists, at Cambridge, Sheffield and more widely, should not be underestimated.

Key Legacies of the Palaeoeconomy School

To discuss only the outcomes of the specific British Academy project, in terms of the legacy of the palaeoeconomy school of thought, would be much too limiting. However, since there are still many active palaeoeconomists, of the first, second and third generations, some limits must be applied. It seems most appropriate to outline the principal achievements of palaeoeconomists from the end of the Second World War to the late 1980s, when post-processualism was gaining traction (e.g. Hodder 1986) on the one hand, whilst developments in the biological and physical sciences were about to herald new revolutions in bioarchaeology. Another way of looking at this is to think about the major advances made by palaeoeconomists from studying long-standing forms of physical evidence such as plant macrofossils, pollen, soils and faunal remains in the days before theoretical challenges from within archaeology and biomolecular advances from outside the discipline.

Since the early history of agriculture was the focus of the original project, this seems the best place to start. The British Academy project itself resulted in three edited volumes, *Papers in Economic Prehistory* (Higgs 1972), *Palaeoeconomy* (Higgs 1975) and, published after Higgs' death, *Early European Agriculture: Its Foundations and Development* (Jarman et al. 1982). The first of these volumes was divided off into three sections dealing with theory, methods and case studies (Higgs 1972). Perhaps the most striking aspect of the theoretical section is the careful consideration of territories, in an environmental and economic sense, with consideration of human mobility and change over time (Higgs and Vita-Finzi 1972). These considerations, of course, once many more data were available, became central to understanding the relationship between the origins of agriculture in the Near East and the detailed sequence of vegetation change through the late Pleistocene (see Hillman 1996). However, 'site catchment analysis', the specific application of these considerations to individual archaeological sites to understand 'the relationship between technology and those natural resources lying within economic range' (Vita-Finzi and Higgs 1970: 5), also became something of a hallmark of palaeoeconomic studies (see Fig. 1.2).

Site catchment analysis features in the case studies section of the first volume in relation to the Neolithic site of Tell Gezer (Webley 1972). This early application of the method considers also modern land use by traditional farmers and, hence, adds an ethnological aspect, as well as considering the evidence for environmental change within prehistoric periods. In the second project volume, exceptionally detailed use is made of site catchment analysis to elucidate settlement patterning in prehistoric Italy by both Barker (1975) and Jarman and Webley (1975), whilst Dennell and Webley (1975) applied the method to southern Bulgaria. This book concludes with appendices on how to carry out site catchment

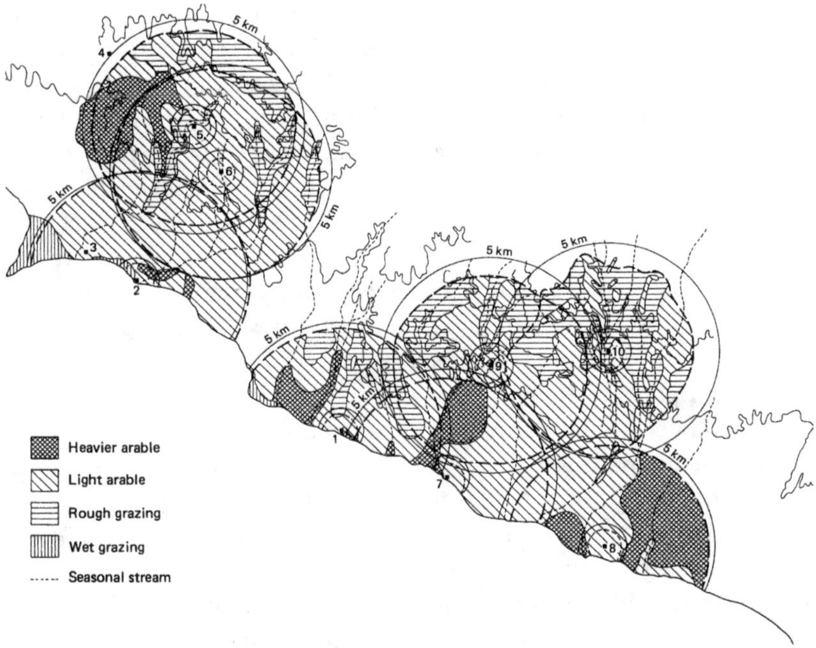

FIGURE 1.2 Site catchment analysis of a series of late Neolithic and early Bronze Age sites from central Macedonia: 1 Nea Kallikratia; 2 Kritsana; 3 Apanomi C; 4 Playiari; 5 Mesimeriani Toumba; 6 Mesimeri; 7 Veria; 8 Phloyita; 9 Nea Syllata; 10 Neo Triglia. Outer solid-line circles represent 5 km radius whilst dashed lines represent territories that could be walked within one hour. The 'one hour exploitation territories' are characterized by land type (reproduced with permission from Jarman et al. 1982: Fig. 60).

studies (Higgs 1975: Appendix A). Such analyses, and the more general mapping of geographical zones by economic potential, contributed very significantly to our understanding of the spread of farming societies within Europe and elsewhere. A clear example of the use of such an approach are the extensive palaeoeconomic discussions of the relationship between *Linearbandkeramik* (LBK or Linear Pottery Culture) settlement patterning and loess soils in Central Europe (e.g. Clark 1952; Barker 1985), a pattern first observed by German archaeologists (Buttler and Haberey 1936). Such observations regarding the ecological zones targeted by early farmers led to important new models for how colonization by farmers, or the adoption of agriculture by indigenous hunter-gatherers, may have proceeded. Simple models such as the 'wave of advance model' (Ammerman and Cavalli-Sforza 1973) were being challenged by more nuanced models, such as the 'pioneer colonization model' (Dennell 1985) that allows for selective colonization of fertile regions, delayed adoption of farming in areas sub-optimal for agriculture and continued occupation of some enclaves by hunter-gatherers. The 'availability model' (Zvelebil and Rowley-Conwy 1984, 1986; Zvelebil 1986) extends these principles further to consider a blurred boundary between farming and hunter-gathering where, between the two extremes, there are areas where agriculture is being adopted, the 'substitution phase', and regions where hunter-gatherers are in contact with farmers, known as the 'availability phase' (Fig. 1.3). During the availability phase the fundamental subsistence base has not yet changed, but the contact between groups inevitably has both social and economic implications, as later discussed in detail by Zvelebil (1998).

The final project volume (Jarman et al. 1982) features site catchment analysis on its cover and almost ubiquitously throughout. By the late 1970s, site catchment analysis was also gaining traction within America (Roper 1979) with leading 'New Archaeologists' such as Kent Flannery (1976a, 1976b) making significant, if not uncritical, use of the technique. One can have endless arguments over how best to undertake site catchment analysis, technically, or how to interpret the information gleaned, theoretically, but few would disregard the concept entirely, and viewing a site within its immediate environmental surroundings is now a routine aspect of archaeology.

The methodological section of *Papers in Economic Prehistory* (Higgs 1972) is quite heavily concerned with improving the recovery of environmental remains through such techniques as 'froth flotation' with chemical additives to improve retrieval of charred plant remains (H.N. Jarman et al. 1972) and understanding the biases caused by a failure to screen for small bone fragments (Payne 1972a). Clearly, an issue facing the new palaeoeconomy movement was the fact that most earlier excavations had not employed the techniques necessary to recover, or fully recover, the key forms of evidence they were interested in. The problem was particularly acute for the advancing environmental archaeologists, because, whereas ceramics specialists might happily be able to visit old museum collections of pottery and make good use of them, providing the provenance was sound, environmental specialists would need to carry out new fieldwork to make real progress. Two individuals associated with the British Academy project, Tony Legge and Gordon Hillman, saw their chance to do just that at Tell Abu Hureyra situated on the middle Euphrates in Syria. They joined with Andrew Moore to begin their own excavations on this important site, which spanned the critical periods from the Epipalaeolithic through to the ceramic Neolithic (Moore et al. 2000). This team's campaign of excavations

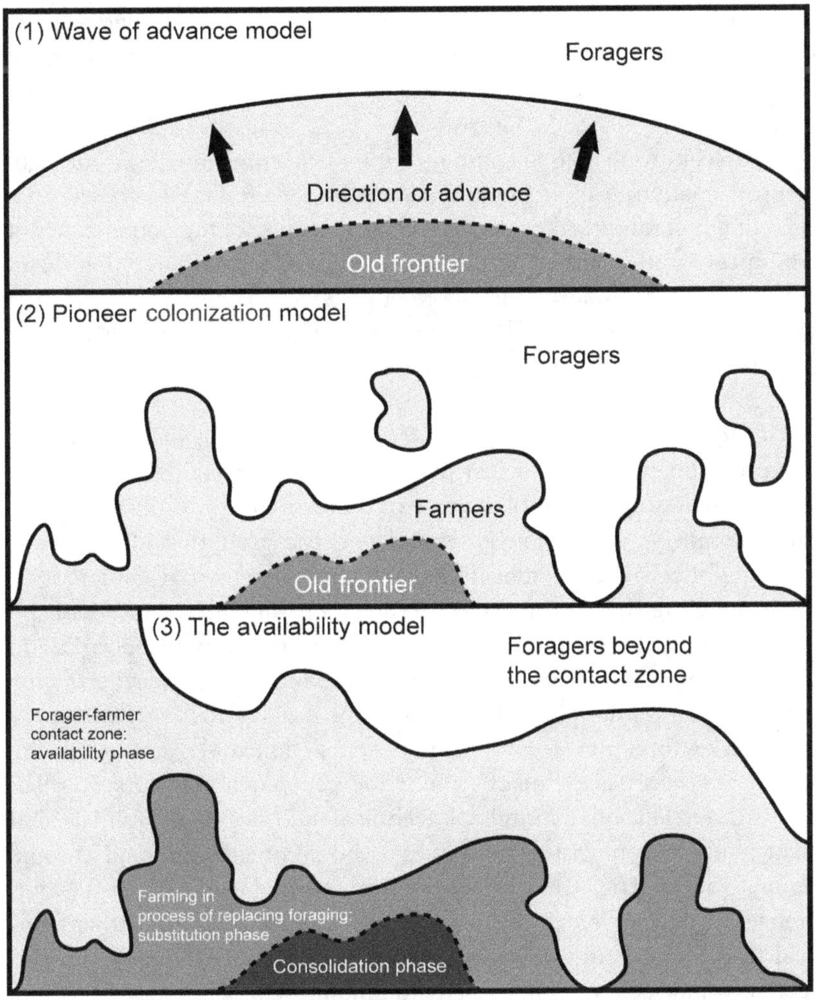

FIGURE 1.3 Different models for agricultural frontiers: (1) Wave of Advance; (2) Pioneer Colonization; (3) Availability (after Zvelebil 1986: Fig. 2).

at the site started in 1972 and was over by the end of 1973, but, with robust recovery techniques, the site yielded staggering amounts of environmental and economic data very quickly, leaving the team with a vast analytical task. Whilst a preliminary report was quickly published (Moore et al. 1975), money had to be raised to conduct the detailed study of the plant and animal remains during the 1980s. Hillman was joined by de Moulins in analysing the archaeobotanical remains, whilst Rowley-Conwy joined Legge in studying the faunal material (Moore et al. 2000). The amazingly detailed new economic sequence that emerged could be considered alongside ecological models of climatic and environmental change that might explain the initial impetus for agricultural origins in the Fertile Crescent (e.g. Henry 1985, 1989; McCorriston and Hole 1991). In so doing the Abu Hureyra team were able to come up with an exceptionally powerful argument in relation to the specific sequence at the site that was based on a great depth of empirical evidence and remains one of the cornerstones of our current understanding of Old World agricultural origins (Moore and Hillman 1992; Hillman 1996; Moore et al. 2000). The final full report, a 585-page volume entitled *Village on the Euphrates*, was eventually ready to be published some twenty-five years after the initial interim report (Moore et al. 2000).

The 1970s and 1980s were, in general, decades when methods for the interpretation of archaeological plant and animal remains saw very fast development. Key authors of major texts on these topics during this period came from a very wide range of academic backgrounds and schools of thought (for example regarding faunal remains: Chaplin 1971; Binford 1981; Klein and Cruz-Uribe 1984; Davis 1987 and for plant remains: van Zeist and Casperie 1984; Hastorf and Popper 1988; Zohary and Hopf 1988; Harris and Hillman 1989). As such, it would be wrong to claim that the palaeoeconomy school itself revolutionized these fields, but it did particularly develop a series of key interpretive tools. One of the significant advantages of the palaeoeconomists, also true of some of the new processual work, was that they moved beyond constrained technical knowledge of animals and plants, held by zoologists and botanists, who dominated the field in some regions. Indeed, Higgs insisted on training bone and seed specialists within Archaeology rather than making use of existing specialists from other fields (Halstead pers. comm.). Palaeoeconomists were interested more in human economy and society, within its environmental setting, rather than in the past plants and animals in-and-of-themselves. Hence, they were strong on the development of models to interpret empirical environmental evidence in terms of key features of human subsistence and settlement within the landscape as it changed over time.

The first British Academy project volume contains a methodological summary by Sebastian Payne on the information that can be retrieved from faunal assemblages (Payne 1972b). In this broad summary he considers the methods for establishing herd structures, in terms of age and sex ratios, and what they might mean. He was not the first to consider such issues. There had already been sound empirical work done on establishing age and sex ratios within the herds of some domestic animals (e.g. Higham 1966, 1968a,

1968b, 1969; Higham and Message 1969; Silver 1969) and also examples of understanding such patterning in wild animals. An example of the latter, in North America, was the study of age structures within bison at 'jump' type kill-sites (Frison and Reher 1970). However, building on earlier work (Ewbank et al. 1964), Payne (1973) was about to make a step change in the field by developing a rigorous new scheme for establishing age at death of sheep and goats from mandibular tooth eruption and wear. This ageing scheme became very much a standard method for zooarchaeologists, but, more importantly, Payne had developed a series of models that might allow one to understand whether the herd had been optimized for the use of meat, milk or wool. The models were constructed to show how the bone assemblages (deadstock) would accumulate if farmers managed their livestock towards a particular economic goal. In simplified terms, if a farmer is most interested in wool then they will keep both females and males alive to produce annual coats and will only kill animals once they are barren or no longer produce good wool. In the meat model females are kept alive, whilst fertile, to regenerate the herd whilst all but a few males, kept for breeding, are slaughtered when they reach full size and will yield no more meat. For a pure milk model, most males are killed close to birth to free up the mother's milk, apart from a few breeding males (Payne 1973) (Fig. 1.4). Zooarchaeological reports had so frequently, in the past, represented little more than a list of animals that people ate, kept, rode or hunted. This new kind of approach had massive potential to provide significant details about the big questions in the development of human economies.

Tony Legge also contributed significantly in this field. Early work on age profiles amongst gazelle in the Levant made him wonder if they had become semi-domesticated (Legge 1972), but later work at Abu Hureyra appeared to indicate that, in fact, early agriculturalists had stressed the gazelle population through over-hunting prior to the domestication of cattle, sheep and goats (Moore et al. 2000). At least as significant was Legge's work on interpreting the functions of cattle herds within British prehistory, particularly their use for dairying (Legge 1981). Around the same time, using a rather different evidence base, Andrew Sherratt had proposed a 'secondary products revolution' in the European Bronze Age, whereby he proposed that the human exploitation of animals intensified significantly to encompass the use of milk and other products, like labour, that could be gained without slaughtering the animal (Sherratt 1981, 1983). This was an influential and worthy theory, that holds reasonably true for some areas, but zooarchaeological herd-structure research very quickly started to question the simplicity of that model. Halstead (1989a) had studied

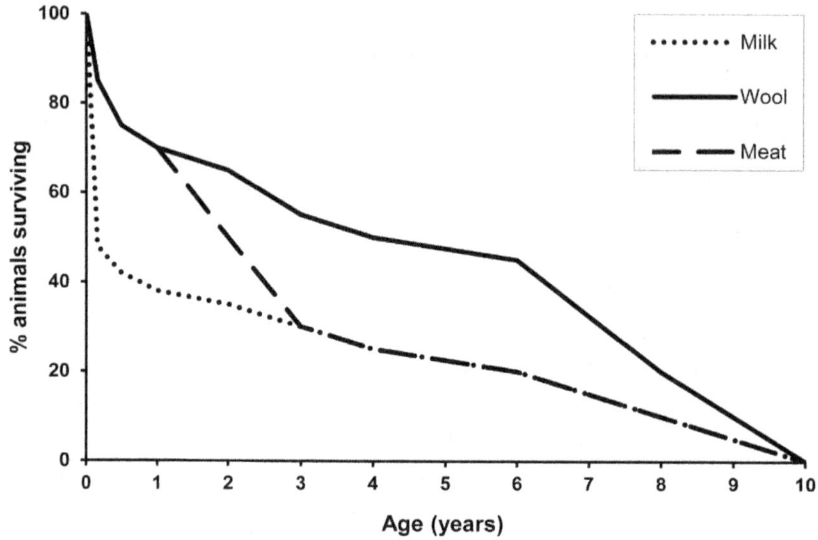

FIGURE 1.4 Models showing expected kill-off patterns of caprines if managed to maximize production of meat, milk or wool (following Payne 1973).

caprine herd structures in Neolithic south-east Europe and noted regions where there were hints at much earlier exploitation of milk, such as in the Alpine Foreland. It seemed more likely that the development of secondary product use was earlier than thought, in general, but also more patchwork in relation to the local environment and economic context, something Legge (1981) also stressed with regard to cattle husbandry in the Swiss Alpine Foreland.

Many mainstream archaeologists may have been sceptical over the reliability of such methods, but, in fact, much of this early herd-structure work has now been shown to be valid by recent intensive studies of ceramics for the absorbed lipid residues of dairy products (Copley et al. 2003, 2005a, 2005b, 2005c; Evershed et al. 2008; Cramp 2014). These studies support widespread dairying in Britain in the early Neolithic (Copley et al. 2003, 2005a, 2005b, 2005c; Cramp 2014) and, from some of the very earliest pottery available in the Neolithic of the Near East and south-east Europe, but with significant regional variation. In particular, it seems that cattle-dominated north-west Anatolia exploited milk much more extensively in the ceramic Neolithic (Evershed et al. 2008) than other regions, underlining the point about the environmental-context-specific nature of the secondary products revolution, at least if one assumes that there is not a radically different way in which pottery is utilized. Herd-structure analysis remains a key feature of current zooarchaeological studies, but the methods, resolution of data and interpretative models are being refined and debated (e.g. Vigne and Helmer 2007; Marom and Bar-Oz 2009; Brochier 2013; Gerbault et al. 2016).

In relation to the zooarchaeology of hunter-gatherer societies, the palaeoeconomists' impetus to refine methodologies had their roots in Clark's Star Carr excavations (1954). The bone assemblage at this early Mesolithic site in north Yorkshire was both large and well preserved, due to waterlogged conditions. This was certainly a rarity in Britain and so the assemblage offered a significant opportunity to understand Mesolithic economy and settlement in far more detail. The original faunal report was undertaken by Fraser and King (1954), who were zoologists from the British Museum Natural History (now the Natural History Museum, London). It is a detailed, if largely descriptive, report, that offered a significant interpretation with regard to the seasonality of the site. This interpretation was based upon the presence of the antlers of different deer species that shed at different times of year (Fraser and King 1954: Fig. 31). Clark later noted that he had particularly queried Fraser and King over the seasons of site use, so they took 'great trouble' over addressing that issue (Clarke 1972b: 23). To its credit, this study must be viewed as being amongst the first to deal with site seasonality through zooarchaeology. However, the basis for the conclusions was soon to be questioned on the grounds that antler might not be the best indicator of season and hunting activity levels because it might be collected and, indeed, curated (e.g. Caulfield 1978; Pitts 1979; Grigson 1981).

Partly because of the number of speculative reinterpretations of the Star Carr fauna, Legge and Rowley-Conwy (1988) decided to reanalyse the bone assemblage fully and applied many new techniques developed with the palaeoeconomy community, but also coming out of American processualist work, particularly that of Lewis Binford (1978, 1984). The result was highly innovative and represented one of the most detailed considerations of a faunal assemblage from that period. One of the novel aspects regarding their approach to the issue of seasonality was the use of tooth eruption sequences to establish the age of death of immature specimens of the different deer species present (Legge and Rowley-Conwy 1988) and thus work out the likely season of death based upon adding age to likely season of birth. This was a very significant methodological advancement, though it requires the acceptance of some uniformitarian assumptions, and arguments over Star Carr's seasonality continued (e.g. Carter 1997, 1998). Legge and Rowley-Conwy (1988) also addressed site function in detail by considering the relative abundance of skeletal parts and butchery patterns. To aid their interpretations, they made considerable use of ethnoarchaeological observations and utility indices in Binford's (1978) landmark work *Nunamiut Ethnoarchaeology*. Their final conclusion was that Star Carr had been a summer hunting camp (Legge and Rowley-Conwy 1988). Using zooarchaeology to understand economy, seasonality and settlement function was a significant advance on simply understanding which animal species people ate.

Rowley-Conwy (1987) went on to discuss the implications of the use of such methods for understanding the Mesolithic in North West Europe, more broadly, and applied his new methodologies to well-preserved sites of the Ertebølle Culture in southern Scandinavia (e.g. Rowley-Conwy 1998a, 1998b). Beyond merely representing methodological development within zooarchaeology, this work helped to characterize temperate late Mesolithic societies that did not resemble the classic, ethnography-based understanding of what hunter-gatherers societies should be like (e.g. Service 1966; Lee and DeVore 1968). Unlike the common perception of hunter-gatherers as mobile bands, Ertebølle peoples appeared to be much more sedentary, like native groups on the north-west coast of America (Rowley-Conwy 1981a, 1983). It was necessary to accept a much wider range of variability within hunter-gatherer societies (Rowley-Conwy 1986) and, in particular, no longer necessarily to view the more settled, ceramic-using societies of the later Mesolithic as simply being examples of cultures on their way to becoming farmers. This way of life could instead be seen as a relatively stable adaptation to the generally rich economic environment they inhabited, meaning, if anything, that farming represented much less relative advantage (Rowley-Conwy 1981a, 1986). This new understanding of temperate European Mesolithic societies goes a long way in explaining the significant hiatus between the rapid spread of *Linearbandkeramik* farmers and the eventual adoption of farming in North West Europe (Rowley-Conwy 1998b, 2001).

Experimental archaeology was another sub-field of the discipline that was significantly promoted within Cambridge at the same time as Higgs' tenure at the helm of the 'Early History of Agriculture Project'. In this instance, John Coles was the primary source of impetus, publishing *Archaeology by Experiment* in 1973 and *Experimental Archaeology* in 1979. It was during this period that experimental centres like Butser Ancient Farm were set up and began to produce interesting results (Reynolds 1979, 1981). The potential for experimental archaeology was also understood by the group of palaeoeconomists. For instance, the first volume of the early agriculture project contains a chapter that summarizes various experiments, around the world, into the domestication of different animal species (Wilkinson 1972). Experiments were, perhaps, more important to increasing our understanding of early cereal agriculture. For example, systematic experiments on wild wheat and barley were able to demonstrate the rate at which certain harvesting techniques followed by planting would result in the selection of the critical, tough-rachis phenotype that denotes domestication (Hillman and Davies 1990a, 1990b). Since plant remains are frequently preserved by charring, experiments into that process and its particular taphonomic biases were invaluable (Boardman and Jones 1990). Data from long-established agricultural experiments at Rothamsted could be used to re-evaluate the need for slash-and-burn agriculture in prehistoric temperate Europe, particularly given the availability of manure (Rowley-Conwy 1981b).

As well as interest in experiments, palaeoeconomy-minded archaeobotanists were also particularly interested in what could be learned about traditional agriculture from ethnoarchaeology. This approach predates Binford's (1978) ethnoarchaeological study of hunter-gatherers, and the sub-field of 'palaeoethnobotany' was first named by Danish scholar Hans Helbaek (1959). The integration of ethnology is so important that this term features heavily in the titles of major volumes on the study of ancient plant remains on both sides of the Atlantic (e.g. Hastorf and Popper 1988; Renfrew, 1991; Pearsall 2000). This approach was particularly fruitful in gaining a thorough understanding of the different stages to crop processing and, crucially, what the by-products or waste from each stage looked like (e.g. Hillman 1981, 1984; Jones 1984). This information would allow archaeobotanists to understand not just which crops were being consumed, but also how and where they were processed and stored, and in what form they were stored (e.g. Dennell 1976). It was becoming clear that it would be possible to reconstruct many more details of crop husbandry practices (Hillman 1981).

Further to understanding the botanical specifics of agriculture, ethnography is also extremely valuable in considering traditional agriculture more holistically, including consideration of the way household economies are run to serve both subsistence and social needs. A pre-eminent example of this is Hamish Forbes' work on traditional Greek rural communities (Forbes 1989), where he particularly considers individual farms' economic strategies to perceived risks. This study appeared in a volume entitled *Bad Year Economics: Cultural Responses to Risk and Uncertainty* (Halstead and O'Shea 1989a), which represents the inception of another key strand of the palaeoeconomy school's legacy. The economic models contained in this volume show very clearly how economic strategies relating to 'risk buffering' can elicit different cultural responses that can lead to significant social change (Halstead and O'Shea 1989b).

Perhaps one of the most powerful concepts presented in that volume was that of 'normal surplus' (Halstead 1989b). Considerable debate can be had over what constitutes a 'surplus' or, indeed 'affluence' (see Sahlins 1974), but, nonetheless, few would maintain an argument against the notion that agriculture has greater potential and tendency to over-produce relative to subsistence need, than does hunting and gathering, whether or not that makes one more affluent. The potential role that surplus could have played in facilitating social change, following the adoption of farming in the Neolithic, has long been appreciated. While some have seen surplus as an essential precursor to the rise of elites (e.g. Childe 1954), others have emphasized the role of elites in encouraging, possibly demanding, intensification to increase surplus (Sahlins 1974). Competitive 'peer polity' interaction would have led to greater complexity and specialization (Renfrew, 1982). Without the need to deny these mechanisms of change, what Halstead (1989) was arguing, based upon the kind of data generated by Forbes (1989), was that the day-to-day practice of cereal farming would tend to create surplus *without* the need for a specific impetus to create greater wealth or pressure from elites. On a household level, farmers plan to be able to withstand hazards and must decide how much grain they will need to replant to generate sufficient in next year's crop. They must make allowance for such disasters as bad weather, disease and animal trampling, but also the need to meet unforeseen social obligations related to such events as marriages. The result of building all these contingencies into an annual plan at a household level *normally* results in surplus, but the reason is risk buffering, not necessarily an explicit desire to become wealthier or develop elites (Halstead 1989). Forbes (1989: 91) shows that amongst the traditional Greek households he studied, the mean overproduction was 63%, with farmers stating that their motivation was defence against uncertainties rather than the desire to sell the excess for cash. Of course, a very small number of farmers still fared badly, having an insufficient buffer against what befell them, whilst others had exceptional good years. The concept of 'normal surplus' is exceptionally important, because it has the power to explain the origins of both surplus and inequality in early agricultural systems, that could later have led to significant social changes through mechanisms such as elite competition.

Above, some of the major achievements of the palaeoeconomic school have been outlined. An increasing interest in the application of science, combined with new theoretical frameworks resulted in a very productive period for economic archaeologists between the end of the Second World War and the 1980s. In terms of the philosophy of science, this is a good example of a period of 'normal science' (see Kuhn 1996). There was a post-war paradigm shift towards scientific approaches and a group of scholars worked productively within that paradigm in a general atmosphere of mutual methodological understanding. However, through the 1980s and increasingly in the 1990s, the whole area of study became considerably more theoretically complex. On the one hand, post-processualists were presenting significant criticisms of that scientific paradigm as well as proposing myriad new ways to approach the past. Post-processualism cannot be described easily for what it *is*, as it is defined by what it is *not*. Of course, scientifically minded processualists and palaeoeconomists continued their work, but there was by then a notable schism between different sections of the archaeological research community, often talking past each other and working independently, with rather different publishing patterns. This was also a period when new scientific methods were being developed and applied to archaeological questions from outside the discipline. The biologists, chemists, physicists and environmental scientists in question were clearly even more 'scientific' in outlook, but also less informed about the theories of archaeological interpretation. Economic archaeologists very happily worked with these scientists, which only accentuated some of the differences within the field.

The current situation is perhaps even more complex, with a vast array of different theoretical approaches being exploited and fascinating patterns of both co-operation and exclusion that, interestingly, affect different time periods and regions of study in different ways. This environment has significantly impacted on the sorts of questions that are in vogue within any given sub-field. When there are pressures to conform to particular research fashions, there is a danger that both stronger and weaker aspects of past research agendas will similarly be rejected to maintain the appearance of being 'on trend'. At this point, it seems that the great strengths of the palaeoeconomic school need to be restated, and the best aspects of it taken forward, whilst the key criticisms need to be either rebuffed or taken on board. Below there is a short discussion of key criticisms of scientific and economic approaches.

Criticism of Economic Approaches and its Impact

In a general sense, the post-processual movement in archaeology emerged as a result of the more widespread post-modernist (see Lyotard 1984) attack upon positivist (see Popper 1959) approaches to scientific enquiry. The post-modern criticism went further than simply questioning the objectivity of human scientists, and whether or not hypothesis testing and falsification were always possible in practice, and proposed a relativist world where almost anything goes. An early example of this genre would include Paul Feyerabend's 1975 volume *Against Method: An Outline of an Anarchist Theory of Knowledge*. However, as Johnson (1999) makes clear, post-modernism influenced post-processualists, but the two things are not synonymous, and not all post-processual work is relativist, indeed only a very small minority of such scholars could be characterized in such an extreme way. There is also much variation in perspective within post-processual thought (Hodder 2012), making it unwise to generalize too widely, other than to note that those who call themselves post-processualists shared a dissatisfaction with the rigidity of scientific hypothesis testing, as it was being practised, and the processualist adherence to claims of objective knowledge and metanarrative. They objected to narrowly functionalist and other reductionist approaches. They not only questioned what was being presented as objective fact, but also began to 'question the question' (Johnson 1999: 177). This is not the place to resolve these debates, but it is worth considering the specific criticisms made of economic approaches, and the effect they had on research trends within the discipline.

An early direct criticism of economic archaeology came from Tilley (1981) in a paper entitled 'Economy and Society: What Relationship?' It explicitly targeted the palaeoeconomic school of thought as well as other ideas that were ecologically framed or applied a systemic framework. This paper shared the post-modernist disdain for positivist hypothesis testing and falsification, but the main thrust of objection related to the reductionist nature of many economic models and interpretations. Such approaches, he argued, turn human actors into 'helpless spectators always subject to external forces over which they have very little control' suggesting that 'human intentions, motivations and meanings become dependent variables, functions of social, psychological or biological forces' (Tilley 1981: 131). Perhaps some in the palaeoeconomy school would simply have agreed with him and not understood why this was a criticism, but he goes on to counter that 'man is not a natural entity if we accept the primacy of sentience, intentionality, linguistic and symbolic communication' (Tilley 1981: 132). Hodder (1986: 4) argues that 'aspects of culture are *irreducible*' because 'cultural attitudes…cannot be predicted from or reduced to an environment' as 'cultural relationships are not caused by anything outside themselves'. The criticism of the palaeoeconomic approach hinges almost entirely around the charge of environmental determinism coupled with its perceived failure to acknowledge the impact of human agency or ask more social questions. The authors of this volume first studied environmental archaeology and palaeoeconomics in the 1990s when there was a particular trend, at least in the UK, to damn any work deemed to be 'environmentally determinist'. The criticism was influential and resulted in significant modifications to the way many environmental specialists conducted their work, either by changes being made to the types of questions being asked, or, where the line of enquiry was predominantly economic, great care in how conclusions were expressed.

From this period onwards there was an increasing trend for specialists in environmental forms of evidence to accentuate social research questions and present that research agenda as moving 'beyond' the preoccupation with environment, economy or diet (e.g. Palmer and van der Veen 2002; O'Day, et al. 2004; Russell 2012; Overton and Hamilakis 2013). Specific consideration of cultural and non-economic roles of plants, animals and landscapes can only be considered to be a positive addition to the field, though it could be argued that integrated and holistic study of these classes of evidence might be a better way to proceed than going 'beyond'. The frequent use of 'beyond', in this context, implies the replacement of core questions, rather than addition, but even if social questions should be foremost, it seems that understanding environment and economy provides, if nothing else, a useful contextual framework. Some of these works, therefore, could be charged with over-compensation for perceived earlier imbalance.

The reactionary effects of the 'determinism' criticism were even more dramatic within the works of those who associated themselves directly with post-processualism. Hodder (1990) rethought the origins of agriculture in terms of a symbolic domestication of society, inventing the term '*domus*' to represent this concept. Rather more clumsily, in discussing the transition to the Neolithic in Britain, Thomas (1999: Fig. 2.1) produced a diagram that showed instant change in material culture at the start of the Neolithic and only very gradual change in economy, which only becomes fully agricultural by the middle Bronze Age. This very conscious uncoupling of economy from material culture was not, even then, well supported by the empirical evidence, and one could suggest that it was a deliberately provocative reaction to the paradigm of the time. In response to this, plant and animal bone specialists (Bogaard and Jones 2007; Parmenter et al. 2015) have carried out direct, quantitative comparisons of aspects of the physical evidence for early Neolithic domestic production in Britain and Central

Europe, where an agricultural economy has rarely been disputed. There is little difference in the actual levels of evidence, so it can be argued that the different interpretations are principally born out of theoretical perspective. Whilst the palaeoeconomic view of the evidence may have needed balancing with other factors, in this case, the pendulum swung too far. Thomas's (1999) argumentative conceit was to divorce economy and culture and create a false dichotomy, which was neither constructive nor evidence-based.

As observed by Hodder (2012: 8), theoretical differences are often exacerbated by people talking across each other and there is some recent evidence that a degree of convergence across the processualist–post-processualist divide is possible. The perspective of this volume is not that archaeology should, in terms of theoretical approach, return to the 'golden days' of the palaeoeconomy school, but, to put it colloquially, the 'baby should not be thrown out with the bath water'. Many of the approaches and models developed at that time continue to be powerful. Quite a lot of the work of palaeoeconomists did engage with cultural and social issues. Environment does at times impose limits and provide opportunities, but it always provides a context. The key to gaining the most from economic approaches, however, lies in addressing the whole issue of 'environmental determinism' in much more detail, before economic models can meet their full research potential. This is the topic of the next chapter.

CHAPTER 2

Is Determinism Dead?

> *"...however unfashionable the term and ideas behind determinism may be, the very existence of natural laws presupposes a degree of determinism."*
>
> Higgs and Jarman 1975: 2

One criticism of economic and processual approaches to archaeology is that they tend to focus upon settlement and subsistence, whilst giving scant attention to hugely important cultural issues, such as belief systems (Trigger 1989: 327). This is largely a function of the interests of the researchers and the nature of the evidence they specialize in. Equally, one might argue, there are many works that concentrate upon religion or aesthetics, with scant regard given to economic or environmental context. In so much as it is true that different specialist branches of archaeology have a tendency to focus on one particular type of evidence, from their perspective, it seems that palaeoeconomists do not significantly stand out in this regard. Such biases are, in fact, relatively unproblematic at the level of highly specialist and technical discussions, if these are judged for what they are. These focused pieces of research are the essential building blocks for the creation of more synthetic works that aim to provide a more holistic consideration of particular archaeological questions. At this higher level, a much more balanced consideration of factors clearly becomes desirable, indeed essential. When our understanding of past human cultures begins to rely upon overly simplistic, environmental causal mechanisms, the intellectually serious charge of 'determinism' is frequently levelled (see Sluyter 2003; Judkins et al. 2008). This is a valid criticism. Of course, equally simplistic causal mechanisms, such as for instance considering 'friction internal to society' (Thomas 1999) to be the cause of the origins of agriculture, whilst dismissing environmental change as a relevant factor, are suspect, because they, too, represent a form of unjustified reductionism.

There is no doubt that many of the models regularly used by both palaeoeconomists and processual archaeologists employ causal relationships between environmental or economic variables and their resultant socio-cultural effects. Indeed, the application of a series of such models to significant periods of environmental change can result in metanarratives about human development that are vast in scale and impact. However, these are clearly flawed if the underlying assumptions of causality cannot be maintained, or if there is the potential for equifinality. However, the simple fact that these models make use of environmental and economic causation does not automatically make the research 'deterministic', since there are very different ways in which the results of such modelling can be used. The way the models are employed makes all the difference between intellectually problematic and simplistic reductionism, and the powerful use of a valuable research tool. There is also a clear difference between a fatally flawed method and a poorly applied one. Additionally, the charge of environmental and economic determinism can be too broadly and unthinkingly applied. Just because some causal links can be demonstrated to be too simplistic, does not mean that all such arguments are false. There is a danger that the accusation of determinism can be used to oppose such research findings without establishing the individual merits of a particular case. In such a way, the charge of 'determinism' becomes a lazily applied dogma rather than a valid criticism. Whilst most relationships involving culture are indeed complex, such dogma unjustifiably assumes that no variable is ever capable of determining an outcome.

The following chapter addresses several key questions in relation to determinism. Does the 'determinist' criticism of palaeoeconomy broadly apply, or is it more of a reaction against poor examples of the genre? Are there aspects of human culture that *are* determined by environment or economy? How should palaeoeconomic metanarratives be viewed? How can causal models involving economic and environmental variables be used to best effect in the study of archaeological questions? In what ways can environmental and economic models be integrated with cultural factors? In order to establish a useful way forward, it is first necessary to examine some of the key models that are frequently applied by palaeoeconomists, particularly those that might be open to the charge of being 'deterministic' in nature.

Key Models

Site Catchment Analysis

Site catchment analysis (SCA) is, as discussed in the previous chapter, one of the very particular legacies of the palaeoeconomic school of thought. It aims to establish the nature of the environment surrounding a specified archaeological site, with the extent of that catchment being defined by those areas which could have been habitually and easily exploited by people living at the site. The distance included in the survey is usually modelled upon assumptions related to acceptable travel times, based upon ethnographic analogies. These can involve a set radius or, because of varying ease of mobility over different terrain, a travel time limit in each direction, which results in a more complex catchment shape (Higgs and Vita-Finzi 1972; M.R. Jarman et al. 1972; Roper 1979). Whilst establishing the most applicable parameters could be endlessly debated (see Roper 1979), the purpose of the model is relatively simple. It puts the site in a broader environmental and economic context, highlighting variability in the site's hinterland in terms of terrain, soil types, likely vegetation cover, ease of mobility and probable availability of natural resources. The resulting assessment of resource availability sets up expectations than can potentially be tested against other lines of evidence.

There is no question that having this information provides a much more contextualized and data-rich approach than the earlier habit of focusing solely upon archaeological sites, themselves, with little regard to their landscape setting. Vita-Finzi and Higgs (1970: 28) underlined this point by suggesting that the positions of sites themselves are not very representative of the average environment around because they are 'preferred locations atypical of the zone' that are 'commonly located at the junction of very different habitats, the integration of whose resources results in a viable economy'. It is clear that the method of SCA, in-and-of-itself merely provides interesting contextual data through which a site can be better understood, and any resulting inference can be tested against other data. There is no *a priori* reason to view such analyses as being deterministic. Our attention must focus on the way in which the data produced by such analyses are interpreted. It is clear in the quotation above that Vita-Finzi and Higgs do think that site location primarily relates to economic viability. The implication of their statement is that sites tend to be located where their occupants will have efficient (within easy reach) access to a range of economic resources. Their framework of interpretation is clearly functionalist, where human actors are expected to be economically rational and the landscape features worthy of note relate to nature resources or economic potential. They do not hint at alternatives, where the reasons for location might relate to defence, display, view-shed, social connections, traditional usage, sacred places or, indeed, are simply irrational. It is also clear that many such social or cultural factors were not explicitly discussed by early proponents of the method (e.g. Webley 1972; Barker 1975; Jarman and Webley 1975; Rossman 1976; Zarky 1976), leaving these works open to criticism.

However, whilst such studies are weakened by their failure to consider a holistic range of human motivations, they avoid the direct charge of determinism because they frequently stress the hypothetical nature of their work. Higgs and Vita-Finzi (1970: 28) were clear that the purpose of SCA was 'furnishing a hypothesis in need of testing', and they characterized the results of their very first analysis as a 'very speculative possibility' (Vita-Finzi and Higgs 1970). Barker (1975: 164) modestly states that his work in central Italy 'cannot be more than preliminary hypotheses: although the data are now too complex to fit the simplistic models used in the past'. In this instance Barker is attacking a series of 'models of rigid cultural and economic stages' in favour of more complex and nuanced data. At the time this work was produced, it was opening up the range of considerations, rather than narrowing them. He does, however, also discuss 'predictive locational models' (Barker 1975: 164), whilst Higgs and Vita-Finzi (1970: 28) talk of 'the drawing of generalizations'.

Site catchment analysis itself is categorically not a deterministic technique. It just identifies the potential resources that the particular choice of site opens up, and those potential resources simply become another field of choices for humans to make (Davidson 1981: 26). Whilst early proponents may have had a bias towards the economic utility of landscapes and site location, the data produced by SCA could equally be used to support an argument that a site location was chosen for a non-economic reason. A lack of economic rationality for a particular position could be used in conjunction with other evidence, both on the site and in the surrounding landscape, to argue that social and cultural factors could have been more important than economic considerations. As Bintliff (1981) notes, if a site's location implies that its population would outstrip local resources, then this forces archaeologists to examine more closely the nature of the tenure of that settlement or what its network of external links might have been. Furthermore, the use of such analyses to generate hypotheses, to be tested against further evidence, also mitigates against simplistic causal explanations that become deterministic in nature. However, the use of data generated by SCA to populate wider models and make generalizations provides both increased potential for the method as well as an increased risk of employing deterministic lines of thought.

The principles of SCA have regularly been used to produce generalizations of where sites of a particular culture or type might be found, which in turn can be used as a predictive tool for the locations of such sites. Perhaps one of the classic examples of this is the association between *Linearbandkeramik* (LBK) settlements and loess soils in Central Europe (Clark 1952; Barker 1985), though acknowledgement of this association predates formal use of SCA analysis (Buttler and Haberey 1936, cited in Barker 1985). As well as predicting site location, such generalization of the most appropriate site catchment for that site type also feeds into models for understanding the nature of the spread of agriculture, such as in Dennell's (1985) pioneer model. In this model, certain environments are seen to favour faster spread of agriculture than others, and a key way of modelling this on the ground would be SCA. Perhaps another key example of generalization and prediction of likely site locations relates to sedentary hunter-gatherer sites. Often employing SCA, it has frequently been argued that such sites, for example of the Ertebølle Culture, are often located in estuarine or fiord zones where there is high ecological productivity, with access to both terrestrial and aquatic resources, shelter and good access for boats (see Clarke 1976; Paludan-Müller 1978; Rowley-Conwy 1983). Such inferences are based upon empirical correlations between site type and environmental conditions. SCA can be used both to establish the pattern and, potentially, to identify new likely locations for currently undiscovered sites. Like all inductive research this practice is probabilistic, working on the logic that because *most* known sites follow a particular pattern that yet-to-be-found sites *might likely* follow the same pattern. This line of argument would only become deterministic in nature if the generalization were formed into a law whereby sites would only ever be interpreted as being of a particular nature and function if they possessed the specified catchment parameters. Perhaps a greater danger for inductive research in archaeology is that fieldwork might then be limited only to locations fitting the generalization to produce a self-fulfilling and self-strengthening feedback loop. This issue is in no way limited to environmental and economic approaches, but applies to all inductive enquiry, making it essential to incorporate appropriate sampling strategies to test assumptions. In scientific terms, control samples are needed.

An early criticism of SCA (Hodder and Orton 1976) appears to base its argument on three pillars; they argue that it is environmentally deterministic, that inappropriate assumptions are made and that there are clear examples where the logic of the models is contradicted in real life. In support of the first assertion they quote early proponents of the method making what they view to be deterministic statements about the effect of the landscape setting upon the culture of its inhabitants. There is no shortage of statements that show a strong bias towards environmental influences upon culture and some are deterministic is nature, but Hodder and Orton (1976) confuse the views of users with the actual method itself. This seems to be a naïve logical fallacy. Just because the method can be used by some in a deterministic fashion does not mean that the method itself is deterministic. Instead of directing the criticism at the method, there would have been greater intellectual merit in discussing how to use it better. It is worth highlighting this particular fallacy of argument, as it is too often repeated in relation to a number of potentially valuable modes of archaeological enquiry. A similar point can be made regarding underlying assumptions. They suggest that it is dangerous to assume that sites operate within closed systems and that there are risks in using modern landscapes to model past environments. These points are very true, but again they are not actually reasons not to carry out SCA, but speak to a range of better underlying assumptions when making interpretations.

Their third line of argument (Hodder and Orton 1976) relates to a series of ethnographic examples in tropical Africa where the land nearest to settlements appeared to be the poorest, with good agricultural land being some distance away (Jackson 1972). Hodder and Orton (1976) suggest that this contradicts the whole logic of SCA and the concept of locating sites in relation to the efficient use of resources. Their particular example is purported to contradict the principles of distance and land use laid out by Chisholm (1962), an economic geographer who was an influence on early palaeoeconomists. In the first place, such an observation is only a problem if SCA was being used deterministically to create laws. If not, the more imaginative might see the method as having flagged up an interesting phenomenon worthy of further investigation. Bintliff (1981) did just that and followed up primary sources about the particular sites and cultures in question. He found a fascinating story of land use and change over time. Settlements had initially been located in good agricultural land, but the operation of an infield/outfield system had strained the more intensively farmed infield leading to degradation of its fertility. When the soil becomes too poor the communities move and start the cycle again. One of the original papers on this topic, consulted by Bintliff, actually concludes that the 'land use systems in tropical Africa are nonetheless rational to a considerable degree in a strictly economic sense' (Jackson 1972: 261). If used to best effect, SCA actual provides a baseline of data that is exceptionally valuable in drawing attention to and understanding such interesting processes of landscape use.

Optimal Foraging Theory

Site catchment analysis is only one way that archaeologists have modelled the environmental context of humans from an economic perspective. A more quantified and mathematical way of doing this is through a series of models that fall under the general heading of optimal foraging theory (OFT). These models originally derive from biology (Bettinger 1991) and were designed to model the behaviour of non-human animals within the sub-field of behavioural ecology. The potential of these methods to study the behaviour of human hunter-gatherers became apparent to anthropologists who adopted OFT (Kelly 1995) and the term 'human behavioural ecology' is now in use (Codding and Bird 2015). The origin of the use of these models in archaeological applications lies in the much closer relationship between archaeology and anthropology within North American academia, and most of the earlier work that makes use of these techniques is American. OFT models always assume that there is a rational goal to explain behaviour, as measured in some form of quantifiable currency in relation to a series of constraints (Kelly 1995). The goal could be reproductive fitness, but, in the majority of archaeologically applied cases, it is maximum efficiency in gaining food, as measured in calorific yield relative to the time spent in foraging and preparation. It is obvious from the outset that these models can be used in an extremely deterministic way, since they were designed to model behaviour of non-human animals, which lack complex culture and can be observed in the modern day. The models make clear, mathematically based predictions of behaviour based upon a limited set of ecological variables. The use of such models is deterministic if their predictions are used as the actual answer to a research question without further consideration. However, OFT does not have to be used in a simplistic way, so theoretical evaluations of applications need to be undertaken on a case by case basis. There is quite a wide range of OFT models and their variants, so not all can be discussed in detail here. The examples discussed below are *diet breadth*, *marginal value theorem* and *linear programming*, because these are some of the most relevant to archaeological investigations.

The logic behind the diet breadth model, as it is now known (Bettinger 1991; Kelly 1995), was first formulated by biologists MacArthur and Pianka (1966) and Emlen (1966). It is designed to predict which edible items, from the list of those available in the local environment, will actually be chosen for exploitation when a goal of maximum return efficiency is assumed. In order to do this, dietary items are put in a rank order according to their post-encounter calorific efficiencies. This measure includes the time it takes to process the foodstuff (e.g. butchery, extraction, detoxification, etc.) as well as its innate calorific value. The foodstuff with the highest energy return rate will be ranked first, and most likely to be exploited, with less efficient foods ranked below. Calculations of efficiency have been made during ethnological research on a wide range of resources (see Kelly 1995: Table 3.3 for examples). Merely establishing rank order, however, does not determine where the cut-off point in exploitation should be. As food items are added to the diet, the post encounter efficiency will drop as less efficient foods are included, but there is an increased chance of encountering resources if the diet is less specialized, so the search time will drop. Since time spent on processing less efficient foods will increase as more items are included, time spent foraging will reduce. At a particular point in this process, the combination of these two factors will yield the most efficient diet set. The graphical solution for this model can be seen in Fig. 2.1. It is worth noting that season will affect both the dietary items available and their calorific value, so diet breadth may change from season to season. Equally, factors such as climate change, erosion or, indeed, human impact or over-exploitation, will affect the mathematics of the model leading to different optimal diet breadths. In the case of human behavioural ecology, one also needs to take account of changing technology and the effect that could have upon processing and acquisition efficiencies. Mass capture can make a massive difference to efficiencies compared to individual encounter acquisition, as demonstrated in an archaeological diet breadth study in the Great Basin (Schmitt and Madsen 1998). In that example, the mass collecting of grasshoppers, when in swarm, actually begins to outrank large game on the diet breadth model and such hunting appears to be largely abandoned at times when there is large-scale evidence of grasshopper exploitation.

One of the most impactful uses of the logic that lies behind diet breadth models, within archaeology, is the concept of the ‘broad spectrum revolution’. Kent Flannery (1969) coined the term, though fellow leading processualist Lewis Binford (1968) also noted the same phenomenon. In summary, diet breadth appeared to have increased at the end of the Palaeolithic such that a wider range of species was being exploited using an

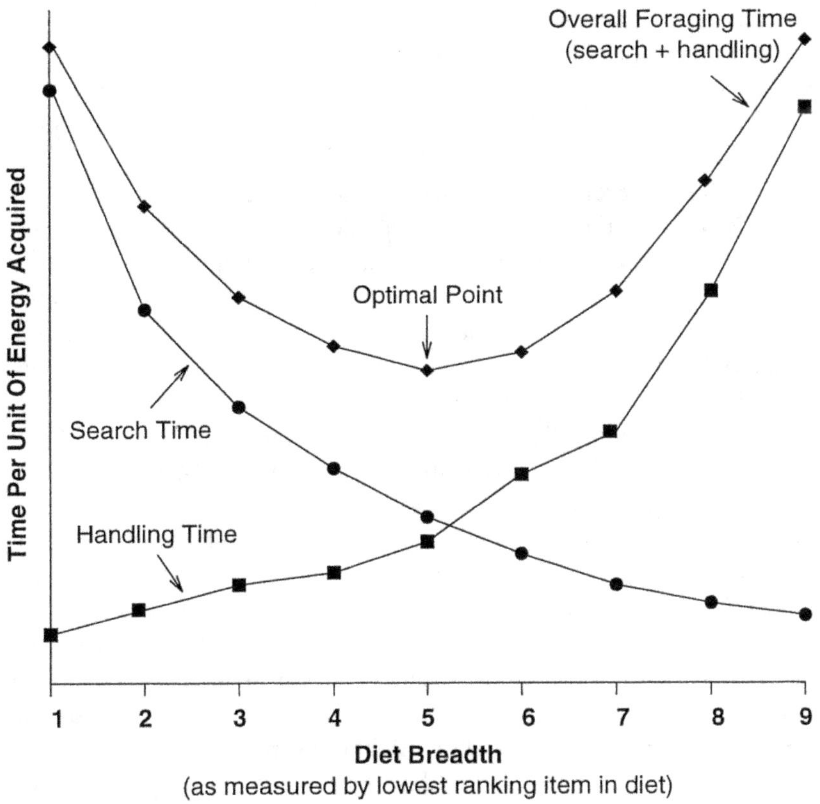

FIGURE 2.1 A graphical representation of the diet breadth model (after MacArthur and Pianka 1966).

increased range of technologies, including food-processing methods. This subsistence diversification was seen as a reaction to population pressures on the environment's carrying capacity brought on by climate change. Such evidence of subsistence pressure might be seen as prefacing (necessitating) the development of agriculture (Stiner 2001). This theory has been hotly debated ever since on both theoretic and empirical grounds. A particularly interesting aspect of the application of diet breadth to human populations is the way in which humans can manipulate the environment or alter the efficiency calculations through the use of technology. As such, unlike animals, human cultural attributes have the ability to manipulate the baseline figures in the model just as much as can environmental change. As a result, it can be argued that diet breadth OFT is insufficiently sophisticated to deal with the complex behaviours involved in this particular question and, perhaps, the alternative concept of 'niche construction theory', which also derives from evolutionary biology, is more appropriate (Smith 2009, 2011; Zeder 2012a).

Niche construction will be discussed in more detail later in this chapter, but it is also relevant to discuss it here, since aspects of it act as a criticism of OFT. According to proponents of niche construction, diet breadth theory is inappropriate for the consideration of complicated processes, such as the origins of agriculture, because of its simplistic assumptions that movements in the landscape are random, energetic efficiency is the only concern in resource selection and that human actors have no ability to manipulate their environment (Smith 2009). They predict instead that a broad spectrum revolution might actually be indicative of an abundant supply of predictable resources from a mosaic of ecozones that can be accessed from settlements with reduced mobility (Zeder 2012a). It is interesting to note that this echoes the expectations discussed above, derived from site catchment analysis, in relation to the locations of sedentary hunter-gatherer bases in Mesolithic North West Europe (Clarke 1976; Rowley-Conwy 1983). If this is correct, then was the application of OFT to the broad spectrum revolution of no research value? It seems likely that the logic behind the diet breadth model does not adequately explain the motivations behind the broad spectrum revolution in the Epipalaeolithic Near East, but use of the model did highlight very significant patterns in the economic evidence, allowing debate over their causation. This is a very important point, since there is a significant distinction to be made between saying that a modelling tool does not provide the best explanation for a pattern in data, and saying that the use of that model in investigating the question was of no value. One could also point out that the two theories are not actually mutually exclusive, since a rich, predictable, diverse resource landscape might have been selected as a part of niche construction, but the support of a more settled and larger population might simultaneously imply a wider diet breadth through OFT principles. An ecosystem can be simultaneously rich, predictable, diverse and put under pressure by human populations' subsistence needs. Furthermore, increased population or deleterious environmental change might have resulted in a series of possible outcomes, such as either a return to mobile lifestyles, further increase in diet breadth or change in the technological basis of food production (i.e. agriculture). Indeed, not to be environmentally determinist, such pressures could also have led to a violent religious cult and the eventual failure of that society. Debate over the broad spectrum revolution continues.

Diet breadth can also be used in a series of less complex situations to model the intensity of resource use and relate this to possible instances of economic and dietary stress. One way of doing this is to consider the intensity of exploitation of the ranked constituent components of a particular resource, rather than the diversity of different resources. An example of this is the selection for utilization of particular body parts from hunted large mammals. Binford (1978) studied the decisions Nunamiut Inuit made in relation to transporting different portions of caribou that they had hunted at kill-sites back to their camps. Just in the same way as different types of food have different exploitation efficiencies, so too do different parts of a dead animal. Each element will have different amounts of meat on it, as well as marrow fat and potential quantities of rendered bone grease. This led Binford (1978) to generate 'utility indices' for caribou based upon measuring the food potential of portions of the body associated with each skeletal element (as the bones provide the surviving archaeological evidence). Since then, the 'economic anatomy' of many other species has been studied, with some variation in methodologies (e.g. Metcalfe and Jones 1988; Savelle and Friesen 1996; Outram and Rowley-Conwy 1998; Rowley-Conwy, Halstead and Collins 2002). Theodore White (1952, 1953) had much earlier noted that hunters tend to make selections relating to which body parts were most worth transporting in relation to their utility, but Binford (1978: Fig. 2.18) added to this observation by creating a set of model graphs that related the numbers of different elements selected for transportation with their food utility. In these models he proposed that, if the hunters' needs were being easily met by the kills available to them, they would only exploit the richest body parts. He called this the 'gourmet strategy', which is not a commonly observed pattern in archaeological assemblages. Heavy under-exploitation of carcasses has been noted in some mass kill assemblages of larger animals, such as the horses at the Palaeolithic site of Solutré in France (Olsen 1989), though there are also ethnographic accounts of bison hunters in North America taking only the tongues of animals as delicacies (Verbricky-Todd 1984: 169). Exploitation of all but the very lowest ranking elements is categorized as a 'bulk strategy' and this is much more commonly seen in archaeological assemblages and this pattern was what Binford (1978) witnessed as the Nunamiut practising. There is clearly a wide spectrum of possibility depending upon the relative need of the hunters concerned. Speth (1983), at the bison kill site of Garnsey in New Mexico, even notices a different set of hunters' exploitation decisions in relation to the sex of the animals, with lower intensity of processing and transport of smaller, possibly less fatty, females.

The logic Binford (1978) employs to underpin his body-part transport models clearly relies upon the same principles as diet breadth in OFT (Bettinger 1991), with the 'bulk strategy' equating to increased diet breadth since lower efficiency food sources are exploited as a result of increased subsistence needs relative to the food supply available in the environment. There are many technical zooarchaeological problems in applying such models simplistically in terms of taphonomy and the production of indices (see Outram 2004a) and other complicating factors, such as prey size, number of hunters and distance from the camp (Schoville and Otárola-Castillo 2014), but there are also obvious theoretical objections. Clearly, people have tastes in foodstuffs, a need to balance nutrition and the potential to select different parts of the body for utilization for crafts, fuel or symbolic/ritual purposes. The value of diet breadth modelling, therefore, lies in its ability to generate a hypothesis that might be tested, rather than a simplistic end interpretation.

Another OFT technique worthy of discussion is marginal value theorem (MVT), which was originally designed by Charnov (1976). MVT is relatively easily explained and most people that have ever undertaken a task like berry picking will appreciate its concerns. The model predicts when it is most efficient for a forager to leave a particular resource 'patch' (e.g. berry bush) because they will get a better rate of return from another patch, whether that new resource is of the same type or a different one within the diet breadth being exploited. The method works for patches where there are diminishing returns. As one picks berries from a bush the rate declines because those berries most easily seen and reached are taken first, leaving fewer and more difficult to obtain fruits. At some point, before all berries are picked, one is likely to move on and try to find an alternative bush. In MVT, the optimal time to leave is when the diminishing return rate reaches and begins to drop below the average rate of return for the environment, taking into account both the time needed to find a random new resource and collect from it. The graphical solution for MVT can be seen in Figure 2.2. This particular OFT method has, perhaps, had less impact on archaeology than diet breadth, but has seen a range of applications, not only in relation to food. For instance, it has recently been used in the modelling of stone tool life histories (Kuhn and Miller 2015). Outram (2004b) noted that rather than using diet breadth to model hunters' body-part transport choices, one could treat the dead animal as a patch and view the rank order indicated by food utility indices as a progression of diminishing returns. This approach has since been applied in fully worked examples (e.g. Burger, Hamilton and Walker 2005). Perhaps this is more

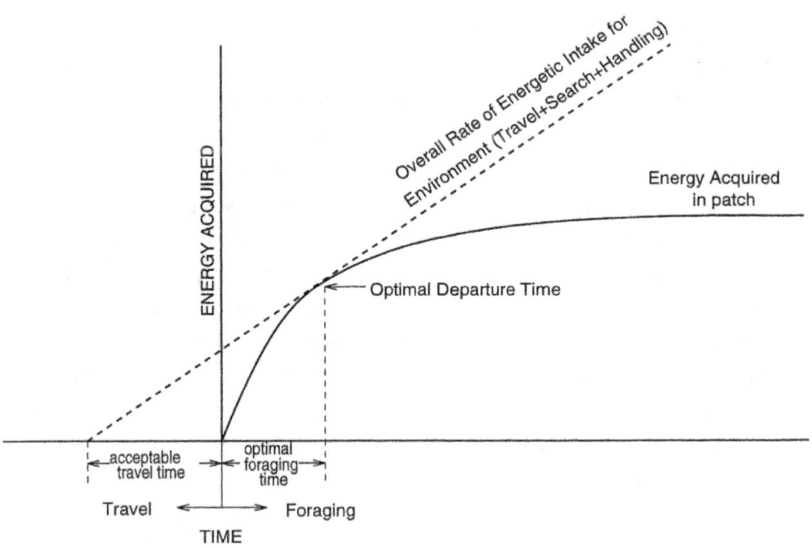

FIGURE 2.2 A graphical representation of the marginal value theorem (after Charnov 1976).

appropriate because MVT explicitly deals with the most efficient intensity of exploitation of a particular resource when encountered, which matches well with an animal kill, whereas diet breadth is actually more about the diversity of resource types. Nonetheless, similar criticisms with regard to goal assumption can apply.

An even more specific application of the MVT model can be applied to evidence for the exploitation of bone fats (Outram 2001, 2002) in the assessment of potential levels of subsistence stress (Outram 2004b). Bone fat exploitation lends itself very well to this kind of the study for several reasons. First, the exploitation of fats from within bones requires extraction, in the form of marrow fracturing or bone grease rendering, which leaves identifiable patterns in the archaeological record in the form of fracture types and fragmentation levels. These patterns can be discerned with careful analysis alongside other taphonomic factors. Second, bone fats were a regularly exploited, very important source of high-calorie food (see Speth and Spielmann 1983), but also one with a clear rank order of extraction efficiency. It is exceptionally easy to break a large long bone and instantly poke out a large amount of highly nutritious marrow, but rendering out small amounts of bone grease from the broken up articulations of long bones is very arduous and time consuming, as well as using up fuel. An even more extreme activity is the boiling of shaft fragments and ribs for very meagre resources. Ethnographic support for the association of certain bone fat exploitation practices with dietary stress is very abundant in the literature (see Outram 2004b). Archaeological studies of this issue in relation to medieval Norse settlers on Greenland, who operated a struggling economy poorly adapted to the climate and available grazing, needed to go to extreme lengths to exploit bone fats, whereas locally adapted Paleoeskimo groups employed a less intensive regime (Buckland et al. 1996; Outram 1999). On the other hand, on Iceland, where the environmental conditions were more favourable to pastoralism and there is more evidence of extensive fishing, there was only a small amount of evidence for simple marrow extraction and no rendering (Outram 2003). Whilst it must be noted that fat can also be used for fuel and craft purposes, the linkage between extreme bone fat exploitation patterns and dietary stress through OFT mechanisms appears to work well in both ethnographic and archaeological case studies. Context remains very important, however, and significant bone grease production in some circumstances could relate to trading activities, such as at the Initial Middle Missouri agricultural and bison hunting site of Mitchell, South Dakota (Karr et al. 2010, 2015), where it has been suggested that grease or pemmican could have been traded along river systems to regions with less access to bison products. Interpretations are often deeply affected by the degree to which subsistence economies are open or closed.

The final OFT method that will be covered here is linear programming, a mathematical method co-opted into archaeology and anthropology in the late 1970s (e.g. Keene 1979; Reidhead 1979). Whilst the process itself was generally designed to solve multiple linear equations relating to many variables, the common OFT use is to evaluate diets in terms of whether they can supply all essential nutrients (Kelly 1995). This model differs from the others in that it is not about maximum efficiency, but about establishing whether diets are viable or not to support human life, long-term. It establishes base-line requirements and allows dietary scenarios to be evaluated against them. The model is justifiably deterministic and goes to the heart of the quotation (Higgs and Jarman 1975) that begins this chapter. Cultural variability has limits determined by viability. Social agency is curtailed by death.

The crux of the matter is that OFT can be used in an inappropriately simplistic, deterministic fashion, but it does not have to be. It can set baselines for viability and it can produce reference points for efficiency. Archaeological interpretation is difficult and multifaceted, so the ability to construct clear points of reference using logical principles is extremely valuable. Such rare frameworks allow us to generate hypotheses that can be tested and illuminate anomalous patterns that might indicate particularly interesting cultural phenomena. Whilst all variables needed in such models might not be available in archaeological case studies, they still can act as analogues (see Foley 1985) against which to compare empirically observable aspects of the past through environmental and economic reconstruction. The value of such frames of reference is discussed further at the end of this chapter.

Models of Ecological Productivity, Predictability and Territoriality

In addition to OFT, anthropology has also introduced into archaeology a series of more qualitative models that categorize environments with regard to factors like ecological productivity, resource density and foraging predictability and then relate these categories to aspects of human behaviour, such as territoriality, reciprocity, exchange, food storage, warfare, wealth and social hierarchy (see Kelly 1995). Like OFT, these models are most commonly applied to hunter-gatherer societies, but application does extend to early agricultural societies and, in particular, they are often discussed in relation to periods immediately prior to the advent of farming (e.g. Rowley-Conwy 2001).

One of the earlier of such models to emerge was the 'economic defensibility model' (Dyson-Hudson and Smith 1978) which focuses on the role of ecology in influencing degrees of territoriality (see Fig. 2.3). The model uses the logic that, whilst defence of local resources has its benefits, it also comes with costs in the form of either physical boundaries or the threat of violence or warfare. It is only economically rational physically to defend a territory where there is a high resource density and those resources are predicable (quadrant B in Fig. 2.3). If the resources are sparse then the size of an area, extensive enough to contain sufficient resources to be worthy of defence, would be physically too large to defend. It is equally unwise jealously to guard an area where resources are unpredictable, as later in the year the best resources might be on the outside of one's territory (and in somebody else's). Where resource density and predictability are low (quadrant C), high mobility and dispersion are predicted, whilst if resources are sparse but predictable, there might be the notion of a 'home range', but not one worth physical protection (quadrant D). Where resource density is high but predictability is low, probably as a result of seasonal variations in the resource schedule, mobility will be required, but temporary notions of territory might be exerted (quadrant A). A good example of the last category might be the Akulmiut Inuit, who are territorial in relation to places

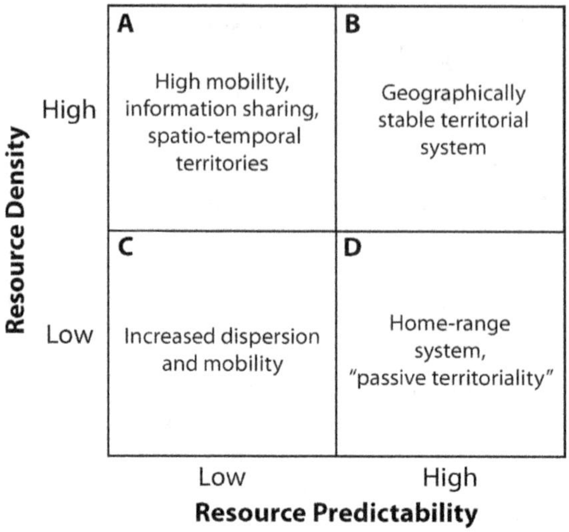

FIGURE 2.3 The economic defensibility model (after Dyson-Hudson and Smith 1978).

on rivers where fish can be obtained in large numbers during particular seasons (Kelly 1995: 191).

In researching the ecology and territorial behaviour of Bushmen of the Kalahari, Cashdan (1983) noted that the model did not always appropriately predict territoriality. Cashdan's analysis highlighted that Bushman groups often employ 'social boundary defence' to maintain the notion of a territory. Social boundary defence is mediated through outsiders asking permission, which is usually granted, to forage in a particular area, but maintains notional rights of groups to a territory without the costs of physical defence (Kelly 1995). Cashdan notes that, since social boundary defence is not costly, the degree to which it features within cultures cannot so easily be modelled based upon a ratio of resources to land area (Cashdan 1983). It is important to note this, as it is an example of how human cultural systems can differ significantly from those that might govern simpler life-forms. However, Smith (1983) points out that the 'economic defensibility model' is designed to deal with instances of enforced, physical defence, while the peoples studied by Cashdan live in very similar, low-resource-density environments for which a lack of territorial defence would be predicted within their model. Cashdan (1983b) replied with a further model that very usefully clarified when social boundary defence might be prevalent (see Fig. 2.3). Where competition for resources is negligible, there is no need for any form of territoriality, but where there is competition, social boundary defence will be used when the territories have few resources and are large, whereas physical defence will occur in smaller, rich regions. This further contribution on the topic is important because it highlights that simply modelling the ecology of the area immediately surrounding an archaeological site might not yield the correct predictions, unless the wider economic and cultural context is also understood, including the potential for interaction with others.

As with OFT, the economic defensibility model should not be simplistically applied with the expectation that, once the resources available to people in a particular archaeological example are understood, we will then know what their territorial behaviour would have been. Having undertaken palaeoenvironmental reconstruction and site catchment analysis, models like economic defensibility assist in interpreting what the implications of the environmental setting might be. This can be formally treated as a hypothesis and tested against a range of other evidence, such as for fortifications or warfare, or simply viewed holistically alongside all other evidence to reach the most parsimonious interpretation. If one takes the example of the Ertebølle Culture of late Mesolithic southern Scandinavia (see Rowley-Conwy 1983, 1998b, 1999), the economic defensibility model is just one portion of the evidence cited for the presence of some permanent settlements and stable territories, alongside other indicators such as evidence of season-round occupation, regional styles and the presence of cemeteries. The model provides the ecological context necessary to make such an interpretation, but does not alone determine that interpretation.

Winterhalder (1986) takes a rather different approach to how environmental context might influence cultural practices such as exchange, storage, sharing and migration. He looks at economic strategies from the perspective of risk reduction by examining the extent to which an individual forager's success will vary from day to day (intra-forager variance), in a given environment, and whether others in the same social group are likely to have had a similar degree of success at the same time (inter-forager correlation). Environment affects this significantly depending upon how predictable resources are and how they are distributed within the landscape (to what extent does a forager rely on luck?). In this model (see Fig. 2.4), where an individual's foraging success is relatively uniform (low intra-forager variance) and their peers perform similarly (high inter-forager correlation) there would be little need to migrate, exchange or store, as there is a steady supply of foods in the locality and little inequality (quadrant C). If the reverse is true and a forager has high variance, but that performance is not positively correlated to their peers', then it makes

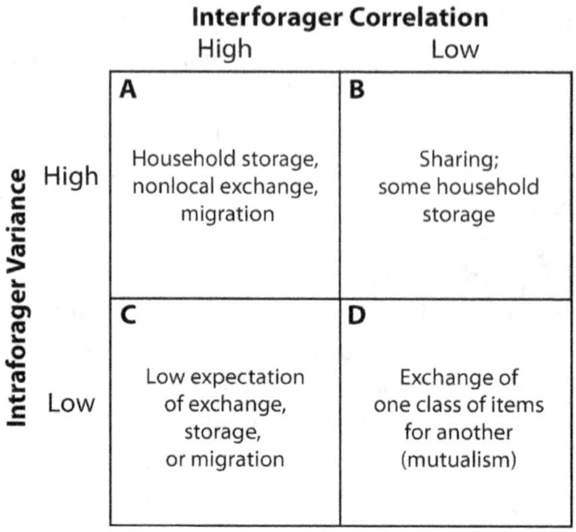

FIGURE 2.4 A model for risk and variance reduction amongst foragers (after Winterhalder 1986).

sense to share reciprocally, hence providing a mutually beneficial mechanism for reducing risk and providing a steady supply of food. Some storage might also be useful, to make use of one day's overabundance to provide a cushion against dearth in the near future (see quadrant B). If a forager has variable performance but that co-varies with that of peers (quadrant A), then sharing with one's immediate fellows will not help, because they have a dearth in resources at the same time and have nothing they can provide. Possible solutions here include migration to better resources, exchange with non-locals who forage in a different area (a more extensive reciprocal system) or buffering through storage. If a forager's variance is low, but correlation between foragers is also low, it suggests that different foragers are targeting different resources. The logical thing to do here is exchange different resources to diversify diet (quadrant D).

This model was designed to predict a series of logical behaviours within a small foraging band, and aspects of it can clearly be applied in considering archaeological scenarios. However, because of the nature of the evidence, greater archaeological application is possible if similar logic can be applied to social groups as a whole. Kelly (1995: 198) presents just such an adaptation of the model (see Fig. 2.5). This is a simple adjustment of the model that looks at variance in the groups' overall acquisition of resources (intra-group variance) in relation to how that matches up with neighbouring groups (inter-group correlation). Many aspects are

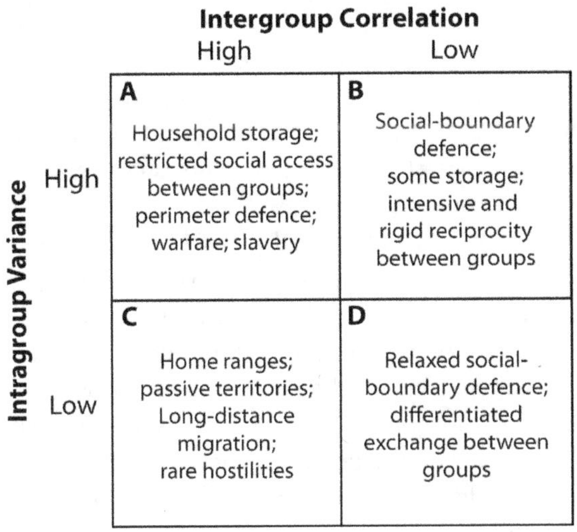

FIGURE 2.5 A model for risk and variance reduction amongst hunter-gatherer groups (after Kelly 1995: Fig. 5.6).

similar to the forager model, but, at the group level, there are some serious additional implications related to competition between groups. When intra-group variance and inter-group correlation are both high it suggests that whole groups will be in direct competition for resources in periods of dearth, suggesting greater potential for warfare, the possibility of slavery and the need for boundary defence (quadrant A). This is the most significant difference to note, whilst the other quadrants simply express similar behaviours to the forager model, but at a group level. None of the other scenarios requires physical defence of territory, but they suggest different levels of mobility, storage and exchange (Kelly 1995).

The Winterhalder (1986) risk reduction model and its Kelly (1995) variant, are based upon expected rational behaviour given particular scenarios of environment and neighbours' environments. Keeley (1988), on the other hand, took an empirical approach and widely surveyed the ethnographic accounts of 94 different hunter-gatherer cultures to establish correlations between variables relating to such issues as latitude, continentality, different measures of resource productivity, nature of diet, population density, population pressure, sedentism, dependence on storage, exchange and levels of socioeconomic hierarchy. He later extrapolated from his generalized data to model possible behavioural changes at the end of the Pleistocene in Europe (Keeley 1991). Some of the key trends in the data that relate to behavioural aspects are that sedentism, population pressure, levels of storage and presence of wealth and hereditary social classes are all positively correlated (Keeley 1991). All of these factors are also positively correlated with more productive and reliable environments (Keeley 1988). These data are for hunter-gatherers, but the arrival of agriculture, where storage is essential, surplus is 'normal' (Halstead 1989b) and aspects of land tenure are implicit, is arguably a game changer.

This is a brief simplification of a very detailed piece of work, which contains more nuances, but it is clear that these data are broadly in line with the predictions made by the economic defensibility model (Dyson-Hudson and Smith 1978) and risk-/variance-reduction models (Winterhalder 1986; Kelly 1995), though they only share some of the same variables. It is fairly clear that there is good evidence for a generalized relationship between certain aspects of behaviour and certain environments, so dismissal of the value of such modelling in addressing broad questions seems unwise. However, like OFT, the models should serve as a point or reference, a source of hypotheses or part of wider contextual argument rather than as a simplistic determinist answer. Keeley's (1988) data show generalized support for such logic, but also interesting variation. His work is inductive, and aids us in making inferences regarding the best explanation, whilst recognizing that the existence of exceptions precludes the formation of a law.

Carrying Capacity and Population Growth

If it is possible to use a device such as linear programming to model whether a given set of resources will meet human biological requirements, then an obvious next step is to work out the maximum number of people a given environment could support. The concept of carrying capacity originates within the field of ecology (e.g. Odum 1959) and defines the point at which significant population increase is prohibited by a lack of available natural resources. Early, explicit, use of the concept within archaeology dates back to the 1950s and 1960s (Glassow 1978) and this included some applications to farming societies (e.g. Conklin 1959; Carneiro 1960). Whilst not generally referring to the ecological concept by name, work on carrying capacity was also a feature of the research of the Cambridge palaeoeconomy school. Sturdy (1975), in researching prehistoric reindeer economies in Europe, considered how many animals environments might support and the implications for possible human population levels. Calculations demonstrating that some environmental contexts would be likely to support larger, and indeed more sedentary, hunter-gatherer populations are not uncommon (e.g. Rowley-Conwy 1983). In relation to early farmers, speculative models to reconstruct likely crop yields, based upon ethnographic examples and site catchment analysis (e.g. Dennell and Webley 1975; Jarman et al. 1982), were used to evaluate good areas for supporting significant populations of agriculturalists. In most of these cases, the mathematics of such modelling did not extend as far as setting absolute numbers for carrying capacities. Instead, the arguments tended to more relative in nature.

Early objections to the concept of carrying capacity concentrated on practical difficulties of obtaining sufficiently accurate data to make the use of the method effective. Hayden (1975), in fact, recommends that the whole idea should be abandoned as impractical. Instead he suggests that lines of evidence such as rates of mortality resulting from subsistence deficiency should be used to investigate issues relating to population pressure and resources. However, simply because something is difficult to do does not mean it should not be attempted, particularly as methods and sources of data might improve with time. Furthermore, to assume that rates of subsistence-related mortality indicate the same thing as carrying capacity is very simplistic (see Glassow 1978), particularly as comparing carrying capacity to mortality levels might lead to the most interesting conclusions. There is no doubt that it is extremely difficult to generate models that take into account the right variables and then obtain values for those variables related to a past period. The same difficulty applies to OFT, but models provide a useful framework for investigations and frequently allow at least discussions of relative values and rank order. Furthermore, both environmental reconstruction and complex modelling techniques have advanced significantly, opening up new possibilities.

Putting aside practical criticisms, it is worth considering the theoretical value of modelling carrying capacities. The concept is clearly always deterministic in the sense that, if correctly calculated for the environmental and technological context, the carrying capacity is a limit. This constraint on human behaviour is totally defensible in exactly the same way as setting the minimum required to live through linear programming. It is only deterministic in relation to what is not possible, but is permissive in allowing a wide range of viable population variation between zero and the carrying capacity. However, quite commonly, the underlying assumption expressed by palaeoeconomists was for '…the demographic tendency of human populations to stabilize around an optimum density which achieves a full exploitation of the available food resources' (Bailey et al. 1983). This may be true in some cases, but this is a risky, determinist assumption. Like OFT, carrying capacity is best used as a constraint and as a point of reference.

As noted above, when dealing with human populations, it is necessary not only to understand the environmental context accurately, but also the technological context. Some early critics of the method stressed the need to consider changes in modes of subsistence, farming practices and subsequent dynamics affecting such factors as soil fertility (Street 1969; Glassow 1978). Clearly, non-human organisms have minimal agency over environmental carrying capacities, and changes are only likely to be driven by long-term effects caused by forces external to them, such as climate change or, indeed, human impact. Human cultures have significant ability to modify their landscape and use technology to extract higher productivity and raise carrying capacities. At first, this seems to invalidate the whole notion of studying carrying capacities for human populations, but actually this leads to a very rich vein of research that speaks to some of the biggest transformations in human societies and economies. It is possible to conceptualize differing carrying capacities in differing environments, but also differing carrying capacities in the same environment employing different modes of subsistence and technology. How does population growth relate to environmental change, and how do both those factors relate to technological change?

Boserup (1965) challenged the Malthusian perspective that food supply inflexibility governed population growth and would only be able to expand substantially if there was some fortunate innovation in food production. She inverts the argument to suggest that population can grow independently, putting pressure on current carrying capacities, becoming 'a major factor determining agricultural developments' (Boserup 1965: 11). In a later work, she suggests that the 'prehistoric shift to food production was preceded by a period of acute population pressure on the supply of wild food' (Boserup 1981: 26). This influential metanarrative has been the subject of massive debate ever since. It fed into existing ideas within archaeology that there was unidirectional evolution of society from band to tribe to chiefdom and, finally, state (e.g. Service 1962). Combining these concepts creates a rigidly progressive view that is determinist in nature. It assumes that, as populations grow and reach the environment's carrying capacity, there will be a one-way incremental change towards greater socioeconomic complexity. This notion received early criticism from palaeoeconomists: 'the belief that all agricultural systems must have been bound by, and have developed through, a rigid series of steps of increasing intensification seems logically dubious and ignores concrete examples to the contrary' (Jarman et al. 1982: 144). It should be noted that the palaeoeconomy school was not always in favour of reductionist

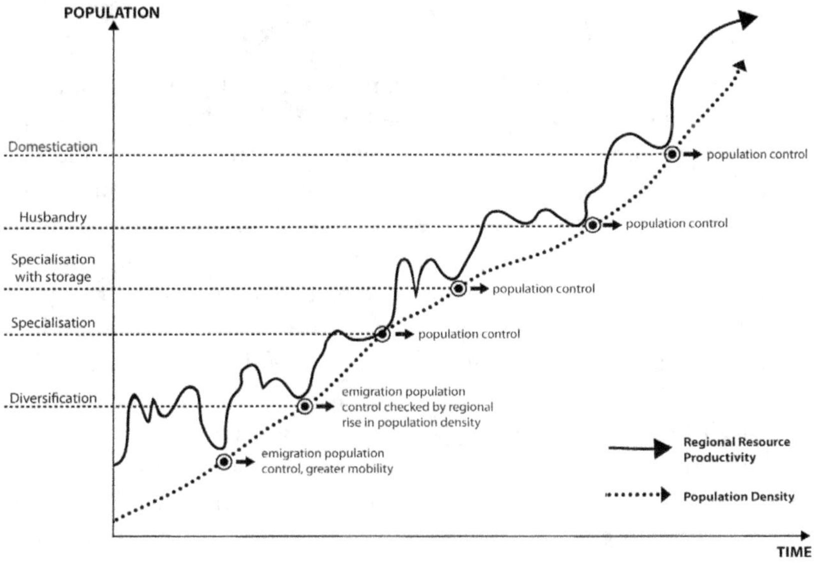

FIGURE 2.6 A model relating population density increases over time to episodes of population control overcome by changes to resource-use and productivity (after Zvelebil 1995: Fig. 2).

arguments. However, progressive models of population growth coupled to increased complexity persist and are still debated. Zvelebil (1995), whilst acknowledging possible variability, presented a generalized model where population increases to create particular pressure points that precipitate, in order: diversification (i.e. broad spectrum revolution), specialization and storage, husbandry and, finally, domestication (see Fig. 2.6). Rowley-Conwy (2001) strongly argues against this, pointing out many examples where such development never occurred, or where there was reversal from farming back to hunting and gathering. He argues that the conditions that led to the origins of agriculture in the Near East relate to a very specific sequence of environmental, economic, social and population factors pertaining to that region at that time. In particular, he argues that complex hunter-gatherers in North West Europe should not be viewed as being on an inexorable track towards farming (Rowley-Conwy 2001); indeed these were amongst the hunter-gatherer societies that resisted that transition the longest within a temperate European setting. Whether such models are globally applicable or not, however, the notion of carrying capacity plays a pivotal role in understanding the interactions between population, environment, modes of subsistence and social change.

Niche Construction Theory

Niche construction theory (NCT) also, not surprisingly, derives from evolutionary biology and was first proposed by Lewontin (1982, 1983). This relatively new concept has only very recently been applied to the discussion of archaeological questions. NCT recognizes that non-human organisms do not merely adapt to their environments, but their adaptation, both physical and behavioural, can, in turn, modify their ecosystem. An excellent example of this is the dam-building behaviour of beavers, which not only improves the immediate reproductive fitness of the individual animals, but also greatly modifies the dynamics of the whole surrounding ecosystem (see Laland and O'Brien 2010). It is almost redundant to point out that, if the effects of beavers' ecosystem engineering are substantial, then humans must be the 'ultimate niche constructors' (Smith 2007: 195). Since this way of thinking can encompass the complex and dynamic interplay between environment, genetics and behaviour (culture), it has lent itself particularly well to the consideration of the origins of agriculture (e.g. Smith 2007; Rowley-Conwy and Layton 2011; Zeder 2012a; Smith and Zeder 2013). NCT provides rich potential for the integration of future archaeological investigations because it holistically considers environmental and economic factors, whilst making full allowance for the impact of human agency. Furthermore, it does so in a way that can be well integrated with the vast raft of new genetic information that is currently flooding into archaeological research. An additional strength is that studies carried out within the framework of NCT are context specific, so avoid the pitfalls of overarching and dogmatic laws and generalizations. Whilst NCT represents an excellent theoretical way forward, that does not actually imply that earlier modelling techniques are not worth pursuing. They can still be used to understand the role of particular variables within a more complex argument.

Conclusion: Constraints, Frames of Reference and Metanarratives

In answer to the question posed in the title of this chapter, determinism is not dead. This proposition is supported by two rather different lines of argument. First, overly simplistic causal models have been applied by economic and environmental archaeologists in the past and, unfortunately, this practice continues in some work today. However, palaeoeconomists do not have a monopoly on work that can be criticized in this way, and there have been many scholars in the field who never fell into that trap.

Environmental and economic models do not have to be used simplistically, so it is unjust to dismiss the whole field by employing the charge of determinism lazily. Second, some matters *are* determined by environment or economy, following the logic of the quotation at the start of this chapter (Higgs and Jarman 1975). The aspects of human life that can be determined are the limits of viability. Models can establish the constraints within which a diverse and variable range of human cultural systems and behaviour can live out their lives.

The great strength of understanding environmental context in order to establish the limits to cultural variability, rather than determine actual behaviour, was recognized at the very beginning of economic studies within geography, archaeology and ethnography. It was something particularly stressed by Forde (1934), and it is worth reciting a paragraph from the conclusion of his *Habitat, Economy and Society* volume:

> *Although the adaptation of culture, and particularly of crafts and economy, to the habitat exists everywhere, and is usually (in its outlines) obvious enough, the whole complex of the physical environment does not affect human activity in any single and comprehensive way. It is necessary to distinguish the negative conditions that are limiting factors at all stages of culture, and which demand special efforts to overcome (such are, for instance, difficulties of terrain, climatic restrictions on particular plants and animals), from those that acquire positive significance only in connexion with specific cultural achievements. This distinction may be expressed by saying that physical conditions have both restrictive and permissive relations to human activities.*
>
> (Forde 1934: 463)

Concepts such as linear programming can be used to establish the minimum quantity of any particular diet required to survive, whilst detailed environmental reconstruction then also allows at least some notional modelling of maximum carrying capacity. Somewhere between the minimum resource required to support the smallest viable population and the maximum community that can be supported in an environment, including its wider economic connections, must exist the full range of possible forms of subsistence and society. Dramatic change in environment, whether brought on by climate change or human agency, is likely to alter those constraints. If the change is for the better, then new ways of living might be permitted, but if the environment becomes more restrictive, then some lifeways become non-viable in that context, whether that leads to adaptation, exodus or oblivion. In making similar points about the nature of the interplay between environmental limits and culture, Dennell (1983: 7) uses the example of Norse settlers on Greenland who attempted to eek an existence from pastoralism, with some hunting, in a landscape and climate that did not make that easy. There were other ways of living in that environment, as demonstrated by indigenous Inuit, so environment did not determine culture, but both these cultures were within the limits of viability. With the later onset of the Little Ice Age the climate deteriorated, as did the productivity of pasture (see Buckland et al. 1996), and a pastoral way of life began to fall outside those limits. Furthermore, long-distance economic support from Scandinavia, derived from walrus ivory trade, seems to have fallen away at the same time, as that product was increasingly sourced from the White Sea (Frei et al. 2015). The Norse could have adapted and stayed, but it appears that their cultural preferences were rigid, and they chose to abandon the settlements on Greenland. There are few clearer examples of people resisting the logical influence of environmental and economic factors over their way of life, up until the point where they were constrained by the limits of viability.

Beyond the determination of constraints, economic and environmental models also provide valuable frames of reference and points of comparison. Models like OFT indicate what rational behaviour, with a particular goal in mind, might look like. The model is neither good nor bad. Like any tool, its usefulness is determined largely by how, and for what, it is used. Such models should rarely be used with the simple expectation that actual behaviour will conform, but their use provides a fixed point of reference to aid discussions of competing interpretations of the archaeological record. If we consider, for instance, a deposit of animal bones, it could represent the remains of a normal meal, a feast or a ceremonial deposit. The particular animal from which the bones came may have been valued for the calories it provided, the craft materials obtained, its great taste or its totemic potency, among other things. One source of reference in debating these possibilities could be ethnographic analogies, but another could be models based upon a series of observable variables. Economic models are not about establishing that all behaviour relates to economy, but in fact are exceptionally useful in observing when it is not. Such frames of reference provide a much more compelling, evidence-based way to throw light on cultural phenomena than the assertions and storytelling of relativists.

Given the above, how should one view the major metanarratives of human development that are based primarily upon environmental, economic and demographic factors? Once again it depends on how they come to be used in ongoing research. If such metanarratives are used as a hypothesis, to be evaluated constantly against new evidence, then they remain useful in the framing of research questions. If contradicted by the record, then they must be amended, or rejected and replaced. For instance, the 'secondary products revolution' (Sherratt 1981, 1983) has proved a most valuable hypothesis in the conception and stimulation of many research projects, but new information from the application of new techniques has necessitated adjustment and nuancing of the original idea (see Vigne and Helmer 2007; Evershed et al. 2008; Outram 2015), but, in fact, not complete replacement. The danger with wide-scale generalizations and metanarratives is that they become dogma and are used as inflexible laws, expected to work in all contexts. This is when deterministic approaches are most deserving of criticism. However, the labelling of environmental and economic models as being 'deterministic' has itself become something of a dogma, yet that criticism is often unjustified and leads to the stifling of rich veins of research that can significantly add to our understanding of human cultural variability, within sound theoretical frameworks for evidence-based enquiry.

CHAPTER 3

Incorporating New Methods I: The Stable Isotope Revolution

'*Der Mensch ist was er ißt*' (Feuerbach 1850), commonly translated as 'you are what you eat', has become something of a repeated rallying cry for archaeological scientists and biogeochemists specializing in stable isotope research (Bogaard and Outram 2013; e.g. DeNiro and Epstein 1976; Kohn 1999; Tykot 2004). The revolutionary discovery was that stable isotope ratios in preserved biological tissue contained direct evidence for aspects of past diet. Prior to this, diet had to be extrapolated and inferred from the analysis of possible food remains. Proxy evidence from bones and seeds provides considerable evidence for food production strategies, but it is exceedingly difficult to model from those data alone what the total diet looked like. Stable isotope analysis suddenly opened up the possibility to understand not just what a community's general diet looked like, but also what specific individuals consumed. This had huge ramifications for understanding social and cultural, as well as economic questions pertaining to food supply and consumption. As research in the field developed it became clear that the power of the method extended beyond a narrow understanding of diet and could tell us much more about the lives of plants, animals and humans and their interactions. At the same time, as with most new methods, there has been a realization that some of the initial assumptions were overly simplistic and ever more complex analyses and models are necessary to get the best out of the data. This chapter will first outline the origins and scientific foundations of stable isotope research, before addressing its key contributions to establishing, first, how plants and animals were connected in food webs. Then *what* people ate will be addressed, before discussing how isotopes also contribute to understanding migration and seasonality through understanding *where* and *when* that food was eaten. In addition to addressing cultural and economic questions, the chapter will also touch upon how stable isotope analysis has contributed to understanding human health and also plant and animal husbandry. It will also tackle some of the weaknesses of the approach, and ways to address them, as well as discussing the considerable refinement of methodology that might be offered through compound-specific analyses alongside a fuller understanding of metabolic systems. Compound-specific stable isotope analysis has also revolutionized the study of organic chemical residues (Evershed et al. 1994), but discussion of that will be reserved for Chapter 4. Stable isotopes have additionally contributed much to palaeoclimatic reconstruction; this chapter will not focus upon that subject in detail but will consider it in relation to understanding economic questions related to environment as well as use of climatic proxies in establishing migration and patterns of seasonality.

A chemical element is defined by its atomic number, which relates to the number of protons in its nucleus, but its atomic mass refers to the number of protons and neutrons in the nucleus (Brown and Brown 2011). If the number of protons changes, so does the atomic number and it becomes a different element, but if the number of neutrons changes it becomes a different isotope of the same element, with the same chemical properties, but a different mass. The existence of isotopes was first fully described by Frederick Soddy in a letter to *Nature* (1913), the name having been suggested by Dr Margaret Todd from the Greek *isos topos* meaning the 'same place' – i.e. in the periodic table – (Nagel 1982). The same year as Soddy's breakthrough, Sir Joseph Thompson, experimenting with very early mass spectrometry, demonstrated the existence of stable isotopes (Thomson 1913). Whilst radioactive isotopes, of course, eventually became the mainstay of many scientific dating methods, the fact that other isotopes remain stable over time is fundamentally important to reconstructing the circumstances of significant past chemical reactions, irrespective of age. From the start (Soddy 1913), it was recognized that whilst isotopes of an element would chemically react in essentially the same way, there would be some instances where physical properties might be directly dependent upon atomic mass. We now know that some of the effects of differing atomic mass are non-trivial and biases in rates of reaction between heavier or lighter isotopes create different isotope ratios through a process called 'fractionation' (Brown and Brown 2011). Fractionation effects on different elements in particular contexts tell us a wide range of archaeologically useful things about environmental conditions, sources of nutrients and metabolism. Fractionation, however, is not the only cause of differing stable isotope ratios. Just a year after Soddy and Thomson's work, it was discovered that different isotopes of lead were generated by the radioactive decay of other elements (Richards and Lembert 1914). Such isotopes, which relate to the abundance of parent radio-isotopes within the local environment or geology, are now referred to as being radiogenic isotopes (Banner 2004). Radiogenic isotopes are most significant in determining the geographical origin of inorganic materials based upon parent geology and organic materials based upon the bioavailable radiogenic stable isotope ratios of local geological origin that enter through diet. Despite this early understanding of stable isotopes, application to archaeology was much delayed.

Whilst Willard Libby developed an understanding of the cosmic production of radiocarbon (^{14}C) and its potential for dating archaeological materials by the mid 1940s (Libby 1946; Arnold and Libby 1949), archaeological applications of fractionation effects in stable isotopes took much longer to develop. By the 1950s, understanding of the biogeochemistry of stable carbon isotopes was increasing (e.g. Craig 1953) followed by appreciation of trophic level shifts in stable isotope ratios of nitrogen by the 1960s (e.g. Miyake and Wada 1967). However, it was not until the late 1970s that dietary reconstruction in relation to ancient material was considered and undertaken (Vogel and Van der Merwe 1977; DeNiro and Epstein 1978; Van der Merwe and Vogel 1978), with early applications combining consideration of both carbon and nitrogen stable isotope ratios following in the early 1980s (e.g. DeNiro and Epstein 1981). Knowledge of atmospheric oxygen isotope ratios and climatic fractionation effects increased through the 1950s and 1960s (e.g. Dole et al. 1954; Dansgaard 1964), with the idea of using ancient osteological material to establish palaeoclimate and seasonality gaining traction in the 1980s (e.g. Longinelli 1984; Koch et al. 1989). In relation to radiogenic isotopes, the use of lead isotope ratios to source material culture got under way in the mid 1960s (e.g. Brill and Wampler 1965, 1967) whilst use of strontium isotope ratios in bioarchaeology, to look at residence patterns of ancient humans, did not develop until the 1980s (e.g. Ericson 1985).

'You are What You Eat' and Beyond – Reconstructing Plant, Animal and Human Diet, Foodways, Health and Husbandry

This section will establish what isotopic analysis has added to the study of past diet and related topics as well as highlighting exciting new avenues for future investigation. However, it will also critically evaluate the limitations of the approach and the need for integrated consideration of complementary information from established lines of bioarchaeological evidence, alongside other novel approaches. Before embarking on this, it is worth briefly outlining some of the key principles behind stable isotope dietary reconstruction. Stable isotope determinations for dietary reconstruction can be undertaken on any preserved organic materials but are most commonly undertaken on bones and teeth. For dietary reconstruction work, as with radiocarbon dating, it has been found to be generally more reliable to extract just the collagen for determination, and hence avoid some significant problems with diagenetic effects and contamination that can be associated with the inorganic components of bone (Sealy 2001). The two most valuable isotope ratios for dietary reconstruction are $\delta^{13}C$ and $\delta^{15}N$ values (Sealy 2001; Makarewicz and Sealy 2015), with the 'delta' representing a function of the difference in observed ratios to an internationally recognized standard ratio of $^{13}C/^{12}C$ or $^{15}N/^{14}N$ (Sealy 2001).

$\delta^{13}C$ values in food webs tend to be depleted (negative) due to fractionation favouring the lighter isotope during plant photosynthesis at the base of the food chain. However, there are two major ways in which plants photosynthesize: C_3 or C_4 pathways. The C_3 pathway is much more discriminatory in terms of fractionation than the C_4 pathway, hence C_4 plants end up with considerably less depleted $\delta^{13}C$ values, as do animals who feed upon them. The vast majority of human food crops are C_3, but a small number of highly significant crops are C_4, most notably maize in the Americas, along with sugarcane, and sorghum and millets in the Old World (Sealy 2001; Brown and Brown 2011). Therefore, one key set of archaeological questions the method can address relates to the introduction and scale of consumption of key C_4 crops. However carbon stable isotopes additionally help with the identification of marine diets. Whilst marine carbon systems are complex (Sealy 2001), most marine foodstuffs tend to display less depleted values (relative to terrestrial C_3 diets), so investigation of the exploitation of sea foods also becomes possible (Brown and Brown 2011). Alongside these causes of major shifts in $\delta^{13}C$ values there are smaller variations caused by local environments and food webs.

The stable isotope ratios of nitrogen provide different types of information. $\delta^{15}N$ values in food webs generally tend to be positive values that can be further enriched through several different mechanisms. Marine environments tend to have slightly enriched values (Schoeninger and DeNiro 1984) as do plants in very arid areas, along with the animals that feed on them (Sealy 2001; Brown and Brown 2011). However, $\delta^{15}N$ values have been most used in archaeology as an indicator of trophic level, as there are successive enrichments in values up the food chain from plant to herbivore to carnivore and so on (Minagawa and Wada 1984; Makarewicz and Sealy 2015). A similar effect is visible in $\delta^{13}C$ values which become

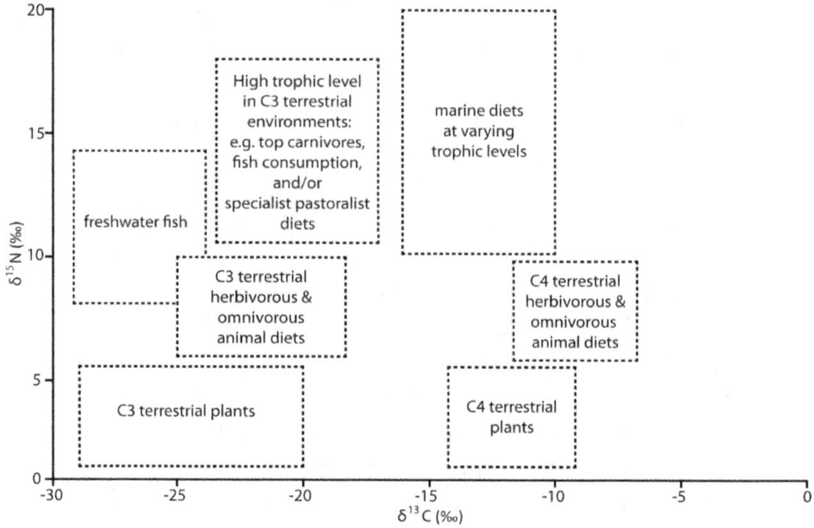

FIGURE 3.1 An approximate and generalized representation of the relationship between δ^{13}C and δ^{15}N values in organisms with different diets.

successively less depleted (Brown and Brown 2011), but the effect is not quite so pronounced. So a common use of δ^{15}N determinations in archaeology has been establishing how much dietary protein may have resulted from plant or animal or marine/aquatic sources at different trophic levels. A diet of carnivorous marine fish would, therefore, produce one of the most pronounced enhancements in δ^{15}N values (Wada et al. 1991).

Further advantage is gained through plotting δ^{13}C against δ^{15}N determinations from the same samples, since combined consideration helps eliminate some areas of potential equifinality; C_4 and marine diets could look similar if only carbon is considered, but are distinguished by the addition of nitrogen isotopic values. Figure 3.1 displays the common positions of key dietary sources on a scatter plot of δ^{13}C against δ^{15}N values. The complexities of archaeological interpretation of such diagrams will be critically discussed below, but it is worth noting, purely in relation to technical aspects of biochemistry, that many early applications employed the above principles of fractionation in an overly simplistic way and a much more sophisticated understanding of metabolic systems and food webs is developing but is far from complete. What is becoming increasingly apparent is the need to carry out a detailed assessment of local ancient food webs through the comprehensive analysis of surviving plant, animal and human tissues. It has often been common practice to examine human diet by simple reference to local herbivore animal values, but we now know that different husbandry systems and seasonal movements through different ecosystems do not necessarily make such samples a suitable baseline for comparison (Makarewicz and Sealy 2015). Indeed, even food crops are susceptible to human isotopic manipulation through differing forms of husbandry. The isotopic effects of such manipulations are interesting in and of themselves in addressing important archaeological questions, as will be discussed below, but it is clear that simplistic comparisons should be replaced by more holistic consideration of whole food-web systems from natural local vegetation upwards. Unfortunately, overly simplistic work is still not uncommon, sometimes as a function of the level of scientific understanding or logistic limitations, but perhaps more often as a result of the high financial and time costs of fully comprehensive studies.

In addition to carbon and nitrogen, there are a few other stable isotope ratios that are of value in establishing what was eaten in the past. Sulfur is worth particular mention. $\delta^{34}S$ values may well prove to be most significant as a further indicator of marine food consumption due to enhancements in marine ecosystems (Nehlich 2015). In addition, sea spray effects in relation to $\delta^{34}S$ values might also help to distinguish marine, coastal and terrestrial diets in a way that $\delta^{13}C$ values will not. $\delta^{34}S$ values also express some degree of trophic level enhancement, but much more research is required to understand the many potential influences on sulfur isotope ratios (Nehlich 2015). Significant trophic level fractionation has also very recently been noted in $\delta^{88}Sr$ (Knudson et al. 2010) and now verified in controlled feeding experiments (Lewis et al. 2017). Already, $^{87}Sr/^{86}Sr$ radiogenic isotope ratios of strontium were a mainstay of investigating geological sources, but the use of $\delta^{88}Sr$ stable isotope values shows some promise in assisting with equifinality of interpretations based upon $\delta^{15}N$ determinations. Clearly, the future lies in multi-proxy approaches to dietary reconstruction based on stable isotope determinations.

Given the above range of technical possibilities, how successful have stable isotope proxies been so far in answering major archaeological questions about past diet? In relation to the spread of maize agriculture in North America, the earliest archaeological dietary application (Vogel and Van der Merwe 1977), results were exceptionally clear. They were of importance because they tended to push back the date, in relation to the conventional wisdom at the time, of significant maize consumption in both Mexico (DeNiro and Epstein 1981) and more northerly regions where the crop was later adopted (Vogel and Van der Merwe 1977). In contrast, such as in earlier Hopewell individuals, maize was found not to be a major component of diet despite some prior speculation that it might have been (Bender et al. 1981). It is clear there were some very quick wins from early research in North America with studies progressing on to address social dimensions of food consumption. For instance, in Cahokia mound burials, $\delta^{13}C$ and $\delta^{15}N$ determinations on skeletal collagen used together showed that apparently low status individuals seemed to rely almost entirely upon maize for sustenance, whereas high status individuals obtained considerably more of their protein from the meat of animals grazing on C_3 plants (Ambrose et al. 2003). Limitations to archaeological methodologies may come in many forms: in the case of stable isotope research into prehistoric human diet in North America these were not related to technical issues, preservation of materials or failure of middle range theory, but the need to carry out destructive analysis on human remains. The political context and ethical concerns related to such work vary considerably in geopolitical terms, especially in relation to rights of indigenous peoples. Whilst human dietary reconstruction continues at pace in some regions, it has almost ceased in others.

In the Old World, the arrival of cereal agriculture is not so easily marked out in isotopic terms since the most important staples, wheat, barley, oats, rye and rice, are all C_3 plants (Sealy 2001), but there have been attempts to track the introduction of some novel C_4 crops such as millet that appear to have been traded into Europe from the Far East by at least the Bronze Age (Jones et al. 2011). There are apparent early archaeobotanical finds of millet in both central Asia (Frachetti et al. 2010; Miller et al. 2016) and Europe (Hunt et al. 2008), although some of the Neolithic dates from Europe have now been questioned following direct dating of the charred grains (Motuzaite-Matuzeviciute et al. 2013). Furthermore, the isotopic evidence for a significant accompanying C_4 isotopic signal is patchy (Lightfoot et al. 2013; Matuzeviciute et al. 2015; Nitsch et al. 2017; Ananyevskaya et al. 2018). This work is useful as it appears to show that millet was rarely a staple, though perhaps a few individuals ate more of it, but these results are much less clear cut regarding the economic and dietary status of millet than American studies of maize. Stable isotopic signals are not particularly good at picking up lesser components of diet and, in some cases, there is potential for confusion and equifinality resulting from complex mixed diets with marine components. Furthermore, in interpreting these data, one should not make the mistake of equating lack of significant C_4 signal, and thus millet not being a staple, with lack of economic importance. For instance, millet is fast-maturing and can produce high yields in limited growing seasons, making it ideal as a risk buffer, particularly in regions with short or dry summers (Jones et al. 2011). Furthermore, purely pragmatic aspects of economy could be secondary to the social prestige often attached to exotic crops when first introduced to new regions (see Boivin et al. 2012). The comparison between isotopic stories of maize and millet starkly contrast in terms of the definitive progress that can be made through dietary isotope work alone. In the case of millet it is not merely clear that isotopic results must be integrated with a wide range of other evidential forms, but actually that answering some of the key questions lies outside the frame of resolution afforded by isotopic methods as they currently stand. There are only limited occasions in archaeology when new methods are truly 'magic bullets'.

Early successes with dietary isotope research in the Old World revolved much more around identifying shifts in the use of marine resources in the transition from hunter-gatherer to farming societies. For instance, early applications in coastal regions of western Europe appeared to show an abrupt cessation in the exploitation of sea food with the arrival of farming ways of life (e.g. Tauber 1981; Lubell et al. 1994; Richards and Hedges 1999). These results were a dramatic new entrant to heated debates over the spread and nature of economic shifts at the start of the Neolithic. An abrupt shift in diet rather favours the argument that the Neolithic package arrived from outside and represented discontinuity from what had gone before, something counter to popular arguments at the time (see Thomas 1991, 1999). It is not surprising that other studies were undertaken with a view to testing this emerging picture. In southern Scandinavia (Lidén et al. 2004), new work illustrated a more complex picture with some Neolithic coastal sites, particularly of the Pitted Ware Culture, showing considerable exploitation of marine food. Whilst this paper was presented as challenging the above characterization of a fast dietary change at the start of the Neolithic, it was really further elucidating an already observed pattern of reversion to some hunter-gatherer behaviours in the middle Neolithic Pitted Ware Culture (see Lindqvist and Possnert 1997; Rowley-Conwy and Storå 1997). A more complex picture in Scandinavia can be readily accepted. In relation to the British Isles, counter arguments focused much more on issues of the representativeness of samples and the sensitivity of the method (Milner et al. 2004). From a technical point of view there was the suggestion that a shift to a very low-protein diet could be masking a continued input of marine foods (Milner et al. 2004). Such an argument would still need to admit considerable shift towards terrestrial plant diets, but would allow some greater level of continuity in coastal exploitation. The ability to pick up smaller scale levels of resource exploitation is certainly an issue in this case, as it is with the identification of millet consumption. Nonetheless, a recent, large-scale, multi-proxy study of this issue applied to the northern British Isles and archipelagos, that examined faunal assemblages, lipid residues and stable isotopes, concluded that all the lines of evidence demonstrated an abrupt move away from marine resources at the start of the Neolithic (Cramp et al. 2014). Sea food, in fact, is close to absent from the Neolithic record whilst it slowly increases into later prehistory and even more so in the Viking age, but never returns to late Mesolithic levels (Cramp et al. 2014). Even at the periphery of the Neolithic world, on the Shetland Islands, the sudden shift to a terrestrial diet is evident in isotopic data, with evidence only for sporadic use of marine resources, perhaps in times of famine (Montgomery et al. 2013a). Whilst it appears that the early impactful results on this topic largely hold true still, the challenge of masking in low-protein diets and identifying smaller components of diet remain. Recent controlled pig-feeding experiments to investigate marine signals (Webb et al. 2017) further illustrate the difficulties with diets low in protein and the detection of marine diet proportions of below 20%; however, the use of multiple isotopic proxies and/or compound-specific approaches (see below) to stable isotope research present possible ways forward (Webb et al. 2017).

Human dietary reconstruction has frequently been undertaken to address questions related to subsistence economics, but some dietary patterns relate to health, the way people are cared for and social structures, whilst other patterns are principally driven by cultural practices and differences. Stable isotope analysis is a massively powerful technique for addressing such questions because it is capable of generating information about individual people from direct analysis of their tissues. When combined with osteologically determined age, physical or genetic criteria for sex and descent, alongside archaeological context, stable isotope data can penetrate demographic, socioeconomic and cultural questions in a way that traditional methods of dietary and subsistence reconstruction simply cannot.

Some health issues are directly related to diet and have particular isotopic signatures. In cases where individuals are under severe nutritional stress, particularly in relation to protein intake, then they enter a state of 'catabolism'. This involves reuse of amino-acids from existing bodily protein resulting in additional fractionation that resembles upward trophic level shift with enriched $\delta^{15}N$ values (Fuller et al. 2005; Reitsema 2013). This effect has been established to occur in cases of starvation (and severe dieting), eating disorders such as anorexia (not bulimia), morning sickness during pregnancy and diets that severely lack protein but which are still calorifically adequate (Reitsema 2013). Systematic investigations of starvation cases in archaeological contexts have not yet been undertaken, but there is awareness of this effect in relation to the potential identification of cases of malnutrition, but also as a complicating and rather counter-intuitive factor in dietary reconstructions. Particular medical conditions can, in some circumstances affect isotopic fractionation in very particular ways. Some such conditions are known within medicine to affect isotope ratios in urine or plasma (see Reitsema 2013), but in many of these cases it is not yet clear whether an effect is also observable in tissues that would survive archaeologically. One such example that has been noted is the increase in $\delta^{15}N$ values of the bone protein in an osteomyelitic lesion (Richards and Montgomery 2012), which demonstrates the point that isotopic analysis is not just specific to an individual, but also to particular tissues in relation to the timing and circumstances of their formation.

Another cause of increased $\delta^{15}N$ values that relates strongly to the timing of tissue formation has been quite extensively researched. When an infant is being fed with its mother's milk this also represents a trophic level shift, so breastfeeding infants show elevated $\delta^{15}N$ values compared with their mother. These values return to normal once weaning has been completed, so if stable isotope data is added to age at death then weaning ages can be determined (Katzenberg et al. 1996; Herring et al. 1998; Schurr 1998). This provides exceptionally valuable information in relation to social organization, health, issues of fertility and population dynamics, which are often closely associated with weaning practices (see Liamputtong 2007; Quinlan 2007). In archaeological cases it might not be possible directly to match mother and infant, but the method has generally worked very well in identifying breastfeeding and weaning by comparison to the general adult range of $\delta^{15}N$ values (e.g. Clayton et al 2006; Nitsch et al. 2011), although there have been curious cases where infants and adults in mortuary contexts do not relate well to each other isotopically in relation to either $\delta^{15}N$ or $\delta^{13}C$ values (Jay et al. 2008). Such problems could relate to sample selection and contextual issues, but another important fact to consider is that these are the infants that died, rather than survived, so a risk of this method is extrapolating too much about the whole population from a potentially abnormal sample that died young. Methods for examining weaning have been improving, however, and instead of undertaking a single determination from each individual and using its age at death, it is possible to take multiple samples from different teeth, largely deciduous ones, to show the weaning sequence within a single individual (e.g. Dupras and Tocheri 2007) allowing intra-population as well as inter-population comparisons. Furthermore, methods for micro-sampling within the first molar, that record different ages when the tooth was developing (see Eerkens et al. 2011), allow sampling within individuals that survived beyond infancy, hence removing the bias discussed above. Some studies appear to show two distinct timings for weaning (e.g. Clayton et al. 2006) and this could potentially indicate differential weaning times in infants of different sex. When micro-sampling within molars is used to examine adult skeletons for their infant dietary record, their sex can also be determined. Just such a study of Holocene hunter-gatherers from California showed that boys were weaned much later than girls (Eerkens and Bartelink 2013). A new method that allows sex determination based upon chromosome-related peptide markers in tooth enamel (Stewart et al. 2017) opens the possibility of establishing the sex of infant remains and this information could be combined with isotopic data in future studies. Such resolution regarding an issue so critical to understanding the interplay between environment, health, demographics and culture is a remarkable step forward.

Stable isotopic indicators of status and social differentiation have already been touched upon in relation to protein intake and status in the Cahokia burial mounds of the Mississippian (Ambrose et al. 2003), but there has been abundant research in this area. Studies range from dietary differences relating to Church burial position in post-medieval Belgium (Quintelier et al. 2014), to analyses of a Viking cemetery in Sweden (Linderholm et al. 2008) and Iron Age inhumations in the Czech Republic (Le Huray and Schutkowski 2005), to mention but a few. All these examples show not only differentiation by status, as indicated by burial position or grave goods, but also differences between the sexes. Variations in diet between populations with different religions have also been noted. For instance, in late medieval Spain the Islamic *mudéjares* population appears to have consumed more C_4 plants than local Christians (Alexander et al. 2015). This difference might relate to the historically known *mudéjares* association with sugarcane production, and hence be more related to socioeconomic associations of cultural groupings than it is to faith *per se*. Another study indicates no significant change in diet accompanying Viking change of faith from pagan to Christian on Gotland (Kosiba et al. 2007) and that the diet of early Christians in Rome, possibly high in freshwater fish, was most likely a function of economic situation, but could have undertones of faith (Rutgers et al. 2009). The issue of whether the previously discussed avoidance of fish in early Neolithic Britain represented some form of taboo belief has even been mooted (see Thomas 2003; Richards and Schulting 2006). Whilst the potential for isotopic investigation of cultural preferences, taboos and expressions of faith through foodways remains an intriguing line of enquiry, differentiation between faith and socioeconomic factors will always be exceedingly difficult and highly dependent upon detailed arguments pertaining to archaeological context and a holistic consideration of lines of evidence.

Diligent stable isotope research will involve determinations to cover most of the relevant local food web, including flora and fauna. Whilst, in many cases, this is undertaken to understand properly human food consumption, significant archaeological questions about the diet of plants and animals themselves are now of increasing interest. Dietary reconstruction of animals is partly about understanding their movements in the landscape (see discussion below), but there are also significant questions stable isotopes can answer in relation to diets associated with domestication, commensalism and different husbandry regimes, for instance. In the case of both dogs and cats, isotopic reconstruction of diet has been used as a line of evidence for identifying early domestication (e.g. Germonpré et al. 2009; Hu et al. 2014) based upon assumption that diets in the wild would significantly differ from those obtained through strong association with humans and their subsistence activities. One of the established routes to domestication is the 'commensal pathway' (Zeder 2012) where close association and interest in human food waste can eventually lead to domestication. This pathway is certainly very pertinent to dogs and cats and clearly a change in diet to include foods deriving from human subsistence practices could be an indicator of domestication in progress. A study of dietary changes in cats in China (6th millennium BP) identified one older cat that apparently ate very little meat, but quite a lot of C_4 millet, perhaps showing reliance on human foods in old age, and therefore possibly domesticity (Hu et al. 2014). This remains a valid hypothesis, though others have pointed out that commensalism and use of human food waste do not necessarily imply domesticity and, whilst in some cases it might lead to domestication, in others it does not (O'Connor 2013; Bar-Oz et al. 2014). Transition in diet upon domestication could be relevant for other species too, as well as changes in food supply brought about by evolving husbandry practices. There are applications of such studies that relate to much later archaeological periods. One example examined the changing methods of husbandry of pigs during the transition from the high to late medieval periods. A study from Flanders, Belgium (Ervynck et al. 2007) suggests a shift in diets consistent with a change from forest dwelling towards being foddered on farms during this period. Something similar is noted in England at around the same time by a decrease in dietary diversity accompanied by other evidence for more controlled and enclosed pig husbandry practices (Hamilton and Thomas 2012).

As with humans, the timing of weaning can also be studied in some animals and early demonstrations of this were in cattle (Balasse et al. 1999, 2001). Establishing weaning patterns in cattle can be particularly interesting because early weaning has the potential to be associated with dairy husbandry strategies where the herder is trying to reserve more of the milk for human consumption (Balasse and Tresset 2002). Just such a potential pattern was argued to exist at the Neolithic site of Bercy, France (Balasse and Tresset 2002). Another study that integrated detailed attention to age at death patterns with stable isotope evidence at the Chalcolithic site of Borduşani-Popină in Romania (Gillis et al. 2013) suggested a complex mixed model of husbandry. The herd structure contained females that were kept to advanced age for milking whilst much slaughter of males occurred between 6 and 12 months (relatively early for meat production) or from 12 to 24 months (potentially prime meat production). This suggests a mixed use of the animals for meat and milk. In this case, it seems that weaning did not occur particularly early, possibly as a strategy of having calves present to facilitate milk let-down in this breed, thus implying that the milk produced here needed to be shared between calves and herders (Gillis et al. 2013). There is much to learn about the complexities of different past husbandry strategies and studies of this type are in their infancy, but it is clear that there is now the potential to tackle them through integrated methodologies.

Food plants are also affected by changes to their nutrient and water sources. This tells us about processes of ancient crop husbandry, but it is also significant because of the effects it can have further up the food chain. Areas of particular focus have been on identifying evidence for the irrigation and manuring of crops. Changes to levels of water supply can be detected in $\delta^{13}C$ values, which become less depleted if the plant is water-stressed. However, since $\delta^{13}C$ values in plants can also be affected by changes in atmospheric carbon isotope ratios over time, that factor needs to be taken into consideration This is done by using ice core data to model changes in atmospheric $\delta^{13}C$ values through the Holocene and by expressing the determination in ancient crops as a function of the difference between the crops' values and atmospheric values at the time, to produce a $\Delta^{13}C$ value. This value increases with more water input (Ferrio et al. 2005; Wallace et al. 2013). This proxy can be used to compare growing conditions in different places at different times, or for different crops at the same time and place that might be grown under different husbandry regimes, and potentially to identify the effects of deliberate irrigation. One such study relating to sites in Bronze Age Mesopotamia and the Levant (Riehl et al. 2008) indicated generally increased aridity in the middle Bronze Age, but also noted high standard deviations in values at some arid sites that might suggest that some crops were receiving irrigation whilst others were not. Another study has suggested the selective irrigation of faba beans during the Bronze Age in the Iberian Peninsula with no other crop displaying enhanced $\Delta^{13}C$ values (Araus et al. 1997).

In plants, $\delta^{15}N$ values can be related to nutrient availability but can be particularly enhanced by the manuring of fields. This is because of the fractionation effects of ^{15}N-depleted volatile forms of nitrogen in animal dung leaving in gases resulting in relatively higher $\delta^{15}N$ values in the residue (Bogaard et al. 2007). The effects of this process are now reasonably well understood through experimental crop trials in different environments under different manuring regimes (Fraser et al. 2011). Another factor that needs to be understood, before applying such methods to charred archaeobotanical specimens, is whether charring itself creates further fractionation. This too has been tested experimentally (Styring et al. 2013; Nitsch et al. 2015) and the off-set is relatively small but sufficient for correction to be advisable. It is becoming clear from examination of a number of sites in Neolithic Europe that early mixed farmers were making intensive use of manure to enhance crop production, often through strategic application to specific crops and/or parts of the landscape (Bogaard et al. 2014b). Manuring is not evident everywhere, however, and a study that makes use of both $\delta^{15}N$ and $\Delta^{13}C$ values considers changing agricultural conditions at an early agricultural site in south-east Spain (Aguilera et al. 2008) where, whilst hydrological conditions remained fairly constant, $\delta^{15}N$ values dropped in later periods showing possible loss of fertility or the use of more marginal lands. A recent study made use of further multi-proxy, modern, experimental comparisons in Morocco, incorporating the study of weed ecology as well as crop stable isotopic determinations, to examine plant husbandry at early Bronze Age Tell Brak in Syria (Bogaard et al. 2018). A complex and highly detailed pattern of exploitation over time, comparing different crop types, could be established. In general the city appears to have subsisted from relatively low-intensity, rain-fed, extensive fields, though there is 'sherd scatter' evidence for spreading settlement waste on infields in the later phases studied. Similar results have now been found at a range of other tell sites (Styring et al. 2017a). Studies like these, that elucidate issues such as agricultural extensification and the use of manuring, have recently been used to underpin the major conclusion that there was greater wealth disparity among early agriculturalists in Eurasia than in North America or Mesoamerica (Kohler et al. 2017). This research clearly indicates what can be achieved in terms of resolution of data from a multi-proxy approach underpinned by solid comparator information.

The obvious strength of the isotopic approach to dietary reconstruction is that it provides direct and specific information about individual people, plants and animals. Its weakness is that the information can be somewhat vague and open to equifinality. It is worth exploring these two issues a little further. Stable isotope values are not only specific to individuals but indeed to the precise tissues sampled. This is of great benefit to the study of factors that require a time sequence, such as weaning or seasonal movement (see below), and should largely be seen as a further strength. Indeed specificity to particular pathological tissues could also be highly informative. However, this all depends upon us having a sound understanding of how and when tissues are formed and, whilst we have established quite a lot, there are still some significant gaps in knowledge. These are things that isotope specialists will need to continue working on, but archaeologists interpreting isotopic studies also need to be suitably aware of the issues and understand exactly what a determination on a particular tissue might mean. This is very similar to the learning curve exhibited in the development of radiocarbon dating, in terms of sample selection and understanding precisely what moment was being dated, for instance a twig from a 400 year old oak, as opposed to its heartwood.

The individual specificity of stable isotopic approaches allows us to tackle time series, but it also allows us to see demographic differences and compare diets of the old and young, male and female, high status and low status, the indigenous and alien, as well as different cultural groupings. However, the understanding of diet provided only relates to broad food groups and food sources such as marine versus terrestrial, amounts of protein in diet or plant groups according to photosynthetic pathway. Alone, stable isotopes do not tell us about the species exploited, never mind precise foodways. In an American context, for instance, we can only be totally certain that the major shift in $\delta^{13}C$ values seen in many regions in prehistory relates to the introduction of maize because there are additionally finds of preserved cobs. In many other cases it is far less straightforward and there is a very high degree of equifinality possible in resultant whole-diet signals from different mixtures of foods, which becomes particularly complex to deal with if marine, freshwater, terrestrial and C_3/C_4 issues are all in play simultaneously. Careful consideration alongside the traditional faunal and floral evidence for hunting, gathering, herding and farming activities will in most cases largely resolve the problem, particularly if the consumption of particular foods is also established through organic residue chemistry techniques (see next chapter). Then there is the clear potential to understand exactly which species were being exploited, how they were being consumed and what the resulting dietary patterns were in different individual plants, animals and people.

There are, however, sometimes occasions where the different forms of evidence do not match up well. For instance, isotopic studies of later prehistoric steppe pastoralists in central Asia appear to frequently show significant consumption of freshwater fish, based upon inference from elevated $\delta^{15}N$ values in relation to the rest of the food web (e.g. O'Connell et al. 2003; Lightfoot et al. 2015), but studies of faunal remains and ceramic lipid residues reveal very little evidence for fishing. Very small numbers of fish bones have been recovered at sites, which represent an insignificant proportion in terms of numerical abundance in the assemblages, and an even smaller proportion of diet if respective meat weights and secondary products are taken into consideration. Fish bones are frequently underrepresented where recovery methods are poor but representation is still very low, even at sites with rigorous sieving and good preservation. Lipid residues studies in the region have not identified any pots that appear to be particularly associated with freshwater aquatic food processing (Outram et al. 2012). Could this be caused by heavy consumption of processed dairy products? Processing by fermentation and cheese making can cause very small uplifts in $\delta^{15}N$ values, but these are not apparently sufficient to create the effect seen (Privat et al. 2005). However, Mackarewicz (2018) notes that there are examples of pastoral societies exhibiting $\delta^{15}N$ values that are enriched to the same degree as major fish consumers, even in circumstances where there is good reason to rule fishing out, such as historic Bedouin from Jordan, known not to consume significant aquatic resources (Gregoricka and Judd 2016). There is a clear potential problem of equifinality in the central Asian example therefore. It could certainly be the case that many fish bones have been lost, or were disposed of in such a way that they are not being recovered. This would need to be happening on a fairly large scale for fish to become a significant proportion of total diet. Equally, it is possible that fish were generally not cooked in pots, but simply roasted. On the other hand, extreme reliance on pastoral animal products might be influencing $\delta^{15}N$ values along with unaccounted for environmental effects. A complex combination of effects is also possible. In many cases, holistic integration of multiple lines of evidence will produce a coherent and rich picture. In other cases it will suggest useful lines for future enquiry.

'You are Where and When You Eat' – Migration, Seasonality and Socioeconomic Landscapes

This section moves away from diet to address spatio-temporal issues of mobility throughout landscapes and how those can be isotopically reconstructed through diet and water sources. Establishing patterns of mobility in an individual requires some form of serial sampling of tissues (Makarewicz and Sealy 2015) that allow one to establish a known temporal sequence of isotopic intake. Indeed such a sequence of $\delta^{15}N$ values and $\delta^{13}C$ values might show differences if diet varied over time in relation to changes in foods available in particular places at particular times. However, what people chose to eat is subject to many socioeconomic and cultural factors which may not always directly relate to geographical position or time of year. As such, a different suit of isotopic approaches can be added that speak more directly to place and time as expressed through geology and climate.

In relation to geological origin, the radiogenic isotopes of two elements, strontium ($^{87}Sr/^{86}Sr$) and lead ($^{206}Pb/^{204}Pb$; $^{207}Pb/^{204}Pb$; $^{208}Pb/^{204}Pb$), are of particular interest. These radiogenic isotopes are products of the radioactive decay of unstable elements and they provide a fingerprint for particular underlying geologies. Strontium is most used in archaeology to identify the regions individual organisms came from because bioavailable strontium is taken in through diet and therefore $^{87}Sr/^{86}Sr$ ratios will represent the local geology of dietary sources (Ericson 1985; Bentley 2006). Deposits of different geological age tend to show the biggest variation in strontium isotope ratios (Burton and Hahn 2016). It is necessary to avoid being overly simplistic in making the assumption that the precise $^{87}Sr/^{86}Sr$ ratios seen in the geology will necessarily be reflected in the tissues of food consumers above. Whilst feeding experiments (e.g. Lewis et al. 2017) show generally good correlation between $^{87}Sr/^{86}Sr$ ratios in diet and those assimilated into tissues, considerable diligence needs to be shown with respect to understanding local geological variation and what the 'bioavailable' $^{87}Sr/^{86}Sr$ ratios are as displayed by local plants, which might not be quite the same, sometimes as a result of atmospheric inputs such as sea spray (Bentley 2006; Burton and Hahn 2016) and these factors need to be taken into account through appropriate reference work. Stable isotope ratios of lead can be used in much the same way, but their use to complement strontium data in bioarchaeological mobility studies, as opposed to material culture sourcing, is a relatively recent development that only began to gain traction in the late 1990s (Montgomery et al. 2000). Whilst there are recent archaeological studies making full use of both strontium and lead (e.g. Turner et al. 2009; Shaw et al. 2016), the vast majority of such studies still focus on strontium alone. Indeed a number of reviews of stable isotope techniques do not mention lead (e.g. Sealy 2004; Makarewicz and Sealy 2015) though modern experimental studies show a good relationship between lead isotope ratios in the meat of animals reared in different locations and their local geology. It appears that lead isotope ratios in animals are geogenic in origin, with assimilation occurring through both food ingestion and inhalation of dust and soil particles (Evans et al. 2015). It is worth noting that in periods following the introduction of metallurgy that environmentally available lead sources might well have been modified by that industry (Budd et al. 2000) and use of lead vessels, pipes and paints and so on will have a direct effect on ratios (Montgomery et al. 2010).

Oxygen isotope ratios, on the other hand, reflect variation in temperature during the precipitation of water and $\delta^{18}O$ values in biological tissues reflect the water being ingested and hence its climatic signature (Sealy 2004). This mechanism has been used as a mainstay of long-term climate reconstruction studies but can also be used as a form of dating (Aitken 1990) for archaeological tissue samples from deep time by assigning oxygen isotope stages that correspond to various major phases of glaciation as reconstructed from sea and ice core measurements. However, in mobility studies we are interested in changes related to climate in different latitudes, altitudes and seasons (Sealy 2001; Makarewicz and Sealy 2015; Mayur et al. 2016). Likely geographical sources of diet can then be best determined by a combination of $^{87}Sr/^{86}Sr$ ratios (perhaps complemented by lead isotope ratios) to identify likely geogenic sources, and $\delta^{18}O$ values to identify likely climatic ranges. Clearly, the more proxies that are included the narrower will be the final mutually valid range of possibilities. Evidence for changing C_3/C_4 plant intake and aridity levels might additionally be indicated from $\delta^{13}C$ and $\delta^{15}N$ values providing further evidence for likely locality. Isotopic mapping is more or less developed in different regions of the world, and some 'isoscapes' (Bowen 2010) present more heterogeneity and specificity than others. In some cases it might be possible to suggest specific source regions with a reasonable degree of confidence within the context of the study, but frequently, conclusions might be restricted to 'local' and 'non-local'.

Whilst $\delta^{13}C$ and $\delta^{15}N$ values in mammals can be determined from extracted collagen, and such determinations have been found to be a good proxy for original diet, strontium and lead isotopes need to be determined from the inorganic fraction of bones and teeth. This has presented some significant problems, because relatively early on in such studies it was established that processes of diagenesis and later contamination from ground water could significantly affect ratios of radiogenic isotopes (Nelson et al. 1986), as indeed could some forms of sample treatment (Koch et al. 1997). The end conclusion is that tooth enamel, which is much more resistant to diagenetic alteration, is a reliable source for isotopic determinations for strontium, lead and oxygen, whilst extracted collagen is the best source for carbon and nitrogen determinations (Nelson et al. 1986; Koch et al. 1997). This has immediate repercussions for archaeological applications because tooth enamel isotopes relate to diet and residency when the tooth was being formed in a juvenile, whilst bone collagen isotope ratios inform us about the last few years of life. This means that only childhood residency can be established from radiogenic isotopes whilst the dietary information gained from analysing collagen refers to later stages of life. However, a limited residency time sequence can be established by looking at different teeth that form at different times in line with eruption sequences (Ericson 1985). Additionally, seasonal patterns of movement can be established through micro-sampling a single tooth to look at variations as that tooth formed (Makarewicz and Sealy 2015).

There are very large numbers of applications of stable isotopic signatures to compare locality of deposition or burial with where an individual person or animal originated in youth. Illustrative examples include consideration of evidence for immigration at Machu Picchu in Peru and whether patterns might relate to socioeconomic classes (Turner et al. 2009). This investigation concluded that there was evidence for a range of origins but that there was no correlation with class. Another case study pertains to identifying migrants to Roman London (Shaw et al. 2016) where it was concluded that, whilst there were individuals of local origin, there was a very cosmopolitan mix then, as now, with far-flung likely origins including Rome itself. Richer understanding of mobility and how it might relate to economic factors can be gained from considering the origins of both plants and animals. Looking at human migration alone rather lacks context and without further data it might be unclear whether patterns observed relate to culture factors, marriage practices, colonization, economic migration or be tied to economically or environmentally driven mobility patterns. Viewing human movement alongside the mobility patterns of economic resources, both ecofactual and artefactual, allows a deeper understanding. The origins of both plants and animals were considered at the early Neolithic site of Vaihingen in Germany (Bentley et al. 2003). In this case it was found that exogenous human individuals were more likely to be buried in outer ditches of the settlement, possibly indicating a cultural practice, within the context of a society whose animals showed a variety of isotopic signals indicating some mobility in herding practices. At Neolithic Çatalhöyük in Turkey, both animals and plants have been considered (Bogaard et al. 2014a). Charred plant remains can also yield strontium isotope determinations that might indicate geogenic origins and which of the outlying areas were in use for agriculture, and potentially which crops. In this case, the pilot data revealed that the plants probably originated from fields on the surrounding plains and not more distant areas to the south, and that whilst both local uplands and lowlands may have been used for animals, summer movement to the mountains can be excluded.

These studies indicate start and end points, which is useful for identifying migrants and resource sources, but not so useful in establishing the nature and timeframe of movement. Within animals and humans, multiple determinations from different teeth which develop in sequence during youth, will show movement during a particular timeslot in the development of a juvenile, in addition to knowing the end point of deposition. A fascinating case study employing this approach captured a very significant movement event. Whilst it is clear that fallow deer in Britain (*Dama dama*) are largely descended from animals introduced during the medieval period (Sykes 2004), there were a small number brought into the country by wealthy Romans, with a limited number of specimens in the assemblage at Fishbourne Roman Palace. An early-dated specimen exhibits isotopic evidence that it started life outside Britain and was transported to Fishbourne as a fawn. Later specimens demonstrate a stable isotopic pattern consistent for the local area at Fishbourne, suggesting that those deer were not imported, but bred locally (Sykes et al. 2006). Another example of this type of work, undertaken on both humans and animals from the British Neolithic (Montgomery et al. 2000; Neil et al. 2016), shows that, whilst some groups of animals and humans maintained the same isotopic signature over time and may have been sedentary, a higher proportion demonstrated mobility during a relatively short time window, suggesting a certain degree of residential mobility. However, when it comes to understanding fully the details of regular mobility, such as seasonal transhumance, pastoral nomadism or the settlement patterns of hunter-gatherers, far more resolution is desirable. This requires micro-sampled sequences that can tie dietary and geogenic signals to seasonal climatic signals.

Tooth enamel is formed in a sequence from the top of the crown (cusp) downwards to the base (cervix) such that an isotopic time sequence is established (Koch et al. 1989; Zazzo et al. 2012; Montgomery et al. 2013b).

This sequence can be studied by drilling or grinding small samples of the enamel at intervals down the tooth (e.g. Bendrey et al. 2014), a process usually called micro-milling. An alternative is taking the sequence of samples through laser ablation (e.g. Montgomery et al. 2013b; Reitmaier et al. 2018), which can sample with high resolution by evaporating or subliming a target spot with the resulting gases being analysed through mass spectrometry. Whilst the intention might be to compare light isotopes (e.g. of carbon and oxygen) and heavier isotopes (e.g. of lead and strontium), these currently require the use of different types of mass spectrometer, which adds to the cost and time required for multi-proxy studies. A longer sequence can be obtained by 'wiggle-matching' the sequence from successive molars that form at different times (e.g. Bendrey et al. 2014), in rather the same way that dendrochronological sequences are created from overlapping the records of successive trees (Aitken 1990). Clearly, the larger the teeth are, in the species being studied, the easier it is to take a long sequence of samples.

Such methodologies have very wide potential applications related to the seasonal movements of different animals in many different archaeological contexts. Establishing whether or not major prehistoric prey species were migratory will serve as a good case study. We have an understanding of the migratory patterns of modern examples of particular species, but it is often unclear how the same species would have behaved in past environments with less anthropogenic impact on the landscape and enclosure. For instance, in North America, there has been significant debate regarding the past behaviour of bison (*Bison bison* L.), in terms of whether this species, which was once superabundant on the plains, engaged in significant long-distance, north–south migration. Some early ethnographies implied that they did and these references have persisted in the literature, but they have been questioned by modern plains ecologists who favour a normal behaviour of year-round presence in particular regions within limited ranges, with small movements to more favourable environments locally (Hart 2001). The study of sequential tooth samples of bison from a number of mid Holocene plains sites for $\delta^{13}C$, $\delta^{18}O$ and $^{87}Sr/^{86}Sr$ appear to support the modern ecologists' view, providing only evidence for limited local ranging (Wigda et al. 2010). Interestingly, a very similar study has been undertaken on European bison (*Bison priscus* Bojanus) for late Pleistocene specimens on the steppes of eastern Europe. This study produced a very similar result that also suggested the species occupied limited ranges with little seasonal movement (Julien et al. 2012). Evidence from strontium isotopes determined on middle Palaeolithic specimens of reindeer (*Rangifer tarandus* L.) from France, on the other hand, appear to show that they did undertake long-distance movement, whilst a bison specimen in the same study presented local signals (Britton et al. 2011). This very coherent set of results demonstrates the potential of the method well and the number of applications is fast increasing. It is worth noting, however, that none of the studies so far undertaken are particularly large scale in terms of numbers of animals studied or comprehensive coverage of a culture and period in a region. Clearly such work, that uses the full range of isotopic-proxies, alongside other evidence, could produce massively rich datasets that provide an in-depth, holistic understanding of economy, mobility and landscape use. It is possible that this has not happened yet because the methods are still new and undergoing development, but a key reason has to be cost. This approach uses a large number of isotopic determinations for each animal specimen studied, potentially requiring different instrumentation for the light and heavy isotopes, so costs mount quickly. The question needs to be of sufficient significance to justify the costs.

Methods are very much still being refined and we are only just gaining a grasp on some fairly fundamental issues affecting the reliability and interpretation of high resolution approaches to sequential sampling. As a result there has been much recent experimentation to test assumptions and refine techniques. Some of that experimentation has been related to sample depth (Guiry et al. 2016) with consideration of the way dentine forms in layers across the tooth. When studying $\delta^{15}N$ values in dentine sequences it appears that shallower samples might reflect the time sequence better, and have less 'lag' in relation to diet over time. Other studies have looked at which part of the tooth should best be sampled for enamel (Zazzo et al. 2012) and it was concluded that for sheep teeth the best sequence for light isotopes comes from the mesial surface. It is also now clear that teeth do not form in direct proportion to time, but display exponential growth patterns in both sheep and horses (Zazzo et al. 2012; Bendrey et al. 2014). Perhaps most seriously, in terms of implications, a consideration of strontium isotope sequences in cattle teeth suggests that these heavier isotopes might be affected by longer-term retention and recirculation leading to averaging and lag effects (Montgomery et al. 2010). As such, very high-resolution sequences might not be entirely synchronous with lighter isotopes or as time-specific, but nonetheless significant differences should present themselves over longer timeframes. Further work on all these issues is necessary to realize the full potential of high-resolution sequential approaches. The technical advancement needs to be matched with equivalent academic prowess in identifying the big questions that would be worthy of the attention of (currently) high-cost methodologies.

Ongoing Revolution – Compound-Specific Stable Isotope Analysis and Novel Proxies

Radiocarbon dating was a revolution in archaeology, but the realization that ^{14}C levels in the atmosphere were not constant and calibration was necessary (Aitken 1990) produced a secondary revolution. Does anything similar lie in store for stable isotope research? The cutting edge of stable isotope research at present perhaps relates to compound-specific determinations (Makarewicz and Sealy 2015). Whilst stable isotope research into protein sources, for instance, usually involves collagen extraction, rather than bulk determinations on bone, the collagen itself still represents an integrated bulk value for a wide range of different amino-acids which might all have different pathways involving different mechanisms of fractionation. This leaves the possibility that very valuable specific information is being ignored in bulk collagen values, but also the possibility that bulk collagen values do not best reflect dietary intake. A new stable isotope revolution might arise with expanding understanding of dietary routing and the contributions of macronutrients to specific bodily tissues (e.g. Howland et al. 2003; Corr et al. 2009; Fernandes et al. 2012; Kendall et al. 2017; Webb et al. 2017, 2018).

In a recent controlled pig-feeding experiment, undertaken to better understand the effects of different diets on isotope values in different tissues and compounds, it was found that bulk protein $\delta^{13}C$ values related to marine diet input could be misleading without thorough understanding of specific protein sources (Webb et al. 2017). The key factor in play here was possibly an increased routing of glycine, a non-essential amino acid that tends to be isotopically heavy (Webb et al. 2017). Whilst it is still clear that large-scale shifts in marine diet are visible in $\delta^{13}C$ determinations from bulk protein, the lack of understanding of such relationships severely limits resolution and precision of dietary reconstruction to broad brush conclusions, as there could be very significant equifinality in what drives smaller-scale variations. Other recent examples of compound-specific applications include plants and soils. Field-based manuring trials, that examine both bulk $\delta^{13}C$ values and those specifically from dung-derived lignin, have indicated that bulk determinations might underestimate manuring levels (Dungait et al. 2008, 2010; Styring et al. 2014a, 2014b). In relation to the interpretation of trophic levels from $\delta^{15}N$ values, the specific consideration of $\delta^{15}N$ determinations from particular amino-acids, particularly glutamic acid, in plants, animals and humans, has indicated that unless amino-acid-based approaches are further developed and applied, the proportions of plant versus animal protein sources might not be modelled correctly (Styring et al. 2015). Whilst these issues might currently represent problems, once fully understood there might also be the potential to answer much more detailed and targeted questions about particular aspects of diet, representing a significant step forwards.

Ongoing revolution might also revolve around the regular use of a wider range of isotopic proxies in concert. The addition of sulfur isotope ratios, alongside carbon, to the consideration of marine input, and the routine addition of lead alongside strontium in radiogenic, geogenic provenancing, has already been discussed. Another element worthy of consideration is hydrogen and its heavy isotope deuterium. Values for δD or $\delta^{2}H$ (depending on preference) are related to climate and precipitation in a similar way to $\delta^{18}O$, and the mapping of δD in climatic studies is relatively well developed (Makarewicz and Sealy 2015). Hydrogen is plentiful in organic compounds, whilst in some cases there will be little oxygen available on which to carry out determinations. δD values have not as yet been studied in many archaeological scenarios, but there is potential to use this approach particularly on organic materials. One recent application used $\delta^{13}C$, $\delta^{15}N$ and δD values to provenance the origin of medieval wool textiles in Europe (von Holstein et al. 2016) with clear clustering seen by region. In the same way that seasonal fluctuations in climate can be seen in sequential sampling for $\delta^{18}O$ in teeth, it has been demonstrated that such patterns can also be detected successfully in human and animal hairs (Sharp et al. 2003), though a recent study of Irish sheep's wool seasonality (Zazzo et al. 2015) found that, whilst seasonal variation existed, the δD values had a more complex relationship to climate, likely related to greater dietary influence on δD, than $\delta^{18}O$ values. Whilst δD values are more complex to understand, they represent an alternative proxy for climate (see Roffet-Salque et al. 2018), and, once fully understood, any difference between $\delta^{18}O$ and δD levels may in-and-of-itself be informative. Another recent application of δD determinations (Outram et al. 2009) relates to lipid residues and is discussed in the next chapter.

Conclusion

The arrival of stable and radiogenic isotope techniques to archaeology has revolutionized our understanding of what was eaten, by whom, and where and when they ate it. It has provided an insight into major economic transitions as well as provided an excellent framework for understanding cultural and demographic factors in foodways, through determinations that are specific to individuals of known descent, class, sex or age. It has provided a window into aspects of human health and childcare, as well as the techniques of plant and animal husbandry. We can also understand much better the issues of migration, seasonal mobility and spatial aspects of resource supply. In early palaeoeconomic work, site catchment analysis was used as a way to integrate evidence from bones and seeds related to the exploitation of plants and animals. The equivalent for isotopic research is a sound reconstruction of the regional isoscape in terms of bioavailable geogenic sources and climatic maps, alongside a thorough understanding of local food webs.

Key themes for future research will include continued experimental programmes to better understand how the isotope record is formed. It is necessary to increase our understanding of how specific macronutrients, at a compound-specific level, are routed from diet into specific bodily tissues. This will address potential issues of equifinality and signal masking and establish if these problems might be resolved. For studies requiring sequential sampling to establish a time series, we need further to develop models of tissue deposition rates and the resolution with which those tissues record dietary input of isotope ratios from different elements. The use of multiple isotope proxies is likely to aid further in the resolution of issues of equifinality, so the more routine application of a fuller range of currently available proxies is likely to become standard, alongside work on new proxies. It is increasingly clear that interdisciplinary teams are essential to deal with such complexity successfully and to best effect. The only drawback to the need for large teams using complex methods and instrumentation is one of financial limitation, but this is the way in which the best research is likely to be realized.

A key point to recognize is that stable isotopic research does not replace the traditional study of archaeobotanical and faunal assemblages, because these forms of evidence provide specificity in totally different ways. Bones and seeds provide us with specific evidence for exploitation and husbandry at a species, even breed, level, but do not tell us who ate what. Isotopes provide us with relatively vague dietary information, but it is highly specific to the individual people, plants or animals studied. It is essential to consider these forms of evidence in an integrated way in order to gain a rich and detailed picture of economy, society and foodways. Between production and ingestion lie food storage, cooking and consumption. The study of chemical residues from vessels provides an invaluable way to investigate this set of linking processes, as well as a way to identify the exploitation of very specific food products. The next chapter addresses that line of evidence.

CHAPTER 4

Incorporating New Methods II: Residue Chemistry

The ability to recognize and identify the presence of organic substances, not just from the survival of macroscopic or microscopic remains, but also from chemical fingerprints, has been a game changer within the first part of the 21st century. Attempts at identifying organic residues date back much earlier than this (e.g. Condamin et al. 1976; Morgan et al. 1984), but, until more recently, only a small number of fats, waxes and resins could be unambiguously identified from molecular signatures. Earlier studies employed gas chromatography followed by mass spectrometry (GC/MS) to identify characteristic molecules from particular organic sources, a method that worked for substances such as pine pitch (Evershed et al. 1985; Robinson et al. 1987), human faecal-derived coprostanol (Bethell et al. 1994), beeswax (Evershed et al. 1997c; Salque et al. 2015) or frankinscense (Evershed at al. 1997a). Many animal and plant fats, oils and waxes, however, leave very similar decay products, making specific identifications difficult. This chemical equifinality could, however, be addressed by determining the stable isotope ratios of specific decay compounds (using GC-C-IRMS) (Evershed et al. 1994), revolutionizing the identification of fats and oils from different groups of species and also allowing the recognition of certain food types, such as dairy products (Dudd and Evershed 1998). Methods of protein residue analysis were also developing during the same period, initially making use of immunoassay (see Gernaey et al. 2001; Smith and Wilson 2001), with increasing development of mass spectrometry based methods of peptide 'barcoding' (Buckley et al. 2010, 2014; Collins et al. 2010; Hendy et al. 2018c) in more recent years.

These methods provided another way to evidence the production and exploitation of different plant and animal products, including those that were previously difficult to demonstrate directly, such as milk (Dudd and Evershed 1998; Craig et al. 2000; Copley et al. 2003; Warinner et al. 2014;

Hendy et al. 2018b). Beyond that, however, one of the most significant contributions made by residue chemistry has been to associate items of material culture directly with particular foods and other organic products. In some cases, form and function can be linked, such as in the case of speculative *Linearbandkeramik* dairy sieves (Bogucki 1984), which have now been proved to be just that (Salque et al. 2013). In other cases (e.g. Mukherjee et al. 2008), consideration can be given to whether there is any cultural association between product type and material culture styles. The importance of creating this linkage between economy and material culture cannot be underestimated in the way it provides a more holistic and integrated view of human cultural systems and change. The technique unites the interests of a wider range of archaeological specialisms. At times, critics of economic approaches have sought to devalue the significance of economy and subsistence by artificially disconnecting them from arenas of culture, such as material culture, which they wish to stress as being of more importance. A key example of this is Thomas's (1999: 16, and Fig. 2.1) attempt to suggest that the early British Neolithic was marked out by almost immediate material culture change, with economy lagging a long way behind. Such a notion, theoretically driven rather than soundly based in evidence, no longer needs to be researched in the abstract, but can be tested directly. Indeed a recent study of both dietary isotope and lipid residue evidence points to an immediate change in both material culture and subsistence base (Cramp et al. 2014), bringing Thomas' viewpoint into clear question (see also Parmenter et al. 2015).

Chemical residue methods have captured the imagination of environmental and economic archaeologists, because once invisible resources are now revealed and long held theories can now be tested. However, whilst there have been many excellent collaborations between chemists, archaeobotanists and zooarchaeologists, the chemical evidence for plant and animal exploitation has generally remained outside the direct theoretical purview of zooarchaeology and archaeobotany. As organic residue chemistry becomes more ubiquitously applied within the field, this should change and there needs to be appropriate development in the understanding of the middle range theory associated with these lines of evidence, and how they can be integrated with established techniques in broader interpretative frameworks (see Outram 2017). Therefore, this chapter draws out the different strengths and weaknesses of the new and traditional methods in relation to a variety of questions. Key issues include identification, reference material, inherent biases, taphonomy, quantification of the economic and cultural significance, association with material culture and context, dating, and environmental reconstruction. The chapter will first address lipid residues before moving on to consider proteins.

Lipid Residues and Zooarchaeology: Critical Comparison

Lipids occur ubiquitously in plants and animals in the form of fats, oils, waxes and resins (Evershed et al. 2001). As an organic material they are liable to chemical or microbiological decay, but are generally more resistant to degradation than other classes of organic compounds. Where there is good organic preservation, lipids can be recovered directly from plant material or as amorphous deposits (of resins, tars, etc.), but in less favourable conditions they can frequently also be recovered from bones, pottery and some stones and sediments. In particular, the small spaces in the fabric of unglazed pottery provide a very good environment for lipid preservation, and absorbed residues are usually in much better condition than those on the surface, though surface residues do sometimes survive and can be analysed (Evershed et al. 2001). Whilst lipid residue analysis has so far contributed greatly to the identification of a wide range of organic products (see Evershed 2008a), it is arguably the case that the use of compound-specific GC-C-IRMS analysis to identify the particular origins of animal fats has had the most impact on palaeoeconomic archaeology. As such, it seems appropriate to commence discussion with a critical comparison of the analytical and interpretative frameworks relating to the study of animal bones and fat residues.

The first challenge facing both zooarchaeologists and residue chemists is that of identifying the origin of the remains under analysis. Zooarchaeology relies largely upon the morphological recognition of bone fragments and assignment of identifications, where possible, to animal species and skeletal part. Analysts are aided in this task by reference collections of mainly modern specimens of the species being studied and by bone identification manuals and atlases that have been illustrated and annotated to highlight reliable features for distinguishing differences between taxa. Such atlases are often tailored to different regions of the world (e.g. Olsen 1964; Schmid 1972; Matsui 2008) or the specific consideration of mammals, birds, fish or reptiles (e.g. Cohen and Serjeantson 1986; Cannon 1987; Gilbert 1990; Sobolik and Steel 1996). The vast majority contain idealized drawings of bones that emphasize the key criteria, whilst others rely on photography (e.g. France 2009). There are positive and negative aspects to both means of representation, but both types of manual are limited by two-dimensional representation, though developments in laser scanning and photogrammetry alongside three-dimensional printing and virtual reality technology are likely to revolutionize standardized reference material in the future. In some cases, metrical criteria have been used in addition to morphological criteria to help distinguish similar species, such as sheep and goat (Boessneck 1969; Payne 1969). However, zooarchaeological identifications have been, for the most part, made on the basis of subjective and qualitative judgements of an analyst.

The accuracy of zooarchaeological identifications depends greatly upon how well trained the analyst is, how experienced they are and the level of care they take over their work. Their performance will be affected by the quality of the reference collection available to them and whether good bone atlases, containing reliable criteria, have been constructed for the species and region in which they work. Zeder and Lapham (2010) conducted a series of multi-analyst blind tests of criteria for distinguishing sheep and goat elements and found that whilst the criteria were generally robust, as applied by different analysts, some were better than others and, for some elements, identification errors above 20% were encountered. Zooarchaeologists, of course, also work with fragmentary material, not usually whole bones, so taphonomy plays a big role in what can be identified, both in terms of average fragment size, but also how well diagnostic features have been preserved on bone surfaces. Yet a further challenge is that most reference materials come from modern animals, even though they may be primitive breeds, so there can be significant differences between reference material and ancient specimens. Variation in morphology caused by sex and age add further complication still. Since time and cost will remain a significant factor, qualitative identification is likely to remain the mainstay of zooarchaeology for some time, but fast methods of collagen fingerprinting (e.g. Buckley et al. 2010, 2014) or aDNA screening (e.g. Murray et al. 2013) may well play a greater role in the analysis of difficult or highly fragmented assemblages in the near future, as will the use of scanning and three-dimensional geometric morphometric (GMM) techniques to bin species groups statistically using multivariate techniques (see Haruda 2014, 2017).

In significant contrast, the identification of lipid residues to species and animal product is not qualitative or subjective, but rigorously objective. This observation alone speaks to the value of applying and comparing both methods to the consideration of ancient animal exploitation. However, this does not mean that recognition of lipid residues is simple or devoid of significant challenges and there are some problems of equifinality. As in osteological identification, taphonomy, regional differences and appropriate reference material are all significant factors that deserve consideration. Indeed it is impossible, not merely difficult, to separate some species by lipid residue analysis. If animal fats were perfectly preserved, as fresh, it would be possible to distinguish some differences between species and different animal products from the ratios of different fat molecules present. Fresh fats are made up of predominantly triacylglycerols (TAGs: three fatty acids ester bonded to a glycerol molecule). The fatty acids can be of different carbon chain lengths and contain different numbers of double bonds (saturates with no double bonds, monounsaturates and polyunsaturates) and appear in different combinations to form different triacylglycerols (see Evershed et al. 2001). Ratios of different TAGs can sometimes be indicative of different species and products, but over time these usually degrade. During diagenesis TAGs hydrolyse, producing free fatty acids and mixtures of diacylglycerols (DAGs) and monoacylglycerols (MAGs). At the same time, more reactive unsaturated fatty acids tend not to survive well at all. The end result is that degraded animal fats are largely characterized by large quantities of two saturated free fatty acids, palmitic acid ($C_{16:0}$) and stearic acid ($C_{18:0}$), alongside a mix of surviving TAGs, DAGs and MAGs, that no longer indicate anything very reliable about their origin, other than that this is a classic pattern for degraded animal fat (Evershed et al. 2001).

Establishing the origin of degraded animal fats requires the additional determination of carbon stable isotope ratios, in order to establish taxonomic groupings or type of animal product (Evershed 2008a). A compound-specific method is used whereby the $C_{16:0}$ and $C_{18:0}$ fatty acids are separated using gas chromatography and $\delta^{13}C$ values are determined for each of them through isotope ratio mass spectrometry. Differences in $\delta^{13}C$ values can relate to fractionation caused by different metabolic processes employed in different species groups, or in the production of different types of fat within the same species. Differences could also relate, however, to varying diets or environments. When $\delta^{13}C$ values for each fatty acid are plotted on a scattergraph, for samples taken from a single environment, there is a clear separation between groups of species. Problematically, ruminant animals, such as cattle, sheep and goats (amongst others) cannot normally be differentiated by species, due to peculiarities of the ruminant process, but other non-ruminant species, that have different metabolisms, such as pigs (Evershed 2008a) or horses (Dudd et al. 1999; Outram et al. 2009), can be identified. Highly significantly, differentiation between ruminant adipose fats and milk fats can also be made (Dudd and Evershed 1998), because of the different metabolic routes involved in the biosynthesis and deposition of body fats in relation to those produced by mammary glands (Mukherjee

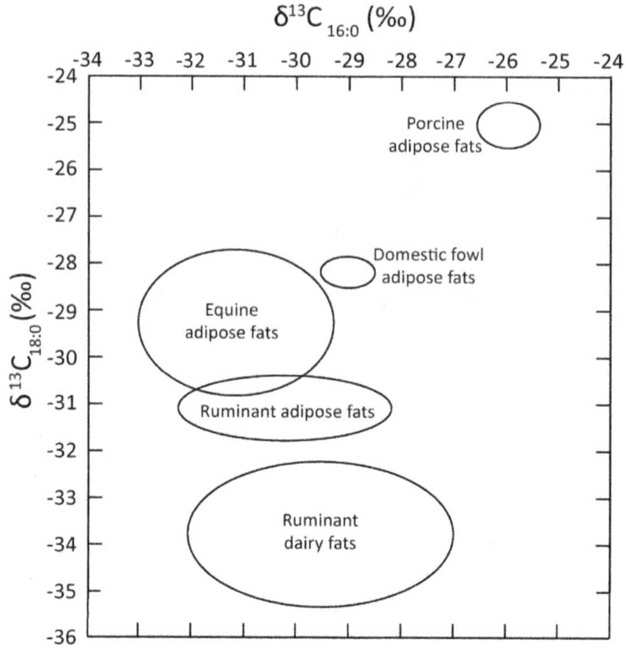

FIGURE 4.1 A graph showing compound-specific $\delta^{13}C$ values of $C_{16:0}$ and $C_{18:0}$ fatty acids obtained from some of the early reference animal fats studied from Great Britain. Ellipses encompass full ranges of values obtained (data derived from Dudd and Evershed 1998; Dudd et al. 1999).

et al. 2005). Figure. 4.1 shows the differentiation of different animal products through these methods as undertaken on some of the early reference fats to be studied from Great Britain. Additionally, aquatic and marine resources can now be identified by establishing the presence of certain marker compounds (Hansel et al. 2004) or from compound-specific $\delta^{13}C$ values in conjunction with $\delta^{15}N$ values on bulk residues (Craig et al. 2007; Cramp and Evershed 2014; Taché and Craig 2015). Like with zooarchaeological analysis, reference materials are required to establish criteria for identification. Reference isotopic values are established from an appropriate sample size of fats from modern animals from the region studied. It is important that the animals studied have been fed on local, indigenous plant materials that would have been present in the ancient diet, rather than on modern feeds of exotic origin (see Roffet-Salque et al. 2017).

If there are large-scale differences in environment and climate, the $\delta^{13}C$ values of fats can shift, making local reference work in the region concerned quite important. In particular, differences in the quantities of

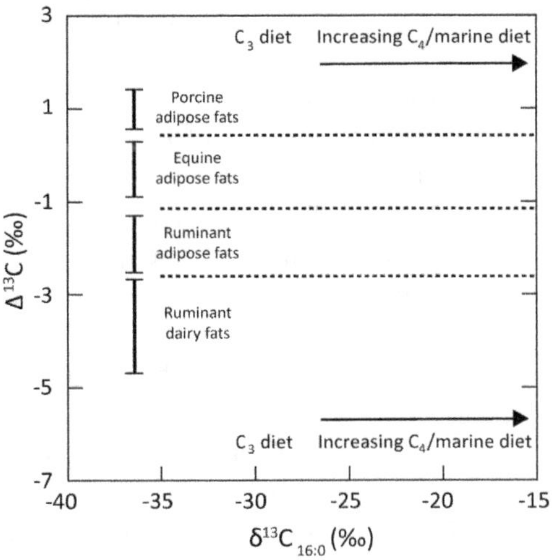

FIGURE 4.2 A graph showing Δ^{13}C values ($\delta^{13}C_{18:0}$–$\delta^{13}C_{16:0}$) that help eliminate environmental variations to show underlying differences in metabolic fractionation that distinguish ruminant milk, ruminant adipose and non-ruminant equine and porcine fats. The values are plotted against $\delta^{13}C_{16:0}$ to allow dietary influences from C_4 or marine diets to be identified (data derived from Outram et al. 2009).

C_3 and C_4 plants can have an effect. It is possible to sidestep this problem to a large degree by calculating Δ^{13}C values ($\delta^{13}C_{18:0}$–$\delta^{13}C_{16:0}$) (Evershed et al. 1999; Dunne et al. 2012) so as to focus only on the metabolic causes of fractionation between the two fatty acids, caused by fractionation within the animal, whilst removing the effect of external, environmentally-derived differences in δ^{13}C values. Now that a good number of reference sampling programmes have been undertaken in different regions of the world with very different environments, such as in Europe and the Near East (Copley et al. 2003; Evershed et al. 2008), central Asia (Stear 2008; Outram et al. 2009, 2012) and sub-Saharan Africa (Dunne et al. 2012), it has been possible to show that the separation of ruminant milk, ruminant adipose and porcine fats through the use of Δ^{13}C values remains highly robust in a wide range of settings (see Fig. 4.2). One of the great strengths of the stable isotope method for examining lipid residues is that it can effectively identify decayed animal products. Being able to establish the presence of dairy products is of great palaeoeconomic importance, but the very reason that this method is robust also creates a limitation. It cannot establish the difference between different types of dairy product (fresh milk, cheese, yoghurt, etc.). Such products, if perfectly preserved, would display differences in molecular make up, but the carbon isotope signature remains the same whether the milk is processed or decayed.

A blind test of identification accuracy, between different laboratories using different techniques, has been undertaken in relation to lipid residue analysis (Barnard et al. 2007). In this test, an unglazed pot was soaked in camel's milk and then artificially aged. Analysts using simple GC techniques were off the mark with their identifications, whereas GC/MS clearly indicated animal fats, though not accurately to precise origin. The use of bulk GC-C-IRMS to establish $\delta^{13}C$ and $\delta^{15}N$ values of the residue, however, yielded the correct conclusion of the 'milk of a herbivore' (Barnard et al. 2007). This shows the value of the stable isotopic approach in dealing with degraded lipids. However, compound-specific analysis, through GC-C-IRMS of the $C_{16:0}$ and $C_{18:0}$ fatty acids, was not included in this study, and this would likely have yielded the slightly more specific determination of 'ruminant mammal milk', though it would not be possible to be as specific as 'camel'. This round-robin test was valuable in some ways, though such a test, where the laboratories have no sense of the question they are trying to answer, is a rather simplistic way of considering how analytical chemistry should be conducted.

The essential lesson is that lipid residue analysis should not be divorced from its zooarchaeological, environmental, palaeoeconomic and cultural context, as Evershed (2008a) makes clear. Analyses cannot simply establish what was in every ceramic vessel, whatever that might be, but can rather answer questions posed within the framework set by a particular research project once appropriate reference material has been analysed. In this round-robin study, the laboratories were not provided with a context that would have made clear the need to develop methods specifically for distinguishing camel products from other locally available foodstuffs. Conventional analyses of faunal remains are still essential in providing the appropriate context for generating pertinent hypotheses and establishing the necessary range of local reference fauna. At some point in the future there might be a highly comprehensive databank relating to the vast majority of species and regions, but at present analytical techniques need to be tailored to address fairly specific questions. The critical difference between bone and residue identification is that an alert zooarchaeologist might well spot a specimen of an unexpected exotic species within an assemblage, but a residue chemist has little chance of doing so, as things stand, without having the opportunity to carry out the appropriate pilot work. As methods improve and reference data increase, the relationship between zooarchaeology and organic geochemistry will mature, but they will always be mutually beneficial in honing research questions and approaches.

A further factor that affects the identification of lipid residues is the issue of mixing and blending. Fragments of animal bones from different species are, of course, very frequently found mixed together within archaeological deposits, but they remain individual specimens that are divisible and separable. Commingled and fragmented assemblages clearly present quite a long list of methodological challenges in terms of quantification (see Ringrose 1993; Lyman 1994, 2008; Reitz and Wing 2008) and detailed discussion of these problems does not need to be repeated here. However, when it comes to lipid residues in pottery, more than one fat-rich material may have been present in any single vessel. The fats not only mix, but blend together and, in most cases, it is not possible to distinguish which fatty acids were derived from one product rather than another. The blended residue therefore presents a single integrated $\delta^{13}C$ value (Evershed 2008a, 2008b) irrespective of the origin of the $C_{16:0}$ and $C_{18:0}$ fatty acids. This integrated value will plot in between the expected ranges of products present, in proportion to their relative abundance (Evershed 2008a) (see Fig. 4.3). This blending process causes a certain amount of equifinality in residue identification results from ceramic vessels of mixed use, depending on the effect of the ratios present. When identifying the possible effects of blending it is worth considering $\delta^{13}C$ alongside $\Delta^{13}C$ values, as the latter alone have the potential to confuse blends of ruminant milk and porcine fat with ruminant adipose fats (see Fig. 4.3).

This phenomenon would have very serious implications for the value of lipid residue analyses were it not for two factors. Firstly, it has actually been shown that a surprisingly high proportion of vessels were, in fact, used for the preparation or storage of single products, where $\delta^{13}C$ values plot entirely within the range for a single residue origin (e.g. see Copley et al. 2005a, 2005b, 2005c; Evershed et al. 2008; Outram et al. 2009, 2012). Maybe we should not be surprised that many unglazed vessels would be retained for a particular purpose, perhaps to avoid the tainting of foodstuffs. Such practices are not unknown even in modern kitchens using materials that are easily cleaned. Indeed, links between forms and particular functions might also result in repeated use of vessels with the same food products. Secondly, the situation can be more easily understood once viewed alongside the zooarchaeological data. For instance, a study of the British, late Neolithic site of Durrington Walls (Mukherjee et al. 2005) shows that, on a site dominated by pig and cattle bones, there are some pots that contain a pure pork fat signal, some that contain a pure ruminant milk fat

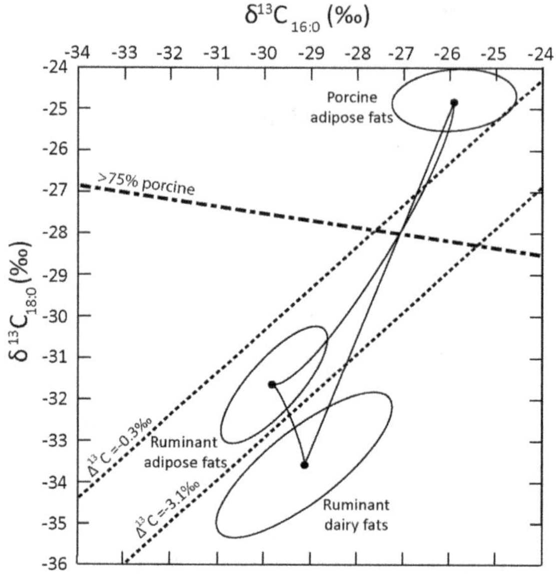

FIGURE 4.3 A graph modelling the effects of admixture of lipid residues from different sources (solid lines between ellipses). In this example, ruminant and porcine data from the full set of reference fats studied from Great Britain are used, displayed in confidence ellipses representing one standard deviation from the mean (data from Copley et al. 2003). Also displayed are dashed lines that separate products based upon $\Delta^{13}C$ values (see Mileto et al. 2017) and a dot-dash line modelling the point at which more than 75% of fats would have derived from pigs (see Mukherjee et al. 2008).

signal, and a significant number of vessels that plot along the line between ruminant dairy and porcine adipose. The faunal assemblage tells us that most of the ruminant lipids are likely to be from cattle, though some sheep and goat fats are also possible. It is also clear that some pots were only used with milk, some just had pork cooked in them, and some were used for both purposes. Whilst the effects of blending do not particularly assist with palaeoeconomic questions, when lipid residues are used in conjunction with faunal data we see both the economic and material culture patterning with good resolution.

Does blending only occur if more than one product is cooked simultaneously in a mixture? Does similar blending occur if single products are cooked at any one time, but different ones are, sequentially, cooked in the same pot? It has been proposed that the remaining residues might be biased towards the substances used in the latter part of a vessel's working life (Craig et al. 2004). Experimental work designed to model these scenarios suggests that both early and later uses are represented in the final blended residue

(Evershed 2008b), although this study was limited in duration and in the range of products, and more experimental work would be useful to understand the implications of multiple uses over the use lives of vessels. Authors such as Legge (2005) have also been concerned regarding ethnographic accounts of the use of milk fats to seal unglazed ceramic vessels. This might result in a residue that relates not to economic or culinary function, but to technological *chaîne opératoire*. This is a valid point, though it should be noted that such a vessel would then carry a blended signal with other later uses, rather than a pure dairy signal. As such it is highly likely that vessels producing pure milk residues were indeed used principally for dairy products. The use of dairy fats as a craft sealant, furthermore, is still highly indicative of the plentiful supply of that product within an economy. Once again, integrated consideration of faunal and residue evidence is likely to assist the interpretation of both lines of evidence.

Most forms of economic evidence suffer from inherent biases. Archaeological animal bone assemblages only evidence where skeletal elements are discarded, rather than where the animals lived or where their products were consumed. They directly evidence the exploitation of primary products such as meat and bone fats and only indirectly evidence the exploitation of secondary products (Sherratt 1981, 1983) such as milk, wool and labour. The inherent biases in lipid residue evidence are entirely different, but fortunately largely complimentary to faunal studies. It is clear enough that lipid residue analyses will only identify products that contain enough fats, waxes or oils to leave a sufficient concentration of lipid residue in the porous walls of unglazed ceramic vessels. Lipid residue analysis can identify the presence of adipose fats, and potentially from which groups of species they come, but it will not identify from what part of the body the fat comes. A great strength of the method has been its ability to identify dairy products directly (Dudd and Evershed 1998), but not the exact form of food that milk could have been processed into. Whilst the early presence of processed dairy products, such as cheese, has been hypothesized from the presence of sieves (Bogucki 1984), which we now know were used to process dairy products (Salque et al. 2013), direct evidence for different forms of cultured dairy produce still proves difficult to pinpoint. It had been hypothesized that the fermentation process could produce enhanced $\delta^{15}N$ values that are large enough to be visible in dietary isotope signals, but exploration of this possibility did not produce results that display a sufficiently clear statistical difference (Privat et al. 2005). The direct evidence of dairy production, whatever its precise form, has been of immense value to zooarchaeologists struggling with complex indirect arguments about identifying dairy herds zooarchaeologically.

Zooarchaeological analyses can furnish evidence of specialized husbandry, from reconstructing herd composition and slaughter patterns, related to the production of particular products such as milk and meat (Payne 1973; Legge 1981, 2005; Vigne and Helmer 2007) and non-food products like wool (Payne 1973). A key problem with these methods is that there is considerable equifinality if the husbandry strategy is not specialized but for mixed uses. The exploitation of meat is evidenced by understanding the nature of butchery marks which have been studied both ethnoarchaeologically (e.g. Binford 1978) and experimentally (e.g. Seetah 2008). Bone fracture and fragmentation patterns can help to identify bone marrow extraction (e.g. Outram 2002; Johnson et al. 2016, 2018) and grease production (e.g. Outram 2001; Karr et al. 2015). If residue evidence is viewed alongside husbandry strategies, and data related to bone processing, the faunal remains help to shed light upon the particular products that most likely gave rise to adipose residues, whilst the lipid chemistry will help to resolve problems of equifinality within mixed husbandry regimes, particularly in relation to secondary products.

Perhaps the most problematic bias affecting lipid residue studies is that only foodstuffs that are processed, cooked or stored in ceramic vessels (or, more rarely, porous stone, etc.) will leave any evidence. It is obvious that ceramics are not present at all in some periods, depending upon the region. Pottery also becomes glazed in later periods whilst ceramic cooking vessels might be replaced with metal cauldrons and there are many organic alternatives that may not survive at all. Storage often takes place in ceramic vessels, but also in a very large range of organic materials (such as wood, horn and skin), which may frequently have been used to make containers to hold key products like milk. The success of lipid residue analysis in identifying very high frequencies of dairy fats in Neolithic *Linearbandkeramik* ceramic sieves (Salque et al. 2013) simultaneously highlights the potential problem posed by the use of organic vessels. The same article also shows that other ceramic vessel types have an extremely low frequency of dairy fats and instead they contain largely meat fats (Salque et al. 2013). It is clear that a vessel must have been used to pour the dairy products through ceramic sieves into yet another vessel. This result is highly suggestive that such vessels were organic, thus there is the risk that dairying is being under-represented in comparison to societies that principally used ceramics to process milk products. Sieves can clearly be organic too, so how visible would dairying be in this culture if that were also the case?

Stews of meat in pots clearly leave residues and meat can also be roasted within ceramic vessels and ovens to leave clear evidence. Different cooking methods have been investigated experimentally during the development of lipid residue techniques to establish the nature of likely absorbed deposits (Evershed 2008b). However, meat or fish can also be roasted over an open fire or with hot rocks in an earth oven. At the British late Neolithic site of Durrington Walls, charred bone ends that would have jutted out from the meat seem to indicate that some joints of pork were being roasted over a fire (Albarella and Serjeantson 2002). As previously discussed, the residue results from that site (Mukherjee et al. 2005) show that there are at least some pots that were used purely for pork processing and many more for mixed uses including pork. The Durrington Walls faunal report (Harcourt 1971) shows that pigs are dominant in the bone assemblage. The relatively low proportion of vessels displaying a pure porcine signal could perhaps be the result of not only the effects of mixed vessel use, but also of the preparation of significant quantities of pork without using ceramics. Each line of evidence alone produced a skewed view of the site's economic and culinary practices, but the combined consideration of all this evidence, coupled with an appreciation of the biases in play, generates an extremely rich insight into food production and consumption at the site.

Given the above issues of bias and blending, can lipid residue analysis extend beyond identifying the exploitation of particular animal products to provide a quantified evaluation of the cultural, economic and dietary significance of particular species or foodstuffs? The current body of evidence suggests that residue results can be used quantitatively, but should not be viewed simplistically. By comparing the proportions of different residue identifications against the relative abundance of different species of animal bone fragments at a selection of British Neolithic sites (Mukherjee et al. 2005: Fig. 15), it becomes apparent that there is a clear relationship between the two. The species ratios are not identical, but as the ratio of species rises and falls within the animal bone assemblages, the residue determinations appear to reflect similar relative trends. It is apparent in that study, but also in a study of Near Eastern and south-east European Neolithic sites based on very large sample sizes (Evershed et al. 2008), that there is a strong relationship between the relative abundance of cattle bones and the quantities of ceramics with milk residues. In another study that combines both methods of quantification to compare settlement and funerary contexts in relation to late Bronze Age Kazakhstan (Outram et al. 2011), it becomes apparent that horse is significantly better represented in both the faunal and residue evidence at the funerary sites. Whilst it is unlikely that either faunal or residue analyses directly quantify either species abundance or economic significance, it is clear that both are good quantitative proxies for those values that are strongly and significantly correlated. Earlier in the development of residue methods some had questioned whether the technique could move beyond demonstrating presence or absence of certain commodities to provide quantitative data (e.g. Legge 2005), but as the body of data expands, it is clear that there is an important quantitative contribution to be made, providing the way the record is formed is correctly appreciated during interpretation.

Quantifying exploitation of different species can be difficult enough, but archaeologists want to be able to move beyond that to establish the significance of species to economy, diet and culture. Despite the long period in which zooarchaeological techniques have been developing, this is not always done well within the field. Simple errors such as failing to take animal size into account in relation to meat yield are surprisingly common, despite the availability of utility indices that provide absolute yield values and so on (e.g. Binford 1978; Metcalfe and Jones 1988; Outram and Rowley-Conwy 1998). Relative contribution to diet cannot simply be calculated by mass either because calorific and other nutritional values relate to the differing composition of different parts of the body. Ratios of fat to protein are very significant because fat contains more calories than protein by a ratio of 9:4 (Erasmus 1986), and the composition of fat (ratios of saturated, monounsaturated and polyunsaturated fats) differs by species and anatomical position (Hilditch and Williams 1964). For example the bone marrow in upper limb bones is very different to that found in more distal elements (Binford 1978; Outram 1998). An even more common error is a lack of appreciation of the difference between 'livestock' and 'deadstock', a critical distinction that Reynolds (1981) makes during his discussion of Butser Iron Age experimental farm, in reflecting on the difference between a living farm and archaeological site formation processes. Halstead (2003) also draws particular attention to this problem whilst discussing how to reconcile historical records regarding livestock with the accumulated deposits of slaughtered animals that archaeologists have to interpret. Unless an entire herd is catastrophically killed in a single event, the archaeological faunal assemblages will not resemble the live populations of animals that resulted in that assemblage. What Rowley-Conwy (1994) terms 'Mary Celeste' assemblages, after the ship found totally abandoned in 1872 with half eaten meals still on the table, exist at times, but are very rare; we instead generally see faunal assemblages that have accumulated slowly according to deliberately skewed patterns of selection for slaughter and consumption. Since different species mature at different rates and have different life expectancies they will naturally enter the record at different rates (e.g. see Outram et al. 2012). Animals with a fast turnover will be over-represented numerically, in terms of what the live herd might have looked like at any one time. This will be further influenced by the husbandry strategy being followed for the production of different animal products. Animals such as pigs, slaughtered fairly young as part of intensive meat production, may well represent diet reasonably well, but will be over-represented in terms of the composition of the live herd when compared against longer-lived animals, such as horses, that might have been kept well into maturity for riding. Quantifying the economic contribution of secondary animal products such as wool, milk and labour creates even more complexity. Whether slaughtered as a juvenile for meat, milked until barren, or exploited for wool or labour through its entire life, a single animal only ever contributes one skeleton to a faunal assemblage. Residue analysis provides us with the opportunity to gauge ubiquity of milk residues within the pots of a particular culture and provide points of comparison between the relative abundance of dairy and adipose fats. Such a ratio will not represent an absolute measure of the extent of dairy consumption, but it is clearly a key proxy for establishing the relative importance of at least one secondary product, which can be viewed alongside herd structure evidence.

A very substantial amount of modelling is required simply to describe economic and dietary value, and this is prior to considering the very complex ways in which animals might gain social significance and cultural value (see Russell 2012) or provide key craft resources (see Hurcombe 2014). Both residue analysis and zooarchaeology provide quantitative data that are highly difficult to interpret, but the information they provide is satisfyingly complimentary and can be further triangulated with isotopic evidence for diet. Whilst the evidence provided tends to show reassuring correlation in the assessment of major trends, the different forms of evidence help answer different questions about the nature of an economic system.

Animal bones and material culture are usually connected only through contextual association, unless the artefact is actually fashioned from bone. This association is perhaps most common in what we would generally perceive to be domestic refuse, notwithstanding debates about structured deposition of bone groups in such contexts (see e.g. Hill 1995; Morris 2008; Parmenter 2015). Ritual deposition and association with specific material culture is more simply demonstrated in clearly funerary contexts. Other associations, related to food storage, processing or cooking, might occur in structures such as cache pits or earth ovens, though these features often have secondary uses, such as for the disposal of refuse material. Different forms of butchery tools will leave marks on bones that might be distinguished from their micromorphology (Greenfield 1999; West and Louys 2007; Bello and Soligo 2008), whilst microwear patterning on tools might indicate use on bone, flesh or skin (e.g. Sano 2012; Miller 2015). Apart from exceptional 'Mary Celeste' deposits, it is rarely the case that it is possible to ascertain with any certainty what the direct association might be between faunal remains and the material culture used to cook or consume animal products. Perhaps methods such as identifying pot polish (e.g. White 1992; Ellis et al. 2011), usually restricted to trying to identify cases of cannibalism, or particular fractures associated with boiled bones (Outram 1998), might help demonstrate that cooking occurred in pots, but not which precise ones. Residue analysis allows us to make a direct connection between foodstuffs and material culture, opening up a window onto a plethora of economic, social and cultural questions.

From the perspective of attempting to connect form and function, residue analysis has, as discussed above, confirmed the use *Linearbandkeramik* ceramic sieves as being related to dairy processing (Salque et al. 2013). In other instances, however, residue research has disproved long-held archaeological theories about the function of vessel forms. Copper Age vessels from Central Europe, traditionally referred to as being 'milk jugs', were found to have very rarely contained milk, whilst many other vessel forms not previously thought to be used for milk frequently contained evidence for dairy products (Craig et al. 2003). In another example, despite the potential for symbolic aspects of material culture to relate to function, an examination of British Neolithic Grooved Ware vessels from different sites (Mukherjee et al. 2008) failed to find any statistically significant relationship between decorative styles and the type of residues present. However, the previously mentioned research in Bronze Age Kazakhstan (Outram et al. 2011) demonstrated an association between ceramics that had been used as grave goods and higher relative abundances of horse-fat residues. Whilst most major residue studies have been conducted with economic and environmental hypotheses in mind, there is clearly massive potential to expand our understanding of cultural aspects of human–animal relations and the social contexts of food consumption.

The relationship between associated items of evidence and the actual contexts of past human activities is complex. Merely establishing a direct link does not tell the whole story. Just as we cannot simply assume that bones found in a classic cache pit context were stored there, since the pit could have been reused for refuse, similar mistakes must be avoided with regard to interpreting residues. Taking the above study from Bronze Age Kazakhstan as an example (Outram et al. 2011) (see Chapter 8 for further details), there appeared to be a clear association between both bone and residue evidence for higher representation of horse remains within funerary contexts, relative to settlement ones. It is tempting to think that funerary rites tended to involve feasting on horsemeat and, indeed, this remains one viable possibility. The animal bones in question were not actual grave goods, but more generally associated with features within the clusters of kurgans. They are there in higher proportions than in settlement middens, but their precise function at the cemetery, as offerings or feasting debris, is a matter for speculation. The relationship between the lipid residues and the funerary context is even more complex. The pots from which the residues came were grave goods, directly associated with the interment, but this does not directly imply that the residues within the pots are associated with the funerary rites themselves. If the vessels were produced specifically for the purpose of including them in funerary rituals, then the food they contained might be either offerings or the leftovers from mortuary feasting. However, it seems likely that many such vessels were not new when deposited, and indeed some had been repaired with bronze staples (Outram et al. 2011). As such, the higher proportion of equine lipid contents would relate to the vessels' use prior to being selected for inclusion in a grave. The consumption of horse may still be related to important social events and that may still influence the selection of 'special' vessels for funerary deposition, but researchers clearly need to avoid simplistic inferences. Lipid residues provide direct associations with material culture, but the context of that association remains in the realm of interpretation, potentially guided by other sources of evidence.

The direct association that lipid residues can have to items of material culture is additionally useful in the sphere of dating. Pottery manufacture dates must provide a *terminus post quem* for the cooking of the fats absorbed therein, so ceramic seriation schemes can have a clear bearing on the dating of economic evidence without the need for direct scientific dates. Of course, animal bones can be similarly dated by association with artefacts in contexts, but there is much higher risk of error caused by residuality. In many cases, dating can work the other way around, with radiocarbon determinations on organic materials, such as bones, being used to provide an absolute framework for relative seriations of items of material culture, that are found in association with bones. Potential problems of residuality apply here too. Radiocarbon dating of bones has been routinely undertaken since early in the development of the method, but the accuracy and earliest dating limits for application of the technique have both been improved much more recently through the development of compound-specific accelerator mass spectrometry radiocarbon determinations (AMS) and processes such as ultra-filtration (Higham et al. 2006). Compound-specific AMS dating can also be undertaken on fatty acids from ceramic residues (Stott et al. 2001, 2003; Berstan et al. 2008). Dates that have been derived this way have been found to correlate quite well with other absolute dates, such as from dendrochronology, that relate to the same contexts, and the method has recently been improved further such as to generate dates consistent with bulk dates on associated archaeological material (Casanova et al. 2018). The date derived from this method will pertain to the death(s) of the animal(s) that provided the fat, and blending of lipid sources will produce an average of such dates in relation to the proportions of each source present. As well as providing a direct date for the exploitation of animal resources, such a determination also provides a *terminus post quem* for the *use* of the pot containing those products, but not its date of manufacture. This technique has not been widely applied, largely because of cost and the complex sequence of laboratory processes required as well as a lack of infrastructure for that service to be routinely offered. This is likely to change imminently, however, with considerable impact on dating sequences.

As well as being dateable through radiocarbon determinations, organic materials can also be carriers of isotopic proxies for climate and environment. Bones, particularly teeth, are well-known carriers of climatic (e.g. $\delta^{18}O$ values) and geological (e.g. $^{87}Sr/^{86}Sr$ ratios) (see Chapter 3) proxies that allow us to research past environmental change and movements of people and animals (e.g. Lang et al. 2013). High-resolution sampling and a better understanding of the chronological development of teeth have been providing ever more accurate seasonal isotopic sequences (e.g. Zazzo et al. 2012; Towers et al. 2014), and such work is now being integrated with detailed consideration of mortality profiles and husbandry strategies (e.g. Gillis et al. 2013). Fatty acids do not contain geological signatures and the quantities of oxygen present make the use of $\delta^{18}O$ values more difficult, though not totally unfeasible. Lipid residues also do not produce the incremental sequences that teeth do. However, they can still produce valuable information on climate and environment through deuterium ratios (δD). Such determinations on lipids have been used on peat sequences for some time, as an environmental proxy of temperature and precipitation (e.g. Xie et al. 2004). Similar applications on archaeological lipid residues from ceramics are much more recent. δD values have been used to help distinguish summer-produced equine milk from year-round integrated signals produced in equine adipose fats (Outram et al. 2009). Development of the potential of lipid residues as an environmental proxy is still in its infancy, but recent progress has been made in marrying the δD record from lipid residues with other environmental proxies in an archaeological context (Roffet-Salque et al. 2018).

Lipid Residues and Archaeobotany

The vast majority of the observations made with regard to animal bones and fat residues equally pertain to the archaeobotanical consideration of residues of plant oils, waxes and resins. However, whilst lipid residue analysis has very usefully identified the exploitation of a series of plant products in particular cases, it has not had quite the revolutionary effect on the field of archaeobotany that it has had on zooarchaeology. In part, this must simply relate to the much greater presence of fats in animal products and the relative domination of animal fats found in archaeological residues. One has to wonder to what extent faunal derived lipids mask much more subtle signals from plants in blended residues. There are certainly far fewer archaeological examples where it seems that important research questions can be answered, at least quantitatively, by studying lipid residues from plants. Beyond the identification of tree tars, pitches and resins (e.g. Evershed et al. 1985; Robinson et al. 1987), used in craft activities, significant plant food products to be identified through lipid residues include the waxes from leafy vegetables (Evershed et al. 1991), olive oil (Condamin et al. 1976) and palm fruit (Copley et al. 2001) grasses and aquatic plants (Dunne et al. 2016), amongst many others.

Perhaps one of the most significant crops to be studied this way is maize. Methods for identifying maize lipid residues were developed some time ago (Reber et al. 2004; Reber and Evershed 2004a), though not without difficulty. During experiments conducted in the development of the method (Reber and Evershed 2004b) it was noted that maize contains low proportions of lipids and these degrade relatively quickly. As a result, they will indeed be easily masked by other lipid bearing products. Where lipids are present, a combination of looking for marker compounds and establishing $\delta^{13}C$ values can identify maize, largely as a function of maize being a C_4 plant (Reber and Evershed 2004b). Some studies have concentrated on compound-specific determinations (e.g. Reber and Evershed 2004a) whilst others have used bulk carbon methods, because, although less precise and more open to contamination, there is greater potential for extracting sufficient lipid to undertake analysis (e.g. Seinfeld et al. 2009). Recent experimentation (Hart et al. 2009) has suggested that bulk $\delta^{13}C$ values are potentially subject to too many variables to make them a reliable method for identifying maize. Whilst compound specific approaches are not similarly dismissed, these authors conclude that the low yield of lipids is likely to make microscopic recognition of starch grains and phytoliths from residues the most promising avenue for that field of research. Some lipid research in this area, however, continues (e.g. Lantos et al. 2015; Reber et al. 2015).

Whilst discussing C_4 plants, it is also worth noting that the plotting of $\Delta^{13}C$ values ($\delta^{13}C_{18:0}$–$\delta^{13}C_{16:0}$) against $\delta^{13}C_{16:0}$ (see Dunne et al. 2012; Outram et al. 2012) for animal fat residues allows for the identification of the residue according to metabolic fractionation on one axis, whilst providing a proxy for C_3/C_4 plant ratios in animals' diets on the other axis. As such, lipid residues provide some proxy information in relation to local vegetation and animal fodder. As well as incorporating isotopic signals from plants, livestock also contribute to the isotopic signals found in crops if manuring is practised. Identifying the use of manuring is significant to understanding ancient agricultural systems, and it has now proved possible to see its effects in the $\delta^{15}N$ values obtained from charred cereal remains (Bogaard et al. 2007; Fraser et al. 2011). A recent study using this method shows that manuring was apparently quite common in Neolithic Europe (Bogaard et al. 2014b). In relation to lipid residues, however, it is also possible to identify specific biomarkers of faecal lipids within palaeosols, providing they are sufficiently well preserved (Evershed et al. 1997b; Bull et al. 1999).

Protein Residues

Protein residues can also, in theory, be recovered from ancient ceramics and, indeed, the presence of prehistoric dairying has additionally been evidenced in that way (Craig et al. 2000). The method used to identify the presence of proteins in this case was immunoassay, where proteins of specific origin are identified by their ability to induce an antibody response (Gernaey et al. 2001). In general, the discovery of particular protein residues in ancient ceramic vessels has the same palaeoeconomic and archaeological implications as finding lipid residues, but there are a few significant differences. The most important advantage of immunoassay techniques is their potential ability to identify residues to much finer resolution in terms of species. Craig et al. (2000) were able to identify bovine casein, so we know that the Iron Age inhabitants of Cladh Hallan were specifically milking cattle, not just ruminants in general. A further possible advantage of this approach is that it is not affected by the blending of food products. It should provide an indication of the presence or absence of all proteins for which an antibody test has been developed regardless of admixture. Given these apparent methodological strengths, why is it that since 2005 or so, the vast majority of ceramic residue work has largely focused on lipids? Why has immunoassay not taken off as a regularly used method?

Immunoassay residue studies rely upon establishing that the particular proteins which one wishes to identify (antigens) will elicit an immune reaction in another species (frequently rabbit) to produce antibodies that are specific to that protein and not likely to cross-react with other proteins from different sources (Brown and Brown 2011). Having successfully established this, two different forms of immunoassay test have been commonly used in archaeological work: crossover immunoelectrophoresis (CIEP) and enzyme-linked immunosorbent assay (ELISA). ELISA is possibly more appropriate for archaeological work because it is more sensitive than CIEP (Gernaey et al. 2001) and has greater potential to provide a quantified result, rather than just a positive/negative result (Brown and Brown 2011). Great care, not always evident in all archaeological studies, needs to be taken when using these methods to include appropriate control samples covering fresh and ancient material, environmental controls and samples that should provide a negative result, in order to confirm that cross-reactivity is not a problem and that there is no contamination (Gernaey et al. 2001). However, even in a well-conducted study, diagenesis of an ancient protein may present significant difficulties. Antibodies recognize very specific shapes on the surface of the antigen, called epitopes, and as the protein decays the epitopes may be altered producing a false-negative result, or worse, the new shape might display non-specific cross-reactivity with other antibodies leading to misidentification and false positives (Brown and Brown 2011: 50; Barker et al. 2015). Few studies have applied both lipid and immunoassay techniques to the same ceramic fragments, but Craig et al. (2003) did so in a Bronze Age context that was specifically targeting milk and found a certain degree of discrepancy between the two methods. This could have been caused simply by differential preservation, since proteins are more prone to decay than lipids, by false results caused by diagenesis of epitopes or by the milk detected by the lipid method being derived from sheep or goat milk, rather than cattle. Immunoassay methods work in theory, particularly if great care is taken, but they will only identify products that one is specifically testing for with appropriate antibodies. There is also a higher risk, particularly on very early sites, that preservation will be inadequate, and there will always be a question mark over reliability in relation to diagenesis and its effect upon cross-reactivity. These challenges have limited the usefulness of its application within archaeology, hence its very limited current use, though it may still prove useful as a rapid screening method before the application of other techniques.

Recent work on protein residues has begun to focus on proteomics instead of immunoassay (Hendy et al. 2018c). This exciting new field of research identifies the source of proteins by creating a detailed profile of all the individual proteins present in a very complex mixture that is indicative of a particular source. This is called peptide mass fingerprinting (Brown and Brown 2011) and has been made possible by separating the proteins with liquid chromatography followed by identification of the individual proteins in a new type of mass spectrometer capable of dealing with large molecules, such as matrix-assisted laser desorption ionization time-of-flight mass spectrometry (LC-MALDI-TOF/TOF-MS) (Brown and Brown 2011; Hong et al. 2012; Barker et al. 2015). This method has recently been applied to the identification of cattle, sheep and goat milk caseins dating to the first millennium BC, with apparent success and good correlation with ELISA results on the same samples (Hong et al. 2012). Most recently there have been highly valuable applications to the detection of a range of specific food products in ceramics from Neolithic Çatalhöyük West (Hendy et al. 2018a) and tracing dairying practices amongst Bronze Age steppe pastoralists (Jeong et al. 2018). As such, the additional, species-specific potential of protein residue analyses is starting to be realized, providing that the preservation is good enough in the time periods relevant to the most significant research questions. Generally, however, poor preservation levels of proteins in ceramic residues remains a potential limiting factor and recent experiments show that there is rapid degradation of proteins within ceramics and thus a need for caution (Barker et al. 2018). Other recent applications of peptide finger-printing to identify milk consumption has been on dental calculus from both prehistoric and medieval specimens dating back as far as 3000 BC (Warinner et al. 2014). Dental calculus is a form of residue that has massive potential to reveal exactly what was being consumed by individuals, though not necessarily in what proportion. The value of the ability to demonstrate directly that individuals consumed very specific food products should not be underestimated, and this is not duplicated by other methods. The combined study of calculus residues and isotopic values in human teeth and bones may well provide a good balance of specificity and quantification.

The above discussion relates to protein residues in ceramics, but, in fact, the detection of blood residues on ancient lithic artefacts using immunoassay has a longer history, dating back to the 1980s (Loy 1983). Clearly, the potential ability to link tools used in hunting and butchery to particular animal species is very exciting. Pot residues do not help much if a society is aceramic, and they tell us about processing and consumption rather than prey acquisition. Ceramic residues have informed us mostly about early farming and herding societies with much smaller amounts of information having been gleaned about rarer ceramic hunter-gatherer societies. Indeed, it is also worth noting that the earliest agriculturalists in the Near East were aceramic. As such, the study of protein residues from stone tools could revolutionize our understanding of many hunter-gatherer societies, particularly those whose sites frequently contain little more than lithic scatters, not always accompanied by faunal remains. However, the immunoassay recognition of blood from stones has caused controversy ever since the method was developed (Brown and Brown 2011: 38). Critics have seriously questioned the durability of protein residues on lithic surfaces, in part based upon experimental trials, and have stressed the need for blind testing and repeatability (e.g. Downs and Lowenstein 1995; Fiedel 1996). Exposure to UV light appears to be a particularly destructive agent to the immunoreactivity of blood (Tuross et al. 1996). Other works argue that, if good protocols are followed, residues do survive in controlled experimental tests (Kooyman et al. 1992; Reuther et al. 2006). The method continues to be used, and some recent studies have produced apparently sensible results (e.g. Yohe and Bamforth 2013), but, because of the possibility of cross-reactivity of degraded protein epitopes (Brown and Brown 2011; Barker et al. 2015) and worries about diagenesis on stone surfaces, there will continue to be concerns about the reliability of individual results using this approach. Ideally, confirmation from other techniques in needed. Perhaps the best use for immunoassay methods in archaeology is for the rapid mass screening of artefacts for proteins to be later targeted with other methods for verification, if available.

Conclusion

Residue analysis has revolutionized aspects of economic archaeology through directly demonstrating the exploitation of secondary products and through the direct associations it may make between food resources and material culture. If one analyses the strengths and weaknesses of both the macrofossil and residue evidence, it is clear that, in many cases, where one is weak, the other tends to be strong and complementary. The implication of this is that the new lines evidence cannot really be used to replace the traditional ones, but instead their combined use vastly increases the quality and reliability of findings. Studying plant and animal remains tells us most about procurement, husbandry, processing and storage, whilst chemical residues tell us most about processing, storage and the material culture contexts of consumption. If blood residue analysis on stone tools is trusted enough to be added to this mix, then residues also inform us about the material culture used in animal processing and procurement. Additionally, studying dental calculus residues informs us about some specific foodstuffs consumed by individual people, whilst the determination of isotopic ratios in human bone tells us about generalized human diet. Holistic use of multiple proxies will yield the richest results and decrease uncertainties caused by evidential equifinality.

Notwithstanding a number of excellent contributions on other topics, the lion's share of chemical residue work, particularly in relation to ceramics, has related to lipid residues and the study of zooarchaeological questions. This is most likely the result of lipid residues having generally better levels of preservation than proteins in ceramics from early periods that relate to some of the most important economic transitions. The more fatty nature of animal products has lent itself better to the application of this technique than the study of plants. Now that proteins have the potential to be more reliably analysed, with ever-improving instrumentation, through proteomic approaches, it is very likely that work in this area will expand rapidly and achieve important results. The analysis of dental calculus for proteins and other biomolecular and microscopic evidence is also likely to be a major growth area with the potential to add very significant new insights not afforded by other approaches.

CHAPTER 5

Incorporating New Methods III: Answering Palaeoeconomic Questions with Molecular Genetics

Deoxyribonucleic acid (DNA) was first isolated during research into leukocytes in 1868/9 by Swiss medical doctor Friedrich Miescher (Dahm 2008), with the structure becoming fully understood by the 1950s (Watson and Crick 1953). The first sequencing of DNA became possible in the 1970s (Sanger and Coulson 1975; Sanger, Nicklen and Coulson 1977), with attempts to extract and sequence ancient DNA (aDNA) getting under way by the 1980s (e.g. Higuchi et al. 1984; Pääbo 1985, 1989). That decade also saw genetic profiling first successfully used by forensic science (Gunn 2009). Ever since, there has been extremely rapid development in the field that has particularly accelerated after the development of 'next generation sequencing' (NGS) (Linderholm 2015) or 'high-throughput sequencing' (HTS) (Leonardi et al. 2017) since 2010 or so. These approaches allow much faster and cheaper study of large numbers of samples, including whole genomes, such that the scale and scope of current research projects represents a step change from what has gone before. This chapter, more than any other, risks being out of date between being written and published. However, archaeological science has already learned many very important lessons about the application of genetics to ancient questions. It is clear that the field is having a revolutionary impact on our understanding of key palaeoeconomic themes, but there are also some significant cautionary tales to tell.

A highly significant proportion of earlier genetic papers addressing archaeological questions reached the wrong conclusions. This appears to be a very dramatic statement to make, but one that is clearly demonstrable. In most scientific fields published work may not turn out to be entirely correct, and it is normal to see incremental improvement over time. This is largely true of the data presented by archaeogeneticists, but in that field there has been an unusual frequency of cases where completely contradictory conclusions are reached in studies undertaken in parallel or quick succession. A good example of this is in papers that address whether there was a significant degree of admixture between anatomically modern humans and Neanderthals. Earlier studies that considered only mitochondrial DNA (mtDNA) from the maternal line (e.g. Currat and Excoffier 2004) generally concluded that there was little evidence to support significant interbreeding, whilst more recent whole genome studies make it clear that there was but debate the level of potential admixture (see discussion for example in Hodgson and Disotell 2008; Wang et al. 2013; Schaefer et al. 2016; Hajdinjak et al. 2018). Within whole genome work, papers have presented rather different pictures; key papers published in the same year showed significant inconsistency (e.g. Green et al. 2006 compared to Noonan et al. 2006), most likely as a result of differing amounts of modern human contamination, as well as methodological differences (see Wall and Kim 2007; Hodgson and Disotell 2008). Given that such papers are often published in high profile journals and frequently present apparently firm conclusions that are widely reported in the press, this pattern of rapid contradiction has become a source of increasing concern to many archaeologists.

The paragraphs below outline how archaeogenetics can contribute to palaeoeconomic research, followed by a discussion of the possible pitfalls that have been exposed since the final years of the 20th century. However, there is a positive case to be made that the field is now moving beyond some of these earlier problems and is now radically advancing knowledge. The rest of the chapter provides more detail on key areas of development within the field including cutting-edge approaches and future avenues for research.

Archaeogenetics and Economic Questions

Before highlighting how palaeoeconomic questions can be addressed through genetic research, it is worth quickly outlining the different things that can be studied and the types of information that may result (see Brown and Brown 2011; Matisoo-Smith and Horsburgh 2012; Linderholm 2015 for general reviews of methods). The DNA of plants, animals including humans, along with their associated bacterial microflora, can all be studied in modern day populations and also in ancient samples, where preservation is good enough. The study of very small amounts of surviving aDNA was made possible after the development of a process called polymerase chain reaction (PCR) in the 1980s (Mullis et al. 1986; Mullis and Faloona 1987) which facilitated amplification through synthetic cloning of DNA fragments such that there was sufficient to allow sequencing. The entirety of an organism's DNA is its 'genome', but that can be subdivided. In multicellular animals, cell nuclei contain two sex chromosomes (X and Y) and a much larger number of autosomes. The mitochondria in cells also contain DNA that is only passed down the female line (mtDNA). The DNA in Y chromosomes, on the other hand, is only passed down the male line. Total chromosome numbers vary by species and are more variable in plants than animals (Brown and Brown 2011; Matisoo-Smith and Horsburgh 2012). Genes are particular sections of the DNA that contain, either individually or collectively with other genes, codes that govern particular functions, and once physically expressed in the organism result in different traits or 'phenotypes' (e.g. eye colour). The different variants of a gene that lead to different phenotypes are called 'alleles' and the collective set of gene information is called the 'genotype'. There is also much 'intergenic' DNA that does not have a fully understood function and the entire DNA sequence carries mutations and copying errors that generate uniqueness and allow ancestry to be tracked (see Brown and Brown 2011; Matisoo-Smith and Horsburgh 2012).

Much archaeological work on human DNA has explored patterns of evolution, dispersal, migration and ancestry. A lot of earlier work in this area involved inferring past patterns from studying variation in limited portions of DNA, such as mtDNA, Y-chromosome or a particular gene, in modern populations and using assumptions about mutation rates to estimate the dates of likely past events (e.g. Chen et al. 1995; Harding et al. 1997). The integration of information from modern populations combined with consideration of a number of aDNA samples provides a considerably more grounded picture, much less reliant upon models based on assumption. For example, the first study of ancient mtDNA from Neolithic populations in Europe produced quite a different picture in reality from some of the expectations arising from modelling only modern mtDNA patterns (e.g. Haak et al. 2005; Bramanti et al. 2009). Recent approaches, facilitated by next generation sequencing techniques and advances in computing, have been able to study similar questions based upon much larger numbers of ancient samples that can consider the whole genome, not just a single chromosome, gene or the mitochondria (e.g. Allentoft et al. 2015; Haak et al. 2015), to reveal much richer patterns that are far less based upon projected models and assumptions. The problems with modelling backwards from modern DNA will be a specific topic for discussion below, as will the relative value of studies based upon selected portions of DNA (e.g. mtDNA or chromosomes) versus whole genome approaches that include all the autosomes in addition.

The clear value in modelling human migrations in relation to palaeoeconomic questions is in circumstances when the impetus for population expansion or migration relates to significant changes in subsistence base (and *vice versa*), such as the adoption of agriculture (e.g. Bramanti et al. 2009; Haak et al. 2015) or new forms of pastoralism (e.g. Allentoft et al. 2015; Haak et al. 2015). A clear understanding of population dynamics significantly aids our appreciation of the demographic effects of economic change, but also elucidates long-standing debates about whether it was the idea of particular economic practices that spread or its practitioners themselves. Intellectual fashions have alternated from one extreme to the other in favouring colonization or indigenous adoption but aDNA research can actually now begin to answer these questions. We already have some answers for some regions of the world, but there is much patchiness yet to be filled in. It is already clear that in certain regions, such as Central Europe, there is considerable evidence for population replacement with the first arrival of farming (Bramanti et al. 2009; Haak et al. 2015) and then considerable additional later input deriving from Bronze Age pastoralist groups from the East European steppes (Allentoft et al. 2015; Haak et al. 2015). On the other hand, areas like the Baltic zone see more continuity of local hunter-gatherer populations through into the Neolithic, although there is still evidence for later steppe input (Jones et al. 2017). It is remarkable that after so many years of debate, we finally have access to direct evidence to help answer such a fundamental economic/demographic question, though there is still need for some interpretative caution.

There are also smaller scale demographic and ancestry questions that relate environmental and socioeconomic factors to kinship. For instance, post-marital residence patterns are widely affected by the relative importance of different subsistence practices and environmental conditions in circumstances when there are gender-specific roles (Kelly 2013, 227). To generalize for hunter-gatherer groups, patrilocal residence might prevail where stability in male specialist knowledge in food procurement was most significant, and matrilocal systems where women are primary providers of sustenance. Bilocal systems can be more common where there are fluctuating environments and uncertainty. It is clear too that a shift from hunting and gathering to farming could also alter such social arrangements. There is also a good statistical correlation between modes of subsistence and the extent to which polygyny is practised (Schutkowski 2006: 231). Genetics can be employed to establish kinship relations, spatially, within cemeteries such that reconstructing post-marital residence patterns and kinship groups becomes feasible. This can be best achieved by combining genetic studies of kinship with isotopic evidence for region of origin. There is the exciting possibility of identifying intermarriage between differing groups, such as between farmers and neighbouring hunter-gatherers in a more detailed and contextualized way than simply establishing levels of genetic admixture.

One recent example of work in this area has revealed sex-biased migration and admixture amongst the earliest farmers in what is now Estonia (Saag et al. 2017) and it did so purely through consideration of population genomics. By studying the whole genome and then comparing the differences in patterning seen in the autosomal DNA versus mtDNA and X and Y chromosomes, it was possible to establish that the majority of the genetic make-up was derived from hunter-gatherer and steppe peoples, whilst there was some input of Anatolian farming groups through female lines. The precise cultural mechanism for this needs further elaboration. Where studies can also integrate spatial relationships within cemeteries, physical anthropology and isotopic information with analysis of aDNA, more specific conclusions can be reached. The Neolithic site of Eulau in Germany (Haak et al. 2008) provided genetic evidence of a nuclear family buried together and, whilst men and children tended to be of local origin, females tended to have different isotopic signatures. This provides clear evidence for patrilocal post-marital residence practices. Whilst studies of this type are still limited in number, evidence of matrilocal residence has also been detected at a 5th millennium BP site in Shangdong Province, China (Dong et al. 2015) where mtDNA variation was particularly low, and indeed there was little evidence for even married-in males being buried with matrilineal family groups. Alternative hypotheses would require a severe population bottleneck reducing lineages, but other evidence for that is lacking.

Moving away from the topic of kinship and ancestry, another way to answer palaeoeconomic questions from genetic research is to consider particular genes that may have co-evolved with changes in economy and subsistence practices. For this to happen, a particular phenotype must present a sufficient advantage to those practising a particular economic activity such that it leads to significant positive selection of the particular alleles responsible for that trait. The most discussed example relating to this is the lactase persistence gene. Prior to the use of domestic animals to provide milk for human consumption, humans were all lactose intolerant as adults since the ability to produce lactase stops following weaning. At some point certain human populations evolved high frequencies of alleles that allowed the continued synthesis of lactase into adulthood, thus allowing discomfort-free consumption of dairy products. In Europe, a single mutation is responsible, but in other regions, such as sub-Saharan Africa, multiple alleles are associated with this ability (Gerbault et al. 2011). It has been hypothesized that, whilst it is possible to derive nutrient value from milk whilst suffering from lactose intolerance, and that its effects can be reduced considerably by the manufacture of cheeses and other products, there would have been a significant subsistence advantage afforded to lactose tolerant individuals in a society that could intensively exploit domestic animals for dairy products. As a result, positive selection for the lactase persistence mutation would go hand in hand with the introduction and intensification of that economic practice. Some models for this have suggested that in a European context the initial locus for that co-evolution could have been the *Linearbandkeramik* (LBK) of Central Europe (Itan et al. 2009; Gerbault et al. 2011; Leonardi et al. 2012). However, whilst there is residue evidence for some milking in the LBK (Salque et al. 2013), direct detection of early examples of the lactase persistence allele in aDNA has proven elusive. Indeed, even by the Bronze Age, frequencies are still very low (and only imputed), even in some steppe 'pastoralist' societies that have been studied (Allentoft et al. 2015). However, given that some pastoralist societies today do not have particularly high frequencies of lactase persistence and it is proving rather hard to find in ancient genomes, perhaps the selective pressures behind its varying frequency in different populations are not as simple as first assumed (Ségurel and Bon 2017). It is clear that there was indeed significant selective pressure in some societies, but perhaps the economic niche in which strong selection occurred was more specific than simply exploiting dairy products to a high degree. This remains a hot topic on the interface between archaeogenetics and palaeoeconomics.

In some respects, the study of the genetics of plants and non-human animals can speak more directly to palaeoeconomic questions, since they concern the actual subsistence resources put under selective pressure by human economic activity. When thinking of hunter-gatherer modes of subsistence, there is frequent debate about whether human hunting pressure or natural environmental change resulted in a given extinction event (Eren and Outram 2012). Phenotypic changes could be utilized to help understand these processes, though current applications of genetics have been more focused on identifying the taxonomy, ancestry and population diversity of now extinct species, along with providing a means of establishing latest appearance dates. For instance, Bayesian modelled spatio-temporal patterns of musk ox population diversity were found not to support the hypothesis of significant contribution of human hunting to that species' extinction from much of its former Pleistocene range (Campos et al. 2010). In this case, there appeared to be no correlation between evidence of human expansion and reductions in diversity within mtDNA lineages. Ancient DNA analyses can clearly help identify late appearances of extinct species through verifying identifications on specimens too small to allow accurate morphological identification, but recent applications have gone further by identifying the presence or absence of species' amplified aDNA from dateable sedimentary layers, known as 'sedaDNA' (Graham et al. 2016). Examples of studies targeting sedaDNA include one demonstrating later than expected survival of mammoths and horses in Alaska that implies several millennia of overlap with human occupation of the area (Haile et al. 2009). Another, using multiple environmental proxies correlated with sedaDNA presence/absence patterns, investigates the very late survival and final extinction of relict woolly mammoth populations on St. Paul Island, Alaska (Graham et al. 2016). As well as sediments, DNA can be recovered for other media such as ice cores. DNA recovered and amplified from environmental samples, whether ancient or modern, can be referred to as 'eDNA'. This is a relatively new field and one for which taphonomic biases in different deposit types, reference datasets and issues of contamination all need further attention (Pedersen et al. 2015).

The study of plant and animal domestication processes, however, has been by far the most prolific field of palaeoeconomic enquiry within archaeogenetics, and a number of detailed reviews of approaches are available in the literature (for plants see Emshwiller 2006; Allaby 2014; for animals see Bradley 2006; MacHugh et al. 2017). Many earlier studies focused on using mtDNA and Y-chromosome phylogenies, reconstructed from ancient and/or modern DNA, to identify wild progenitor species and the most likely geographic locus for original splits between wild and domestic lineages. If domesticated animals spread out in a simple radial fashion from a centre of domestication, then individual breeding populations will separate in sequence, with the latest splits being the most peripheral and the first split representing the locus of the initial domestic founder population (MacHugh et al. 2017). The spread of domestic taurine cattle is a good example of earlier work on this type of question that was largely modelled from modern specimens, with mtDNA lineages indicating that European cattle were most likely initially domesticated from wild *Bos primigenius* in the Near East (Troy et al. 2001), while African cattle had a different lineage, the result of either independent domestication or significant local introgression of wild stock (Bradley et al. 1996). Indeed, additional consideration of Y-chromosomes suggests that west African cattle also have introgression from male Indian zebu cattle (*Bos indicus*) (MacHugh et al. 1997). Another example is solving the long-standing debate over origins of domestic camelids in South America. Both alpacas and llamas were once assumed to be domesticated varieties of guanaco, whilst vicuña were thought never to have been domesticated. Analysis of modern mtDNA and microsatellites (short repeated tracts of DNA with high mutation rate), however, suggested that alpacas indeed derive from vicuña but with much hybridization with guanaco (Kadwell et al. 2001), and that it is possible that there is more than one centre of llama domestication (Barreta et al. 2013). This sort of approach has, in some cases, produced clear results that match well with the zoological subfossil and archaeological records. However, when there are potentially several independent domestication events or a complex pattern of spread, population admixture and selection, interpretation can become more difficult. For instance, similar work on dogs has been used to argue for different single or multiple domestication events in Europe and/or east Asia, or central Asia without firm agreement (MacHugh et al. 2017).

Similar studies have been applied to the consideration of plant domestication. In the case of maize, there has long been a debate over whether that crop is domesticated from an annual teosinte grass or whether those lines diverged prior to domestication, with domestic maize coming from an already distinct wild maize. Whilst the latter theory is much less in current favour, issues of hybridization have left room for continued debate (Emswiller 2006). On the other hand, microsatellite analyses have suggested a single point of origin in the Mexican highlands (Matsouka et al. 2002). In the case of rice, early phylogenies indicated independent origins of domestic *Oryza sativa japonica* and *O sativa indica* in China and India, respectively, but the pattern could be more complicated. There is the alternative hypothesis that later *O sativa indica* domestication could have resulted from hybridization between *O sativa japonica* and local wild strains rather than as an entirely independent event (Gross and Zhao 2014). Whilst this type of approach has certainly yielded success, there has been the tendency for simple phylogenetic models to be complicated by bottlenecks and hybridization.

Understanding of introgression is certainly much improved when aDNA from the actual period of the populations' potential overlap is studied, rather than modelling from the modern end result. Whilst the Near Eastern origin of most European key domesticates has remained fairly clear since early mtDNA models, debate over the extent of domestic admixture with local wild populations has been a hot topic. In the case of sheep and goats, the lack of local wild variants rules out admixture, but that is not the case with cattle or pigs. If we take cattle as the example, what evidence is there for interbreeding with local wild aurochs (*Bos primigenius*), which co-existed in the landscape for millennia? Ancient mtDNA analyses originally led to the conclusion that prehistoric domestic cattle were husbanded in such a way as to make introgression of aurochs exceedingly rare (Edwards et al. 2007). However, once a whole genome became available for *Bos primigenius* (a 6,750 year old specimen from Britain), it became clear that there was significant admixture with domestic stock in prehistory, at least in the British Isles (Orlando 2015; Park et al. 2015). This could have been deliberate restocking with aurochs from the wild or a loose system of husbandry. This example speaks to limitations of uniparental lineages in recreating the entire ancestry of individuals and to the advantages of whole genome research (Park et al. 2015). Lineages of Y-chromosome and mtDNA have some advantages in understanding aspects of phylogenetic events, because of constraint and relative simplicity. Quite clearly they help identify sex-biased mechanisms of introgression, but it is clear that the full story requires consideration of this alongside the broader pattern that includes the autosomal DNA as well.

Ancestry aside, initial domestication and the later creation of different domestic strains and breeds clearly results in the selection of particular physical and behavioural characteristics. As such, the genotypes in domesticates should reflect such selection for phenotypes. That selection might be inadvertent and the result of a founders' effect and inbreeding of a limited initial genepool, or the result of the unintentional removal of natural selective pressures through husbandry. On the other hand, it could be very deliberate human positive selection for desired traits. If the alleles responsible for particular phenotypes have been identified, the relevant allelic frequencies can be spatio-temporally mapped through aDNA studies. This line of evidence is very clear in some domestic plants. In maize there is a series of domestication-related loci within the genome including alleles related to exposing rather than encasing kernels and others relating to ear shattering and starch biosynthesis, amongst others (Jaeicke-Despres et al. 2003; Ramos-Madrigal et al. 2016). In rice, alleles responsible for preventing shattering are particularly important to prevent loss of seeds during harvest, but at some point there was also selection in favour of mutations that yielded white and glutinous rice (Gross and

Zhao 2014). Like rice, wheat has also undergone selection that prevents spikelets shattering and spilling seed upon harvest, but there are also many other gene loci of interest that govern other aspects of spikelet architecture associated with ease of threshing, as well as others related to yield and nutrient composition (Peleg et al. 2011; Peng et al. 2011).

In animals, one of the most discussed phenotypes, in relation to domestication, is coat colour (Linderholm and Larson 2013). Alleles responsible for controlling coat colour have been identified and it is clear that there is often a rapid increase in unusual coat colour allelic frequencies following domestication, most likely as a result of human selection. An example of this is seen with a sudden shift in horse coat colour allelic frequencies following domestication around 5,000 years ago (Ludwig et al. 2009). Along with desired selection of particular positive traits, processes such as domestication, husbandry and later selective breeding can remove negative selection against deleterious mutations that are responsible for unwanted conditions and diseases. The same processes introduce genetic bottlenecks and inbreeding that leaves populations with increased deleterious mutation loads (MacHugh et al. 2017). Such patterns can be seen in both plants and animals and represent another way of interrogating domestication events and the creation of breeds in relation to their genetic cost.

Whilst some of the details differ, there are many similar approaches to the archaeogenetic study of both plants and animals. However, collecting aDNA from plant samples is more of a challenge than from animals. Bones regularly survive in the archaeological record and, whilst preservation of DNA varies tremendously in relation to burial environment and temperature, collagen frequently survives within bones allowing ancient DNA to be amplified and sequenced. Whilst plant organics occasionally survive because of desiccation, freezing or waterlogging, and may well have good DNA preservation, these circumstances are far rarer than the survival of bones. Plants frequently only survive in the archaeological record in a charred state. Charring may not involve the complete destructive distillation of all organics, and thus the interior parts of plant macrofossils can potentially be analysed, but with challenges. Since DNA is very susceptible to heat damage, charring processes are highly likely to destroy most or all DNA present. In addition to that, chemical reactions between the carbohydrates and proteins caused by heating result in some products that act as inhibitors to the PCR process needed for aDNA amplification (Giles and Brown 2008). However, it is reported that small amounts of DNA have been successfully extracted from experimentally charred grain using carefully designed PCR procedures (Giles and Brown 2008). Next generation techniques have also apparently recovered aDNA from charred macrofossils (Bunning et al. 2012), though both these sets of authors were at pains to point out the severe risk of contamination when such sensitive amplification techniques are required. More worryingly, a more recent study investigating whether next generation, high-throughput methods might assist in this problematic area (Nistelberger et al. 2016) concluded that the vast majority of DNA extracted was not endogenous to the specimen and likely to be spurious. They urged extreme caution in relation to the analysis of charred macrofossils. Clearly, solving this problem would revolutionize the field in terms of the data available, but it is not yet clear whether this will occur.

As well as studying the DNA of individual people, plants and animals, it is also possible to study associated preserved bacteria, where they survive. Bacteria could be environmental, related to decay processes or part of the body's natural microbiome. The genetic significance of microbiomes will be revisited below, but other types of bacteria that could be present are those associated with infectious disease. Clearly studying disease in the ancient world is a topic of archaeological interest, but in some circumstances it is also of particular palaeoeconomic interest. Some infectious diseases and parasites are zoonoses, meaning that they have been transferred from animals to humans. The shift from hunting and gathering to farming involved significantly closer human–animal relations as well as interaction with a different range of species and food products (e.g. milk), thus changing and enhancing the vectors for disease transmission (see Jones et al. 2013). An example of disease that may have increased in humans as a result of the transition to animal husbandry is brucellosis (Fournié et al. 2017). *Brucella* spp. aDNA markers have been detected in bones displaying appropriate osteological palaeopathologies from a medieval cemetery in Albania (Mutolo et al. 2012), whilst unaffected bones and individuals all produced suitably negative results. Even earlier Brucellosis DNA has been reported from 3,500-year-old skeletons in Iran (Kafil et al. 2014). Brucellosis has not, however, been the most commonly studied disease that is regularly transferred from livestock. Tuberculosis (*Mycobacterium tuberculosis*) has been identified many times in both skeletal material and mummies bearing physical signs of the disease. This bacterium lends itself to aDNA study because its structure makes it relatively resistant to taphonomic degradation (Anastasiou and Mitchell 2013). The earliest archaeological human material from which *M. tuberculosis* aDNA has been recovered is from 9250–8160 cal BP at Atlit-Yam in the eastern Mediterranean. However, now that the whole genome of both *M. tuberclusosis* and *M. bovis* have been studied, it appears that the human form is more ancestral and thus people may be responsible for transferring the disease to cattle, rather than the other way round (Hershkovitz et al. 2015; Spigelman et al. 2015). Cattle, particularly after the advent of widespread dairying, could then have become a significant vector for the spread of infection.

Pitfalls and How to Avoid Them

From its earliest days the 'Achilles heel' of aDNA research has been contamination, so this pitfall should be discussed first. In 1994 much excitement surrounded the purported successful PCR amplification and sequencing of a portion of mitochondrial aDNA from 80 million-year-old dinosaur bones from Cretaceous deposits in Utah (Woodward et al. 1994). However, subsequent cladistic analyses by a number of other scholars quickly showed that, in fact, what had been sequenced was of human origin and therefore a contaminant (Allard et al. 1995; Hedges and Schweitzer 1995; Young et al. 1995; Zischler et al. 1995). Mistakes of this kind, reaching print, became a very significant risk in the field, leading Cooper and Poiner (2000) to compose a letter to *Science*, designed as a wake-up call, entitled 'Ancient DNA: Do It Right or Not at All'. In this they urged the use of a rigorous set of protocols and checks that had not been routinely undertaken in many early studies.

DNA contamination can occur at many different stages, from the original deposition of materials in the past through to excavation and from the laboratory itself (see discussion in Brown and Brown 2011: 137). Depending upon funerary rites or waste deposition practices, the DNA of multiple individuals and species might end up being very closely associated in a burial context with cross-contamination highly likely. During diagenesis a bone, or other potential subject for analysis, will be infiltrated by a vast array of environmental DNA from soil microbes and so on. Once excavated, an archaeological context will be opened up to the above ground environment risking further contamination, not least from the excavators themselves. Sampling for DNA might happen at that point, but frequently there will be stages of finds processing, washing and handling for other forms of analysis and museum storage. Once in the laboratory there is a risk of further cross-contamination. Original commingling of materials cannot be controlled for and so must be a factor for consideration in analysis and interpretation. The other contamination risks can be addressed in various ways. For instance, removal of the outer 2 mm of bone before extraction significantly reduces contamination levels (Brown and Brown 2011: 42) and archaeologists and laboratory workers can wear gloves, masks and suits to prevent them leaving their DNA, but it is difficult to eradicate all contamination. There are contamination risks for all types of material studied, but clearly the study of human aDNA is most at risk, since archaeologists and laboratory technicians tend to be human. Given the potential presence of contamination, no matter how careful one has been, it is necessary to tailor the amplification and sequencing techniques and develop ways of recognizing contaminants versus the genuine endogenous DNA of the sampled material (Brown and Brown 2011; Matisoo-Smith and Horsburgh 2012).

The enrichment of endogenous DNA, selective non-amplification of exogenous DNA and recognition of authentic aDNA have all improved massively with the introduction of next generation sequencing with ability to sequence far more and gain a much richer dataset to analyse (Llamas et al. 2017). For example, laboratory protocols used in extraction and amplification can be tailored to exploit subtle differences in methylation markers between bacteria and multicellular organisms to enrich the latter (Seguin-Orlando et al. 2015) and it is also possible to target only specific regions of interest resulting in selective capture (e.g. Enk et al. 2014). Once sequenced, it should be possible to eliminate content that is clearly from the wrong species, and question that which makes no phylogenetic sense (Matisoo-Smith and Horsburgh 2012). Ancient DNA also tends to display a very particular pattern of miscoded lesions that are a result of its degradation relative to new contaminants (Brown and Brown 2011: 142) and some of these patterns have a correlation with age (Llamas et al. 2017). In this way, recent contamination might be recognized and disregarded, though where the contamination is itself old it might also display some ancient characteristics (Matisoo-Smith and Horsburgh 2012). Clearly, in this respect, recently excavated remains analysed following good DNA sampling protocols are preferred subjects of study. Cross-contamination from aDNA amplicons in aerosols from previous analyses in the same laboratory remain an ever-present risk and this cannot be spotted during authentication work, but can be limited by good laboratory protocols between processing individual samples (Brown and Brown 2011: 143).

Even though many sources of contamination, at least modern ones, can be eliminated from study after the sample has been taken, doing this adds considerable expense (Llamas et al. 2017), meaning that sampling procedures should remain rigorous to avoid inflating project costs at that stage. Whilst archaeologists are becoming more cognizant of appropriate procedures in particular projects and circumstances, good practice in this area of work is still far from widespread, and there are significant practical issues in maintaining such standards for all organic materials that may need to be analysed at some point for aDNA. There can also be conflicts of interest between the needs of different specialists. Geneticists may prefer bones not to be washed (Llamas et al. 2017), but an osteoarchaeologist wishing to study surface modifications and lesions might require clean bones. One way around such issues, in the context of a research excavation with defined goals, is co-ordination of expert needs in advance. For instance, when excavating skeletons, full aDNA protocols could be maintained until the best target element for aDNA sampling (e.g. teeth or petrosal bone) can be lifted and recorded. The aDNA sample can be taken in the field with the least chance of contamination, then allowing the rest of the excavation and analysis to continue as normal. This clearly cannot be applied in all field scenarios. Figure 5.1 shows the sampling of a horse petrosal bone with appropriate anti-contamination protocols.

Other legitimate criticisms that can be levelled at some past archaeogenetic work relate to over-interpretation and unwarranted certainty in conclusions. Not infrequently the genetic analyses will be sound but inferences made from them much less safe as a result of unrepresentative samples or insufficient consideration of context. There are numerous studies presenting high profile findings where whole populations are represented by the analysis of a single specimen, or a very small number (e.g. Green et al. 2008; Rasmussen et al. 2010, 2014; Gallego Llorente et al. 2015). Whether firm conclusions should be reached from such studies, without highlighting significant areas of assumption, depends very much on the specific points being made, the extent to which the cultural affinity of the individual is relevant, and whether the sample can be considered representative. The issues here are slightly different depending on whether the research is merely targeting the recognition of mtDNA or Y-chromosome haplogroups, or some other particular marker, or the sequencing of whole genomes. If the study is directed at generalizing about haplogroups or particular allelic frequencies, then it is clear that sample size is highly relevant, and any study with very limited numbers or with significant spatio-temporal gaps, should be accompanied with due statistical caution. However, when whole genomes are studied, other arguments come into play. An entire genome cannot be considered to be one data point; there is a really vast amount of data, not just about that individual but also about the much wider ancestral population that individual derives from. Thus, it can be argued that study involving a single ancient genome does not represent a small sample size and, at least in terms of ancestry, it could be representative with regard to the conclusions being made. This

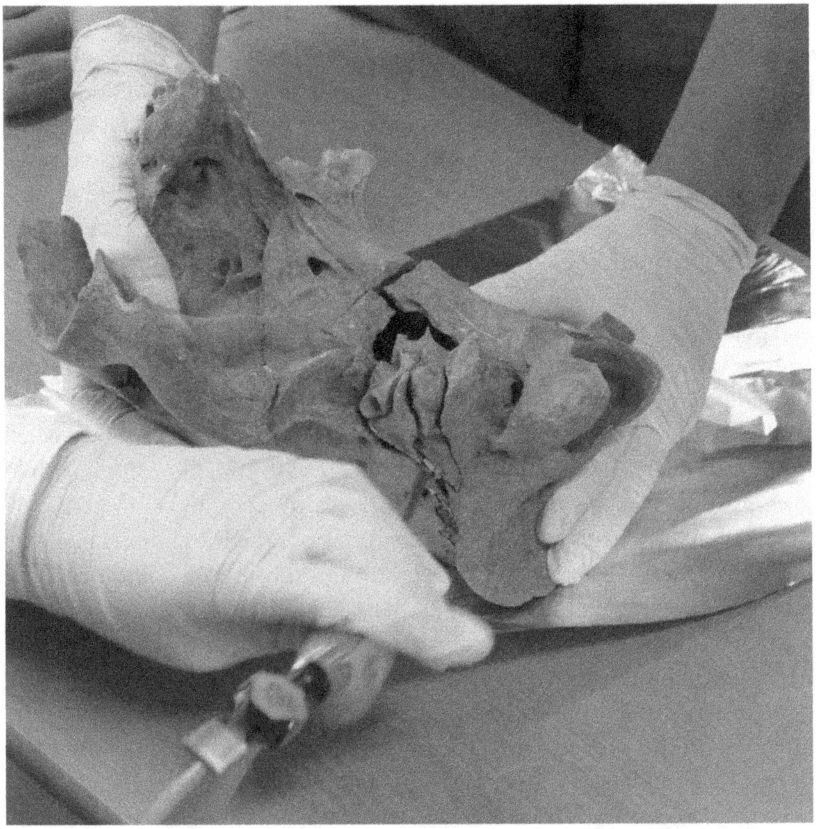

FIGURE 5.1 A photograph showing the removal of the petrosal bone from an Eneolithic horse cranium in Kazakhstan. Equine petrosal bones are one of the best elements of skeleton for good preservation on ancient genomes and they can be carefully dislodged for study without wider damage to the cranium. Sampling precautions included double gloving, use of clean aluminium foil under the specimen and cleaning of tools prior to use with a bleach solution formulated to destroy DNA.

argument is legitimate, but only to a certain point, and that is where the correct consideration of archaeological context becomes important.

If we accept that a whole genome provides rich data on a population, the find spot is known, and the bone has been directly radiocarbon dated, is there any potential problem? This is where geneticists have on occasions been over-strident in deciding all is well, with minimal archaeological input. That genome might tell us much about the population it comes from, and it clearly comes from that time and place, but it is more difficult to assert from a single individual that it is representative of a particular cultural or economic phenomenon that actually makes the research significant. Let us assume a situation where a human skeleton is being analysed as part of an investigation of the nature of population movement during the adoption of agriculture. It has been recovered from an early agricultural site that otherwise provides evidence for the introduction of agricultural material culture and domestic plants and animals. The direct date on the skeleton has a range consistent with the agriculturalists' arrival. Without further consideration of the archaeological context it is still not safe to assume that single individual represents that early farming community. The potential confounding mechanisms are, in fact, multiple. Radiocarbon dates in prehistory can have calibrated ranges of several hundred years. Is the skeleton in some way directly associated with the farming culture, perhaps by burial rite or associated finds, or could it be from a slightly earlier hunter-gatherer occupation of the same locale within shallow stratigraphy? If we assume that the timing of the burial is indeed during the agricultural settlement's use, the assumption is still not safe. If the individual was buried in a non-normative fashion for the culture, it is possible that they are, in anthropological terms, 'other'. They could be an enemy victim of violence, or a captive. Let us assume further that the burial rite was normative for the culture and there is every contextual reason to assume that s/he was interred by the agricultural society as part of their own community. Even in this scenario the individual might still be informing us about the wrong population. That society might have patrilocal or matrilocal marriage customs that frequently involve exogenous spouses. Even with whole genomes, safely linking population data to particular cultures and economies can only be done safely when context is fully understood and, ideally, multiple individuals, of both sexes, have been studied, preferably from normative burials. Thus there can be a point of disconnect between excellent genetic work and the final stage of interpretation linking those data to archaeological research questions.

Similar arguments can be applied in some circumstances to plants and animals. Whilst less applicable to wild floral and faunal populations, domesticates can be transplanted on an individual basis at great speed by human action, and the context of deposition is also important to interpretation. Recently, eleven horses from the Iron Age site of Berel in Kazakhstan were sampled for whole genome sequencing (Librado et al. 2017). Eleven is an impressively high number of ancient genomes and one might reasonably assume the safe characterization of horse herds from around the site of Berel at the time. In this instance, the authors demonstrated excellent awareness of context. They observed that since the horses were in a high status burial context, not a domestic one, and that Herodotus refers to Scythian sacrifices of horses given as gifts by allies, this assemblage might represent a much wider selection of Iron Age horses from the region, rather than purely local herds. That potential interpretation is supported by limited evidence for kinship within this group (Librado et al. 2017).

As discussed above, one of the most important contributions made by genetics to palaeoeconomic studies has been to the consideration of plant and animal domestication processes. Such processes cause phylogenetic splits and phenotypic changes that can be recognized in the genetic record. However, whilst these may be excellent lines of evidence for or against domestication, such events and traits could have other potential causes and thus context and other lines of non-genetic data also need to be considered. For instance, isolation of mammoths on Wrangel Island in the Russian Arctic (Fry et al. 2017) had some of the same effects as domestication bottlenecks, in terms of reduced genetic diversity and deleterious allelic loads, but context in this case provides a blatant case for mechanisms other than mammoth domestication. A more subtle case study can be taken from work relating to the domestication of wheat in the Near East, which is of equal relevance to the interpretation of genotypes as well as the study of their phenotypic expression as studied in preserved macrofossils.

A key phenotypic change frequently taken as a crucial indicator of wheat domestication is the change from a brittle to non-brittle rachis (Hillman and Davies 1990a, 1990b). Wild grass seeds were harvested prior to agriculture, but the defining feature of farming cereals is the replanting of a portion of the harvest deliberately to ensure a future crop. Thus, only seeds successfully harvested can be replanted, producing a strong selective pressure. If brittle rachis wheat is harvested and it breaks apart, those seeds will plant themselves, as if wild, and will be lost to the harvest and not included in replanting. The harvest will have a strong bias towards non-brittle plants and so those will preferentially be replanted, potentially leading to a fast transition to a majority of plants displaying non-brittle characteristics (Hillman and Davies 1990a, 1990b). As well as being recognizable in macrofossils the alleles responsible for this characteristic have also been identified (Peleg et al. 2011; Peng et al. 2011). There is no question that this criterion is a good one for recognizing clearly domesticated wheat, but, more strictly speaking, it is only evidence for the use of particular harvest methods under a farming regime. There are two key ways whereby wheat could be farmed but not produce this phenotypic change. First, if wheat were harvested in other ways, such as by beating spikelets into a basket, rather than sickle harvesting, then both brittle and non-brittle forms would be selected for replanting (see Moore et al. 2000: Fig. 12.9). Second, the brittleness of rachis is highly sensitive to the time of year, so early harvest might not produce significant selection (Peleg et al. 2011). As such, this marker might be indicative of the earliest wheat agriculture, or a later change in harvest form or intensity of exploitation after a period of farming under a different regime. The message here is simply that phenotypic markers cannot be used alone as simplistic markers of domestication in isolation from other lines of environmental and archaeological evidence.

Some of the possible interpretative pitfalls described above can be exacerbated by pressure to arrive at the clear and impactful results that are desired by the editors of the highest ranking journals. Editors' selection of reviewers may also result in more or less attention to different aspects of technical arguments. Whilst geneticists have been guilty of archaeological naivety at times, it is true that archaeologists can also lack the scientific literacy required to appreciate the genetic arguments being made. Just as contamination problems can be reduced by early collaboration in projects between archaeologists and geneticists, close working in interdisciplinary teams should also ensure appropriately contextualized interpretation. These issues are far from unique to this area of interdisciplinary science, and there are many examples of good work, but this field has been more prone than some to this type of disconnect, at least in its early development.

Another potential pitfall in archaeogenetics has really only started to reveal its full extent relatively recently, as the databank of aDNA samples has become much larger, principally as a result of new high throughput techniques. It is becoming increasingly apparent that modelling major events in deep time, such as domestication and migration, based upon modern geo-spatial patterning in the DNA of modern populations alone, is risky in the extreme. For instance, recent sequencing of a large number of modern and ancient horse genomes has revealed the surprisingly recent loss of male lineages and the relatively late arrival of high deleterious mutation loads and some other allelic frequencies associated with positive selection of traits (Librado et al. 2017). Until Librado et al's paper, it had been commonly assumed (e.g. Warmuth et al. 2012), quite reasonably, that modern mtDNA and Y-chromosome haplogroup patterns owed much to the selection processes of initial domestication. Similarly, it might have been assumed that high deleterious mutation loads were introduced largely as a cost of initial domestication, since that is a common hypothesis, but in this case it appears they are mostly the result of much later intensive breeding (Librado et al. 2017).

Another very good example of this problem comes from the study of pig domestication. Examination of the mtDNA of 686 modern wild and domestic pigs from across Eurasia (Larson et al. 2005) appeared to show that modern domestic stock in western Europe was related to European wild boar, not Near Eastern domestic stock. This quite reasonably led to the hypothesis that there was a separate domestication event in Europe, rather than replacement of local wild populations with domesticated ones from the East, as had happened with cattle. However, when ancient samples were added to the picture (Larson et al. 2007) this view required significant revision. It became apparent that Near Eastern pigs were present in the Neolithic, possibly leading to additional domestication of local wild boar and admixture. The newly domesticated European pigs almost totally replaced the Near Eastern stock surprisingly quickly leaving only the slightest significant trace of their Neolithic presence in modern stock. In fact, we now know that there were even some pigs of domestic Near Eastern origin in the hands of Ertebølle hunter-gatherers, presumably as a result of trade with farmers to the south (Krause-Kyora et al. 2013), though, of course, they were not necessarily being husbanded by Ertebølle people. It is becoming increasingly clear, in both plants and animals, that significant introgression between wild and domestic stock is common and can easily be confused with independent domestication (Larson and Fuller 2014). Patterns in modern DNA, it is now clear, cannot resolve this equifinality, and, indeed, extremely important portions of the narrative can be entirely masked. The study of ancient DNA is therefore necessitated, but by extension of the above logic, we should also be wary of large temporal gaps within sets of aDNA data, as similar masking mechanisms might lie within those unstudied time periods.

Despite there being some significant pitfalls and interpretational problems during the development of archaeogenetics, there is now every reason for optimism. The arrival of high-throughput, next generation sequencing helps immensely because it allows large numbers of whole ancient genomes to be sequenced in an affordable way. Simply the possibility to have so much more data removes many problems of equifinality and allows gaps in datasets to be closed more easily, based upon good sample sizes. Being able to study whole genomes opens up so many more avenues of investigation than earlier work on uniparental lineages or limited targeted loci (see Linderholm 2015; Leonardi et al. 2017; MacHugh et al. 2017). Increased datasets also make it easier to process out possible contamination (Llamas et al. 2017). However, none of this removes the need for good interdisciplinary co-operation in both sample collection and interpretation, and the need for holistic integration of all lines of evidence.

At the Cutting Edge and Future Directions

Genotypes and Phenotypes: Integrating Genomics with Geometric Morphometrics (GMM)

Certain genes control phenotypes related to physical development and thus the size and shape of an individual plant or animal. Where that particular morphological trait is heavily dependent upon genotype and less affected by plastic changes during life that are a result of states of nutrition, health and activity, then that trait may well correlate with ancestry. Bioarchaeologists have routinely recorded sets of metrical data for the specimens they analyse, since the very birth of these disciplines. Such data generally consist of series of well-defined linear measurements (e.g. von den Driesch 1976), but in the wider world of biology during the 1980s and 1990s there was a revolutionary shift away from linear measurements towards the new technique of 'geometric morphometrics' or 'GMM' (Adams et al. 2004). The problem with a series of linear measurements is that they are not ideal for describing the subtleties of shape, while differences in gross size cause considerable allometric problems when wishing to examine shape alone. Progress can be made when linear measures are converted into ratios, and many measurements or ratios are considered together using multivariate statistical methods, but significant limitations remain. GMM instead considers a set of well-defined landmarks and all the geometric relationships between those landmarks, and is a much more powerful approach to the subject (Adams et al. 2004).

Despite its earlier development in biology, its use in archaeology has really only begun to build since 2010. For instance, it has been noted that GMM applied to enamel fold patterns in teeth of horses appears to show up differences in breed that might be of use in archaeological applications (Seetah et al. 2014). This kind of study is two-dimensional GMM that analyses perpendicular photographs of tooth occlusal surfaces. Other recent studies are three-dimensional and based upon laser scans, such as GMM analysis of sheep and goat astragali to help separate the two species (Haruda 2017) or even distinguish between apparent local landraces of sheep (Haruda 2014). These advances make the combined use of GMM and aDNA analysis an obvious next step. For instance, another recent study of horse teeth tested the reliability of GMM correctly to group a series of equids according to genetically verified phylogenetic relationships (Cucchi et al. 2017). The results were very promising, and GMM, verified by genetics, might be applicable where cost or the prohibition of destructive sampling prevent aDNA analysis. Alternatively, both forms of analysis can be applied across a study such as in a recent investigation of domestic pig dispersal in Eurasia (Ottoni et al. 2013). Beyond identifying traits for the purposes of tracking ancestry, the combination of ancient genomics and GMM has great future potential to examine the selection of specific morphological phenotypes that relate to domestication or the subsequent creation of specialized breeds. Particular allelic frequencies might be correlated with observed morphological changes and not others. Where GMM criteria correlate well with genetics, specimens that can only be studied that way might augment the dataset available. The combination of these two methodologies is a common approach in a number of ongoing large projects which are yet to report.

Epigenetics and Microbiomes

It has long been understood that there is not always a simple and direct relationship between genotype and phenotype. The coding in genes has to be physically expressed, and the form of expression can be interfered with by environmentally induced chemical modifications to loci in the DNA or other key reagents. Originally, the term 'epigenetics' was applied to describe in general the processes of expression from genotype to actual phenotypic traits then displayed. However, the term is often now used more specifically to describe patterns of chemical modifications to DNA that can potentially be heritable (see Bird 2007; Heard and Martienssen 2014). These modifications are not to be confused with mutations in the genetic code (Bird 2007), but instead are other chemical modifications, such as the addition of a methyl group to a particular locus in the DNA molecule. Whilst the gene sequence is unaltered, the presence of modifications like methylation can repress the transcription of gene. One can distinguish between 'intergenerational' effects caused by environment (e.g. nutrition, stress, hormones, etc., *in utero* during development) and 'transgenerational' effects that are inherited epigenetic changes observable in future generations that were never subjected to environmental factors that first caused that modification (Heard and Martienssen 2014). Many types of stress can be related to epigenetic tagging, such as methylation, in humans, including physical exertion, trauma, malnutrition, drug use, sleep disorders and even social stress (Denhardt 2017). Much of this is inheritable to some extent. Epigenetic patterning has been extensively studied in some plants and animals too (Rival et al. 2010; Jensen 2014) and it is clear that such patterning could be highly relevant to selection during domestication (Jenson 2014). Just as examples, wild and domestic epigenetic patterns for wolves versus dogs (Janowitz Koch et al. 2016) and red junglefowl versus chickens (Nätt et al. 2012) have been compared, with clear, heritable differences noted. The clear conclusion is that epigenetics plays a part in domestication processes and certainly has resulted in distinctive patterning in modern plants and animals.

The potential relevance to palaeoeconomic archaeology is obvious. Epigenomes could be as interesting as genotypes in understanding domestication processes and resulting phenotypes (Piperno 2017), particularly as the act of domestication is likely to have confronted species with new types of environmental, physical, disease or social stressors (MacHugh et al. 2017). However, until very recently, methods had not been developed that allowed patterns of epigenetic tagging to be mapped across ancient genomes. From around 2010 onwards, it has become possible to identify some types of epigenetic marker in aDNA and begin to reconstruct partial epigenomes (Orlando and Willerslev 2014; Gokhman et al. 2016). In the case of methylation, this is approached by using the different way in which a portion of DNA decays, when methylated or not, to identify loci which once had such tags (Orlando and Willerslev 2014). Improved tools that employ degradation patterns to reconstruct ancient epigenetic maps are being developed to aid genome-wide mapping (Hanghøj et al. 2016), though clearly these are early days with considerable need for further experimental work. Early ancient human applications have included the study of a 4,000-year-old Paleo-Eskimo (Pedersen et al. 2014) and specimens of both a Denisovan and a Neanderthal (Gokhman et al. 2014) with meaningful patterns being observed. For example, one pattern of interest, from a palaeoeconomic standpoint, is that the archaic humans being studied shared aspects of epigenetic tagging associated with low calorie intake with modern hunter-gatherers who suffer seasonal subsistence stress (Gokhman et al. 2017). Due caution is required in such a new field, but much potential has been demonstrated.

A major influence on gene expression and epigenetics has been found within the body's 'microbiome'. This is the suite of bacterial flora particularly in the gut but also elsewhere. This is a hot topic in medical science because of apparently significant effects on the progress of a wide range of diseases and health issues (e.g. Hullar and Fu 2014; Blackman 2016; Kim 2017; Lee et al. 2017). Clearly microbiomes have a role to play in understanding ancient epigenomics as well as past diets and health. It is also the case that the DNA of ancient bacteria can be sequenced and studied, but is it feasible to study the microbiome associated with an individual animal or human in any meaningful way? By sampling preserved human faecal material, coprolites, and sequencing the bacterial aDNA present it is possible to gain an insight into the ancient gut microbiome (Tito et al. 2008, 2012; Warinner et al. 2015b), whilst oral microbiomes can be preserved within dental calculus (Warinner et al. 2015a, 2015b). This area of work is not without its challenges. Methodological work is ongoing to establish laboratory techniques that do not skew taxonomic data (see Ziesemer et al. 2015). The taphonomy of flora in coprolites and calculus needs also to be understood, alongside sources of exogenous bacteria from the environment (Warinner 2015b) and therefore it is advisable to collect control samples that might reflect local environmental bacteria (Warinner 2015a). There is much potential to consider microbiomes routinely alongside genomes and epigenomes to search for patterns and correlations. Ancient microbiome research needs considerably more developmental work to ensure that results are not skewed by differential taphonomy and exogenous sources of bacterial aDNA.

Conclusion

The value of ancient genetics to economic archaeology has never been in doubt. It can revolutionize our understanding of the relationship between economy, environment and human migration, as well as that of the animals and plants people relied upon for food. It is possible to understand extinct species better and reconstruct the timing and location of key changes in key economic plants and animals as they were domesticated, traded and bred for specialist purposes. We can gain broader insights into issues of health and disease and their relationship to subsistence practices. It even helps us reconstruct aspects of social relations and how they contrast in different cultures and economies through studying kinship, differential migration of males and females, along with post-marital residence patterns. Epigenetics might provide an insight into how environment, economy and social structures impact genetic expression and evolution.

This chapter has illustrated a range of past methodological problems and misunderstandings in the field. Many of these problems can now be mitigated. Interpretational issues can be best addressed by good interdisciplinary working and holistic consideration of all lines of evidence. Well-planned research with advanced briefing from specialists can help greatly in ensuring good sample collection practices and the maximum protection against contamination. Next generation, high-throughput sequencing and other new laboratory protocols are helping considerably with the identification and elimination of contaminants, whilst the ability to sequence much larger numbers of whole genomes is helping to remove problems related to low sample sizes and patchiness of data. The vastly increased datasets now appearing are less prone to problems of equifinality, but do need careful statistical handling, meaning that the role of bioinformatics specialists and computational biologists will become ever more important. Some recent approaches to extracting and interpreting aDNA are still very much in their infancy. In particular, sedaDNA, microbiome aDNA and amplifications from charred plant material all need further work to become reliable. Microbiomes and sedaDNA need better understanding of the relative taphonomy of different taxa in particular conditions and all these methods require greater appreciation of the issues surrounding the separation of endogenous and exogenous sources of DNA.

What is clear is that continuing into the 21st century we will see a staggering array of new methods and exciting impactful results. The challenge will be for interdisciplinary teams to stay on top of all the developments they need in order to deliver the most insightful research.

CHAPTER 6

Incorporating New Methods IV: Phytoliths and Starch Grains in the Tropics and Beyond

Grahame Clark declared in 1972 that the 'most striking piece of hardware' in the palaeoeconomists' toolkit was the flotation tank: a means of extracting charred (carbonized) plants remains, along with other small biological and artefactual remains, on a large scale (Clark 1972: ix). Fieldwork featuring extensive sampling and flotation to generate new charred plant assemblages played a central role in the palaeoeconomy project (H.N. Jarman et al. 1972), and in the establishment of economic archaeology as a sub-discipline (Dennell 1983). It produced, for example, new evidence for crop processing and use in Neolithic central Anatolia (French et al. 1972) and Bulgaria (Dennell 1972, 1975), and ultimately formed the basis of a 'fine-grained' perspective on the agricultural transition in projects such as the Tell Abu Hureyra excavations (Moore et al. 1975, 2000).

While the large-scale recovery and study of charred macroscopic plant remains from occupation deposits was relatively novel in the 1970s, plant *microremains* in the form of pollen grains were a long established focus of palaeoecological study (Faegri and Iversen 1950). Harry Godwin's Sub-Department of Quaternary Research at Cambridge was one reason for siting the British Academy-funded 'Early Agriculture' project there (Clark 1972). Pollen cores in south-west Asia offered a means of assessing the potential ancient distribution of wild cereal progenitors (van Zeist 1969), an approach that has continued to be refined (Hillman 1996). While charred archaeobotanical assemblages from settlements offered the more direct route to reconstruction of plant husbandry practices (H.N. Jarman et al. 1972: 39), pollen from lake cores played a key role in establishing regional vegetation patterns and ecologies, for example in prehistoric central Italy (Barker 1975).

Phytoliths constitute another form of plant microremain that was well known by the 1970s, but 'silica skeletons' of plant cells and parts received only passing mention by early palaeoeconomists (Jarman 1972: 25). The geographical bias of the project towards early agriculture in south-west Asia and Europe fostered an interest in charred macrobotanical assemblages. By contrast, the recovery and study of phytoliths developed most intensively in tropical environments unfavourable for the preservation of macroscopic plant remains, such as in Central and South America and south-east Asia (Piperno 2006: 3, 23; Ball et al. 2016). Phytoliths have also played a key role in the construction of off-site vegetation sequences where pollen preservation is poor (e.g. Kealhofer 2002).

Widespread recovery and interpretation of another microscopic form of ancient plant material – starch grains – post-dates the palaeoeconomists' heyday (Torrence 2006: 28–9). The observation that intact starch granules were recoverable from desiccated tubers in Peruvian coastal desert contexts (Ugent et al. 1981) opened the way for studies of starch residues on stone tools, which remain a primary application of this technique (Barton and Torrence 2015). Importantly, archaeological studies of starch, like that of phytoliths, developed especially in regions where forms of preservation and/or plant exploitation were not conducive to a primary focus on charred macrobotanical remains. Moreover, starch analysis allowed investigation of root crops such as taro, yam and sweet potato that do not produce phytoliths (Torrence 2006: 28).

Our aim in this chapter is to consider how plant microremains in the form of phytoliths and starch have not only revolutionized the study of prehistoric plant exploitation in the (sub)tropics, but can also add depth and resolution to questions of resource use and material culture, in much the same way as residue chemistry (Chapter 4). The chapter is divided into three parts: first, a review of the nature and impact of phytolith and starch assemblages for tracing early agriculture in the (sub)tropics; second, a comparative assessment of the formation processes that give rise to phytolith, starch and charred macrobotanical assemblages; and third, a summary of the emerging strengths and weaknesses of these techniques, and their potential for integration in regions where all three lines of evidence are recoverable, including western Eurasia, the original heartland of palaeoeconomy.

Phytoliths, Starch and Early Agriculture in the (Sub)tropics

Phytoliths are inorganic silica bodies formed in and around the cells of some groups of living higher plants; they occur at high levels in monocotyledonous plants (e.g. grasses and sedges) and some dicotyledonous, gymnosperm and pteridophyte families, too (Piperno 2006: Table 1.1). Phytoliths confer structural and protective advantages to the plant (e.g. increased resistance to herbivory and pathogenic fungi), and are released when the plant dies, constituting 'arguably the most durable terrestrial plant fossils known to science' (Piperno 2006: 5). Nevertheless, phytolith preservation varies by cell type and depositional environment; soils with abundant free iron and aluminium oxides (common in tropical regions) are particularly favourable for phytolith preservation (Piperno 2006: 21). Plants deposit solid silica after absorbing it in a soluble state from groundwater; while preferential deposition of silica in certain cells is genetically controlled, the extent of phytolith formation in others is a useful expression of water availability during plant growth (Madella et al. 2009), a point we return to below.

Phytoliths are produced to varying degrees in different parts of plants, and identification involves allocation of characteristic shapes to anatomical part as well as to taxonomic level. Crops have been the focus of much phytolith taxonomic work, and distinctive morphotypes, increasingly characterized using morphometric approaches, enable identification to species level for some crops, including maize (especially cob phytoliths) and rice (especially glume phytoliths) (Piperno 2006: 60–79; Ball et al. 2016: Table 1).

Taxonomic work to distinguish phytoliths of domesticated maize (*Zea mays* L.) from those of its wild progenitor and other wild grasses in Central and South America has been extensive (e.g. Iriarte 2003; Pearsall et al. 2003; Piperno 2006: 60–5) and opened the way for tracking the early spread of maize. Poor preservation of carbonized maize cobs in tropical and subtropical climates limits the macrobotanical record in occupation deposits, and phytoliths (together with starch – see below) have played a key role in addressing that gap (e.g. Iriarte et al. 2004). Moreover, phytoliths alongside pollen and microscopic charcoal from 'off-site' contexts have provided important evidence for regional land-use patterns. A study of coastal savanna grassland landscapes in French Guiana (Iriarte et al. 2012) revealed pollen evidence for pre-Columbian establishment of intensively managed raised fields, together with maize phytoliths from raised field sediments. Rather than Boserupian 'progression' from slash-and-burn to intensively managed raised fields (cf. Boserup 1965), this sequence works in the opposite direction, with raised field agriculture and deliberate fire limitation prior to European contact, followed by a dramatic increase in landscape burning (encouraged by a long dry season), as pre-Columbian systems were abandoned from the 16th century AD and modern forms of swiddening were established.

Phytolith-based study of early rice agrosystems in east, south and southeast Asia provide an Old World comparator to work on maize in the

Americas. Much research has focused on taxonomic separation of cultivated rice (*Oryza sativa* complex) and wild forms (e.g. Zhao et al. 1998; Gu et al. 2013). Phytolith-based studies place the origins of the *japonica* rice domestication process in the Lower Yangtze valley much earlier – from 10,000 BC (Wu et al. 2014) than studies of charred spikelet bases (dehiscence) in macroscopic assemblages – 6th to 5th millennia BC (Fuller et al. 2009), though both approaches converge on the view that domestication was a gradual process. The chronological discrepancy requires further investigation using an integrated approach incorporating macroscopic and microscopic plant remains from the same sites and sequences (cf. Weisskopf et al. 2014). Similarly, the arrival of rice in Thailand appears much earlier on the basis of phytoliths than on macroscopic remains. Rice phytoliths are known from lake cores and alluvial deposits in the north and central parts of the country from the early to the mid Holocene (Kealhofer 2002), whereas the earliest charred macroscopic evidence for domestication (of *japonica* rice) dates to the earlier 2nd millennium BC (Castillo 2011).

Whereas harvesting of maize cobs does not lend itself to the (inadvertent) collection of arable weeds, harvesting of rice plants intercepts the weed flora, enabling their preservation on archaeological sites. Arable weeds provide a key opportunity to observe the ecology of crop fields; while some charred macroscopic weed seed assemblages associated with rice have been interpreted as evidence of rain-fed versus irrigated systems (e.g. Castillo 2011), recent discussion has mostly focused on phytolith assemblages. Weisskopf et al. (2014) used proportions of phytolith morphotypes diagnostic of broad groupings (Cyperaceae, hydrophilic species, panicoid grasses, etc.) to distinguish relatively wet and dry rice regimes in the Neolithic Yangtze valley and in Neolithic northern/eastern India, respectively. A complementary approach is to compare ratios of phytoliths from grass cells genetically programmed to produce phytoliths to those that only form phytoliths under high conditions of sufficient water uptake (Madella et al. 2009; Jenkins et al. 2016). Weisskopf et al. (2015) applied this method and detected hydrological shifts in rice growing in the Lower Yangtze valley sequence, from Neolithic flood/drainage systems to irrigated paddy rice (Weisskopf et al. 2015). A strength of the phytolith assemblage-based approach to agroecology is that it can be used to recover evidence from small-scale excavations and sections, though isolation of the 'weed' flora from phytoliths derived from other forms of vegetation needs to be considered (see discussion of formation processes below).

In addition to these and many other seed crops, phytoliths have also made a major contribution to studies of squashes and gourds, root and tree crops that have limited to no representation in the charred macrobotanical record. Analysis of phytoliths from squashes and gourds of the Cucurbitaceae has made it possible to trace the history of the multiple species domesticated in the Americas, including indications of squash alongside maize during the early 9th millennium cal BP in south-west Mexico (Piperno et al. 2009). Taxonomic work to distinguish true banana from its wild relatives enabled the detection of banana phytoliths from Kuk Swamp, an ancient agricultural field site in Papua New Guinea; cultivation is inferred from 6950 to 6440 cal BP, when high levels of banana phytoliths in palaeosols and agricultural feature fills coincide with pollen evidence of regional grassland vegetation (Denham et al. 2003). Tropical root crops of the Americas such as arrowroot and illerén, canna and manioc produce silica bodies that are sufficiently diagnostic to trace their use archaeologically (Piperno 2006). Other applications of phytoliths in palaeoecological research include measurement of $\delta^{13}C$ values in bulk phytoliths from sediments to detect changing proportions of C_3/C_4 taxa through time, and of $\delta^{18}O$ values to assess environmental conditions, though interpretation of the latter is notably complex (Kelly et al. 1991; McClaren and Umlauf 2000; Webb and Longstaffe 2000; Hodgson et al. 2008).

Archaeological interest in starch began relatively recently, in the 1980s (Torrence 2006: 27–9). Ancient starch studies have opened up new avenues of enquiry into plant use in tropical parts of the world, especially in residues on artefacts, but increasingly also in more 'sealed' contexts like dental calculus, charred food crusts and coprolites (Barton and Torrence 2015). Analysts have also tackled persistent concerns over starch preservation and assemblage formation processes (Haslam 2004; Collins and Copeland 2011), including contamination from modern starches in the laboratory and the landscape (Crowther et al. 2014; Mercader et al. 2017). We discuss comparative understanding of the taphonomy of starch, phytoliths and other plant remains below.

Starch granules are the plant's reserve glucose, and are concentrated in storage organs such as seeds, fruits, roots and tubers, but also occur in other plant parts such as starchy stems (Gott et al. 2006). Starch is semicrystalline, consisting of two forms of glucose (amylose and amylopectin molecules) that form harder 'shells' and softer amorphous layers within each granule. Starch's molecular structure confers birefringence, such that granules appear white against a dark background under polarizing light. The extinction cross, appearing as a dark feature, is a key diagnostic zone for distinguishing plant taxa based on the relative length and angle of the arms. Various forms of staining and microscopy are used to enhance diagnostic features (Barton and Fullagar 2006). Starch is insoluble but is subject to (reversible) swelling since it is permeable to water, and gelatinizes under heat and/or certain chemical conditions. Ethnobotanical research on plant processing and food preparation has identified certain forms of damage to starch granules (producing 'modified' as opposed to 'native' starch granules) that may be useful for inferring ancient processing (Samuel 2006), but these effects need to be assessed against diagenetic changes in ancient and contaminating industrial starch (Collins and Copeland 2011; Crowther et al. 2014). Given that starch granules act as food for many organisms, their apparent survival over millennia is remarkable and remains unexplained (Mercader et al. 2017).

Kuk Swamp in Papua New Guinea offers an illustrative example of the potential impact of starch research for understanding early agriculture in Oceania. The site was made famous by the discovery of successive drainage systems indicative of agricultural land management, the earliest dating back to 10,000 BP (Denham et al. 2003). In addition to the banana phytoliths mentioned above, analysis of starch grains extracted from stone tools enabled investigation of root crops that do not produce phytoliths. The recovery of taro (*Colocasia esculenta* (L.) Schott) starch grains from stone tools indicates its presence at Kuk Swamp from the beginning of the sequence, though its status as a cultivar or domesticate at this time is unclear (Fullagar et al. 2006).

Research into the origins and spread of maize further demonstrates the potential of combined phytolith and starch research for tracing early agriculture in tropical regions. Macrobotanical remains of maize cobs from arid highland Mexico, dating back as far as *c.* 6200 BP (Benz 2001), attest to early partially to fully domesticated forms (Vallebueno-Estrada et al. 2017) and for decades focused attention on that region as a likely centre of maize domestication (MacNeish and Eubanks 2000). Meanwhile geneticists identified the progenitor of maize as Balsas teosinte (*Zea mays* subsp. *parviglumis* H.H. Iltis and Doebley), which is endemic to tropical south-west Mexico (Matsuoka et al. 2002; Doebley 2004). Renewed archaeological focus on the central Balsas river region of south-west Mexico identified a lengthy human occupation sequence in the Xihuatoxtla Shelter, dating back to 8700 BP (Ranere et al. 2009). In a microbotanical study of the site, Piperno et al. (2009) recovered maize starch grains from stone tools, using a needle probe to retrieve grains from deep cracks and crevices, and observed that starch grains originated from tool facets with use-wear traces. This method of retrieval and emphasis on recovery from working facets of the tools reflect ongoing concerns with modern starch contamination, particularly from ubiquitous present-day crops such as maize. Phytolith morphotypes likely derived from maize were also found in association with the same tools and in the sedimentary sequence, and were regarded as key corroborating evidence for this early case of maize use at the Xihuatoxtla Shelter (Piperno et al. 2009). The extended sequence of maize use, and absence of starch and phytoliths indicative of teosinte, the wild progenitor, is interpreted to suggest that early 9th millennium BP maize was domesticated. However, macroscopic remains of (desiccated or carbonized) cobs, which are not preserved in this sequence, still provide the most direct evidence of domestic status, through morphology and ancient DNA (Benz 2001; Vallebueno-Estrada et al. 2017).

To sum up, phytoliths and, more recently, starch have revolutionized the study of prehistoric plant exploitation in (sub)tropical regions of the world, where the species being exploited do not always produce remains likely to survive as a result of charring and/or where organic preservation is often poor. Inorganic phytoliths, recovered from sediments, or from vessel or tool residues, have opened a new window on our understanding of key domestic species including seed crops like maize and rice, and root crops such as manioc. Phytoliths also have the potential to shed light on crop growing conditions, particularly hydrology (i.e. irrigation, drainage). Identifiable starch grains can also be recovered from residues, providing important evidence for the exploitation of starchy plants like taro that do not produce phytoliths. Currently these lines of evidence are tracing the origins of agriculture back into the early Holocene in tropical regions of Central and South America, and in Oceania, suggesting a similar timeframe to that established in south-west and east Asia (Denham et al. 2003; Hastorf 2009; Piperno 2017).

Phytolith and Starch Taphonomy: A Critical Comparison

The biases inherent in the formation of charred macroscopic plant assemblages are well known: only the denser parts of plants tend to be preserved, and those species stored and used year-round are more likely to be represented (through accidental charring, or as processing waste in rubbish/fuel discard) than plants exploited for their vegetative parts and/or consumed primarily in season. Here we consider the formation of phytolith and starch assemblages in order to specify inherent biases, before identifying the comparative strengths and weaknesses of these approaches.

Turning first to phytolith taphonomy, a key contrast with charred macroscopic plant remains is that heating is not required in order for these inorganic remains to be preserved. Phytoliths are released as plants decompose and disaggregate. There are, however, inherent biases towards certain plants and plant parts in phytolith assemblages, since many families produce few to no phytoliths, and underground storage organs generally do not produce phytoliths (Piperno 2006: Table 1.1, 104). Moreover, taxonomic work is oriented especially towards crop plants, though the range of taxa with recognized diagnostic morphotypes will continue to broaden (e.g. Ball et al. 2016).

When phytoliths are released from a decayed plant, they tend to be dispersed locally since they are 'heavy' and, unlike many pollen types, are not designed for wind dispersal (Madella and Lancelotti 2012). Two dispersal-related factors, however, can complicate the interpretation of phytolith assemblages: strong winds especially in open, desert environments; and vertical movement due to post-depositional bioturbation. Moreover, the 'phytolith pool' in soils can change dramatically as a result of dissolution under certain conditions of pH, moisture and temperature (Madella and Lancelotti 2012).

In archaeological/anthropogenic deposits, human action is assumed to be the major factor determining phytolith assemblage distribution and composition (Madella and Lancelotti 2012). A major challenge and potential of archaeological phytolith work is to conduct 'micro-sampling' that is sufficiently fine-grained to disentangle individual depositional episodes, such as fine ash lenses in a midden deposit. Soil micromorphology and microstratigraphy offer an important control to achieve this surgical precision. Micro-sampling of late Neolithic ash mound sites in southern India, for example, has enabled identification of individual cattle stabling episodes (Madella and Lancelotti 2012: Fig. 10).

Phytolith recovery is another taphonomic filter that has an important effect on the assemblage and its interpretation. Jenkins (2009) showed, for example, that extraction of phytoliths by wet-ashing breaks down articulated/conjoined phytoliths, generating more single-celled phytoliths and complicating previous attempts to interpret the presence of large multicell phytoliths as evidence of wet growing conditions (Rosen and Weiner 1994). It is worth noting that the alternative approach of inferring water availability from ratios of genetically 'fixed' to environmentally 'sensitive' phytolith types (Madella et al. 2009) is not vulnerable to this same recovery bias.

To summarize this brief discussion of phytolith taphonomy, it is clear that this approach is oriented to the recovery of remains from particular plants and plant parts; that phytoliths are subject to certain 'natural' agents affecting their distribution; and that unpicking the complexity of anthropogenic patterning in assemblage formation is enhanced through integration with other approaches such as soil micromorphological studies.

While the taphonomy of phytolith assemblages is complex, there is no question that their inorganic nature and chemical composition are conducive to long-term preservation. The same cannot be said of starch granules, which by their nature represent food for a range of organisms; thus, the plausibility of ancient starch *per se* has been raised strongly within archaeology, albeit often in the realm of personal communications. Barton and Torrence (2015: 194) recently observed that incomplete understanding of formation processes and contamination remain key 'roadblocks' in ancient starch research. At the same time, and partly as a result of these anxieties, positive steps are being taken to focus on 'sealed' contexts, integration of starch residues with other corroborating evidence and explicit recognition of contamination in the field and laboratory.

A general model of ancient starch taphonomy has yet to be developed, but promising avenues for explaining the preservation of ancient carbohydrates include sorption to mineral phases and mineral neoformation (Mercader et al. 2017). Meanwhile, experimental work has begun to clarify the conditions under which ancient starch is most plausibly preserved, as native and/or modified granules. Valamoti et al. (2008), for example, showed that heating barley grains to 220°C – within the ideal temperature range for relatively undistorted carbonized cereal grains (Charles et al. 2015) – yields starch granules with intact diagnostic features, but also causes some distortions that might otherwise be interpreted as cooking. Furthermore, gelatinization depends not only on temperature but also on moisture levels and the form (e.g. whole versus ground) in which plant parts are cooked (Crowther 2012). The argument that heat-altered (e.g. swollen) or gelatinized granules reflect cooked starch, while native granules reflect raw starch, is also complicated by differing reactions of individual taxa to cooking (Henry et al. 2009) and by the potential for gelatinization at low temperature over long time periods (Collins and Copeland 2011). Clearly, further study of starch-granule diagenesis is needed.

Current analysis of ancient starch is arguably most reliable in application to 'sealed' contexts such as dental calculus, coprolites and charred or desiccated food crusts on ceramics, the latter also providing a directly datable context for starch that has ranged back to 10,000 cal BP (Barton and Torrence 2015: Table 5). In the case of 'unsealed' starch residues on tools – still the primary application of starch in archaeology – cautionary measures include integration with use-wear and phytolith studies to corroborate inferences from starch analysis. The study of early maize and squash in south-west Mexico by Piperno et al. (2009) provides an example of this integrated approach, though it is notable that here the starch granules were retrieved by needle-probe from groundstone tools, while the phytoliths derived from associated sediments.

In addition to diagenesis, the other major challenge for starch studies in archaeology is the need to document and understand starch contamination, in the laboratory and in the excavation landscape. Two recent studies have shed important light on these topics. Crowther et al. (2014) documented the occurrence of contaminating maize, wheat and potato starch granules in laboratory settings, demonstrating the potential for false positives in ancient starch research. Moreover, contamination starches included both native and modified granules, indicating that mere presence of modified grains is no guarantee of authenticity. Contamination starch appeared to derive from airborne sources as well as laboratory consumables. In addition to particular cleaning protocols, these authors strongly recommend negative controls subjected to the same treatment as archaeological samples, and vigilance where the target species under archaeological investigation are also likely contaminating taxa such as maize, wheat and potato.

In a first systematic study of a 'starch contamination landscape' in the field, Mercader et al. (2017) documented soil-, air- and excavator-borne starch at Olduvai Gorge. They found a predominance of starch from underground storage organs in soils, in various states of diagenetic alteration, and of native cereal grain starch types above ground in airborne samples. They also identified a significant likelihood of contamination by excavators bringing starches from the campsite to the excavation, and highlighted the possibility of contamination of tool residues during excavation that may be difficult to factor out. They conclude that mobile clean-rooms offer an appropriate excavation setting where starch contamination needs to be minimized, albeit at considerable cost (Mercader et al. 2017).

Integrating Phytolith, Starch and Macrobotanical Studies

It is clear from the above discussion that assemblage formation processes for phytoliths and starch granules are very different, and also distinct from those that govern charred macroscopic remains. In this final section we consider how these contrasting biases can be exploited in studies that integrate micro- and charred macrobotanical lines of evidence to build up robust, holistic pictures of ancient plant use. As with other multi-proxy approaches in archaeobotany (e.g. combining charred and waterlogged macroscopic remains – Jacomet et al. 2004, or combining weed ecological and crop stable isotope-based approaches to arable growing conditions – Bogaard et al. 2016, 2018), the clear advantages of a multi-stranded approach are that: (1) the potentials of one method compensate for the limitations of another, and (2) there is scope for cross-validation. Table 6.1 summarizes some of the key parameters that define the potentials and limitations of different botanical strands of evidence. While analysis of multiple macro- and micro-botanical assemblages clearly serves to broaden taxonomic and anatomical understanding of plant use, there is also scope for cross-validation in areas such as plant processing and arable field ecology. We consider a few case studies here to highlight the potential of integrated approaches.

Garcia-Granero et al. (2015) took an integrated macro- and micro-botanical approach to the investigation of plant use at Shikarpur, a Chalcolithic settlement in Gujarat, north-west India. Charred macroscopic preservation was poor but indicated the presence of small millets and pulses; phytolith and starch sampling of grinding stones confirmed the processing of both types, and the dominance of these summer crops over sparsely documented winter wheat and barley.

An integrated multi-site case study from pre-Columbian Llanos de Mojos, Bolivia (Dickau et al. 2012) illustrates the potentials of a combined macro- and micro-botanical approach in the Neotropics. Here charred macroscopic plant remains were recovered from a deeply stratified site, Salvatierra, but not from a shallower, single-occupation site (Granja del Padre). Charred maize remains at Salvatierra were ubiquitous, and other macroremains included peanut shell, squash rind, cotton seeds, palm endocarp and possible chilli pepper seeds. Ceramic colanders, associated with *chicha* beer preparation, yielded starch granules indicative of two possible ingredients, maize and manioc; graters and a clay mano yielded maize and likely chilli pepper starch, including granules with probable grinding damage. Sediment samples yielded maize cob and squash rind phytoliths, supporting macrobotanical evidence for their use. These different lines of botanical evidence therefore provide a cross-check on the ubiquity of likely staples, shed unique light on the use of certain plants evidenced only in one preservational form and provide a link with plant processing material culture.

Integrated multi-proxy approaches to plant use and husbandry are still developing in western Asia and Europe, but Delhon et al. (2008) present a pioneering investigation of Neolithic dung and fodder remains from La Grande Rivoire, a rockshelter used for livestock penning in the Rhône

TABLE 6.1 *Summary of key parameters defining potentials and limitations of forms of botanical evidence*

	Macrobotanical remains			**Microbotanical remains**		
	Charred	*Waterlogged*	*Desiccated*	*Phytoliths*	*Starch*	*Pollen and spores*
Formation	Anthropogenic	Natural(/anthropogenic)				
Preservation context	Aerobic or anaerobic	Anaerobic	Aerobic or anaerobic			Anaerobic
Taxonomic bias	Seed/storable taxa	Minimal	Minimal	High phytolith producers (e.g. monocots)	Starch-producing taxa	Abundant producers (e.g. wind-dispersed tree pollen)
Anatomical bias	Dense plant parts (e.g. seeds, chaff, nutshell/fruitstone)	Relatively dense parts	Minimal	Above-ground parts	Starchy plant parts (e.g. seeds, tubers)	Pollen grains/ spores
Analytical potentials						
aDNA	(y)	(y)	y			y
Arable weed ecology	y	y if weeds can be isolated				
Plant processing & use	y					
Regional vegetation		y but dispersal local				y
(Stable) isotope composition	y (e.g. C, N)	?	y (e.g. C, N)	y (C, O)		

valley, southern France (Delhon et al. 2008). These authors combined sedimentological analysis of dung-rich stratigraphic layers with phytolith, pollen and charred macroremains analysis to identify animal feeding practices. Collection of leafy and flowering tree branches as fodder was evidenced by findings of clustered pollen grains (from whole stamens) and charred macroscopic evidence of wood, bark and associated fruits/seeds, while phytolith remains reflected grass forage but also plentiful dicot material, plausibly from broad-leaved trees.

Combined analysis of charred macrobotanical remains (including charcoal) and phytoliths has also made inroads into understanding of indoor and outdoor space use at Çatalhöyük, in south-central Turkey (Asouti 2013; Bogaard et al. 2013; Shillito and Ryan 2013; Bogaard et al. 2014b). Here, houses were variously preserved by burning or abandoned in a relatively 'clean' state, providing some opportunities to intercept *in situ* activity through burning, preserving charred macroscopic remains, but also scope to assess how far those patterns extend beyond primary burning contexts through phytolith analysis. Both lines of evidence suggests that a range of staple plants (cereals, pulses, nuts) were stored in bin-lined side rooms, sometimes in plant-fibre baskets or bags, and that dehusking of glume wheats (stored as semi-clean spikelets) was concentrated in indoor room spaces. External activity spaces or 'yards', which become prominent in the mid to the later Neolithic sequence, are associated with dung burning alongside craft activities such as bead production, woodworking and clay modelling. Some outdoor food processing is also attested in the mid to the later Neolithic sequence, particularly in association with large outdoor ovens and 'yards' accessed directly by crawl-holes from buildings at ground-level (Bogaard et al. 2014b). The implication is that co-residential households of the later Neolithic preferentially conducted food preparation indoors but also took opportunities to appropriate outdoor spaces for craft and food-related activities, tending to become more isolated from one another.

The examples above demonstrate the potential of a combined micro- and macro-botanical approach for developing a wider spectrum of plant use, and of developing a refined understanding of plant-food preparation and consumption, in a way that is complementary to lipid/protein residues (see Chapter 4). An integrated approach also has the further potential of strengthening investigation of other key aspects of early agriculture that were central to the original concerns of palaeoeconomy: domestication and field ecology.

Phytolith-based (and starch-based) approaches to early maize and rice have identified domestication origins that are millennia earlier than those based on macrobotanical evidence, and a similar situation pertains with the introduction of west-Asian cereals in Africa (Madella et al. 2014). Macrobotanical remains, however, provide the *most direct* measure of domestication status in a strict morphological sense (e.g. loss of dehiscence), and offer scope for extraction of ancient DNA (Table 6.1). In future work, therefore, it will be important to integrate sampling of transitional sequences such that the pace of crop uptake as gauged microbotanically can be cross-checked against the domesticated morphology and genetic changes evidenced directly in the macroscopic record.

Equally, investigations into arable field ecology – crop growing conditions – could benefit directly from independent investigation on the basis of phytolith assemblages (e.g. Weisskopf et al. 2014, 2016) and macrobotanical evidence (e.g. Castillo 2011; Bogaard et al. 2016, 2018). Multi-stranded approaches integrating macroscopic remains and phytoliths need to be ground-truthed in present-day studies that incorporate arable weed surveys alongside sampling of crop grain for stable isotope analysis, and whole plants for fixed/sensitive and isotopic analysis of phytoliths. The studies by Bogaard et al. (2016, 2018), for example, have so far focused on ground-truthing macrobotanical approaches, but included whole-plant sampling for phytolith analysis, which remains a goal of future work.

CHAPTER 7

Integrated Case Study I: Early Farming in Central Europe

In their final volume on the palaeoeconomy project, Jarman et al. (1982: 134) identified Central Europe, and especially the archaeology of the Linear Pottery Culture (here, *Linearbandkeramik* or LBK), as the key arena for reassessing Neolithic European economy. In their influential writings V. Gordon Childe (1929, 1957) and J.G.D. Clark (1952) assumed that LBK farmers lacked the knowledge of rotation and manuring to make continuous cropping sustainable. Shifting or slash-and-burn cultivation was thus regarded as the most plausible means for cultivators to maintain fertility, facilitating the spread of farming across Europe. Jarman et al. (1982: 134) identified the slash-and-burn orthodoxy as ripe for reexamination: 'recent developments have, however, led us to re-examine the data, and it will be seen that other conclusions may be drawn for which there is as much support as for the authorized version'.

The palaeoeconomists' analysis of the Central European lowlands, and adjacent lakeshore settlements of the Alpine foreland, offers a useful starting point for assessing how bioarchaeology in these regions has developed in subsequent decades, and where it is headed. A major limitation of the palaeoeconomists' work, which they acknowledged (e.g. Webley 1972: 160), was that site catchment analysis, no matter how fine-grained, could offer only *speculative* reconstructions of subsistence practice. In the absence of on-site bioarchaeological evidence and relevant analytical techniques to test hypotheses, site catchment analysis effectively translated into determinism (see Chapter 2). There has since been significant expansion in the systematic recovery and analysis of primary bioarchaeological data – on-site macrobotanical and faunal assemblages – on which to base reconstructions of Neolithic plant and animal exploitation and land use in Central Europe (e.g. Jacomet et al. 1989, 2004, 2016; Kreuz 1990, 2007; Arbogast 1994; Schibler et al. 1997;

Bogaard 2004). Equally, the range of analytical techniques that can now be integrated to infer farming practice in detail has expanded dramatically, including approaches such as stable isotope analysis, lipid residue analysis and aDNA, reviewed in previous chapters. Thus, while Jarman et al. (1982) challenged the persistent orthodoxy that early farming in Central Europe resembled a form of shifting, long-fallow or slash-and-burn cultivation (for similar arguments in northern Europe, see Rowley-Conwy 1981b), they could not overturn the model because of a lack of direct evidence. Nevertheless, their close attention to local landscapes and affordances anticipated in many ways the inferences that are now supported by an expanded dataset and toolkit.

A second notable feature of the palaeoeconomists' approach to the Central European Neolithic is their stance as regards the work of Ester Boserup (1965). Jarman et al. (1982: 24) insisted on the 'general value of Boserup's thesis': namely, that population pressure – rather than technology – be regarded as the key underlying variable that shapes farming practice. As already outlined, however, on other grounds they were questioning the view that Neolithic farmers necessarily practised long-fallow cultivation, an inference Boserup made on the basis of (presumed) low population density, ethnographic/historical analogy and the work of Iversen (1941, 1949) on pollen evidence for Neolithic woodland clearance in southern Scandinavia (Boserup 1965: 16–19). Moreover, Jarman et al. (1982: 23) cited Bennet Bronson's (1972) criticism of Boserup, prompting the qualification that her predictions should not be applied 'without modification to all cases'.

In fact, Bronson (1972) was not merely calling for 'modification' of Boserup's thesis. First, he questioned the fundamental assumption that farming practice is governed by the law of least effort, arguing that both this and 'the notion that swiddening is easy' reflected 'the frustrations of [colonial] administrators and the excuses of their subordinates, among whom are numbered many authorities on agricultural development and economic anthropology' (Bronson 1972: 196). Second, he set out a broad anthropological case for why any unilinear model of farming development was bound to be misleading, given the number of contingencies that affect farming practice. Third, he argued that Boserup's scheme in particular was likely to be wrong about the global primacy of long-fallowing, suggesting instead that shifting cultivation be understood as a way of avoiding expropriation and other 'social risks' to security. Fourth, he questioned whether *local* population densities were really low enough to make shifting cultivation plausible even in the Neolithic. And finally, he noted that Boserup's 'taxonomy' of farming systems did not recognize the potential relevance of means other than long-fallowing for maintaining fertility – such as middening and manuring – which would appear 'as easily invented' (Bronson 1972: 207; cf. Grigg 1979).

Though Jarman et al. (1982) did not explicitly acknowledge the paradox of their position – that Boserup's thesis about population pressure as an independent variable was right but that her inferences about Neolithic European farming were wrong – Bronson's critique offered several ways out of the dilemma. Most salient for the palaeoeconomists' focus on site catchment analysis was Bronson's hypothesis that *local* population pressure might well be high, despite modest regional densities, where Neolithic communities targeted circumscribed resources and parts of the landscape (Bronson 1972: 215).

A third notable aspect of Jarman et al.'s analysis of Neolithic agriculture in Central Europe is that it de-centred what is still often regarded as the most important question of European Neolithization: the extent to which it reflects demographic movement of farmers, adoption of farming by indigenous communities or a combination of the two. In this respect the work of the palaeoeconomy school fostered interest in the importance of understanding Neolithic life *per se*, regardless of from where, genetically, these communities derived. Meanwhile, advances in aDNA recovery and sequencing are now making it possible to consider how far demographic movement and understandings of economy and diet might inform one another. The increasing resolution of the data available is also opening up new questions of identity construction and social inheritance, including through food-related practice, as long-term consequences of Neolithization.

This chapter presents, first for the loess lowlands and then for the Alpine foreland (Fig. 7.1), a critical summary of the palaeoeconomists' work on these regions, before outlining key bioarchaeological datasets and techniques that subsequently informed reconstruction of farming and herding practices and the wider economy. By bringing together the palaeoeconomists' focus on site catchment analysis with the evidence now available, the aim is to show how territorial analysis framed useful hypotheses that can now be addressed. In the final section, we consider how the resolution of certain aspects of Neolithic economy is prompting new questions.

LBK Economy

The LBK (*c.* 5500–5000/4900 cal BC) represents the material culture context of the establishment of farming and herding across lowland Central

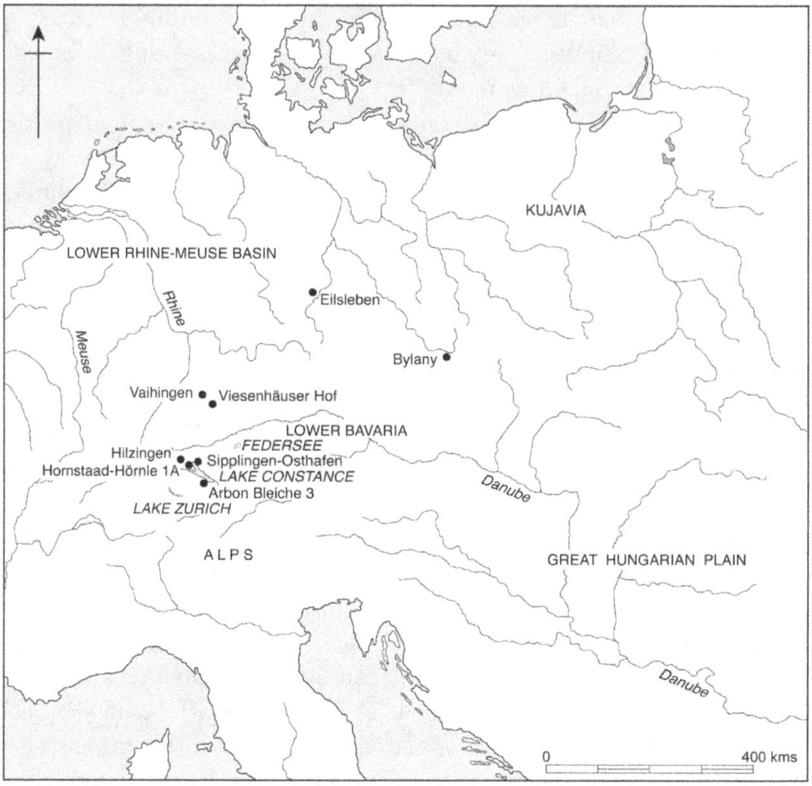

FIGURE 7.1 Map of Central Europe showing the regions and key sites mentioned in Chapter 7.

Europe, eventually extending from the Black Sea in the east to the Dutch coast in the west (Jakucs et al. 2016). It remains one of the best investigated prehistoric archaeological complexes in Europe (e.g. Bickle and Whittle 2013), but formal radiocarbon modelling to establish the start and end dates of settlements and phases has only just begun (Jakucs et al. 2016). Different ways of dividing the period have emerged over the years, but the current literature tends to recognize (minimally) a formative LBK originating in Transdanubia, an *älteste* LBK (äLBK) that spread more than 1,000 km westwards to the Rhine valley and a later LBK that extended across the full distribution area. Initial formal radiocarbon modelling suggests that the äLBK spread was rapid, occurring within a generation or two, beginning in the mid 54th century BC (Jakucs et al. 2016). The äLBK settlements targeted areas of relatively tractable, often loess-based soils and zones of moderate rainfall (Sielmann 1971). In the subsequent LBK the complex extended further to the north, east and west, notably into regions of higher rainfall and more variable soil substrates (Sielmann 1971).

The on-site archaeobotanical and zooarchaeological data available for the LBK when Jarman et al. (1982) formulated their analysis of the Central European lowlands was limited, though more abundant than in many other regions of Europe at the time. The major archaeobotanical work was that by Knörzer (1971) in the Lower Rhine basin, and by Bakels (1978), who conducted a multi-site doctoral study of assemblages in the Dutch Limburg and Lower Bavaria. A general observation was that the glume wheats emmer and einkorn were accompanied in many assemblages by pulses (pea, lentil) and flax/linseed. Primary faunal studies were also limited (e.g. Bökönyi 1974) but the occurrence of cattle, pig and sheep/goat (in order of decreasing frequency) was widely observed.

The major argument put forward by Jarman et al. (1982: 131–46, 168–202) on the basis of the available botanical and faunal evidence was that it documented the *potential* for crop rotation (e.g. between cereals and pulses), manuring (using animal dung) and other forms of crop–livestock complementarity (e.g. use of pigs to clear land and prepare fields). They could not take the interpretation of on-site bioarchaeological evidence for subsistence practice much further, in part because the available assemblages were restricted to a small number of sites, even fewer of which overlapped with those they selected for field walking and territorial analysis (see below). Equally significant were the limitations of analytical techniques available to interpret the on-site evidence in terms of land-use regimes. Knörzer (1971) took an interest in the ancient arable weed flora associated with LBK crops, noting a particular suite of characteristic species for the Lower Rhineland, and suggesting that their regular co-occurrence suggested permanent field cultivation. Bakels (1978: 69) suggested that this persistence could instead reflect consistent conditions among fields that were cultivated for a short period. Jarman et al. (1982: 141) took the view that it was not possible archaeologically to ascertain 'the ways in which soil fertility may have been maintained or enhanced'. They went on, 'in the very nature of archaeological data it is virtually impossible to demonstrate conclusively the existence of [crop rotation and manuring] until there is supporting literary evidence' (Jarman et al. 1982: 142). Their conclusion as regards crop rotation and manuring was that 'it is hard to imagine an archaeological demonstration one way or the other, but commonsense suggests that it is at least reasonable to suggest *a priori* that a degree of manuring took place and that its value was perceived. In fact it is difficult to see how some manuring could have been avoided' (Jarman et al. 1982: 142).

The other key point of the palaeoeconomists' discussion, ground-truthed by field walking of selected site catchments in multiple regions of LBK settlement (the Great Hungarian Plain, Niederösterreich and the Burgenland, the Lower Bavarian Plateau, the northern Upper Rhine valley, the Little Polish Upland, the Aldenvohener Platte), was the high agricultural potential of soils often associated with early Neolithic settlement, including in the Central European lowlands. They characterized this zone as one of 'relatively gentle topography, low rainfall, high temperatures, a long growing season, and well drained tractable fertile soils' (Jarman et al. 1982: 131). Their assessment of agricultural potential emphasized the importance of *both* soil nutrient availability *and* ease of soil working, the often inverse relationship between the two and a general prioritization of tractability over fertility *per se* (i.e. avoidance of fertile clay-rich soils) in the settlement distributions of early farmers (Jarman et al. 1982: 133). An important observation was that LBK settlement did not slavishly target loess, despite the frequent association; rather, relatively light (tractable) soils were preferred, whether loess-based or not, adjacent to productive wet grazing (e.g. in valley bottoms) and surface drinking water (Jarman et al. 1982: 184, 186, 191–2, 196, 198–9). In some regions it was possible to discern a stricter association with loess where zones of higher rainfall were occupied in the later LBK, building on previous observations by Sielmann (1971) in the northern Upper Rhine and south-west Germany (Jarman et al. 1982: 189–93).

Moreover, in the circumscribed parts of the landscape targeted by LBK communities, settlement appeared relatively densely packed (Jarman et al. 1982: 196). The then emerging results of large-scale stripping and excavation (ahead of open-cast lignite mining) in the Aldenhovener Platte region west of Cologne had begun to confirm this 'packing' of settlement in restricted zones, with hamlets and farmsteads strung along stream courses, often within 10–20 minutes' walk of each other (Jarman et al. 1982: 196–9). Relatively high local settlement densities, combined with the affordances of local landscapes (especially soils with high agricultural potential), suggested that more intensive forms of agriculture than slash-and-burn were at least possible (Jarman et al. 1982: 144).

In sum, the palaeoeconomists' reassessment of LBK economy centred on the improbability of shifting cultivation, and the plausibility of alternative methods (crop rotation, manuring) for maintaining soil fertility, based on possibilities raised by the available bioarchaeological data and analyses of selected site catchments in multiple regions of LBK settlement. Because their case rested on *potentials* attested by botanical and faunal assemblages and site catchment analysis, however, it left the way open for continued discussion of shifting cultivation as a characteristic feature of LBK farming (e.g. Whittle 1996: 160–2, 1997).

Given the tendency for soils of high agricultural potential to dominate site catchments, the palaeoeconomists' focus was on arable farming, but they also drew attention to the persistent association of site locations with productive wet grazing in valley bottoms (Jarman et al. 1982: 194–8). They thus excluded as unlikely Kruk's suggestions, based on survey in the Little Polish Uplands, that valley-bottom soils were used for 'low-input' horticulture (Kruk 1973), a view Sherratt (1980) developed into a general theory of agricultural colonization in western Eurasia. Jarman et al. (1982: 192) also speculated that LBK communities in some regions were linked with seasonal transhumant herding to the uplands in summer, as practised in recent times by herders taking their small ruminants into upland areas such as the Vosges mountains and *Schwarzwald* (see also Lüning 2000: 190); as discussed further below, this view has fared less well in the light of recent (bio)archaeological work (Knipper 2011: 113, 357–8).

Since the last decade of the 20th century, work on LBK archaeobotany and zooarchaeology (e.g. Kreuz 1990, 2012; Arbogast 1994; Döhle 1997; Lüning 2000; Bieniek 2002; Bogaard 2004, 2011; Kreuz et al. 2005; Schäfer 2010; Bogaard et al. 2011, 2017a; Kreuz and Marinova 2017) has vastly improved the geographical and chronological scope of primary botanical and faunal evidence for land use, especially for the central and western part of the LBK distribution area. A remarkable feature of LBK farming practice is that it was based on a consistent set of crops: two to three cereal taxa – the glume (or hulled) wheats, einkorn (often dominant) and emmer, sometimes accompanied by a third distinct morphotype ('new type') that can also be traced back to Neolithic western Asia (Jones et al. 2000b; Bogaard et al. 2014b); two pulses of west Asian origin, pea and lentil; the west Asian oil/fibre crop linseed/flax; and, in the later LBK, opium poppy, from the central/western Mediterranean (Bogaard 2011; Kreuz and Marinova 2017). The LBK crop spectrum was thus less diverse than those of the early Neolithic in southern Europe, which featured a broader range of cereals and pulses (Buxó 2007; Peña-Chocarro 2007; Rottoli and Pessina 2007; Kreuz and Marinova 2017). Collection and use of weeds such as *Chenopodium album* likely served to broaden the LBK crop spectrum (Bogaard et al. 2018). The consistency of the LBK arable 'niche' is underlined further by the regionally distinctive composition of associated weed flora, including Knörzer's Bromo-lapsanetum community of the Lower Rhine basin (Knörzer 1971; Bogaard 2011).

Turning to the primary faunal data, there is some chronological and regional variation in the relative importance of hunting, and among the major livestock species. Hunting levels are high in some äLBK assemblages, and the relative composition of domestic taxa variable, but in the two largest assemblages, Eilsleben and Vaihingen, hunting levels are modest and cattle are dominant (Schäfer 2010). On multi-phase sites there is a tendency for smaller stock (pig or sheep and goat) to increase through time, though cattle remain predominant (Schäfer 2010). In the later LBK, levels of hunting and pig husbandry tend to be higher in southern Germany and Alsace than in central Germany, where frequencies of sheep/goat herding are higher and hunting lower (Schäfer 2010). Relatively high levels of pig keeping and hunting have been interpreted as an adaptation to closed woodland formations (Tresset and Vigne 2001), but they could also reflect strategies to increase the meat supply (Bogaard et al. 2017a). A general tendency towards higher levels of hunting at LBK sites closer to the Alps, in south-west Germany and Bavaria may similarly reflect greater susceptibility to climatic deterioration, with negative impact on crop production and a need to supplement the diet with greater consumption of game (Schibler 2001). By analogy with low rates of faunal deposition on the earliest Neolithic lakeshore sites of the Alpine foreland (late 5th millennium BC), it is plausible that LBK stocking levels were low (Schibler 2001).

The greatly expanded bioarchaeological dataset that has accumulated since the early 1980s confirms the potential of crop rotation even within the relatively narrow crop spectrum of the LBK, and the possibility of integrated management of crops and livestock, including use of animal dung to maintain the tractability and fertility of arable soils, as pondered by the palaeoeconomists. But analytical techniques for further assessing the plausibility of such relatively intensive agricultural practices have also developed apace.

Considering first the arable side of the economy, only a few years after the publication of the palaeoeconomists' final volume (Jarman et al. 1982), Halstead (1989a) suggested that the ecology of the weed flora associated with LBK crops pointed to relatively intensive farming (Fig. 7.2). This inference was based on the occurrence of species characteristic of the Chenopodietea phytosociological class, which are today associated with manured and weeded root/row garden crops. A present-day study in central Evvia, Greece, of weed flora associated with winter-sown pulses cultivated under a spectrum of intensities, from manured, hand-dug and weeded backyard gardens to less intensively managed ard-ploughed fields, confirmed that Chenopodietea species were indeed associated with the more intensive

FIGURE 7.2 Charred (carbonized) arable weed seeds, extracted from a sample of the charred chaff-rich by-product of glume wheat dehusking, from LBK Vaihingen an der Enz, Baden-Württemberg (photo: A. Bogaard).

end of the scale (Jones et al. 1999). But because the occurrence of the Chenopodietea could also reflect other factors – including spring sowing – Jones et al. (2000a) applied another approach, based on the analysis of the functional ecological traits of arable weeds, to the Evvia study. This functional ecological method made it possible to disentangle the major ecological components of intensity – soil productivity and disturbance – using relevant functional traits that measured weed species' potential under differing conditions. Small-scale intensive cultivation of spelt in Asturias provided a successful present-day 'test case' for applying the Evvian functional ecological model (Charles et al. 2002), and this paved the way for its archaeobotanical application. Bogaard (2004) showed that LBK weed flora resembled that of the intensive end of the Evvian pulse cultivation spectrum in functional ecological terms, but appeared less intensive than present-day Asturian cereal 'gardening'. In subsequent work comparing present-day intensive Asturian weed flora with those associated with extensive cereal production in Haute Provence (Bogaard et al. 2016), Central European Neolithic weed flora are found to resemble the small-scale intensive system, but align best with the less intensive end of the Asturian spectrum (Figs 7.3, 7.4). This is entirely plausible for two particular reasons. First, Asturian cereal 'gardening' is associated with higher levels of stock-keeping (especially cattle) than is likely for the LBK/Neolithic, and hence very high levels of manuring (Isaakidou 2011; Bogaard 2012). Second, spelt in Asturias is now a minor crop, and often grown on a smaller local scale than is plausible for LBK crop staples (see below), and therefore is more likely to be intensively hand-weeded and managed overall.

(a)

(b)

FIGURE 7.3 Modern cereal fields representing different kinds of production system: *a.* small-scale spelt fields in Asturias, Spain, managed with high labour inputs per unit area; *b.* large-scale einkorn fields in Haute Provence, France, managed with low labour inputs per unit area (photos: A. Bogaard).

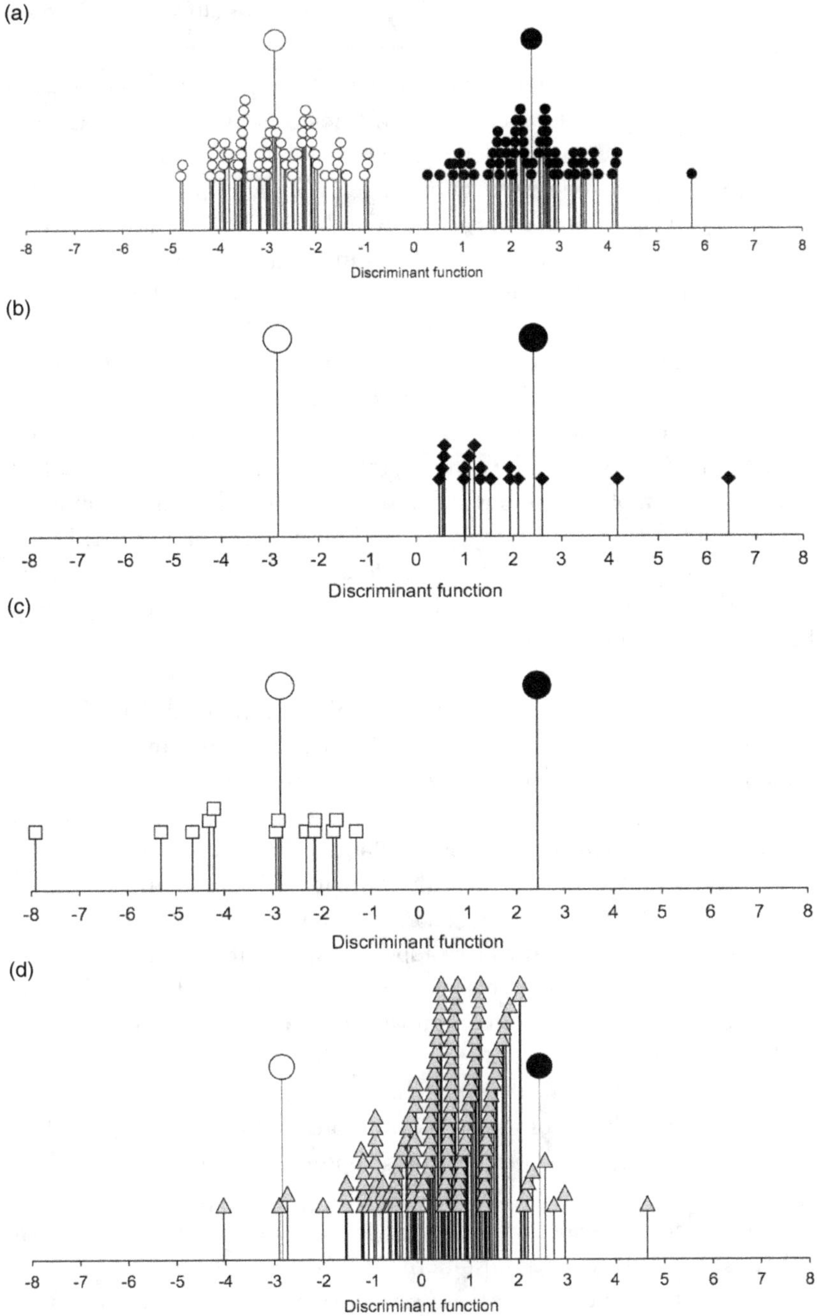

FIGURE 7.4 The relationship of *a.* Haute Provence fields (open circles, n = 56) and Asturias fields (filled circles, n = 65), *b.* Sighisoara fields (filled diamonds, n = 17), *c.* Kastamonu fields (open squares, n = 13) and *d.* archaeobotanical samples from Neolithic Central Europe (grey triangles, n = 141) to the discriminant function extracted to distinguish the Haute Provence and Asturias groups on the basis of semi-quantitative (presence/absence) weed functional attribute scores. Larger symbols indicate centroids for Haute Provence and Asturias (after Bogaard et al. 2016: Fig. 9).

Though the palaeoeconomists despaired of the possibility that manuring and crop rotation could ever be reconstructed archaeologically (in the absence of documentary evidence), stable carbon and nitrogen isotope analysis of crop remains has begun to open up that opportunity (see also Chapter 3). In C_3 plants like wheat, barley and pulses, it has been shown that stable carbon isotope ratios ($\delta^{13}C$ values) in plant tissues variously reflect stomatal conductance, which determines the degree of discrimination against the heavier stable isotope, ^{13}C (Farquhar et al. 1989). How open or closed the stomata are, in turn, is affected in arid regions by water availability and in more humid zones, where water is not limiting, especially by canopy, salinity and other effects (Farquhar et al. 1989). Stable nitrogen isotope ratios ($\delta^{15}N$ values), by contrast, reflect the nitrogen composition of soil, which in arable conditions is determined above all by the addition of organic matter, that is, manuring/middening (Bogaard et al. 2007; Fraser et al. 2011; Peukert et al. 2012). While factors such as shade and topography are clearly more likely to affect LBK crop stable carbon isotope variation than water management, the possibility of manuring can be assessed by measuring stable nitrogen isotope values in grain, and comparing them with present-day manuring effects plus local environmental baselines for unmanured vegetation derived from stable nitrogen isotope measurements of associated herbivore bone collagen, ideally from wild herbivores least affected by any anthropogenic enrichment (Styring et al. 2016a; Nitsch et al. 2017). The plausibility of crop rotation or intercropping – that is, growing of multiple crop species under similar field conditions, and hence potentially in rotation or as a mixed crop – can be assessed by comparing their stable carbon and nitrogen isotope ratios, with the proviso that there are physiological offsets between some crops (i.e. wheat and barley) in their stable carbon isotope ratios when grown under the same conditions (e.g. Wallace et al. 2013).

Like the weed ecological approach, interpretation of crop stable isotope values as evidence of growing conditions and land management in archaeology has depended on present-day observations of cause and effect; agronomic effects on stable carbon and nitrogen isotope ratios are most easily discerned in experimental settings, but 'real world' variation in traditional farming systems, on differing soils and in contrasting climatic zones, is equally crucial as background knowledge for interpreting archaeological values. Reliable interpretation of these values has also depended on laboratory work to establish the effects of charring on grain composition and stable isotope ratios (Styring et al. 2013; Fraser et al. 2013a; Nitsch et al. 2015), the effects of pre-treatment prior to stable isotope measurement for removing contamination (Vaiglova et al. 2014) and possible diagenetic effects during burial (Styring et al. 2013). Finally, integration with faunal isotope measurements is important for assessing unmanured baselines (Styring et al. 2016a; Nitsch et al. 2017), while the combination of complementary weed ecological and crop isotope approaches to a given assemblage offers the robusticity of two independent methods subject to different sources of error and ambiguity (Bogaard 2015; Bogaard et al. 2016, 2018).

For the LBK, stable isotope analysis of crop remains has so far been limited to two assemblages – Vaihingen an der Enz and Viesenhäuser Hof/Stuttgart-Mühlhausen, both in south-west Germany (Fraser et al. 2013b; Styring et al. 2017b) – but with relevant implications for the plausibility of manuring and crop rotation. At both sites, cereal $\delta^{15}N$ values are elevated well above those of herbivore forage, inferred from bone collagen, and especially above those of wild herbivores at Vaihingen (a single, similar wild herbivore bone collagen sample was analysed from Viesenhäuser Hof) (Fig. 7.5). This observation is consistent with manuring. Very few pulse samples have been analysed from either site, but the values available are also consistent with manuring effects. Moreover, the elevation of domestic herbivore $\delta^{15}N$ values above those of wild herbivores at Vaihingen is consistent with some foddering on (manured) crop material; palaeodietary modelling suggests that domestic herbivores at both Vaihingen and Viesenhäuser Hof could have consumed cereal chaff (including stubble in harvested fields) as part of their diets (Styring et al. 2017b: Appendix S.7).

The plausibility of cereal–pulse rotation or intercropping is more difficult to assess, since few pulse samples have been analysed isotopically, and most derive from different archaeological contexts/deposits to the cereals. In any case, the beneficial effect of pulse cultivation on soil nitrogen content depends on the extent to which pulse plant matter is worked into the soil. The plausibility of rotation or inter-cropping amongst the glume wheats, einkorn, emmer (and 'new type'), however, can be assessed, since multi-species, high-density grain deposits, apparently representing dumps of associated charred storage material, were analysed from both sites. While rotation/intercropping of cereals does not have the same implications as cereal–pulse rotation for maintaining soil fertility, it is relevant to consider whether one cereal was preferentially manured over another, as in the late Neolithic of the lakeshore dwellings in the Alpine foreland (see below). The similarity in isotopic compositions within storage deposits at LBK Vaihingen and Viesenhäuser Hof (Fig. 7.5) suggests that emmer and einkorn (and 'new type' glume wheat at Vaihingen) were grown under the same conditions, quite possibly in a mixed/maslin crop given their

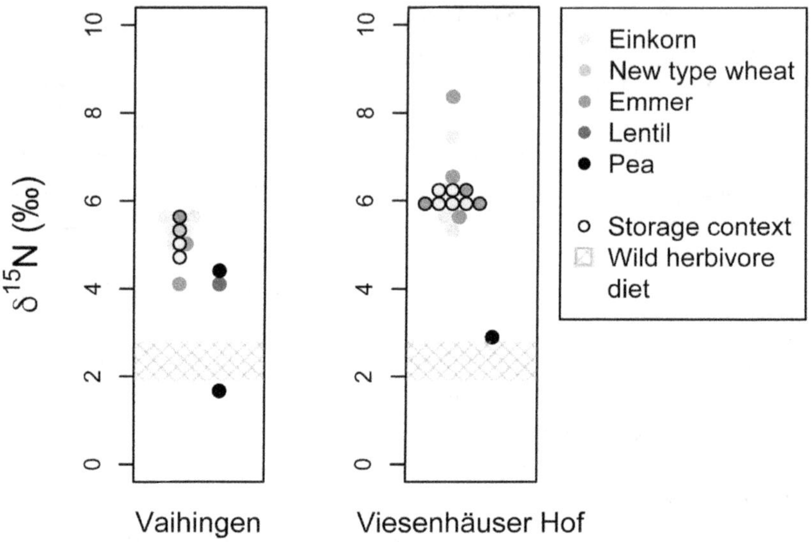

FIGURE 7.5 The $\delta^{15}N$ values of bulk cereal grain and pulse seed samples from LBK Vaihingen and Viesenhäuser Hof, Baden-Württemberg (after Styring et al. 2017b: Fig. 3). Higher $\delta^{15}N$ values indicate higher inputs of organic matter/manure and the grey cross-hatched zone shows the possible $\delta^{15}N$ values of unmanaged vegetation, estimated from wild herbivore bone collagen $\delta^{15}N$ values. Sample data points outlined in black are from high-density 'storage' deposits.

stratigraphic association (Fraser et al. 2013b; Styring et al. 2017b). Whether or not the glume wheats were actually grown together as a mixed crop, the fact that they were apparently grown under similar conditions suggests that LBK farmers here maintained an arable niche that was remarkably consistent, and that did not necessitate separate treatment of relatively more/less demanding crops, as emerges in the later Neolithic of the Alpine foreland (see below). It is plausible that the particularly favourable environments targeted by LBK farmers made this strategy feasible.

Turning to the pastoral side of farming practice, there have been several key developments since the early 1980s. First, as already noted, recovery of many more faunal assemblages from LBK sites confirms the dominance of cattle, but also chronologically and regionally distinctive levels of pigs and small ruminants, and of hunting. Second, ancient DNA studies indicate that early Neolithic cattle and pig were of western Asiatic origin (Bollongino et al. 2006, 2008; Edwards et al. 2007). The genetic traces of the intrusive pigs were overwritten by the later Neolithic through interbreeding with European wild boar (Larson et al. 2007; Ottoni et al. 2012; Larson and Burger 2013; Larson and Fuller 2014). This scenario is highly plausible: it has been shown ethnographically that keeping wild and domestic pigs separate is very difficult (Halstead and Isaakidou 2011). Neolithic domestic cattle appear to have been kept separate from local wild populations based on mtDNA (Edwards et al. 2007; Bollongino et al. 2008), though whole-genome data may reveal a more complex picture (cf. Orlando et al. 2015; Parks et al. 2015). The slow pace of domestic–wild pig introgression, the apparent genetic isolation of domestic cattle and the metric distinctiveness of wild and domestic populations suggest that LBK herding was generally small-scale and intensive (Benecke 1994a: 48–55).

Third, recovery of larger faunal assemblages has enabled the characterization of animal consumption and husbandry in greater detail. In particular, mortality profiles of cattle point to the likelihood of multi-purpose husbandry, featuring the maintenance of older animals for possible use of milk as well as meat (Gillis et al. 2017; Bogaard et al. 2017a). Such multi-purpose husbandry – rather than *specialized* intensive dairying – plausibly forms the context of milk lipid residues detected on ceramic sieves on LBK sites in the Kujavia region of Poland (Salque et al. 2013). *Non*-dairy animal fat residues, as well as plant-derived lipids, were recently detected on ceramics from LBK Bylany in the Czech Republic, suggesting that milk processing was rare or absent (Matlova et al. 2017).

Decorated figurines of cattle (Fig. 7.6) show that they had symbolic significance over and above their economic roles (e.g. Bogaard 2011: Fig. 1.15). The remarkable metric consistency of cattle across many sites (Bogaard et al. 2017a) confirms the likelihood of systematic exchanges and periodic merging of herds, not least to maintain viability (cf. Halstead 1992; Ebersbach 2002). Observations of traction-related pathology are rare (Döhle 1997), while meat-oriented culling patterns and depositional practices at some sites attest to large-scale consumption/feasting (e.g. Gillis et al. 2017). The scale of LBK herding probably remained small (Knipper 2011: 275; Bogaard et al. 2017a; cf. Schibler 2001).

Fourth, analysis of stable (O, C, N) and radiogenic (Sr) isotopes in faunal remains has begun to refine understanding of livestock feeding ecologies and management strategies. Knipper's strontium and oxygen isotope study of LBK cattle teeth in south-west Germany, featuring sequential sampling of tooth enamel to investigate individual life histories, provides a particularly clear example of how isotopic data can be used to test land-use inferences based on territorial analysis/SCA (Knipper 2011). In the case of Vaihingen, with its large and well preserved faunal assemblage, comparison of *potential* foraging zones in 2- and 5-km radii of the settlement with *actual* foraging behaviour as evidenced in the Sr isotope ratios of tooth enamel showed

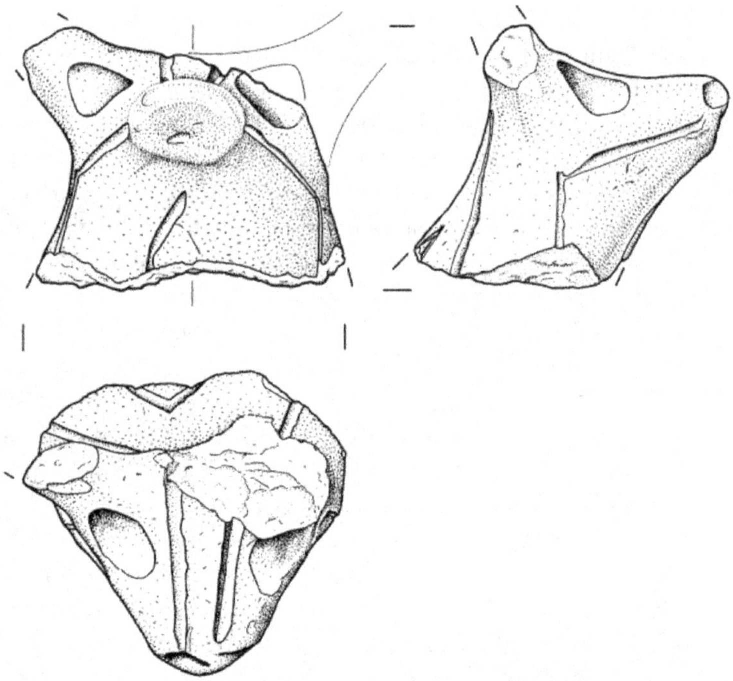

FIGURE 7.6 Head of a clay bull figurine decorated with incised lines from LBK Vaihingen an der Enz (height 5.7 cm, Inv Nr. 4643) (after Krause in Bogaard 2011: Fig. 1.15).

that feeding on loess and shelly limestone of local river valleys was over-represented relative to their availability in the landscape (Knipper 2011: Figs. 9.45–9.46; see also Bogaard et al. 2017a: Fig. 24) (Fig. 7.7). Feeding on geology consistent with upland grazing was under-represented (Fig. 7.7). The implication is that LBK herders targeted the rolling loess landscape surrounding the settlement, nearby streams and the Enz river valley for herding that was likely to have been restricted in scale and integrated with arable activity (Knipper 2011: 278). A smaller set of cattle teeth from Hilzingen suggests targeting of river valleys for grazing (Knipper 2011: Fig. 9.61), further confirming the inference by Jarman et al. (1982: 194–8) that valley bottoms were important sources of productive grazing for LBK herders.

A final aspect of LBK economy with direct bearing on the palaeoeconomists' discussion is the way in which integrated stable carbon and nitrogen isotope analysis of human, faunal and plant remains opens up more explicit testing of dietary scenarios. Though only two assemblages – Vaihingen and Viesenhäuser Hof/Stuttgart-Mühlhausen – have as yet been analysed in

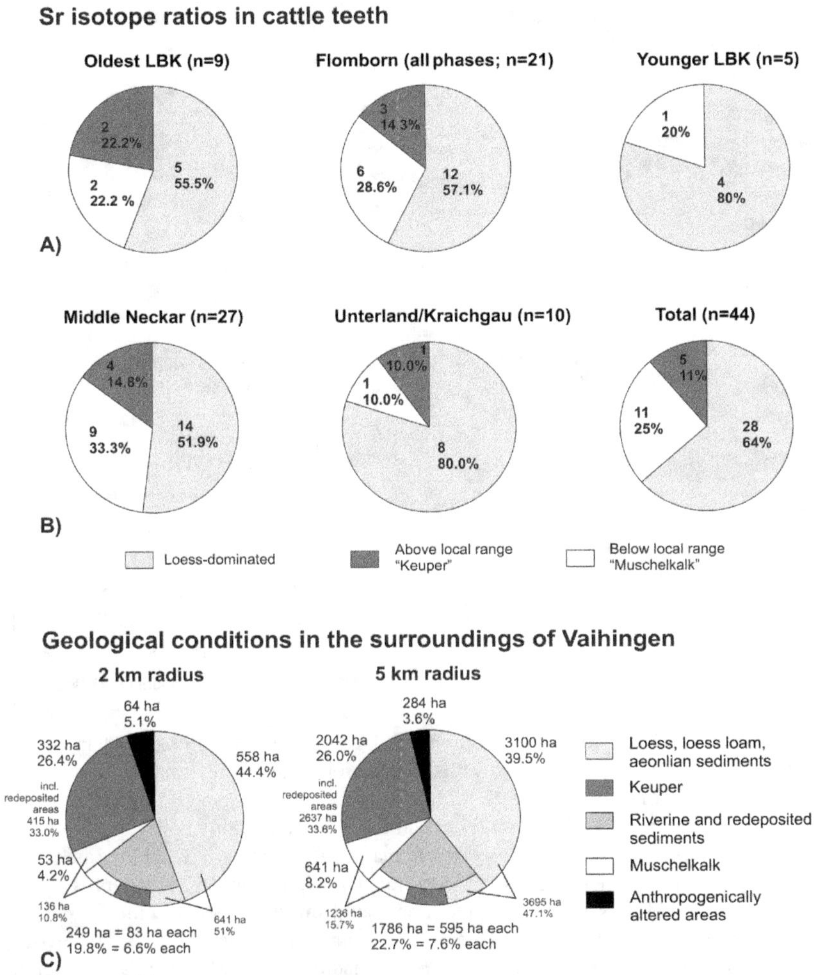

FIGURE 7.7 Distribution of Sr isotope ratios in cattle teeth at LBK Vaihingen by *a.* LBK subperiod and *b.* regional ceramic tradition, in comparison with *c.* proportional areas of dominant geological substrates: loess, shelly limestone (*Muschelkalk*) and Keuper sandstone (after Knipper 2011: Figs. 9.45–9.46; Bogaard et al. 2017: Fig. 24).

this way, the results of both investigations suggest that crops (e.g. an even mix of cereals and pulses) were if anything more important staple foods than livestock meat/milk (Fraser et al. 2013b; Nitsch et al. 2015; Bogaard and Styring 2017) (Fig. 7.8). While lipid analysis results indicate that milking was practised in the LBK at some sites and not others (Salque et al. 2013; Matlova et al. 2017), mortality data show that milking could not have been intensive (Gillis et al. 2017). Low to moderate levels of milk consumption

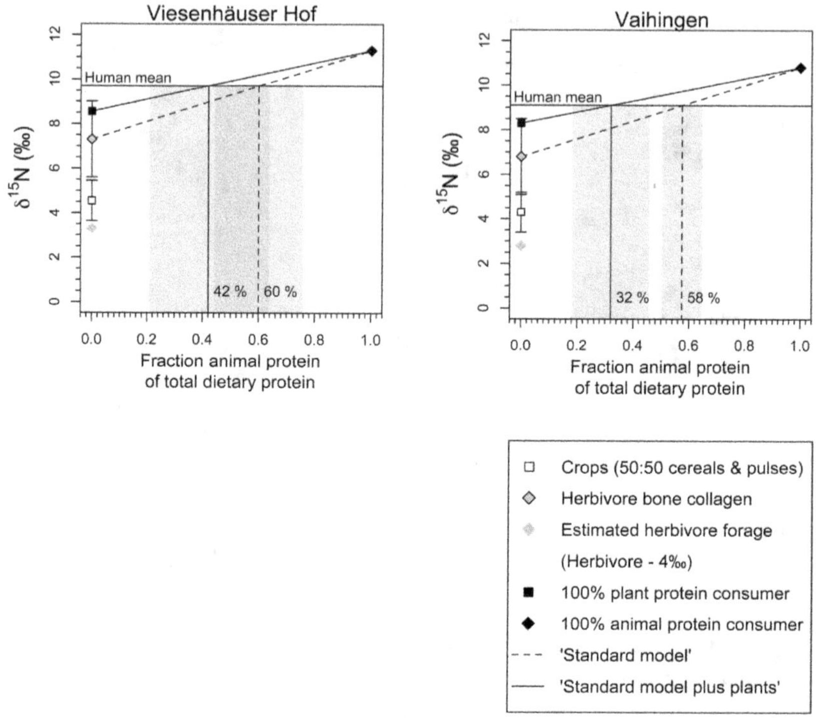

FIGURE 7.8 Palaeodietary models estimating the proportion of animal protein in the diets of Neolithic humans buried at LBK Vaihingen and Viesenhäuser Hof (after Bogaard and Styring 2017: Fig. 14.3). The 'standard model' is based on the assumption that humans eating only plant protein would have the same bone collagen $\delta^{15}N$ value as herbivores from the site and therefore the plants they were eating had the same $\delta^{15}N$ value as herbivore forage (i.e. grasses, leaves and twigs). The 'standard model plus plants' uses the measured $\delta^{15}N$ values of cereal grains and pulses to estimate the $\delta^{15}N$ value of humans eating cereals. Models incorporate data from Fraser et al. (2013), Styring et al. (2015) and Styring et al. (2017b). The grey shading represents the 95% confidence interval for animal protein consumption calculated using IsoError (www.epa.gov/wed/pages/models.htm; accessed 1 July 2016).

can inform understanding of selection pressure for lactase persistence in Central Europe (e.g. Itan et al. 2009; Gerbault et al. 2011). The (as yet) limited number of humans sampled from Neolithic Central Europe has not yielded early examples of lactase persistence, though the relationship with milk consumption is not straightforward (Burger et al. 2007; Liebert et al. 2017). Overall, emerging isotope-based and palaeodietary reconstructions of the LBK appear to confirm the palaeoeconomic hypothesis based on site catchment analysis that the location of sites in zones of high arable potential, combined with productive grazing in adjacent valley bottoms, was central to subsistence.

Neolithic Economy in the Alpine Foreland, with Particular Reference to Lake Constance

In the Alpine foreland (Jarman et al. 1982: 120–9), where the late Neolithic sequence dates are *c.* 4300–2400 BC, Lake Constance (Bodensee) was the focus of the palaeoeconomists' analysis. They noted that Neolithic lakeshore settlements here were conspicuously clustered in a narrow zone of relatively mild climate and low rainfall, especially around the western end of the lake, and that the lighter morainic soils would not be very different in fertility and tractability from the loess. The key limitations were instead imposed by climate and topography away from the lakeshore (Jarman et al. 1982: 122). They inferred that the lakeshore location enabled communities to grow crops and overwinter livestock in a relatively favourable zone, while making use of lacustrine and terrestrial resources. Amongst the individual site territories analysed was that of Sipplingen-Osthafen, on the north-western shore (Jarman et al. 1982: Fig. 42). This site's setting immediately poses the question of where the arable land was located: slopes rise steeply to a plateau a few hundred metres from the shore, creating a narrow strip of *c.* 2 km^2 behind the lake-edge settlement. Though agricultural activity is today concentrated on the elevated plateau, Jarman et al. (1982: 123–5) reasoned that the lakeside strip had the advantages of immediate access and favourable microclimate. We will consider the particular case of Sipplingen later in this chapter.

Since the 1980s there has been an explosion of bioarchaeological research on the lakeshore sites of the Alpine foreland, now listed as a UNESCO World Heritage site (Hafner 2013). Lake Zurich, Lake Constance and the Federsee have been particular focal points, and a nuanced picture of settlement and land-use has emerged, especially from the interdisciplinary work of the Institut für Prähistorische und Naturwissenschaftliche Archäologie in Basel, Switzerland, and the Landesdenkmalamt Baden-Württemberg, Germany. These research groups have handled sampling and primary analysis of bioarchaeological remains from the complex stratigraphic sequences of lakeshore sites, integrated these findings with those of dendrochronological, material culture and palaeoecological studies (e.g. Maier and Vogt 2001; Jacomet et al. 2004) and conducted pioneering applications of many recent analytical techniques, including lipid residue, multi-isotope and aDNA analysis (Larson et al. 2007; Spangenberg et al. 2008; Styring et al.

2016; Gerling et al. 2017). Understanding of daily life and social change in the Alpine foreland is therefore generally more detailed and multi-stranded than anywhere else in Europe. This high-resolution picture is difficult in some ways to compare directly with that reconstructed for dryland settings, including the LBK and subsequent Neolithic of the loess belt. Nevertheless, key inferences on the nature of crop and animal husbandry and its development over time suggest that convergent agropastoral practices developed in both zones of Central Europe (Bogaard et al. 2017b).

A fundamental inference that unites the dryland Neolithic of the loess belt and wetland Neolithic of the Alpine foreland is the rejection of the shifting cultivation model, based on direct evidence of crop-growing conditions (Jacomet and Brombacher 1997; Bogaard 2002, 2004; Hosch and Jacomet 2004). Nevertheless, there has been a revival of the slash-and-burn hypothesis for the Alpine foreland Neolithic based on off-site pollen and microcharcoal data (e.g. Schier 2009; Rösch et al. 2014). Critical reappraisal of on- and off-site data in the Alpine foreland resolves this contradiction: while on-site archaeobotanical data attest to intensively maintained arable conditions (e.g. weeding, likely manuring), the off-site pollen and microcharcoal data plausibly reflect larger scale patterns of land use for livestock grazing, hunting and foraging that included burning parts of the landscape (Jacomet et al. 2016). This integrated understanding of land use, in turn, sheds light on Neolithic lakeshore settlement dynamics. Dendrochronological dating of lakeshore houses and settlements attests to short use-lives and high 'mobility' of settlement, but within long established zones of settlement and land use. An example of this phenomenon on the western shore of Lake Constance is Hornstaad-Hörnle I and its replacement by Hornstaad-Hörnle 3: the earlier settlement was established in 3917 BC, burned down in 3910 and was replaced in 3909 by the later settlement a few hundred metres away (Billamboz 2006). A 'tethering' of shifting settlements to established managed landscapes is also suggested by analysis of the long-term Neolithic sequence at the northern end of Lake Zurich (Ebersbach et al. 2015).

The 1,200-year (4000–2800 BC) multi-settlement sequence at Sipplingen-Osthafen offers a clear example of how archaeological economic reconstruction continues to resonate with site catchment potentials highlighted by Jarman et al. (1982: 123–5), but aims to test these hypotheses using relevant evidence. Baum et al. (2016) have combined agent-based and process-based biophysical modelling to the Sipplingen case, demonstrating how differently a shifting/slash-and-burn versus intensive 'garden' model of cultivation would be accommodated in the surrounding landscape. Their

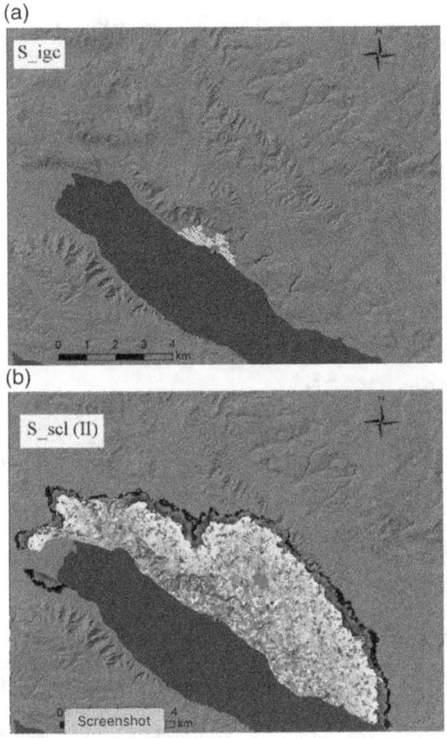

FIGURE 7.9 Simulations of the spatial extents of two different arable land-use models at Sipplingen, Lake Constance: *a.* intensive garden cultivation, *b.* shifting cultivation with long fallow (after Baum et al. 2016: Fig. 9).

quantification of shifting and intensive/permanent arable requirements when settlement reached a maximum (100 households) indicates that permanent cultivation could be accommodated within the climatically favoured 'strip' of light soils immediately behind the settlement, whereas shifting cultivation would extend onto the steeply rising plateau beyond (Baum et al. 2016: Fig. 9) (Fig. 7.9). Baum et al. (2016) also suggest, using biophysical modelling, that manuring was needed to maintain local fertility and yields. A separate study by Styring et al. (2016) used stable nitrogen isotope analysis of charred cereal grains from the various phases at Sipplingen to assess the likelihood of manuring and continuity versus change over the long-term. This study revealed that wheat (initially free-threshing wheat, later emmer) was grown under more intensively manured conditions than naked barley, and this pattern persisted over more than a millennium, including a hiatus in settlement – 3600–3300 BC – (Fig. 7.10).

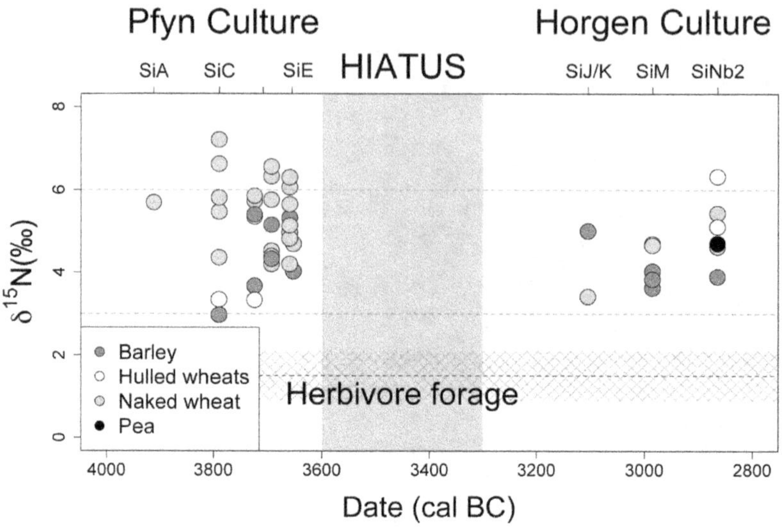

FIGURE 7.10 The δ^{15}N values of bulk cereal grain and pulse seed samples through the occupation of Sipplingen, Lake Constance, *c.* 4000–2800 BC; the dotted black line is the mean estimated herbivore plant diet; the grey cross-hatching is 1 standard deviation; low, medium and high manuring levels are defined from modern, long-term experimental farming plots (after Styring et al. 2016: Fig. 8).

This behaviour makes sense, given that modest stocking levels would limit manure availability, encouraging strategic use of manure on the more demanding/responsive crop.

The strategic approach to differentially manured cereal crops at late Neolithic Sipplingen contrasts with LBK farming practice at Vaihingen and Viesenhäuser Hof/Stuttgart-Mühlhausen (Fraser et al. 2013b; Styring et al. 2017b), where multiple glume wheat taxa were grown under similar conditions, possibly as a mixed/maslin crop. Different explanations of this contrast in approach to cereals are possible, and not mutually exclusive. First, LBK farmers may not have regarded the glume wheats as differentially responsive to fertility, and/or the pronounced dominance of one glume wheat taxon (often einkorn) may have encouraged undifferentiated management. Second, the spread of farming towards the Alpine foreland – associated with a trend towards higher hunting levels within the LBK (Schibler 2001) – possibly entailed adjustments, since farming outcomes were increasingly affected by climatic oscillations (Bogaard et al. 2017b), encouraging a more strategic approach to cereals. Wheat and barley also had distinct culinary uses in the late Neolithic Alpine foreland (Styring et al. 2016). Third, the mechanism(s) and forms of manuring/middening may have differed (Bogaard et al. 2017a).

Finally, turning to the herding aspect of the economy, recent analysis of a lakeshore site on the southern shore of Lake Constance, Arbon Bleiche 3, has shed new light on animal herding and consumption over this settlement's fifteen-year span (Gerling et al. 2017). Arbon Bleiche 3 has been subject to remarkably detailed excavation and sampling, which *inter alia* reveals social geographical patterning across the settlement (Jacomet et al. 2004). In terms of animal consumption, detection of ruminant milk lipids on ceramics (Spangenberg et al. 2008), cattle pathologies suggestive of traction (a wooden yoke was also found) (Leuzinger 2002; Deschler-Erb and Marti-Grädel 2004) and finds of bucrania hung on the outside walls of houses (Deschler-Erb et al. 2002; Deschler-Erb and Marti-Grädel 2004) combine to suggest that livestock, especially cattle, were valued for multiple uses. Gerling et al. (2017) recently investigated cattle-herding strategies in detail using high-resolution sequential cattle tooth enamel measurements of strontium isotope ratios in twenty-five individuals, combined with baseline mapping of Sr variability in the wider landscape. The authors discern three kinds of mobility and herding practice: cattle-keeping immediately around the settlement (cf. overwintering in climatically favourable lakeshore zones, Jarman et al. 1982: 122), seasonal movement beyond the settlement area and non-local herding year-round (Gerling et al. 2017). They exclude large-scale Alpine cattle migration. While some of this patterning may reflect movement of cattle brought in by the settlement's founders, and/or acquisition of animals from other communities, clustering of cattle remains with distinctive herding strategies in the settlement suggests that multiple neighbouring households were engaged in similar practices. This social geographical side of economic practice informs the question of identity construction in Neolithic communities, to which we turn in the final section of this chapter.

Integrated Perspectives on Identity and Inheritance in Neolithic Central Europe

Human aDNA studies, beginning with mitochondrial aDNA and now incorporating genome-wide data, have begun to provide a direct answer to long-standing questions regarding 'colonization versus acculturation' as demographic processes underlying the spread of farming in Europe (see also Chapter 5; Haak et al. 2005, 2015; Bramanti et al. 2009; Lipson et al. 2017). The emerging picture is that in certain regions, including Central Europe, early farmers were descended from 'Anatolians', and hence that the spread of farming involved considerable population movement (Bramanti et al. 2009; Haak et al. 2015). Neolithic populations in different regions reflect varying levels of 'admixture' with local hunter-gatherer populations, and later demographic input from the East European steppe (Haak et al. 2005, 2015; Bramanti et al. 2009; Allentoft et al. 2015; Haak et al. 2015; Lipson et al. 2017). Though the numbers of samples on which these new reconstructions are based are in the hundreds, there is still need for caution in extrapolating from these results, and in interpreting them. It is clear that aDNA studies will increasingly provide direct evidence for human genetic heritage. Equally, Haak et al. (2015) cannot resist interpreting their genetic data also in terms of debate over Indo-European origins, though the specific data they consider do not directly address this debate.

An important consequence of the aDNA breakthrough for palaeoeconomic enquiry is that archaeologists are now increasingly 'free' to interpret bone and seed evidence for land use and food-related practice as precisely that, and not to stretch 'economic' arguments to address questions surrounding the genetic origins of the early farmers (cf. Bogaard and Halstead 2015). As the palaeoeconomists had observed, shifting cultivation as a (problematic) model for the LBK was attractive to Childe (1929, 1957) and Clark (1952) because it helped to explain the (presumed) demographic spread (Jarman et al. 1982: 134). Given the emerging aDNA and agroecological reconstruction for the LBK, it is now apparent *both* that significant demographic spread was likely involved, *and* that people were managing long-established plots with considerable (though variable) labour intensity. Clearly, the LBK farming regime did not directly entail demographic spread in the way it might be argued to do for residentially mobile shifting cultivators (cf. Bogaard 2004: 155). But the detailed history of individual settlements and the way in which households and groups arrived and departed provide important clues to why the LBK spread in the way that it did (Bogaard et al. 2011, 2017a). Explaining this argument requires some additional background on regional and local LBK social geographies.

Detailed study of material culture across LBK settlements has revealed that individual communities could be composed of households/groups with contrasting material culture and different affiliations to regional complexes (e.g. Fridrich 1994; Lüning 2006; Claßen 2011). Intra-site variation in economic practices, such as hunting levels, has also been noted (Hachem 1999, 2000). Integrated bioarchaeological and material culture study at Vaihingen an der Enz, Baden-Württemberg shows that differences in material culture and economic practice coincide to an extent (Bogaard et al. 2011, 2017a). It therefore appears plausible that food-related practice contributed to the construction of social identities and differences within communities (cf. Robb and Miracle 2007). In the earlier part of the sequence, households at Vaihingen belonged to one of two regional material culture traditions, identified on the basis of specific features including stone axe/adze forms: the local Middle Neckar group and the northerly Unterland-Kraichgau group (Strien 2005, 2011, 2014). It appears likely that one particular Middle Neckar lineage founded the settlement. Weed ecological analysis shows that households belonging to the local Middle Neckar group were associated with the most intensively managed plots – probably those located immediately around the settlement (Bogaard 2011; Bogaard et al. 2011, 2017a). Households belonging to the Unterland-Kraichgau tradition, by contrast, were associated with less disturbed conditions, probably reflecting plots that were further away from the settlement. These differences persisted over phases and generations spanning around two centuries, suggesting that they reflect differences in land holdings, and a practice of land inheritance within these groups. When the Unterland-Kraichgau-affiliated households left midway through the occupation sequence, leaving only Middle Neckar households, the persisting arable conditions were exclusively of the intensively managed type. By this time, an oval ditch and palisade that had mostly enclosed the core of the settlement area was abandoned, and its northern half used as a burial ground; the sparse grave goods suggest only Middle Neckar affiliations.

The Vaihingen situation suggests that LBK communities could break down when certain households were disadvantaged in the location of their arable plots, prompting them to found new settlements or to join pre-existing communities elsewhere. An emerging hypothesis is thus that the need for households to be advantageously embedded in communities and local settings, allowing good access to proximate arable land that could be intensively managed, was at least one motivation for the spread of the LBK.

Contrasts are also apparent in the faunal assemblages associated with house groups at Vaihingen (Bogaard et al. 2017a). While cattle-keeping predominated generally, there are differences in the main hunted taxa and preferred secondary livestock. Middle Neckar households are associated with higher levels of red deer hunting and pig-keeping, while Unterland/Kraichgau households targeted hunting of aurochs and relied more heavily on herding of sheep and goats. Hunting of red deer versus aurochs-hunting persisted as a contrast between two Middle Neckar groups in the later LBK occupation. Furthermore, strontium isotope analysis of cattle teeth shows that Middle Neckar households practised year-round grazing on loess, plus some summer grazing in local river valleys and uplands, while Unterland/Kraichgau households focused almost exclusively on loess. These contrasts in practice plausibly reflect different rights held by the two groups, and attempts to exploit the landscape in complementary ways when the community reached its maximum size (around 40–50 longhouses, housing about 300 people).

Intensive bioarchaeological investigation of later Neolithic lakeshore settlements in the Alpine foreland such as Hornstaad-Hörnle IA and Arbon Bleiche 3 has similarly begun to reveal social geographies of food-related practice that formed part of constructed social identities. At Hornstaad-Hörnle IA, differences in material culture amongst individual houses coincide in some cases with differences in stored crop species (Maier and Vogt 2001; Jacomet and Brombacher 2005). Stable nitrogen isotope analysis of the dominant (free-threshing) wheat crop stored in individual houses shows that households harvested plots with distinct land-use histories and likely made their own decisions about arable land management (Styring et al. 2016). Recovery of similar 'toolkits' from individual houses suggests that there was at least an ideal of domestic production and self-sufficiency (Dieckmann et al. 2001). As noted earlier, the immediate replacement of the Hornstaad-Hörnle IA settlement, following its destruction by fire in 3910 BC, with construction of nearby Hornstaad-Hörnle 3 is an example of long-term 'tethering' of lakeshore settlement to established managed landscapes (cf. Ebersbach et al. 2015). This wider cultural landscape, including arable fields, grazing areas and managed woodland, was a key thread of continuity and long-term social identity linking generations of lakeshore dwellers at places in western Lake Constance like the Hornstaad-Hörnle settlements and the long sequence at Sipplingen-Osthafen.

The later 4th millennium BC settlement of Arbon Bleiche 3 on the southern shore of Lake Constance was of short duration (15 years), but meticulous excavation and sampling has revealed fine-grained economic differences amongst houses and areas of the settlement, including specialization in hunting and butchery of game, plant foraging and fishing activities (Jacomet et al. 2004). Another layer of this picture is added by Gerling et al.'s study of cattle mobility using high-resolution sequential measurement of Sr isotope ratios in cattle tooth enamel (Gerling et al. 2017), discussed earlier in this chapter. Clustering of mobility patterns in cattle teeth across the settlement suggests contrasting territorial rights and co-operative links with wider regional networks.

CHAPTER 8

Integrated Case Study II: Horse Domestication and the Origins of Pastoralism in Central Asia

The domestication of any animal or plant species is a significant event in human history worthy of investigation, but the domestication of the horse had particularly important implications for past societies. Horses, once harnessed for riding and traction, revolutionized transport, trade and warfare, with many archaeologists associating these developments with the spread of Indo-European languages, culture and bronze metallurgy (Piggott 1992; Mallory 1996; Anthony 2007). Gaining a thorough understanding of early horse herding societies is a key component of investigating changing human–animal relations, while also feeding into significantly wider debates about the formation of late prehistoric pastoral societies across Eurasia. 'Pastoralism' is broadly defined as an economy based upon the keeping of grazing livestock, which can take many forms (see Outram 2015) including the integration of such practices into mixed farming regimes. Pastoralism is distinguished from hunting by a movement away from predation towards protection and husbandry, and further distinguished from 'ranching', which can be seen as a form of capitalist, 'market-oriented pastoralism' (Ingold 1980). When animal herding is combined with cereal agriculture it is possible to apply the term 'agropastoralism' (Wendrich and Barnard 2008). This chapter, however, focuses upon the development of pastoral societies in the central Asian steppes who were principally dependent upon animals for their immediate subsistence, where evidence of domestic plant use is either totally absent or represents a relatively minor, if sometimes strategically significant, component of subsistence activity.

The link between Indo-European origins and pastoralism in the Eurasian steppes has been the subject of much debate, with other scholars (e.g. Renfrew 1987, 2002a; Gamkrelidze and Ivanov 1995; Bouckeart et al. 2012) favouring Anatolian origins. However, a number of recent, large-scale analyses of human ancient DNA suggest that the development of mobile pastoral societies in the Eurasian steppe was responsible for a major period of human migration into Europe around 5,000–6,000 years ago (Allentoft et al. 2015; Haak et al. 2015) that may well be related to the arrival of Indo-European languages (Anthony and Ringe 2015). Whether or not these migrations are indeed tied to that particular language group, the development of societies, such as the Yamnaya Culture, that were responsible for such rapid expansion, seem to be linked to the domestication of the horse, the use of wheeled transportation and mobile pastoralism. As such, understanding the earliest development of horse husbandry, and how that facilitates pastoral economic systems in the steppes of Eurasia, must be regarded as one of the big questions in Old World prehistoric archaeology. Following on from the arrival of agriculture itself, this development perhaps marks another milestone towards 'anthropocene' impacts on the environment, with vastly increased mobility representing the incipient phases of globalization. Central Asia is a continental crossroads containing crucial east–west trade routes, potentially highly significant in the initial phases of 'Trans-Eurasian Exchange' (Sherratt 2006) that saw agricultural commodities such as wheat reach China from Europe and the Near East, whilst domestic strains of millet came in the other direction (Jones et al. 2011).

Whilst the domestication of the horse has been the subject of considerable scientific research, our understanding of the sequence is far from fully understood. The detailed consideration of the origins of pastoral economies, involving both horses and domestic ruminants, that came to dominate the Eurasian steppes has received far less attention. The application of the most recent analytical techniques and bioarchaeological approaches is only just beginning in some key regions. Whilst much good archaeological fieldwork and analysis of material culture has been conducted throughout the steppes, there has been a general tendency to think of steppe pastoralism as being very homogeneous such that there is a considerable need to better understand its complexities (Frachetti 2009; Hanks and Linduff 2009). In particular, the whole issue of mobility and nomadism needs to be better understood in the context of not only appreciating how the economic system functioned, but also how that affected culture, society and interactions beyond the region.

This case-study chapter will focus geographically on a critical region of central Asia, now largely modern day northern and central Kazakhstan, where a number of key cultures in the story of horse domestication and pastoralism can be found. It will consider how a wide range of approaches have been combined to investigate early equine husbandry, before turning attention to the current state of knowledge regarding prehistoric pastoralists and the potential that exists to use new approaches to revolutionize our understanding of mobile economies. The chapter will also consider how economic understanding can be used considerably to strengthen a social zooarchaeological approach to these societies and investigate the varied ways in which different animal species were seen as significant within human societies. Figure 8.1 is a map showing key sites discussed in this chapter.

Setting the Scene: The Later Prehistory of Northern and Central Kazakhstan

There are two major ecological zones within northern and central Kazakhstan. In the north there is 'forest steppe', made up of a patchwork of grassland with stands of birch and pine trees, whilst in the central region there is relatively treeless, semi-arid steppe. The area was steppe in prehistory also, though there was variation over time in relation to tree cover, with pine generally increasing in extent from the 4th millennium BC through to the Iron Age (Kremenetski et al. 1997). Significant cereal agriculture appears not to have been practised in the region until the Soviet period. We do, however, know from ethnographies that Kazakh pastoralists, particularly in the south of the country, did occasionally grow small amounts of millet, a practice compatible with a semi-mobile lifestyle, because it provides a crop in a very short season (Jones et al. 2011). Recent work has shown that broomcorn millet and wheat were present in south-east Kazakhstan in the 3rd millennium BC (Frachetti et al. 2010; Matuzeviciute et al. 2015) and that a small number of individuals in central Kazakhstan display C_4 plant isotopic signals consistent with some millet consumption by the final Bronze Age (Lightfoot et al. 2015). The earlier adoption of wheat in the south of Kazakhstan, and influences from more southerly agricultural societies, is the principal reason why this chapter focuses on northern and central Kazakhstan, where the economy appears to have been almost exclusively pastoralist. Further north still, societies of the Russian forest steppe appear to have practised mixed plant and animal farming from as early as the start of the 5th millennium BC (Frachetti 2008), but at this date the Neolithic of northern and central Kazakhstan appears to have had an economy based primarily upon hunting animals, such as aurochs, saiga, horse and bison, and on gathering and fishing. Neolithic cultures in the region include the Makhandzhar and Atbasar Cultures, which used domestic pottery vessels characterized by conical bases terminating in a point (Kislenko and Tatarintseva 1999). The 'Neolithic' label,

FIGURE 8.1 A map centred on modern day Kazakhstan showing key sites referred to in Chapter 8.

used in the archaeology of this region, is entirely related to the possession of ceramics, though other aspects of material culture, such as a stone tool tradition that consisted mainly of blade and microblade technology, are more reminiscent of earlier Mesolithic cultures. With a few exceptions, Neolithic settlements are rather ephemeral, and many comprise little more than scatters of material with no current solid evidence for plant or animal husbandry.

Around 3500 BC, however, northern Kazakhstan sees a major new phenomenon with two Eneolithic sister cultures, the Botai (Zaibert 2009) and Tersek (Kalieva and Logvin 1997), manifesting major changes in economic focus, settlement structure and material culture. Pottery use becomes more widespread and lithic technologies change to bifaces and ground stone tools. The Botai Culture develops sizeable settlements that can have more than a hundred semi-subterranean pit houses, which represent a significant investment in what must have been, at the very least, semi-sedentary seasonal residences (Zaibert 2009). The most significant change, however, is a sudden and extreme focus on the exploitation of horses. Horse bones represent the vast majority of faunal assemblages at all Botai sites, and at Botai itself reach the level of 99% (Olsen 2006a; Anthony 2007). The steppes of central Asia had an established population of wild horses that had clearly been exploited by earlier prehistoric groups, in both the Pleistocene and earlier Holocene, as a prey animal. With Botai, however, one sees a sudden focus on that animal, in conjunction with the arrival of large, well-laid-out villages and significant changes in material culture. Since Botai was discovered, in the early 1980s (Zaibert 2009), there has been considerable academic discussion over whether the horses were still being hunted or now herded, and whether they were biologically domestic or still wild. Recent work on this question will be a key focus of the discussion, below.

The Botai Culture ends at the start of the 3rd millennium BC. The following 900 years in this region are extremely poorly understood, with a severe paucity of well-characterized and well-dated sites for the early Bronze Age (EBA). Current synthetic literature (e.g. Benecke and von den Driesch 2003; Frachetti 2008) has had to resort to characterizing this period with reference to a very limited number of sites, such as Sergeevka and Balandino. If we take Sergeevka as an example, it is frequently presented as being late Eneolithic/EBA in date and having a sub-Botai mix of horses and cattle, sheep and goats, the latter possibly having been introduced to the region from the Yamnaya Culture to the west (Frachetti 2008), but we know frustratingly little about this shift in economy. Zaibert (2009) characterizes the site as being multi-phase with a final Eneolithic (post

Botai) layer that is about 0.5 m deep overlain by more than 1 m of late Bronze Age material. The final Eneolithic layer faunal material is still 87% horse, with the remainder being domestic ruminants (Zaibert 2009). Dating the arrival of domestic cattle and caprines is significant, but radiocarbon dating of this phase to the early 3rd millennium BC comes from horse bone (Levine and Kislenko 1997). This is unfortunate because of the possible risk of intrusion of the small amount of ruminant material from the later phases, and confirmation of the early appearance of sheep and cattle would have been valuable. Despite the relative lack of research into this period, detailed discussions with Kazakh archaeologists reveal that, in fact, they know of a significant number of EBA settlement sites, which simply have not been targeted for significant research or absolute dating. In particular, there are many such sites that have been discovered since 2010 in the Pavlodar region, including many along the River Irtysh (Mertz and Mertz 2013). These sites provide the opportunity for a rich vein of future research during this critical period where faunal assemblages transition from equine to ruminant dominance.

The next significant development in the region is the appearance of the middle Bronze Age (MBA) Sintashta and Petrovka Cultures, dating from about 2100–1800 BC (Anthony 2007). The Sintashta Culture is located in the territory between the Ural Mountains and the River Tobol, whilst Petrovka is found in the region of northern Kazakhstan once inhabited by the Botai peoples. These cultures possessed significant, stone-built structures and buried their elite in elaborate kurgan tombs that frequently contained weaponry, horses and, in some cases, possibly the earliest remains of chariots. The economy was based primarily on cattle, but with significant numbers of sheep, goats and horses. Whilst the Botai Culture might present some of the earliest evidence for horse husbandry, the Sintashta and Petrovka Cultures provide very clear early evidence for the integration of equestrianism, and a mixed pastoralist economy, within a culture that appears to have developed a warrior class and the technology to press home military advantage (Anthony 2009). It seems critically important to understand better the earlier development of the equestrian pastoralist package within the EBA 'black hole' in Kazakhstan, as well as in the adjacent Yamnaya Culture on the western side of the Urals (see Shishlina 2003).

The late Bronze Age (LBA – mid 2nd millennium BC) is characterized by the Andronovo Culture and the final Bronze Age (*c.* 1300–900 BC) by the Sargary and Begazy-Dandybaevsky Cultures (Yevdokimov and Varfolomeev 2002). During these periods the economic focus upon the pastoral exploitation of domestic ruminants continues, but the percentage of horses varies considerably from site to site (Outram et al. 2012). Funerary deposits are much simpler than in Sintashta/Petrovka, and do not contain formal horse burials, yet horse bones and horse lipid residues in mortuary ceramics still provide evidence for the continued importance of horse consumption as a significant part of funerary rites (Outram et al. 2011; see below for further discussion). In the following Iron Age, there are, of course, the Scythians with their rich kurgan burials containing gold-clad aristocracy, sometimes with their gold-clad horses (see Lepetz 2013), but this chapter will focus upon earlier pastoralists.

Horse Domestication

Although they originally evolved in the Americas, wild horses spread across to the Old World millions of years prior to human colonization of the Americas in the opposite direction. Horses became extinct on that continent in the final phases of the Pleistocene after a relatively short period of interaction with people (Webb and Hemmings 2006). In many regions of Eurasia, however, horses were a significant source of hunted food throughout the Palaeolithic (Gamble 1979; Olsen 1996; Outram 2006; West 2006) with their presence in the archaeological record of the northern steppes strongly attested over the *longue durée* (Kuzmina 1997). Wild horses were well adapted to the open, tundra-like landscapes of the upper Palaeolithic, but as the environment changed into the Holocene, and the many landscapes became more wooded, horses became a less ubiquitous species (Bendrey 2012). Patchy refugia existed across continental Europe in the Iberian Peninsula and plains of North and Central Europe (Benecke 1994b; Bendrey 2012) with much stronger representation in the steppe zones of East Europe and north-central Asia (Benecke 1994b; Kuzmina 1997). Horse domestication occurred very late when compared to other common livestock, such as cattle, sheep, goats and pigs (Outram 2014). Furthermore, horses appear not to display very clear or consistent metrical or morphological differences between wild and domestic forms, unlike other key food species domesticated in the Near East (Olsen 2006a). As such, research into early horse husbandry has been fraught with difficulty and controversy. The lack of simple markers of domestic status has led researchers instead to weave together complex and multifaceted arguments that consider archaeological, zoological, ethnographic and genetic data holistically, with many of the new approaches featured in this volume playing a part, but none providing the answer in isolation.

For a long time, the earliest indications of human utilization of domestic horses were taken from the first clear depictions of people riding equids, as seen on artefacts such as seals from Mesopotamia in the late 3rd millennium BC (Anthony 1996). However, archaeologists investigating horse-rich regions of the western steppes of the Ukraine began to suggest that riding could have begun as early as 4000 BC in that region (Anthony 1996). At a Copper Age site called Derievka, dating to the turn of the 5th to the 4th millennium BC, a burial of a stallion was recovered that appeared to display clear signs of pathological damage to its teeth caused by wearing a harness and bit (Anthony and Brown 1991; Anthony et al. 1991). The use of bit wear in the identification of domestic horses will be discussed in greater detail below, but this finding was controversial because it seemed so much earlier than when many scholars could see the obvious impact of equestrianism within the archaeological record (see, for example, Renfrew 2002b). In fact, it later transpired that the famous 'cult stallion' burial was an intrusive feature of Iron Age date, as indicated by a series of radiocarbon dates obtained from the animal's skull (Anthony and Brown 2000), though the Eneolithic phases of this site still have great potential in the story of horse domestication. However, Derievka was not the only Eneolithic site where bit wear had been identified. Such pathological traces had also been observed on horse teeth from Botai in Kazakhstan (Brown and Anthony 1998). The arrival of the Botai Culture of the mid 4th millennium BC (Zaibert 2009) heralded a sudden specialist focus upon horses and, with new potential evidence for the use of bits, this culture became one of the key foci for research on horse domestication from that point onwards. During the ten years following the bit-wear study, that evidence was weighed up and discussed by many scholars, as was the circumstantial case for horse husbandry at the site, with different authors reaching different conclusions. What follows is a summary of that debate and subsequently of how our understanding has been radically improved through the application of new methodologies.

Brown and Anthony (1998) identified bit wear by looking for a bevel on the mesial corner of the occlusal surface of the lower second premolar. They had successfully demonstrated that bits could indeed cause this type of wear, even using organic bits (Anthony et al. 2006), but ongoing questioning of that method stemmed from the observation that such bevelling can be observed clearly in wild equids (Olsen 2006a, 2006b). Subsequent zooarchaeological work on equine dental wear (Bendrey 2007a, 2011a) has shown that lower second premolar bevelling can be caused by malocclusion with the upper second premolar that can form a corresponding hook. It is possible to identify whether such malocclusion occurred, or if bit wear is the most likely explanation for the pattern, if both the mandible and maxilla are present and still paired together. However, this was unfortunately not the case with the Botai evidence. The bevel bit wear method has validity, but only provides strong evidence in circumstances where malocclusion can be ruled out. As a result of the uncertainty generated by this critique, a wider range of evidence at Botai was brought to bear on the question.

Staying with the topic of pathologies, it is certainly possible that traction and riding might also produce bone modifications indicative of domestic uses. Traction pathologies have been identified on the metacarpals of cattle as early as the Neolithic in Europe (e.g. Isaakidou 2006), but, without evidence of agriculture, ploughing is unlikely to be relevant in this region of central Asia and there is also no evidence for wheeled transport in the area at this date (Olsen 2006b). Being ridden is the most likely form of equine labour and the resulting load on the spine could cause pathologies. The potential for vertebral pathology as an indicator of early riding has been investigated (Levine et al. 2002, 2005), with some degree of methodological success. There is debate, however, relating to potential differences in likely pathologies generated by riding bareback, using soft pads or different types of saddle (see Olsen 2006a; Bendrey 2007b). A more significant limiting factor in applying this method to sites like Botai, however, lies in the fact that such spinal pathologies can be a result of old age as well as being activity-related (Levine et al. 2002; Bendrey 2007b). Therefore, to apply this method meaningfully one needs to examine the entire spine and have the dentition present additionally in order to establish age at death. This implies the need to have entire axial skeletons buried. Whilst at Botai there can be significant vertebral sections buried in articulation, the required level of completeness is rare. As such, this approach has not yet shed much light upon the earliest phases of horse domestication. Another possible approach could be to look for riding pathologies on humans. Such an approach is equally valid and some very tentative work has been conducted in this field by physical anthropologists (e.g. Molleson and Blondiaux 1994; Baillif-Ducros et al. 2012; Anđelinović et al 2015; Berthon et al. 2018), but human remains are exceptionally rare at Botai (Zaibert 2009) making such a meaningful study difficult as things stand.

From 2000 to 2002, a team led by Sandra Olsen carried out new excavations and geophysical surveys at two Botai Culture sites called Krasnyi Yar and Vasil'kovka (Olsen et al. 2006). This work resulted in Olsen making a wide-ranging archaeological case for horse herding, and the presence of at least some domestic horses, within the Botai Culture (Olsen 2006a, 2006b; Olsen et al. 2006). She argues that the highly organized and substantial settlements of the Botai Culture contrast greatly with the preceding Neolithic period, which was characterized by ephemeral hunter-gatherer camps. The implied reduced settlement mobility does not sit well with the Botai people hunting wild horse herds on foot, but instead suggests a degree of control over the species that had suddenly become the specialized focus of their subsistence economy. Mobility would still have been a likely part of equine pastoralism, but with pastoral husbandry such mobility could be tethered around more permanent settlements. Other evidence is also suggestive of control of horse herds, rather than hunting. Horse skeletal part abundances show none of the differential transport patterns associated with hunting and transporting large prey like horses (see Outram and Rowley-Conwy 1998). Hunters, on foot, will kill animals either where they encounter them, or after a period of tracking an injured quarry, or at a natural topographic feature, such as a cliff jump or natural cul-de-sac. The Botai Culture sites are in very open country with no evidence of cliff jumps or cul-de-sacs and it seems likely that hunted animals would be killed away from villages and require transportation. Horses present major transport problems (Outram and Rowley-Conwy 1998) and so one would expect to see selective transport of body parts as is common in many other archaeological and ethnographic cases (e.g. see Binford 1978). At Botai sites skeletal parts are relatively evenly represented (Olsen 2006a, 2006b) which would be much more likely to occur if horses were herded and could be slaughtered in convenient places. Indeed, riding some horses would further facilitate herding and transport. Hunting is also counter-indicated as the dominant means of subsistence by a relative paucity of projectile points and distinctive impact breaks within the lithic assemblage, whilst scrapers are very common, perhaps providing evidence for extensive hide working (Olsen et al. 2006). There is also some limited evidence for pole-axing trauma to horse skulls (Olsen 2006b), perhaps indicating controlled slaughter within settlements (see Fig. 8.2). Also very common are types of bone tool that were probably used for the production of leather straps, more likely to be associated with animal husbandry (Olsen 2006a). The keeping of horses in close proximity to settlements is also evidenced by soil micromorphology analyses at Botai (French and Kousoulakou 2003) that show the abundant presence of manure within houses. The most parsimonious explanation for large-scale presence of horse dung is that it was abundantly available from nearby corrals or stables and was used in house construction, or simply disposed of in abandoned houses (Olsen

FIGURE 8.2 An example of a potentially pole-axed horse cranium from Botai.

et al. 2006). Whilst the dung of wild animals could be collected from far and wide, that seems less plausible. Potential evidence for the presence of corrals comes from the geophysical observation of a polygonal enclosure at Krasnyi Yar that also yielded elevated phosphorus and sodium levels when geochemically surveyed (Olsen 2006b).

A significant argument that has been mounted against the Botai Culture horses being domestic is that the age structures of horse herds at Botai do not show a pattern consistent with specialized husbandry for meat production. There is not a dominance of the sub-adults one might expect to see if most male animals were slaughtered once they reach maximum size (Levine 2004, 2005). There are indeed more adults present than one might expect for husbandry focused particularly on meat, but it is premature to conclude that this is evidence against domestic status, since there is no reason why Botai husbandry would be so specialized, as it could have encompassed mixed use of primary and secondary food products, as well as keeping horses for riding (Anthony and Brown 2011; Outram 2014). Indeed the picture could also be further complicated by the presence of both wild and domestic animals, since a hybrid situation is not impossible where some domestic stock are used to hunt or herd other horses under looser control (Olsen 2006b). A further argument against the overly simplistic use of herd structure models is that only partial herd structures will be deposited at any given site if there is a seasonal element to mobility. For instance, the cattle at the large late Bronze Age settlement of Kent in central Kazakhstan are clearly fully domestic and lipid residue analysis demonstrates intensive ruminant dairying. However, the age profile for sheep and goats appears more indicative of meat production whilst the cattle are largely adult (Outram et al. 2012). It is most likely that these adult cattle represent a largely female dairy herd and any slaughtering of young males occurred elsewhere and, as such, is not represented in the assemblage deposited at the settlement. Since it would be impossible to suggest that these cattle were wild and hunted, such an argument cannot be applied for the horses at Botai either, without better understanding of economic strategy, patterns of mobility and potential mixture of domestic and wild animals. Whilst the pathological and herd structure arguments presented thus far potentially suffer from problems of equifinality, the skeletal part abundances, settlement structure, plentiful presence of horse dung, tentative evidence for corrals and the tool assemblages of the Botai Culture point towards the control and keeping of horses in close proximity to settlements and a general lack of evidence for hunting. On balance, the evidence points to the keeping of at least some domestic horses.

As these new archaeological and zooarchaeological investigations were ongoing, phylogenetic research into horse domestication was beginning to be conducted too. Studies of the modern mitochondrial DNA of horses suggested that there were several distinct phylogenetic clusters and raised the possibility that there were multiple, independent domestication events, maybe in different localities at different times (see Vilá et al. 2001, 2006; Jansen et al. 2002; Achilli et al. 2012). On the other hand, patrilineal Y-chromosome studies (e.g. Lindgren 2004) revealed a very different pattern, with a far more restricted number of male lines being revealed. Olsen (2006a) suggested that one explanation for such an apparently contradictory pattern could be an initial domestication event in the central Asian steppes followed by the addition of a wider range of female lines through domestic males interbreeding with local wild mares in regions where domestic horses were being introduced. Bayesian modelling of the mtDNA and Y-chromosome data, holistically (Warmuth et al. 2012), suggested that these data were consistent with domestication occurring prior to 3000 BC in the Eurasian steppes, which is also consistent with the Botai representing an early locus for domestic horses. However, the discussion in Chapter 5 warned against the use of modern haplogroup patterning to reconstruct domestication events, using pigs as an example where such assumptions were proved to be incorrect by later ancient DNA work. Indeed, now that there is a larger databank of aDNA profiles, we now have indications that the reduction in Y-chromosome diversity in horses considerably post-dated their domestication (Librado et al. 2017). As such it is becoming ever clearer that patterns in modern animal DNA cannot so readily be assumed to be the result of initial domestication processes, as was common in the literature until now.

From 2007 to 2009 further zooarchaeological research was conducted at Botai that also incorporated lipid residue analyses (Outram et al. 2009). This work yielded three new lines of strong evidence for horse domestication. First, metrical analysis of horse metacarpals, using indices of robusticity, has shown that Botai horses from recent seasons of excavation (Zaibert et al. 2007) closely resemble the slenderness of late Bronze Age domestic specimens from Kazakhstan, and are considerably less robust than Pleistocene wild horses from nearby regions of southern Russia or other Eneolithic horses from the Tersek Culture to the west within Kazakhstan (Outram et al. 2009). Second, in 2007, a novel technique for the identification of bit wear (Bendrey 2007, 2011a) was developed that eliminates the equifinality caused by malocclusion that was a problem for the previous bevel method (see earlier in this section). This new method identifies a parallel strip of wear up the front of the second premolar, which penetrates through both the cementum and enamel, and cannot be caused by malocclusion. Such abnormal wear, in this particular pattern, is not seen in wild or unworked horses (Bendrey 2007). Furthermore, the presence of a bit can also cause exostosis on the diastema bone in front of the molar tooth row, something that is also not seen in severe forms in wild or unworked horses (Bendrey 2007). Recent veterinary research (Cook 2011) also supports the presence of bit wear and interdental periostitis causing changes to the diastema in horses wearing bits, features not found in unworked horses. Both these new forms of evidence for bitting were found in the new material recovered from Botai, which was directly radiocarbon-dated to ensure the material in question was not intrusive (Outram et al. 2009) (see Fig. 8.3). Anthony and Brown (2011) now refer to bevelling as 'type 1' bit wear, the parallel band of wear as 'type 2' and the diastema pathology as 'type 3', with Botai presenting examples of all three.

Finally, lipid residue studies were able to demonstrate that Botai ceramics contained not only adipose fats, but also mare's milk (Outram et al. 2009). Lipid residue methods are able to identify the presence of ruminant animal milk through the study of carbon isotope ratios ($\delta^{13}C$), due to differing metabolic pathways for carbon employed in the animal's production of adipose fats and milk (Dudd and Evershed 1998), but a similar mechanism does not exist for horses, and the carbon isotope ratio ranges for milk and adipose fats overlap in equids. However, the study of deuterium ratios (δD) provides a means of separation, demonstrated in modern samples (see Fig. 8.4), because of the severe continental climate of Kazakhstan. Deuterium isotope ratios preserve a proxy related to climate and precipitation and, whilst adipose fats display an integrated signal for the entire year, milk displays only the seasonal signal related to the time year it was being produced, which tends to be summer. Botai pottery sherds yielded largely equine fats, as expected, based upon comparison with a locally acquired reference fat dataset for $\delta^{13}C$ values (see Fig. 8.5). Those fats securely determined to be equine then further separated into two groups representing integrated and summer only signals based upon δD values, hence implying the presence of both milk and meat fats (Outram et al. 2009) (see Fig. 8.6). The δD values in the ancient samples preserved similar relative seasonal separation of values, but notably the absolute δD values also showed overall climatic differences between the Eneolithic and modern day in line with expectations from palaeoenvironmental reconstructions (Kremenetski et al. 1997; Tarasov et al. 1997). Milking of horses is a common feature of equine pastoralism in central Asia today (see Fig. 8.7), so it is not surprising that it was also present in the past, especially given the very early evidence for ruminant milking in

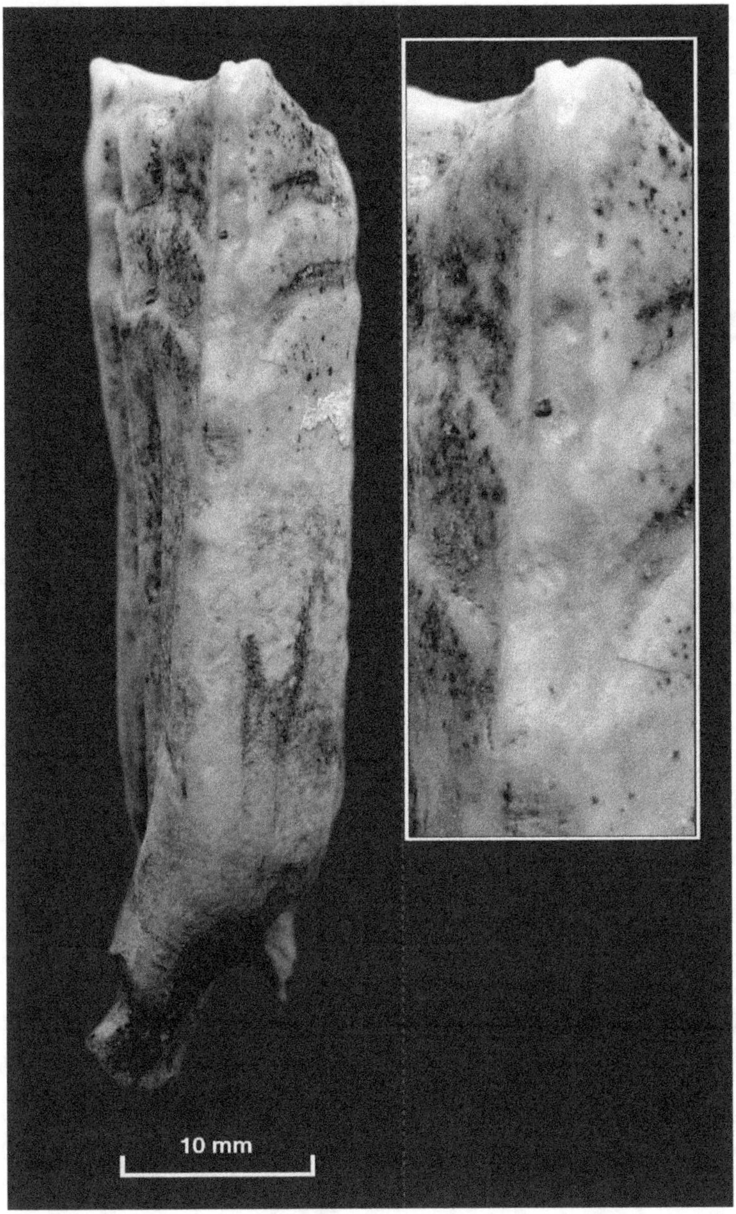

FIGURE 8.3 A close-up of the 'type 2' bit wear identified on the second premolar of a stallion from Botai.

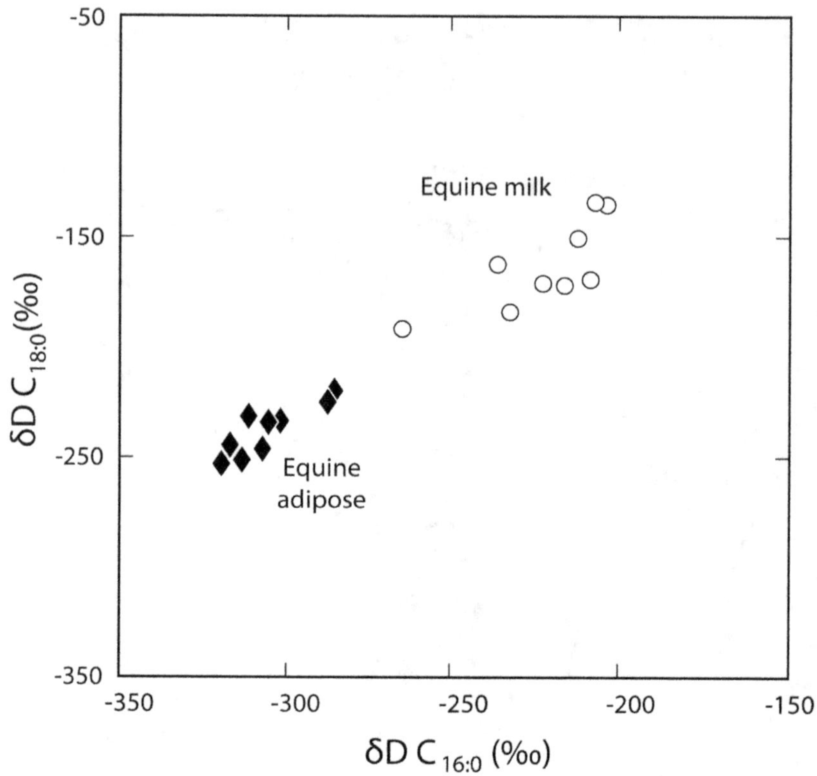

FIGURE 8.4 A graph showing the compound-specific δD values of modern horse milk and meat samples taken locally in Kazakhstan from animals fed on local vegetation (data from Outram et al. 2009).

the relatively early stages of those species' domestication (see Evershed et al. 2008). The presence of mare's milk is very strong evidence for domestication and husbandry. These three new, entirely independent lines of evidence made a very compelling case for domesticated horses within the Botai Culture, particularly viewed alongside all the other contextual evidence (Olsen 2006a, 2006b; Olsen et al. 2006; Anthony and Brown 2011). These arguments were further strengthened by recent genetic research, including ancient DNA from a range of sites and dates across Eurasia, which examined the alleles responsible for the phenotypic expression of coat colour (Ludwig et al. 2009). This work showed a sudden increase in unusual coat colour alleles, that are interpreted to be most likely associated with early domestication founders' effects and breeding, in the forest steppe regions of southern Siberia, some time prior to 3000 BC. Once again this is consistent with the

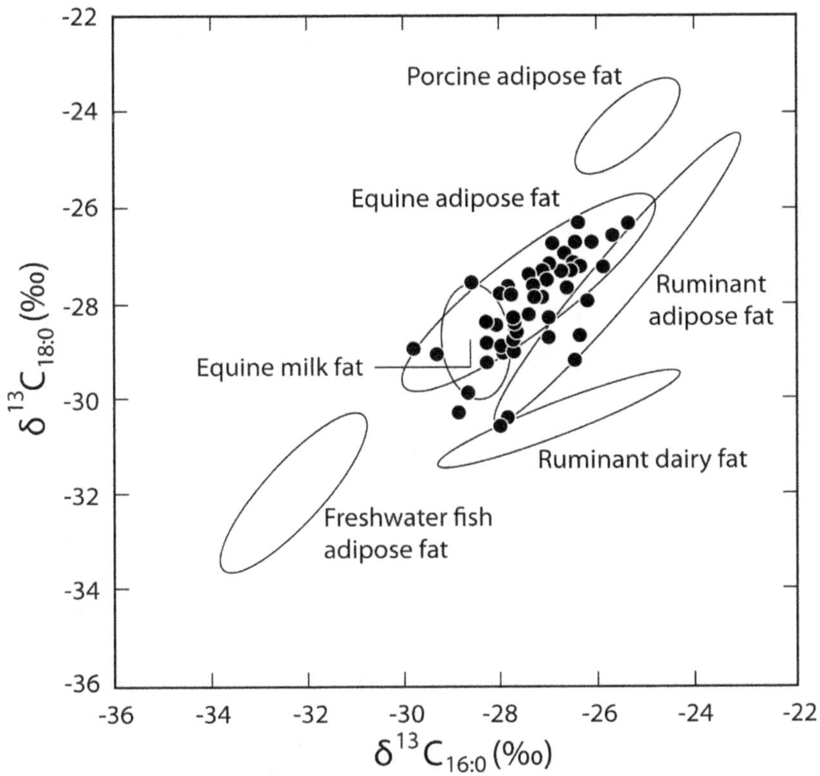

FIGURE 8.5 A graph showing compound-specific $\delta^{13}C$ values of $C_{16:0}$ and $C_{18:0}$ fatty acids obtained from Kazakh reference animal fats in ellipses representing 1 standard deviation from the mean of values obtained. Individual points represent values obtained from lipid residues extracted from Botai pottery (data from Outram et al. 2009).

case for early domestication of horses at Botai, though Botai horses were not themselves sequenced as part of that study.

Underlining the fast pace of such research at present, during the writing of this chapter, the results of whole genome aDNA analysis of twenty Botai horses has now been undertaken using next generation sequencing techniques (Gaunitz et al. 2018). The results of this study are transformative in three ways. First, there is indeed additional evidence for the domesticity of Botai horses in relation to coat colour. There is evidence of insertions associated with the leopard-spotting complex (Gaunitz et al. 2018). When heterozygous in individuals this allele tends to result in patches of white and/or spotting, but when homozygous there tends to be a more uniformly white coat (Holl et al. 2016). It is highly likely that such coat colours

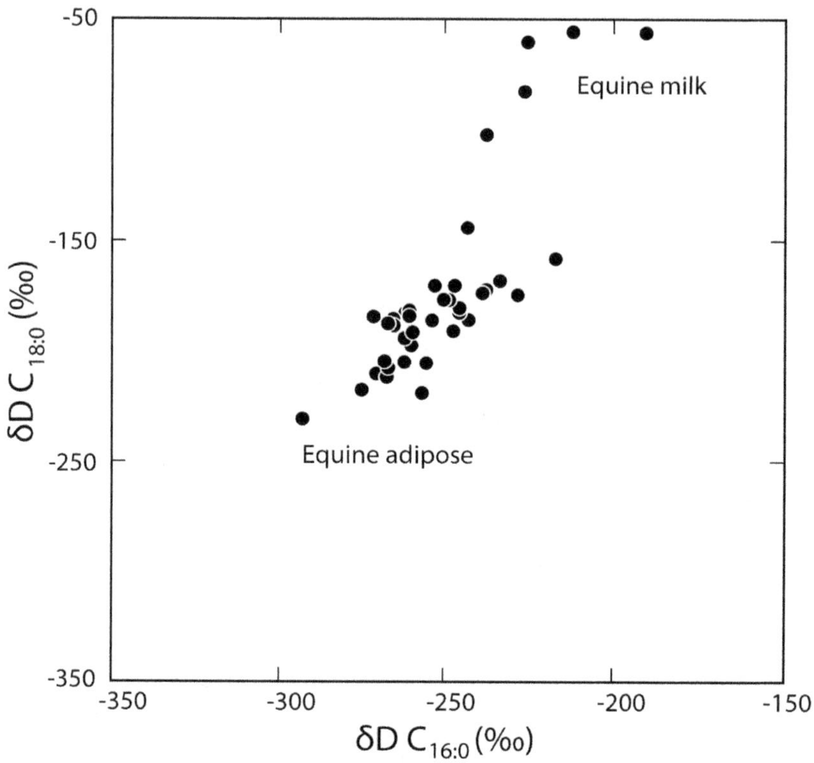

FIGURE 8.6 A graph showing the compound-specific δD values obtained from lipid residues extracted from Botai pottery (data from Outram et al. 2009).

might have been considered desirable and deliberately selected for when breeding, and indeed it has already been noted that there is a high such frequency in other early domestic horses from the Bronze Age (Ludwig et al. 2015). This coat colour, however, also comes with problems. When homozygous it also results in the animal suffering from congenital stationary night blindness (Bellone et al. 2013). This condition specifically means that vision in low light is inhibited, but the condition is also associated with poor eyesight more generally, so in the wild one would expect negative selection against this allele (Bellone et al. 2013). Its presence amongst Botai horses implies a degree of human selection and husbandry (Gaunitz et al. 2018). The selection may have been intentional to increase the number with a desirable coat colour, but husbandry might equally have removed causes for negative selection normally seen in the wild. The same paper (Gaunitz et al. 2018) points to new evidence for corrals at Botai, where

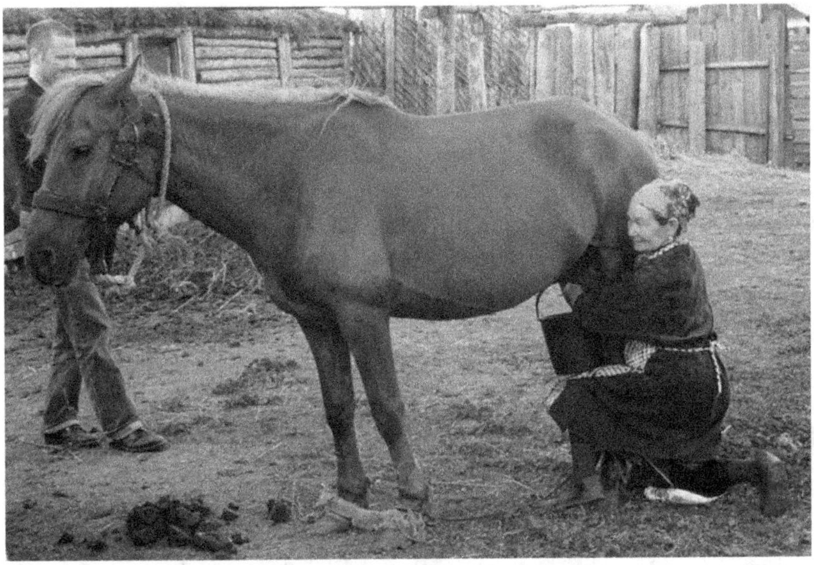

FIGURE 8.7 A horse being milked in a village in Kazakhstan (photo A. Outram).

an enclosure almost identical in size and shape to that previously found at Krasnyi Yar has been identified through geophysics and geochemistry, but also thoroughly ground-truthed by excavation and its date confirmed. Husbandry with corrals provides the practical means by which breeding might be controlled and/or selective pressures removed. Ludwig et al. (2015) note that frequencies of the leopard-spotting complex decline into later periods of prehistory and suggest this could relate to horse breeders' increased awareness of its negative side effects.

Another key line of evidence for domesticity which springs from ancient genomic data is more contextual in nature. Demographic profiles, in terms of changing effective populations, can be modelled over time from levels of genetic drift. Such a Bayesian demographic profile for horses (Gauntitz et al. 2018: supplemental material figure S14; Leonardi et al. 2018) shows a strongly negative trajectory from the last glacial maximum into the early Holocene, something that only reverses again after the spread of domestic horses in the last 5,000 years. The horse went extinct in North America, whilst in Eurasia it appears that populations were also in severe decline and becoming more fragmented. Having been mixed hunter-gatherers through the Mesolithic and Neolithic, it seems almost inconceivable that, faced with plummeting horse populations, they would suddenly focus all their effort on hunting just that species whilst simultaneously becoming less mobile and settling in large villages. On the other hand, if their reaction to the problem was to domesticate the animal, breed it and control it, then this sudden change of lifestyle makes sense.

However, having added yet more strong lines of evidence that Botai horses *were* domestic, this new work also shows that Botai horses *were not* the main genetic source for modern domestic horse stock (Gaunitz et al. 2018). One obvious implication would be that there is a second, and more successful, centre for early horse domestication, and that second clade comes to dominate with only a limited amount of Botai admixture by the Iron Age. If this is indeed the case then the steppes to the west of the Urals need further genetic scrutiny, alongside a few other candidate regions. However, one other possible scenario would be massive introgression from wild stock to replace Botai ancestry over time (see Larson and Fuller 2014), a process that is already known to have obscured the Neolithic presence of Near Eastern domestic pigs in North West Europe (Larson et al. 2007) and thus cannot be discounted. The final key finding is that Botai horses were, however, the ancestors of modern Przewalski's horses, which were once thought to be the only surviving wild horses, but now appear to be feral descendants of an early domestic breed. Interestingly, however, the genetic insertions responsible for the leopard-spotting complex are now absent in Przewalski's, as one might indeed expect as a result of negative selection upon returning to the wild (Gaunitz et al. 2018).

In addition to having whole genomes for Botai horses we now also have three whole genomes for Botai humans, and indeed a series of other Eneolithic and early Bronze Age peoples of the northern central Asian steppe (de Barros Damgaard et al. 2018a). These results are also surprising and significant. They show that the people of this region at this time were effectively a very late relict population that had changed very little over the thousands of years since the Palaeolithic and showed little sign of admixture from outside. There are a series of significant implications to this, but in relation to Botai it tells us something about the possible circumstances of horse domestication in that culture. Zeder (2012b) laid out a number of pathways to animal domestication: 'commensal', 'prey' and 'direct'. Commensal is where an unintended close living association might eventually change into domesticity, with the dog being an oft cited example of this. Prey route is where the relationship with a common quarry changes over time (again potentially unintentionally) to involve more and more control. This is the most common form of domestication relating to food animals and one most frequently undertaken by peoples who were already plant agriculturalists, but still hunted animals (see Outram 2014). Directed pathway domestication implies a prior knowledge of what it is to domesticate an animal and the deliberate act of targeting a species to do that. Zeder (2012b) cites horse as an example of the rare direct pathway and thus suggests that, as a relatively late example of a major domesticate, it was targeted by people with knowledge of the process themselves or through interaction with others, as suggested by Anthony and Brown (2011). However, in the specific case of the Botai, the genetics implies continuity of local hunter-gatherer populations with no evidence for outside contact that left any genetic mark (de Barros Damgaard et al. 2018a). As such this would imply a prey route domestication by local hunter-gatherer populations. This is actually quite rare and its only clear parallel is reindeer domestication (Outram 2014). Reindeer are also animals that were hunted by relict Palaeolithic-derived populations, but can also be ridden and milked. Indeed the close cosmological parallels between reindeer herders and hunters have been noted (Willerslev et al. 2015). One can envisage a very similar process at Botai by hunter-gatherers with similar ancestry, relating to animals that can perform similar functions. Whilst reindeer are common to the taiga, horses are common to the more southerly forest steppes. It now seems, when considering the human and horse ancient genomic data together, that there was a significant population replacement, dating to the middle Bronze Age, that saw peoples like the Botai and their local horse stock replaced by groups migrating from the west with their own horse lineages (de Barros Damgaard et al. 2018a, 2018b; Gaunitz et al. 2018).

Whilst of immense significance to the development of humanity, the investigation of horse domestication has required the application of a vast range of advanced techniques to make any progress. However, though the case for early domestic horses at Botai is now very strong, research in this field is far from complete. Purely in terms of the Botai Culture itself, there is much that is still poorly understood, including mobility patterns and the precise nature of horse husbandry. Much more sampling for aDNA is now needed to fill temporal and spatial gaps in our genomic mapping, particularly to elucidate the dominant source for modern domestic horse ancestry and the nature of early admixture between Botai derived and other horse clades. Further attention will need to be given to other key contenders for early horse domestication centres such as, but not restricted to, earlier phases of the Copper Age in the Pontic-Caspian steppes, west of the Urals (e.g. Anthony 2007; Anthony and Brown 2011; Cunliffe 2015).

Future work is also likely to include a series of methods only just coming into common use in archaeology. For instance, much more work is needed on isotopic sequences in teeth to reconstruct seasonal animal movements (see detailed discussion below). New pathological approaches are also being developed, including exploration of evidence of nasal remodelling caused by harnessing (Taylor et al. 2015) and the identification of interruptions in the formation of dental enamel related to a range of developmental and environmental factors associated with domestic status (see Bendrey 2014). The use of geometric morphometrics (GMM) is being increasingly employed, alongside genetics, to establish domestic phenotypes. Some initial methodological work has been done in this field in relation to two-dimensional GMM on enamel patterns on the occlusal surfaces of second premolars and third molars of horses (Seetah et al. 2014; Cardini et al. 2015), but clearly three-dimensional GMM work on crania (see Heck et al. 2018) or selected postcranial elements could also be more instructive than classical metrical studies have been.

Horse domestication is fundamentally significant to how human societies developed in prehistoric Eurasia in the broadest possible way. The approaches of archaeologists trained in the methods of economic archaeology have been essential in getting to grips with the topic, but in conjunction with the full raft of new scientific techniques. This is a prime example of how economic and environmental understanding does not need to be at the detriment of appreciating cultural or social factors. The relationship between the cultural and economic human decision-making is discussed further below, with particular reference to the significance of horses.

Pastoralism in Bronze Age Kazakhstan: Mobility and Environment

By the Bronze Age in Kazakhstan, pastoralists were herding cattle, sheep, goats and horses (Frachetti 2008; Outram et al. 2012; Outram 2015), accompanied by domestic dogs, and hunting deer, saiga antelope, aurochs and occasional wild boar. Ruminant species dominate, numerically, though horse representation varies considerably from site to site (Outram et al. 2012). Even when not abundant in relative numbers, horses would have had economic significance due to their adaptation to steppe grasslands with cold winters and natural ability to clear snow, aiding the grazing of other less well-adapted species (see Shishlina 2003: 356). Riding horses, of course, would also have been the key means by which mobile herders controlled their stock, along with the use of dogs. Forms of pastoral mobility can vary considerably so it is important not to make simplistic assumptions of uniformity (Frachetti 2009; Hanks and Linduff 2009). Nomadic pastoralism does not necessarily have to involve constant movement and it can be 'tethered' around particularly important resources. It can also be semi-nomadic, with portions of the population remaining sedentary, year round or seasonally. Movement can involve 'vertical transhumance' seasonally between uplands and lowlands, or it can involve horizontal circulation at similar elevations to find sufficient resources (Chang 2006; Wendrich and Barnard 2008). Mobility can also be 'enclosed' by surrounding settled peoples or be 'peripheral' to sedentary agriculturalists (see Wendrich and Barnard 2008, for a useful set of definitions).

Whilst interpretations relating to different models of pastoral mobility are often based upon general archaeological evidence for economy and settlement types (e.g. Chang 2006; Frachetti 2008), it is also possible to demonstrate animal seasonal movement directly through isotopic patterns preserved in teeth. Tooth enamel preserves a record of environmental and dietary change that represents the period of the animal's life during which the tooth was formed. Sequential sampling of tooth enamel provides information on seasonal climatic variation, from stable isotope ratios of oxygen ($\delta^{18}O$), and aspects of diet, from carbon ($\delta^{13}C$) stable isotope ratios, while strontium ($^{87}Sr/^{86}Sr$) isotopic compositions indicate past movements in relation to underlying geology (Balasse et al. 2002; Bendrey et al. 2009). Oxygen isotope composition ($\delta^{18}O$) of meteoric precipitation varies geographically. Such variation is controlled by Rayleigh distillation of atmospheric vapour, driven largely by air-mass temperature, something that is largely dependent on latitude and altitude (Bowen and Wilkinson 2002). Mapping of modern oxygen isotope content of precipitation by the Global Network of Isotopes in Precipitation (GNIP) database confirms that there is a general correlation of oxygen isotope composition of precipitation across the region with latitude. Plants take up bioavailable strontium from the immediate underlying geology, which varies from place to place, and as a result movement of animals between different geologies can frequently be identified from differing strontium isotope ratios ($^{87}Sr/^{86}Sr$) (Balasse et al. 2002; Bendrey et al. 2009). In addition, different environments and geologies may support different plant communities leading to variations in dietary carbon sources. Strontium isotope ratios can either be sampled sequentially, along with samples for $\delta^{18}O$ and $\delta^{13}C$, or summer and winter seasons can be identified from $\delta^{18}O$ patterns and then samples representing the height of those seasons can be analysed to show changes in geology from $^{87}Sr/^{86}Sr$ ratios.

Despite such techniques being available, in theory, since before 2010, there are actually relatively few studies that have employed intra-tooth, incremental study of seasonal variation in isotope ratios to study animal movement within pastoralist societies. Indeed there are none so far that explicitly do so within the region and periods under discussion in this chapter. Possibly the most relevant study of this type that has been undertaken to date relates to movements of horses with an Iron Age pastoralist context in Mongolia (Bendrey et al. 2016). This study did indicate some seasonal movement of horses, but over relatively short distances and thus perhaps was more suggestive of a form of tethered or semi-sedentary pastoralism rather than a regime involving significant horizontal or vertical transhumance or nomadism. Wide-scale applications of such methods to central Asian pastoralists would revolutionize our understanding of how these societies functioned. Perhaps one of the reasons why more such research has not yet been conducted lies in the need to carry out a very large numbers of analyses, for several different isotope ratios, to provide a seasonal pattern for a single animal. In order to obtain significant sample sizes of different species from different sites and time periods, exceptionally large numbers of analyses need to be run resulting in significant costs. Limitations to research can obviously be financial as well as scientific. Without doubt, studies of this type will emerge for the region before long.

One study that directly addresses mobility in the region examined stable isotopes in human teeth from the middle Bronze Age site of Bestamak and the late Bronze Age site of Lisakovsk (Ventresca Miller et al. 2017). Because this study did not look at intra-tooth sequential samples it does not elucidate precise seasonal movements, but does give us a clue as to whether the diets of the people who lived at those sites were local or non-local at the time the teeth formed, based upon $^{87}Sr/^{86}Sr$ and $\delta^{18}O$. The conclusion was that there was very limited evidence for significant migration and most people only undertook small-scale movement local to settlement sites. Whilst not an isotopic study, recent research to reconstruct season of slaughter from tooth cementum analysis of caprines at Tuzasai, an Iron Age pastoralist site in southern Kazakhstan, concluded that there was evidence for year-round slaughter (Schmaus et al. 2018). As such, whilst some people may have moved with herds there was evidence for others being present at the site all the time. Initial findings thus bring into question the tendency to assume simplistic models of nomadism for prehistoric pastoralists.

In addition to thinking about seasonal movements related to animal husbandry, it is also possible to consider other aspects of mobility such as trade and inter-group connections. Traditionally, such matters have frequently been considered in relation to the circulation of material culture types and exotic raw materials, but it is also possible to consider trade in animal breeding stock. Recent research has applied three-dimensional geometric morphometrics to the study of sheep and goat astragali at pastoral sites in Bronze Age Kazakhstan (Haruda 2014). This highly innovative study had the working hypothesis that, if there had been extensive exchange of breeding stock, there would not be major breed differences, as expressed in morphological variation, between different sites. On the other hand, if there was little gene flow between different flocks, regional breed types and morphology might be expressed. This second scenario was fairly strongly evidenced by the study with statistically significant morphological groups being found in the sites studied (Haruda 2014). More work can certainly be conducted in this area, covering a wider range of sites and periods, but also considering cattle, horses and even camels in the more southerly regions. Extending this work may show up temporal variations and levels of stock exchange, but might also indicate different patterns for different species. Were potentially higher-value cattle and horses traded more widely than ovicaprids, for instance? Certainly, the finding from aDNA recovered from the horses buried at the very rich Iron Age kurgan at Berel in the Altai (Librado et al. 2017), that many animals came from different populations, suggests longer-range trade or tribute of those valuable animals. Clearly more studies of this variety could be undertaken through the study of aDNA in combination with GMM, should funds be available.

In the foregoing paragraph, the question of whether different species were valued more than others was raised. Value can clearly relate to a very wide range of factors. In terms of subsistence economy, value can relate to primary products in relation to meat weight, fattiness or the provision of hides or other key craft materials. It could alternatively relate to secondary products such as milk, wool, non-fatal let-blood, hair and labour, including riding. Adaptation to local environments could also be a key requirement in reducing subsistence risk and one species might facilitate the exploitation of others by aiding herding (dogs, horses) or clearing snow (horses). Cultural values might relate to tastes in food, ability to enhance prestige through aiding trade and warfare, exotic rarity, companionship and religious or totemic symbolism, amongst many other things. Is it possible to see any such patterns in species selection at different archaeological sites in the region? Bendrey (2011b) surveyed the proportions of the major domestic species in published faunal assemblages from across the Eurasian steppe for later prehistory. This research noted a very clear relationship between environmental setting and the relative abundance of species. One of the clearest patterns is the greater relative exploitation of cattle in areas with lusher grassland, whereas ovicaprids increase in proportion in more arid regions. Such a finding is not surprising, as such patterns are evident in modern farming systems and other archaeological studies. For instance, if one considers the early Neolithic in south-east Europe and the Near East, cattle are better represented in less arid regions such as north-west Anatolia and, additionally, those regions appear to engage in the highest level of dairying, as indicated by lipid residue analyses (Evershed et al. 2008). Bendrey (2011) therefore argues that there is widespread evidence for a strong degree of environmental determination in at least some matters relating to species selection.

Species representation has been considered in more local detail for the region in question by Outram et al. (2012). This study included a series of new faunal analyses of Bronze Age sites in central and northern Kazakhstan (Outram et al. 2012) and considered these alongside a wide selection of already published studies from the same region and the immediately bordering Trans-Ural region (Tsalkin 1972; Markarova 1976, 1977, 1980; Kosintsev 1989; Akhinazhanov et al. 1992; Germanov and Kosintsev 1995). The 2012 study very much supported the same general conclusions, since cattle were most numerous in the damper forest steppe and Trans-Ural regions, whilst proportions of sheep and goats were higher in the semi-arid steppes of central Kazakhstan (Outram et al. 2012). However, the proportion of horses varied very considerably between just 3.7% and 46.2% of the assemblages by minimum numbers of identified specimens (NISP) and it was noted that there could be considerably different ratios of horses at sites situated not far from each other within similar environmental zones (Outram et al. 2012). It is possible to analyse these data further using correspondence analysis. Figure 8.8 shows a correspondence analysis plot of sites and species, with the sites labelled according to region. It can be seen that the sites clustering closest to cattle are the well-watered forest steppe and Trans-Ural sites, whilst semi-arid sites of central and south-east Kazakhstan cluster around ovicaprids. This analysis also shows an association between semi-arid regions, flocks of ovicaprids, hunted wild animals and domestic dogs. Whilst hunting is clearly more prevalent in these regions, is the higher representation of domestic dogs related to shepherding or hunting or both? What is most notable is that sites rich in horses cluster away from those rich in other species along with sites from a range of different regions and environment types. High proportions of horses do not appear to be simply related to either straightforward environmental factors or the keeping or hunting of other species. Perhaps through understanding the economic and environmental context well, it is possible to argue, with a sounder evidence base, that there might well instead be a particular cultural reason for this pattern that can then be researched through other means.

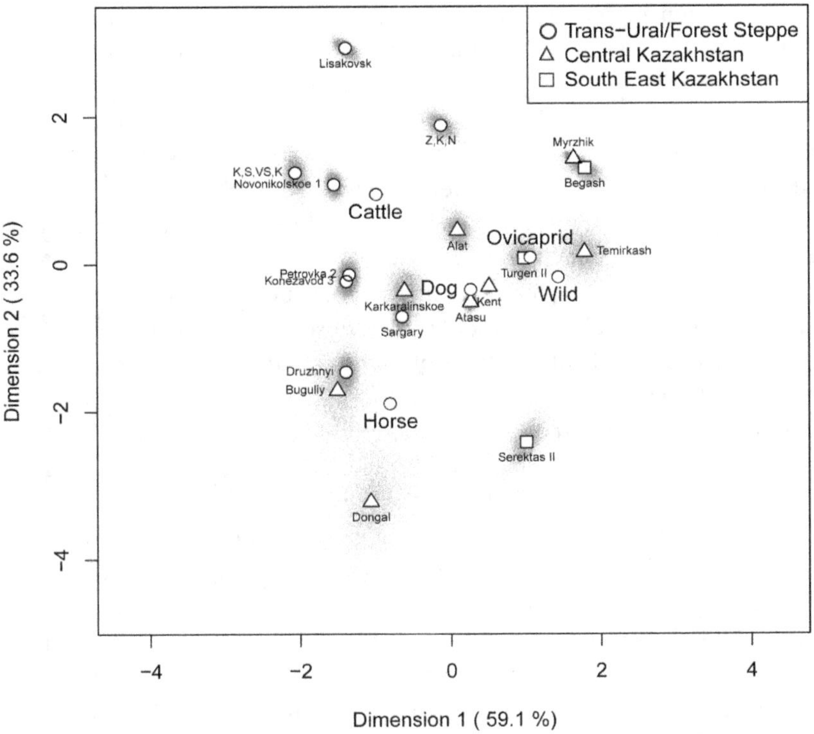

FIGURE 8.8 A correspondence analysis of proportions of species (by NISP) at a wide range of late and final Bronze Age settlements in Kazakhstan and the Trans-Ural region (based upon data from Tsalkin 1972; Markarova 1976, 1977, 1980; Kosintsev 1989; Akhinazhanov et al. 1992; Germanov and Kosintsev 1995; Frachetti and Benecke 2009; Outram et al. 2012; Haruda 2014). Sites with abbreviated names that do not otherwise appear in Figure 8.1 are all Trans-Ural sites in the Cheliabinsk region. This correspondence analysis employs Dirichlet distribution of 30,000 random deviates of the percentages in each class (see method in Gerbault et al. 2016 and Johnson et al. 2018). If scatters remain separated, this predicts significant statistical difference.

Social Zooarchaeology of Horses in the Steppes

If high proportions of horses on pastoralist sites of the Bronze Age do not relate clearly to simple matters of environment or subsistence economy, then finding ways to research other causes for this phenomenon becomes desirable. A distinct possibility that should be considered is whether horses of the later Bronze Age were considered to be a particularly high-status animal, such that their high prevalence might relate to wealth or social standing rather than a means of food production. Whilst horses were, and still are, eaten in central Asia, and so can be treated in a similar way to cattle, they can also be ridden, forming a close bond with the rider. Riding can become associated with high-status pursuits such as warfare, hunting and exotic trade. Maintaining excessive numbers of horses is unlikely to represent the most efficient and risk-free choice, in terms of subsistence economics, so doing so could nevertheless be seen as a means of costly signalling by the wealthy and elites. If the possession of horses were imbued with such meaning, then the slaughter of a horse for food would represent a sacrifice, in either a religious or secular sense, which might well also imbue the resulting cuisine with particular symbolism. Indeed much of this discussion fits very well with features of modern and recent Kazakh culture, but what evidence is there for this in the Bronze Age? The combination of research into burial customs, the faunal record and evidence for food consumption derived from lipid residue analyses formed the basis of recent research into these issues (Outram et al. 2011).

If one examines the role of horses in Eneolithic and Bronze Age funerary rites within Kazakhstan, it is immediately evident that, in various phases, horses played a very significant role. In the Eneolithic Botai Culture there is ample evidence for the decorative or ritual use of horse bones. Pits surrounding houses seldom appear to be filled with random rubbish, but instead there is some evidence for structured deposits of selected materials. In particular, horse skulls are perhaps over-represented (Olsen 2003, 2006b) and some horse frontal bones appear to have been modified to create artefacts that could have been worn as masks (Olsen 2003). On the west side of houses, perhaps the side where the door was placed, pits frequently contain dogs or, at least, dog skulls, often in association with horse skulls, necks, pelves or foot bones (Olsen 2006b). A famous aspect of Botai material culture is the regular decoration of horse first phalanges with incised geometric designs (Olsen 2003; Zaibert et al. 2007). Evidence for human burial customs is very scarce at Botai (Olsen 2006b; Zaibert 2009), however, and it is unclear what the normative funerary rite was. Only Botai itself has yielded human remains and some of these have been disarticulated with little evidence related to accompanying rites (Zaibert et al. 2007), though two disarticulated human skulls had been modified. One had been made into a bowl and the other had an applied clay mask (Olsen 2006b). However, one large pit contained the remains of four people (two adult males, an adult female and a 10–11-year-old child) along with the partial remains of at least fourteen horses, including many skulls, that formed an arc around the feature (Olsen 2006b; Zaibert 2009). It is clear that horses played a significant role in Botai Culture ritual deposits, along with dogs, and that both animal and human skulls held particular significance.

Relatively little is known about the archaeologically poorly represented early Bronze Age, but horses continued to play a very significant role in funerary monuments of the middle Bronze Age Sintashta Culture, dating to 2100–1800 BC (Anthony 2007, 2009). At the settlements of Sintashta and Arkaim, midden material was composed of 60% cattle, 26% sheep/goat and 13% horse. In Sintashta Culture cemeteries, however, horses comprised 39% of the assemblage (Anthony 2007, 2009), potentially indicating that deposits of that species, maybe after feasting, held particular significance. Beyond the general prevalence of horse remains in funerary contexts, some of the richest Sintashta graves contain the remains of chariots accompanied by a number of sacrificial horses, equestrian equipment and weaponry. Graves of this type tend to be associated with adult males and have frequently been seen as relating to warrior elites (Anthony 2007, 2009; Kohl 2007; Koryakova and Epimakhov 2007; Kalekna 2009). In the Botai Culture, horses absolutely dominated both economy and ritual. By the middle Bronze Age, ruminants probably supplied the majority of the subsistence economy, but horses perhaps became more highly valued for their role in warfare and expressing the power and wealth of an elite warrior class, both in life and death. The Petrovka Culture, which dates to the first part of the 2nd millennium BC is found in northern Kazakhstan and was a slightly later derivative of Sintashta (Yevdokimov and Varfolomeev 2002; Anthony 2007). Petrovka graves also contained horse sacrifices, horse tack and chariots (Koryakova and Epimakhov 2007), though there was a decline in the number of horses sacrificed and chariots deposited throughout the period (Anthony 2007).

From the mid 2nd millennium BC, the later Bronze Age Andronovo Culture, which includes the Alakul and Fyodorovo sub-cultures (Yevdokimov and Varfolomeev 2002; Koryakova and Epimakhov 2007), spread across the region. Andronovo graves can include either inhumations or cremations, accompanied by ceramics with geometric designs. The occasional deposition of animals in funerary contexts continued, sometimes involving only the head and lower limbs. This practice did sometimes involve horses, but they were not the most common species. The deposition of whole or partial dogs seems to become more important, as does the role of fire in rituals (Koryakova and Epimakhov 2007). The final Bronze Age (*c.* 1300–900 BC) in Kazakhstan can be ascribed to the Sargary and Begazy-Dandybaevsky Cultures (Yevdokimov and Varfolomeev 2002; Frachetti 2008). Final Bronze Age cemeteries usually involve inhumations with relatively modest grave goods comprising ceramics and occasional ornaments (Yevdokimov and Varfolomeev 2002; Koryakova and Epimakhov 2007). On the face of it, it appears that, in the late Bronze Age, the role of horses in rituals and funerary rites had diminished. However, if one considers the results of faunal and lipid residue analyses of later Bronze Age settlement and cemetery sites (Outram et al. 2011), all is not what it seems.

Figure 8.9a shows the relative abundance of different animal species found in the faunal assemblages from both the Andronovo cemetery and settlement sites of Lisakovsk (Usmanova 2005). Cattle dominate at both sites with ovicaprids being less numerous. This site is situated in forest steppe, not far from the Trans-Ural region, where it is not so arid and cattle husbandry might be expected to flourish. However, what is most striking is the very low representation of horses at the settlement but considerably greater abundance at the cemetery (Outram et al. 2011; Kasparov and Outram 2013). Whilst not necessarily included as sacrifices within the graves themselves, horses feature very prominently in the general faunal deposits around the cemetery. This could potentially indicate that the consumption of horse was a feature of funerary feasting, but much less a feature of everyday diet at the settlement (Outram et al. 2011). Furthermore, if one examines the results of lipid residue analyses of ceramics found in a range of later Bronze Age settlement and cemetery contexts in Kazakhstan, a very similar pattern is revealed: 23% of pots deposited in funerary contexts contained equine fats whilst only between 3% and 7% of pots from settlements contained horse fat (see Fig. 8.9b) (Outram et al. 2011). This underlines a clear relationship between horse remains and funerary deposits that was not immediately obvious through other means.

What exactly, though, is the relationship between the lipid residues and the funerary context? It is possible that ceramics deposited as grave goods were made purely for that purpose and not for prior domestic use. Any residues found in such vessels would relate to the mortuary rite, either in the form of a food offering or the use of the vessel in a funerary feast. However, the pots may also have been used in a domestic setting for cooking or storage before being deposited in a grave. As such, their residues could represent their prior use rather than their funerary role. If the vessels had prior use and a funerary use then the residues would become mixed. (Evershed 2008; Outram et al. 2011). One line of evidence suggests that at least some of the pottery vessels deposited in Andronovo graves were old vessels, long used prior to deposition in a funerary context. A substantial number of pots found in graves have been broken and repaired with bronze

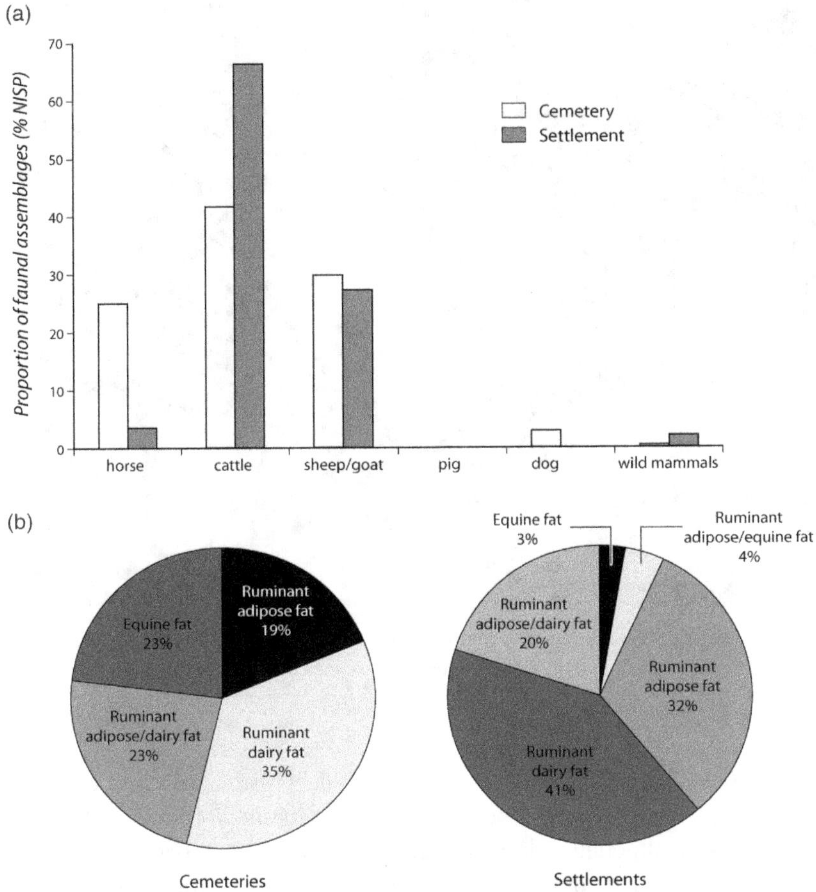

FIGURE 8.9 *a.* Graph comparing the representation of different animal species (by NISP) at the Lisakovsk settlement and cemetery sites. *b.* Pie charts comparing the total proportions of pots containing equine vs. ruminant lipid residues at a number of late Bronze Age settlement and cemetery sites (see Outram et al. 2011).

staples (see Fig. 8.10) before deposition (Bolton 2007). In purely functionalist terms it is hard to understand this practice, because of the substantial amount of effort required to effect such a repair, using valuable bronze, and the unsatisfactory nature of such a repair in terms of usability (Bolton 2007). One might instead speculate that such vessels could be valued heirlooms, associated with particular rituals or significant events. If this is the case then the lipid residues identified in such pots may not relate directly to funerary feasts, but to other culturally significant prior uses, before such vessels were singled out for special treatment and mortuary deposition. Either way, high

FIGURE 8.10 Pottery vessels in an Andronovo Culture, late Bronze Age grave at Temirkash, Kazakhstan. The larger vessel was repaired in antiquity using multiple bronze staples (marked out by white arrows). This is not uncommon.

proportions of use to consume equine products is associated with cultural value through the selection of vessels used in significant social acts. The cultural value attached to horses within these pastoralist societies is sometimes very overt and sometimes less obvious, but detailed holistic analysis of all evidence reveals intriguing patterns in all the varied cultures and time periods discussed.

This case study demonstrates very clearly why theoretical perspectives that seek to examine only the environmental and economic factors, or those that advocate primacy for socio-cultural drivers, are wrong-headed. There is no need to think of 'social zooarchaeology' as having to concentrate 'beyond' economic considerations. Economy, environment and culture need to be considered collectively at all times. The evidence will sometimes lead to the conclusion that one aspect of behaviour had the stronger influence in relation to a particular question, but all aspects are likely to be involved in societies that most likely did not see any simple dichotomous distinction between the economic and social.

CHAPTER 9

Conclusion

The post-war acceleration in scientific endeavour during the 1940s to the 1960s saw the synchronous rise of the 'palaeoeconomy school' and the 'New Archaeology'. Novel scientific techniques afforded much greater ability to study past environments and there was much more attention given to studying the macro- and micro-remains of past diets. Alongside this, radiocarbon dating allowed a reconsideration of chronologies. This combination naturally lent itself, in tandem with models from anthropology and behavioural ecology, to rapid advances in the understanding of past economies in their environmental setting. Much of this progress was empirical in nature; we simply were afforded a better insight into prehistoric food production and the nature of the landscapes and environments people were living in and exploiting. However, such advancement also led to the formulation of metanarratives related to key topics such as population growth and dynamics, the origins of agriculture and the rise of complex societies. Occasionally, what should have remained investigative models, to be put forward and tested, came to be treated as deterministic laws.

Particular criticism of 'determinist' approaches gathered pace during the rise of 'post-processualism' during the 1980s and 1990s. Post-processualism is not one single thing; it is more defined by what it was reacting against than what it proposed. Key themes were a reaction against the perceived way in which economic and environmental factors had been taking precedence over socio-cultural drivers and individual agency. Equally there was a reaction against hypothetico-deductive science in favour of relativist and multi-vocal approaches. Indeed hard evidence and 'facts' seemed out of favour, in a climate of 'anything goes'. During this period it was fashionable to denounce any work that focused upon environment or economy as being 'determinist' whether or not it actually was. Furthermore, determinism was pretty much always seen as being wrong, whether or not there was sound evidence that indeed something was determined by something else. A number of post-processualists presented models that deliberately reversed the relationship to present cultural developments as entirely driving significant transitions, often with economy uncoupled or lagging behind. Many of those who continued to work on diet, environment and economy shifted emphasis in their publications by adding 'social' in front of their sub-discipline, to avoid criticism, or by stating that they were moving 'beyond' mere economy or calories.

It was the case that some palaeoeconomic works had paid too little attention to social factors and that some models were dogmatically and uncritically applied. However, this had never been true of much palaeoeconomic work. Not only was it a mistake suddenly to disregard economy and environment to concentrate on social issues, but in so doing cultural studies actually lost meaningful context and points of reference. It is not a surprise that the pendulum swung too far; that seems to be human nature. It is however somewhat disappointing that the evolution of academic disciplines should have to work that way, rather than by more intelligently acknowledging criticism and moving to a happy medium. Having said that, there were many environmental archaeologists and economic prehistorians who did just that during this otherwise divisive period.

In the first part of this millennium, work has been much more balanced and integrated in theoretical terms, often with large teams working fruitfully together. Over this period, many of the new methods described in this book have been developed, or at least, have seen their first wide-scale use. Some have already radically altered our understanding of key economic issues and transitions in the past, but in many cases the true revolution is yet to come. For many techniques, this period has been characterized by development within particular well-funded projects rather than commonplace and broad usage. The number of laboratories that can carry out certain types of analyses, at least reliably, is still limited. Many are still only available through collaboration in major research projects, rather than as a regular contract service such as is the case for older techniques like radiocarbon dating. Many techniques are still very expensive and require very specialist skills, including the bespoke development of protocols for new applications. However, prices are coming down, technologies, such as next generation DNA sequencing, are increasing sample through-put and academic departments are increasingly hiring new staff who understand these methods. These changes are very fast-paced and the subject will change radically, both in terms of our understanding and the way we work within the coming decade of the 2020s.

The acceleration in new scientific techniques will bring amazing advances, but also significant challenges. The most obvious challenge is funding for ever more expensive laboratories, and to justify this we need to be clear about the impact and benefit of archaeological research to science more broadly and to the public in general. Knowledge is becoming ever more specialized and it is becoming more and more challenging for individuals to stay abreast of developments, so we will need new ways of working. The specialist knowledge required does not just relate to the technicalities of analysis in genetic, residue or isotope laboratories, but also the way we record sites and analyse multiple lines of data. In terms of recording and archiving we need support for digital systems, whilst for multi-proxy studies and meta-analysis we need computational and statistical advice, in the same way that bioinformatics specialists have become so essential within the field of biology. Future archaeology departments will look very different, and there is a risk of divergent trajectories.

In the rest of this concluding chapter there is a consideration of the original key ideas and methods from the palaeoeconomy school and whether they are still relevant to research today. This is followed by a concluding consideration of the theoretical framework that could fruitfully accompany economic approaches to archaeology, and the pros and cons of abstraction, models, metanarrative and culture-specific nuances. The final section addresses future challenges in a little more detail.

Revisiting Key Palaeoeconomic Ideas and Methods

As economic and environmental archaeology flourished during the 1950s to the 1970s, the key lines of evidence for past environment and diet were macro- and micro-scopic subfossils of plants and animals: bones, seeds and pollen. Such remains had been studied much earlier than this, but during this period there was a revolution in appreciating how much information could be gained from their proper study. This went along with vastly better recovery methods and a concerted effort to understand taphonomy and site formation processes. Other microfossils have since been added to the armoury in the form of phytoliths and starch grains (see Chapter 6). Key topics that were addressed during that time included evidence for seasonality to help reconstruct hunter-gatherer mobility and settlement patterns, the domestication of key food species and the development of specialist production strategies through tools like herd structures (see Chapter 1). Given that isotopes (Chapter 3) provide us with proxies for dietary composition and seasonal mobility, whilst residues (Chapter 4) tell us what specific products were being consumed from material culture, and ancient genomics (Chapter 5) provides a direct record of population dynamics and phenotypic changes associated with events like domestication, is there still a need for traditional zooarchaeology and archaeobotany? At the very least, is the role of those sub-disciplines diminished?

The answer is simple: traditional zooarchaeology and archaeobotany are still as important as they were back then, but considerable research potential is lost if they are studied in isolation. Besides the obvious point that subfossil remains are the carriers of the biomolecules being analysed for aDNA and isotopes, and thus they need identifying and contextualizing, none of the lines of evidence actually wholly duplicate each other, thus there is little redundancy. Isotopic data on diet are very specific in the sense that a particular individual's diet is being studied, but exceptionally vague and plagued by equifinality in terms of the specific details of what was consumed beyond broad categories and proportions. Botanical and faunal remains, on the other hand, can be identified to species and part, but it is not clear who ate them and in exactly what proportion. Chemical characterization of food residues tends to be a little more specific than isotopic evidence, but less so than subfossils, though particularly important products like milk can also be recognized. Pottery organic residue techniques are tied to the use of that particular type of material culture, so do not directly quantify dietary consumption. All of these methods are quantitative to some degree, but none provides a simple answer regarding amounts of particular foods produced and consumed. Genetics does not speak directly to dietary reconstruction, but can help with speciation, identifying changes associated with domestic breeding and movements of crops and animals, and human evolutionary adaptation to economy and diet. The more of these methods that can be brought to bear on a case study, the better the holistic picture becomes (as illustrated in the case studies in Chapters 7 and 8). Demonstration of important past transitions and developments becomes much more compelling when many independent lines of evidence tell the same story without risk of methodological circularity.

It is clear that the zooarchaeological and archaeobotanical advances made in those early days are far from irrelevant to modern research. Many of the best recent projects have seen excellent collaboration between zooarchaeologists or archaeobotanists studying the subfossils, and biogeochemists and geneticists studying the biomolecular evidence. However, whilst this has been working satisfactorily, it might be conceptually better if zooarchaeology or archaeobotany were no longer merely thought of as being the study of bones or seeds. Those terms imply the broad research of past plant–animal–human interactions in the past, and the future health of those fields depends upon the holistic integration of all applicable lines of subfossil and biomolecular evidence, though each individual researcher is likely to specialize. Let us briefly consider the impact of holistic approaches on key topics of early palaeoeconomic study, such as hunter-gatherer settlement and seasonality, the origins and spread of agriculture, and specialized use of animals.

With regard to hunter-gatherer economy and use of landscapes, the palaeoeconomy school pushed forward two major lines of methodological approach. The first was site catchment analysis and the second was a suite of ways to establish minimum seasons of site occupation from studying floral and faunal remains. Site catchment analysis, particularly if backed up by palaeoenvironmental evidence to show the past situation, had the power to suggest what resources might be spatially available to people at a particular settlement. This information could be used to construct models regarding carrying capacity and the potential for sedentism and/or territoriality. It could also be used to model possible options for seasonal mobility between different ecological zones. Having created models, these needed testing. Evidence for seasons of occupation from zooarchaeological and archaeobotanical analyses provided a test for some aspects. Furthermore, methods developed by the 'processualists' in North America, such as models for skeletal transport, afforded another way of establishing site function in relation to such models. Archaeological evidence for such things as cemeteries, long-term food storage and regional styles also provided circumstantial evidence to help test models relating to such issues as sedentary occupation or territoriality. If site catchment analysis is used to provide environmental context and any model that is derived from it is then tested against other lines of evidence, then the method is not, in any sense, being used deterministically.

However, a key problem with early applications of site catchment analysis was that frequently the quality of other data analysed was not good enough to support or refute assumptions in models, and in quite a few cases there was not really an attempt to follow through with further investigation at all. If one maintains that site catchment inferences are just models that need testing, then that may not be satisfying but it is not philosophically problematic. However, if conclusions from site catchment analysis slip into being treated as a factual result, then the charge of dogmatic 'determinism' is founded. The greater ability we have to test models deriving from such approaches the less likely we are to slip lazily into such assumptions. Quite clearly with the addition of modern approaches we are in a much stronger position. The value of site catchment analysis itself is in no way diminished, but these days such a study would be undertaken within a geographic information system (GIS) program allowing multiple data forms to be overlain spatially. Physically undertaking such surveys has been made considerably easier by LiDAR, satellite imagery, drones and ever better base maps for geology and so forth. Paleoenvironmental and palaeoclimatic records are also much higher resolution. However, a really critical advance is the ability to think about 'isotopic landscapes' or 'isoscapes' (Grupe and McGlynn 2016). Our novel ability to employ isotopic information to consider what ratios of different resources are being used, and which zones of landscape they might derive from, vastly increases our ability to test models about past use of site catchments. Indeed we can now establish what the *actual* site catchment was, as opposed to making an assumption related to easy proximity. The stable isotopic revolution is also allowing us to track animal movements during the year, thus vastly improving seasonal models, and also allowing us to see long-distance migration or trade. There is much current work dealing with hunter-gatherers, agriculturalists and pastoralists that aims to understand in great detail how people used their settlement's hinterlands. This is site catchment analysis writ large, but in a highly evidence-led, testable way that is far less likely to fall into 'deterministic' traps.

Much of the early work of economic archaeologists was on domestication and the origins and spread of agriculture. Their reliance on site catchment analysis again raised the problem of determinism where hypotheses about land use were not adequately tested. In relation to changes in diet during this subsistence revolution, residue and isotopic studies add new lines of evidence. The identification of products like milk (see Chapter 8) through residue studies can act as something of a smoking gun as evidence for domestication. Principally, however, these additional lines of evidence provide independent confirmation of major dietary transitions. Of all the new approaches, ancient genomics is perhaps most radically advancing our understanding of domestication. It is becoming increasingly possible to identify alleles responsible for domestic phenotypic traits, and such morphological phenotypes can be simultaneously studied on the subfossil remains through techniques like geometric morphometrics. Equally, ancient genomics is recasting our understanding of the farming diaspora, allowing us to interrogate models such as 'wave of advance', pioneer colonization and availability/substitution for Neolithic Europe (Fig. 1.3). The early palaeoeconomists developed a series of models for how farming might have spread from its origins. After so many years of speculation and discussion regarding these models, aDNA is now telling us in which circumstances farming was spread by migration or local adoption. We are now seeing details of the spread of farming peoples and their domesticated plants and animals, and can understand the extent of admixture with local endogenous populations. Perhaps many of us never thought we would actually get to know the answer to such questions after so many years of merely theoretical debate.

Another key strand of earlier economic work related to animal herd structures (e.g. Higham and Message 1969; Payne 1973; Legge 1981). These methods have been modified and improved but are still in use. Indeed, at least in relation to the antiquity of milking (Dudd and Evershed 1998), lipid residue analysis has backed up the usefulness of such approaches. Before there were multiple lines of evidence, many had trouble believing that dairying was so early. This example clearly demonstrates the benefit of multiple, entirely independent, lines of evidence. Current projects investigating the origins of dairying are applying both of these approaches alongside consideration of the ancient DNA record for lactase persistence alleles.

It is clear that the legacy of early economic archaeologists is intact. Many of the questions they thought were important are still being investigated and are still viewed as priority areas of research. Considerable progress is now being made by the combined application of established methods alongside a plethora of new techniques that provide independent lines of verification. Each of these methods has different strengths and weaknesses and can be used in a highly complementary way, without redundancy. Where funding is available, progress is very fast. Furthermore, in the 'anthropocene', understanding humans' economic relationship with environment over the *longue durée* has never been more impactful and relevant.

Striking a Balance in Theoretical Approach

Assumption-based and untested deterministic models are not the best way of proceeding, but the unthinking and dogmatic application of that term 'deterministic' to deride all environmental and economic approaches is equally wrong-headed. Certain lifeways cannot be supported in particular environments. If those lifeways are not biologically viable then no amount of human agency is relevant. Minimum conditions for population survival *are* determined. Different base conditions might be established for different modes of subsistence or states of technology. Equally, upper limits of maximum carrying capacity are similarly determined. However, almost infinite possibilities for cultural diversity exist within these limits of environmental viability. Where a once viable economy becomes non-viable through environmental change (whether human induced or otherwise) then the nature of the response is *not* determined, but some form of change is, whether that is extinction, migration or innovation. Basic limits are determined by environment and economy, whilst viable responses to differing environments may be influenced in varying measure by economic or sociocultural factors, if indeed those two things are separated in the minds of the subjects. Where the likely influence of environment or economy on culture and behaviour has been predicted through modelling, the model needs to be tested with reference to the archaeological record, and the more lines of independent evidence that can be marshalled the better. We now have at our disposal a barrage of techniques that offer different insights to help penetrate the dark veils of site formation processes, taphonomy, diagenesis and equifinality that might plague any single-proxy investigation.

Why go 'beyond' diet, calories and economy, as quite a number of authors (including ourselves) have suggested? 'Beyond' can mean 'in addition to' but also 'apart from' and the latter often appeared to be the drift, with the implication that diet and economy is somehow boring whilst the rich tapestry of culture is fascinating. Diet and economy are fundamentally interesting and deeply embedded in culture, they are furthermore critical to the survival of any society. Additionally, understanding the effects of human economy upon environment, and *vice-versa* has significant modern day relevance. 'Beyond', however it was intended, should definitely be taken to mean augmentation to build on our knowledge, rather than fashionably abandon lines of enquiry for fear of being labelled 'deterministic'. Even where the nuances of cultural variability are the topic of interest, economic and environmental models can provide frames of reference that can help highlight particularly interesting behaviours. Rituals, taboos and cultural preferences are all easier to identify and elucidate in the context of a well-understood economic system.

Ever more nuanced understanding of cultural variability is not an unworthy goal and the resulting rich tapestry is interesting. Is a more nuanced view always the most productive route in academic research? Perhaps not. A recent provocatively entitled but cogently argued paper from the field of sociology (Healy 2017) makes the case that whilst there is nothing *per se* wrong with nuance and it has its place, the fashionable pursuit of it as an end in-and-of-itself is often not the best way to advance this field. Healy demonstrates that use of the word 'nuance' has exponentially increased within sociology publications. This trend is also observable in the world of archaeology and, whilst he is at pains to speak only for his own discipline, the power of his arguments speak equally well to our field. The full argument cannot be rehearsed here, as it dissects the value of nuance in both the aesthetics and strategy of academic discourse in considerable detail and outlines a number of 'nuance traps' (Healy 2017: 118). However, the key point is that *superfluous* nuance acts to inhibit abstraction, and abstraction is essential to good modelling and theory building. He also makes it clear that it could be a mistake directly to associate use of nuance with intelligence.

There is a place for detail and complexity, but there is *additionally* a pressing need for the abstraction that allows learning from one context to be applied to another. This is particularly important if archaeological research is to have relevance to other disciplines and valuable impact in the modern world. Approach must be dictated by the objectives of particular research. Cultural nuances themselves might be the subject of fascinating investigations, but in other cases superfluous detail adds uncalled-for complexity that inhibits the usefulness and applicability of good models and theory. Methodological critique should not be dogmatic, but take account of research aims and also scale. Greater levels of abstraction might be particularly appropriate to deal with a narrow but important question across a broad temporal and geographical scale. Such a circumstance is not uncommon in major palaeoeconomic research projects, the results of which can be highly impactful. Nothing prevents the simultaneous publication of the rich details of individual case studies along with discussion of interesting nuances.

Next Generation Challenges

Much of what will be discussed below will be common to many other disciplines that are adapting to changing technologies and approach. Archaeology, however, does have its own peculiarities and some aspects are unique. Foremost, archaeology has a very broad span across the arts, humanities, social sciences and sciences. Aspects of this are also seen in geography, but it is even more pronounced in archaeology. Even within the non-science portion of the subject one can trace different traditional roots of the subject within either history, classics or anthropology. It is technically oxymoronic to say that one discipline is interdisciplinary, but archaeology is effectively just that. This is a huge strength in terms of effective teamwork to bring to bear a range of approaches and techniques. It is also distinctly advantageous in mediating broader interdisciplinary impacts and communicating the results of research to the general public. The negative side of this, in terms of scientific philosophy, can be a risk of 'incommensurability' (Kuhn 1996), where researchers may not only have different theoretical views but end up without mutual comprehension in their modes of discourse. Archaeology has never quite reached that point, but came close during the 1990s' clash of processual and post-processual thought, and the subject needs to avoid this as ever more technicality and specialization is added to the scientific side of the subject. Perhaps as critical as appreciating possible tensions between humanities and science approaches, is avoiding tensions between studies that possess different scales in terms of scope and detail, or ones full of case-specific nuance versus those involving heavy abstraction for wide application. Such tensions can be avoided if critical faculty is applied when considering the appropriate pathway to particular research aims, rather than lazy recourse to a dogmatic theoretical position.

One thing the whole of archaeology shares is the need to obtain empirical data from fieldwork. Archaeological excavations are the source of the physical evidence analysed in all of the chapters in this book. Whether or not a biogeochemist or molecular geneticist sees themselves as undertaking archaeological work or not, if they need samples from the human past that are of known context and date, then they are dependent upon the good work of archaeologists. They should acknowledge this, and most readily do so now. In the early days of ancient genetic sampling, for instance (they were not the only ones guilty of this), there was at times a tendency to dismiss the role of field archaeologists as not having made a serious research contribution to a given study. It was not an uncommon assertion that they only needed listing in the acknowledgements since *all* they did was provide samples. This utterly failed to understand the depth of knowledge, skill and effort required to locate and painstakingly excavate the material and understand the significance of what had been found. This also ignored what the excavator might have been able to contribute to the better understanding of the results of analysis, had they been invited to contribute more widely. Fortunately, this is largely a problem of the past, and teams from 'big science' now appreciate the role of the archaeologist much better and understand the value they can add.

However, there are new challenges to archaeologists who direct field research. The job of a research excavation director is a challenging one at the best of times. They have to co-ordinate quite large teams of diggers, usually including students, alongside a number of specialists to conduct physically and mentally demanding work in often remote places. This takes place over months or years and involves considerable logistic organization and there is only one chance to get the scientific part right, since excavation is destructive and cannot be repeated in the way a laboratory experiment can. The archaeologist of the 1930s was largely interested in uncovering artefacts and structures, and understanding their context, stratigraphy and dating. Post-war, following the palaeoecononomy school and the 'New Archaeology', excavation became more complex with the need to understand more advanced methods to recover macro- and micro-remains and take specialist samples. Within the first part of the 21st century, this has ballooned with a vast potential array of techniques available that might all require specialist sampling. Some of this can be done *post-hoc*, but many sample types are best taken by specialists on-site, taking particular sampling precautions. Without question, the appointment of and collective consultation with appropriate specialists in advance of opening an excavation is best practice (see, for instance, English Heritage 2008 MoRPHE guidance).

It is increasingly challenging for individual directors to stay abreast of all of the techniques available and, even if they are, there is then the question of funding. Research councils and charitable bodies are funding large-scale projects that apply expensive new analytical techniques. Those projects are utterly reliant on excavated material. However, in general, there has been more reluctance from funders to back major excavation programmes. Such programmes will become ever more expensive as they integrate the full range of sampling now possible and, since excavation is destructive, there is an ethical imperative to carry out good sampling that matches up with the current (and future?) methods available. The backlog of appropriate existing material will become exhausted, and in some cases there will be significant 'black holes' in past work. Furthermore, suitable samples for some techniques just simply would not have been taken in the past. As a result, there must be a shift in funding focus in the future to include significant state-of-the-art excavation programmes that might once again be led by a drive to exploit the very most out of new techniques, as happened during the heyday of the palaeoeconomy school. Whilst this will be necessary to target important research questions and push the limits of new approaches, within major research excavations, vast amounts of new empirical data are also being generated by the professional, developer-funded sector, which takes many different forms in different countries. Such work produces very rich potential for additional research benefit and work is often carried out to a very high standard, within the limits imposed by the commercial context of the endeavour. Academic researchers are already very aware of the need to integrate efforts better with the cultural resource management and professional sectors, whose outputs are often in the form of so-called 'grey literature' archive reports. There are already major synthetic studies (e.g. Bradley et al. 2016) that explicitly extract the impactful work of development-led fieldwork, and some of this research has had a remarkable effect on our broader understanding of economic patterns in prehistory.

In addition to the increasing cost of field enquiry, the standard equipment of a well-found archaeology department has also expanded exponentially in range and expense. Though it is an increasingly scientific discipline, it frequently has a funding base more in line with the humanities and social sciences. Whilst expansion of analytical facilities within research-active archaeology departments is necessary, and some kinds of analysis or sample preparation are easily achievable within that setting, there are other advanced techniques where this is unlikely to be a realistic approach. Some forms of analysis involving complex mass spectrometry or genetic sequencing are much better supported within large science departments that have sufficient resilience in specialist technical support. There have certainly been cases of naïve work where archaeological researchers have unwisely believed that buying an expensive piece of equipment would in-and-of-itself open the door to the application of a new technique. Generally, these are not techniques where you can buy a 'black box' that reliably tells you the answer without need for sophisticated understanding of preparation, calibration and maintenance protocols, alongside a depth of experience and understanding to interpret the results. In most cases collaboration with large 'hard science' departments is the way forward, but even then care is needed. There has been problematic work done in that way too, where, for instance, an archaeologist working with a chemist still did not quite equate to the comprehension of an 'archaeological biogeochemist'. Collaboration with specialist laboratory groups is best to avoid naïve mistakes. However, whilst it is possible to enter into collaboration with those established leading groups through large research grants, there are many techniques where contract services are still not available. That is an important next step if various forms of analysis, for instance residue chemistry, are to become as widely applied as radiocarbon dating.

The final challenge to be noted in this book relates to the processing of ever increasing amounts of data, in many different forms. Much earlier archaeological work did not handle data well, even within the scientific end of the subject. In many cases, eyeballing trends in simple graphs was the order of the day. Embarrassingly, even basic statistical analysis is a relatively recent expectation to pass peer review for publication. In parts of the subject the situation has not much advanced. However, in other areas multivariate techniques such as principal components, correspondence or discriminative analysis or cladistics have become more commonplace. Approaches such as geometric morphometrics and genomics demand sophisticated multivariate techniques. Yet even this is the tip of the iceberg when considered against the availability of computational techniques like machine learning to exploit the full range of variability within multivariate datasets, and many other ways of carrying out sophisticated modelling. Whilst applications of all these techniques have been appearing in archaeological work very recently, and are needed to support the new techniques discussed in this book, the statistical skills base in archaeology is still very patchy. The majority of these advanced techniques are beyond the scope of even expensive standard statistical packages such as SPSS or MiniTab and often require familiarity with program languages such as 'R'. Other subjects, such as biology, faced similar challenges in the past that led to a rise in investment in 'bioinformatics' and 'computational biology' specialists. Something similar might be needed in archaeology, but that is a challenge. Archaeology departments are generally very much smaller than biology departments and lack the resources to invest to the same extent in such specialists. Some departments will and others will need to rely on collaboration and building that expertise into research project designs.

Conclusion

The legacy of the 'palaeoeconomy' and 'New Archaeology' schools is a sound one and the methods developed through the 1950s to the 1970s have been improved but are still of immense importance to modern research. Furthermore, the theoretical approaches to understanding past interactions of economy and environment are also still useful, if the models produced are tested against multiple lines of evidence rather than assumed to be true. Environment and economy do indeed determine limits of viability, but do not determine responses within those limits. However, a sound understanding of economic and environmental context vastly improves our chances of bringing to light fascinating social and cultural variation, rather than obscuring it. The addition of the range of techniques presented in this book has made economic archaeology even more productive because it has provided a wide range of independent lines of evidence against which to test models. These techniques are affected to differing levels by confounding factors such as site formation process or taphonomy and, thus, their combined use helps to cut through many past problems of equifinality. Some techniques, such as ancient genomics and stable isotope analysis, are providing us with clear answers to questions that the original palaeoeconomists perhaps never expected to be answered with any confidence. The future of the sub-discipline is bright; there are challenges related to our funding and skills base; all of these can be solved by good project design and appropriate collaboration. Research into the deep-time relationship between human economies and environmental change has never been of such heightened relevance.

References

Achilli, A., Olivieri, A., Soares, P., Lancioni, H., Kashani, B.H., Perego, U.A., et al. (2012) Mitochondrial genomes from modern horses reveal the major haplogroups that underwent domestication. *Proceedings of the National Academy of Sciences* 109(7), 2449–54.

Adams, D.C., Rohlf, F.J. and Slice, D.E. (2004) Geometric morphometrics: ten years of progress following the 'revolution'. *Italian Journal of Zoology* 71(1), 5–16.

Aguilera, M., Araus, J.L., Voltas, J., Rodríguez-Ariza, M.O., Molina, F., Rovira, N., et al. (2008) Stable carbon and nitrogen isotopes and quality traits of fossil cereal grains provide clues on sustainability at the beginnings of Mediterranean agriculture. *Rapid Communications in Mass Spectrometry* 22(11), 1653–63.

Aitken, M.J. (1990) *Science-Based Dating in Archaeology*. London: Longman.

Akhinzhanov S.M., Makarova L.A. and Nurumov T.N. (1992) *K istorii zhivotnovodstva i ohoty v Kazakhstane (po osteologicheskomu materialu iz arheologicheskih pamiatnikov eneolita i bronzy)*. Almaty: Gylym.

Albarella, U. and Serjeantson, D. (2002) A passion for pork: meat consumption at the British late Neolithic site of Durrington Walls. In: P. Miracle and N. Milner (eds), *Consuming Passions and Patterns of Consumption*. Cambridge: McDonald Institute for Archaeological Research, pp. 33–49.

Alexander, M.M., Gerrard, C.M., Gutiérrez, A. and Millard, A.R. (2015) Diet, society, and economy in late medieval Spain: stable isotope evidence from Muslims and Christians from Gandía, Valencia. *American Journal of Physical Anthropology* 156(2), 263–73.

Allaby, R.G. (2014) Genetics of early plant domestication: DNA and aDNA. In: C. Smith (ed.), *Encyclopedia of Global Archaeology*. New York: Springer. pp. 3004–7.

Allard, M.W., Young, D. and Huyen, Y. (1995) Detecting dinosaur DNA. *Science* 268 (5214), 1192.

Allentoft, M.E., Sikora, M., Sjögren, K.G., Rasmussen, S., Rasmussen, M., Stenderup, J., et al. (2015) Population genomics of Bronze Age Eurasia. *Nature* 522(7555), 167–72.

Ambrose, S.H., Buikstra, J. and Krueger, H.W. (2003) Status and gender differences in diet at Mound 72, Cahokia, revealed by isotopic analysis of bone. *Journal of Anthropological Archaeology* 22(3), 217–26.

Ammerman, A.J. and Cavalli-Sforza, L.L. (1973) A population model for the diffusion of early farming in Europe. In C. Renfrew (ed.) *The Explanation of Culture Change*. London: Duckworth, pp. 343–57.

Ananyevskaya, E., Aytqaly, A.K., Beisenov, A.Z., Dmitriev, E.A., Garbaras, A., Kukushkin, I.A., et al. (2018) Early indicators to C4 plant consumption in central Kazakhstan during the Final Bronze Age and Early Iron Age based on stable isotope analysis of human and animal bone collagen. *Archaeological Research in Asia* 15, 157–73.

Anastasiou, E. and Mitchell, P.D. (2013) Palaeopathology and genes: investigating the genetics of infectious diseases in excavated human skeletal remains and mummies from past populations. *Gene* 528(1), 33–40.

Anđelinović, Š., Anterić, I., Škorić, E. and Bašić, Ž. (2015) Skeleton changes induced by horse riding on medieval skeletal remains from Croatia. *The International Journal of the History of Sport* 32(5), 708–21.

Anthony, D.W. (1996) Bridling horse power: the domestication of the horse. In: S. Olsen (ed.), *Horses through Time*. Boulder, CO: Roberts Rinehart, pp. 57–82.

(2007) *The Horse, the Wheel, and Language: How Bronze-Age Riders from the Eurasian Steppes Shaped the Modern World*. Princeton, NJ: Princeton University Press.

(2009) The Sintashta Genesis: the roles of climate change, warfare, and long-distance trade. In: B.K. Hanks, K.M. Linduff (eds), *Social Complexity in Prehistoric Eurasia*. Cambridge: Cambridge University Press, pp. 47–73.

Anthony, D.W. and Brown, D.R. (1991) The origins of horseback riding. *Antiquity* 65(246), 22–38.

(2000) Eneolithic horse exploitation in the Eurasian steppes: diet, ritual and riding. *Antiquity* 74(283), 75–86.

(2011) The secondary products revolution, horse-riding, and mounted warfare. *Journal of World Prehistory* 24(2–3), 131–60.

Anthony, D.W., Brown, D.R. and George, C. (2006) Early horseback riding and warfare: the importance of the magpie around the neck. In: S.L. Olsen, S. Grant, A.M. Choyke and L. Bartosiewicz (eds), *Horses and Humans: The Evolution of Human-Equine Relationships*. Oxford: Archaeopress, pp. 137–56.

Anthony, D.W. and Ringe, D. (2015) The Indo-European homeland from linguistic and archaeological perspectives. *Annual Review of Linguistics* 1(1), 199–219.

Anthony, D., Telegin, D.Y. and Brown, D. (1991) The origin of horseback riding. *Scientific American* 265, 94–100.

Araus, J.L., Febrero, A., Buxó, R., Rodríguez-Ariza, M.O., Molina, F., Camalich, M.D., et al. (1997) Identification of ancient irrigation practices based on the carbon isotope discrimination of plant seeds: a case study from the south-east Iberian Peninsula. *Journal of Archaeological Science* 24(8), 729–40.

Arbogast, R.-M. (1994) *Premiers élevages néolithiques du nord-est de la France*. Liège: Etudes et Recherches Archéologiques de l'Université de Liège.

Arnold, J.R. and Libby, W.F. (1949) Age determinations by radiocarbon content: checks with samples of known age. *Science* 110(2869), 678–80.

Asouti, E. (2013) Evolution, history and the origin of agriculture: rethinking the Neolithic (plant) economies of South-west Asia. *Levant* 45(2), 210–18.

Bailey, G., Carter, P., Gamble, C. and Higgs, H. (1983) Epirus revisited: seasonality and inter-site variation in the Upper Palaeolithic of North-West Europe. In: G. Bailey (ed.) *Hunter-Gatherer Economy in Prehistory: A European Perspective*. Cambridge: Cambridge University Press, pp. 64–78.

Baillif-Ducros, C., Truc, M.C., Paresys, C. and Villotte, S. (2012) Approche méthodologique pour distinguer un ensemble lésionnel fiable de la pratique cavalière. Exemple du squelette de la tombe 11 du site de 'La Tuilerie' à Saint-Dizier (Haute-Marne), VIe siècle. *Bulletins et mémoires de la Société d'anthropologie de Paris* 24(1–2), 25–36.

Bakels, C.C. (1978) Four Linearbandkeramik Settlements and their Environment: a Palaeoecological Study of Sittard, Stein, Elsloo and Hienheim. *Analacta Praehistorica Leidensia* 11.

Balasse, M., Ambrose, S.H., Smith, A.B. and Price, T.D. (2002) The seasonal mobility model for prehistoric herders in the South-Western Cape of South Africa assessed by isotopic analysis of sheep tooth enamel. *Journal of Archaeological Science* 29, 917–32.

Balasse, M., Bocherens, H. and Mariotti, A. (1999) Intra-bone variability of collagen and apatite isotopic composition used as evidence of a change of diet. *Journal of Archaeological Science* 26, 593–8.

Balasse, M., Bocherens, H., Mariotti, A. and Ambrose, S.H. (2001) Detection of dietary changes by intra-tooth carbon and nitrogen isotopic analysis: an experimental study of dentine collagen of cattle (*Bos taurus*). *Journal of Archaeological Science* 28, 235–45.

Balasse, M. and Tresset, A. (2002) Early weaning of Neolithic domestic cattle (Bercy, France) revealed by intra-tooth variation in nitrogen isotope ratios. *Journal of Archaeological Science* 29(8), 853–9.

Ball, T., Chandler-Ezell, K., Dickau, R., Duncan, N., Hart, T.C., Iriarte, J., et al. (2016) Phytoliths as a toll for investigations of agricultural origins and dispersals around the world. *Journal of Archaeological Science* 68, 32–45.

Banner, J.L. (2004) Radiogenic isotopes: systematics and applications to earth surface processes and chemical stratigraphy. *Earth-Science Reviews* 65(3), 141–94.

Barker, A., Dombrosky, J., Chaput, D., Venables, B., Wolverton, S. and Stevens, S.M. (2015) Validation of a non-targeted LC-MS approach for identifying ancient proteins: method development on bone to improve artifact residue analysis. *Ethnobiology Letters* 6(1), 162–74.

Barker, A., Dombrosky, J., Venables, B. and Wolverton, S. (2018) Taphonomy and negative results: An integrated approach to ceramic-bound protein residue analysis. *Journal of Archaeological Science* 94, 32–43.

Barker, G.W.W. (1975) Prehistoric territories and economies in central Italy. In: E.S. Higgs (ed.), *Palaeoeconomy: Being the Second Volume of Papers in Economic Prehistory by Members and Associates of the British Academy Major Research Project in the Early History of Agriculture*. Cambridge: Cambridge University Press, pp. 111–76.

Barker, G. (1985) *Prehistoric Farming in Europe*. Cambridge: Cambridge University Press.

Barnard, H., Ambrose, S.H., Beehr, D.E., Forster, M.D., Lanehart, R.E., Malainey, M.E., et al. (2007) Mixed results of seven methods for organic residue

analysis applied to one vessel with the residue of a known foodstuff. *Journal of Archaeological Science* 34(1), 28–37.
Bar-Oz, G., Weissbrod, L. and Tsahar, E. (2014) Cats in recent Chinese study on cat domestication are commensal, not domesticated. *Proceedings of the National Academy of Sciences* 111(10), E876.
Barreta, J., Gutiérrez-Gil, B., Iñiguez, V., Saavedra, V., Chiri, R., Latorre, E. and Arranz, J.J. (2013) Analysis of mitochondrial DNA in Bolivian llama, alpaca and vicuna populations: A contribution to the phylogeny of the South American camelids. *Animal Genetics* 44(2), 158–68.
Barton, H. and Fullagar, R. (2006) Microscopy. In: R. Torrence and H. Barton (eds) *Ancient Starch Research*. Walnut Creek, CA: Left Coast Press, pp. 47–52.
Barton, H. and Torrence R (2015) Cooking up recipes for ancient starch: assessing current methodologies and looking to the future. *Journal of Archaeological Science* 56, 194–201.
Baum, T., Nendel, C., Jacomet, S., Colobran, M. and Ebersbach, R. (2016) 'Slash and burn' or 'weed and manure'? A modelling approach to explore hypotheses of late Neolithic crop cultivation in pre-alpine wetland sites. *Vegetation History and Archaeobotany* 25, 611–27.
Bello, S.M. and Soligo, C. (2008) A new method for the quantitative analysis of cutmark micromorphology. *Journal of Archaeological Science* 35(6), 1542–52.
Bellone, R.R., Holl, H., Setaluri, V., Devi, S., Maddodi, N., Archer, S., et al. (2013) Evidence for a retroviral insertion in TRPM1 as the cause of congenital stationary night blindness and leopard complex spotting in the horse. *PLoS One* 8(10), e78280.
Bender, M.M., Baerreis, D.A. and Steventon, R.L. (1981) Further light on carbon isotopes and Hopewell agriculture. *American Antiquity* 46(2), 346–53.
Bendrey, R. (2007a) New methods for the identification of evidence for bitting on horse remains from archaeological sites. *Journal of Archaeological Science* 34(7), 1036–50.
(2007b) Work- and age-related changes in an Iron Age horse skeleton from Danebury hillfort, Hampshire. *Archaeofauna* 16, 73–84.
(2011a) Identification of metal residues associated with bit-use on prehistoric horse teeth by scanning electron microscopy with energy dispersive X-ray microanalysis. *Journal of Archaeological Science* 38(11), 2989–94.
(2011b) Some like it hot: environmental determinism and the pastoral economies of the later prehistoric Eurasian steppe. *Pastoralism* 1(1), 1–16.
(2012) From wild horses to domestic horses: a European perspective. *World Archaeology* 44(1), 135–57.
(2014) Animal paleopathology. *Encyclopedia of Global Archaeology*. New York: Springer, pp. 258–65.
Bendrey, R., Hayes, T.E. and Palmer, M.R. (2009) Patterns of Iron Age horse supply: an analysis of strontium isotope ratios in teeth. *Archaeometry* 51, 140–50.
Bendrey, R., Lepetz, S., Zazzo, A., Balasse, M., Turbat, T., Giscard, P.-H., et al. (2016) Nomads, horses and mobility: an assessment of geographic origins of Iron Age horses found at Tsengel Khairkhan and Baga Turgen Gol (Mongolian Altai) based on oxygen isotope compositions of tooth enamel. In: M. Mashkour

and M. Beech (eds), *Archaeozoology of the Near East 9*. Oxford: Oxbow Books, pp. 262–72.

Bendrey, R., Vella, D., Zazzo, A., Balasse, M. and Lepetz, S. (2014) Exponentially decreasing tooth growth rate in horse teeth: implications for isotopic analyses. *Archaeometry* 57(6), 1104–24.

Benecke, N. (1994a) *Archäozoologische Studien zur Entwicklung der Haustierhaltung in Mitteleuropa und Südskandinavien von den Anfängen bis zum ausgehenden Mittelalter*. Berlin: Akademie Verlag.

(1994b) Zur Domestikation des Pferdes in Mittel- und Osteuropa: Einige neue archäozoologische Befunde. In: B. Hansel and S. Zimmer (eds) *Die Indogermanen und das pferd*. Budapest: Archaeolingua Alapítvány, pp. 123–44.

Benecke, N. and von den Driesch, A. (2003) Horse exploitation in the Kazakh steppes during the Eneolithic and Bronze Age. In: M. Levine, C. Renfrew and K. Boyle (eds) *Prehistoric Steppe Adaptation and the Horse*. Cambridge: McDonald Institute, pp. 69–82.

Bentley, R.A. (2006) Strontium isotopes from the earth to the archaeological skeleton: a review. *Journal of Archaeological Method and Theory* 13(3), 135–87.

Bentley, R.A., Krause, R., Price, T.D. and Kaufmann, B. (2003) Human mobility at the early Neolithic settlement of Vaihingen, Germany: evidence from strontium isotope analysis. *Archaeometry* 45(3), 471–86.

Benz, B.F. (2001) Archaeological evidence of teosinte domestication from Guilá Naquitz, Oaxaca. *Proceedings of the National Academy of Sciences* 98, 2104–6.

Berstan, R., Stott, A.W., Minnitt, S., Ramsey, C.B., Hedges, R.E.M. and Evershed, R.P. (2008) Direct dating of pottery from its organic residues: new precision using compound-specific carbon isotopes. *Antiquity* 82(317), 702–13.

Berthon, W., Tihanyi, B., Kis, L., Révész, L., Coqueugniot, H., Dutour, O. and Pálfi, G. (2018) Horse riding and the shape of the acetabulum: insights from the bioarchaeological analysis of early Hungarian mounted archers (10th Century). *International Journal of Osteoarchaeology*. https://doi.org/10.1002/oa.2723

Bethell, P.H., Goad, L.J., Evershed, R.P. and Ottaway, J. (1994) The study of molecular markers of human activity: the use of coprostanol in the soil as an indicator of human faecal material. *Journal of Archaeological Science* 21(5), 619–32.

Bettinger, R.L. (1991) *Hunter-Gatherers: Archaeological and Evolutionary Theory*. New York: Plenum Press.

Bickle, P. and Whittle, A. (eds) (2013) *The First Farmers of Central Europe*. Oxford: Oxbow.

Bieniek, A. (2002) Archaeobotanical analysis of some early Neolithic settlements in the Kujawy region, central Poland, with potential plant gathering activities emphasised. *Vegetation History and Archaeobotany* 11, 33–40.

Billamboz, A. (2006) Dendroarchäologische Untersuchungen in den neolithischen Ufersiedlungen von Hornstaad-Hörnle. In: B. Dieckmann, A. Harwath, J. Hoffstadt and A. Billamboz (eds), *Hornstaad-Hörnle IA. Die Befunde einer jungneolithischen Pfahlbausiedlung am westlichen Bodensee. Siedlungsarchäologie im Alpenvorland IX*. Stuttgart: Konrad Theiss, pp. 297–414.

Binford, L.R. (1968) Post-Pleistocene adaptations. In: S.R. Binford and L.R. Binford (eds) *New Perspectives in Archaeology*. Chicago, IL: Aldine, pp. 313–41.

(1978) *Nunamiut Ethnoarchaeology*. New York: Academic Press.

(1981) *Bones: Ancient Men and Modern Myths*. New York: Academic Press.
(1984) *The Faunal Remains from Klasies River Mouth*. New York: Academic Press.
Bintliff, J. (1981) Theory and reality in palaeoeconomy: some words of encouragement to the archaeologist. In: A. Sheridan and G. Bailey (eds), *Economic Archaeology*. Oxford: British Archaeological Reports, pp. 35–50.
Bird, A. (2007) Perceptions of epigenetics. *Nature* 447(7143), 396–8.
Blackman, L. (2016) The new biologies: Epigenetics, the microbiome and immunities. *Body and Society* 22(4), 3–18.
Boardman, S. and Jones, G. (1990) Experiments on the effects of charring on cereal plant components. *Journal of Archaeological Science* 17(1), 1–11.
Boessneck, J. (1969) Osteological differences between sheep (*Ovis aries* Linné) and goats (*Capra hircus* Linné). In: D. Brothwell and E. Higgs (eds), *Science in Archaeology*. London: Thames & Hudson, pp. 331–58.
Bogaard, A. (2002) Questioning the relevance of shifting cultivation to Neolithic farming in the loess belt of western-central Europe: evidence from the Hambach Forest experiment. *Vegetation History and Archaeobotany* 11, 155–68.
(2004) *Neolithic Farming in Central Europe*. London: Routledge.
(2011) *Plant Use and Crop Husbandry in an Early Neolithic Village: Vaihingen an der Enz, Baden-Württemberg, Frankfurter Archäologische Schriften*. Bonn: Habelt-Verlag.
(2012) Middening and manuring in Neolithic Europe: issues of plausibility, intensity and archaeological method. In: R.L. Jones (ed.), *Manure Matters: Historical, Archaeological and Ethnographic Perspectives*. Farnham: Ashgate, pp. 25–39.
Bogaard, A., Arbogast, R.-M., Ebersbach, R., Fraser, R.A., Knipper, C., Krahn, C., et al. (2017a) The Bandkeramik settlement of Vaihingen an der Enz, Kreis Ludwigsburg (Baden-Württemberg): an integrated perspective on land use, economy and diet. *Germania* 94, 1–60.
Bogaard, A., Ater, M. and Hodgson, J.G. (2018) Arable weeds as a case study in plant–human relationships beyond domestication. In: C. Stépanoff and J.-D. Vigne (eds), *Hybrid Communities: Biosocial Approaches to Domestication and Other Trans-Species Relationships*. London: Routledge, pp. 97–112.
Bogaard, A., Charles, M., Livarda, A., Ergun, M., Filipovic, D. and Jones, G. (2013) The archaeobotany of mid-later Neolithic occupation levels at Çatalhöyük. In: I. Hodder (ed.), *Humans and Landscapes of Çatalhöyük: Reports from the 2000–2008 seasons*. Los Angeles: Monographs of the Cotsen Institute of Archaeology, University of California at Los Angeles, pp. 93–128.
Bogaard, A., Fraser, R., Heaton, T.H., Wallace, M., Vaiglova, P., Charles, M., et al. (2014b) Crop manuring and intensive land management by Europe's first farmers. *Proceedings of the National Academy of Sciences* 110(31), 12589–94.
Bogaard, A. and Halstead, P. (2015) Subsistence practices and social routine in Neolithic southern Europe. In: C. Fowler, J. Harding, D. Hofmann (eds), *The Oxford Handbook of Neolithic Europe*. Oxford: Oxford University Press, pp. 385–410.
Bogaard, A., Heaton, T.H., Poulton, P. and Merbach, I. (2007) The impact of manuring on nitrogen isotope ratios in cereals: archaeological implications for reconstruction of diet and crop management practices. *Journal of Archaeological Science* 34(3), 335–43.

Bogaard, A., Henton, E., Evans, J.A., Twiss, K.C., Charles, M.P., Vaiglova, P. and Russell, N. (2014a) Locating land use at Neolithic Çatalhöyük, Turkey: the implications of $^{87}Sr/^{86}Sr$ signatures in plants and sheep tooth sequences. *Archaeometry* 56(5), 860–77.

Bogaard, A., Hodgson, J., Nitsch, E., Jones, G., Styring, A., Diffey, C., et al. (2016) Combining functional weed ecology and crop stable isotope ratios to identify cultivation intensity: a comparison of cereal production regimes in Haute Provence, France and Asturias, Spain. *Vegetation History and Archaeobotany* 25, 57–73.

Bogaard, A., Jacomet, S. and Schibler, J. (2017b) Towards an integrated bioarchaeological perspective on the central European Neolithic: understanding the pace and rhythm of social processes through comparative discussion of the western loess belt and Alpine foreland. In: P. Bickle, V. Cummings, D. Hofmann and J. Pollard (eds), *The Neolithic of Europe. Papers in Honour of Alasdair Whittle*. Oxford: Oxbow, pp. 120–42.

Bogaard, A. and Jones, G. (2007) Neolithic farming in Britain and central Europe: contrast or continuity? In: A. Whittle and V. Cummings (eds), *Going Over: The Mesolithic-Neolithic Transition in North-West Europe. Proceedings of the British Academy 144*. Oxford: Oxford University Press, pp. 357–75.

Bogaard, A., Krause, R. and Strien, H.-C. (2011) Towards a social geography of cultivation and plant use in an early farming community: Vaihingen an der Enz, south-west Germany. *Antiquity* 85, 395–416.

Bogaard, A. and Outram, A.K. (2013) Palaeodiet and beyond: stable isotopes in bioarchaeology. *World Archaeology* 45(3), 333–7.

Bogaard, A., Ryan, P., Yalman, N., Asouti, E., Twiss, K.C., Mazzucato, C. and Farid, S. (2014c) Assessing outdoor activities and their social implications at Çatalhöyük. In I. Hodder (ed.), *Integrating Çatalhöyük: themes from the 2000–2008 seasons*. Los Angeles: Monographs of the Cotsen Institute of Archaeology, University of California at Los Angeles, pp. 123–47.

Bogaard, A. and Styring, A. (2017) Plants, people and diet in the Neolithic of western Eurasia. In J. Lee-Thorp and A. Katzenberg (eds), *Oxford Handbook of Ancient Diet*. Oxford: Oxford University Press. DOI:10.1093/oxfordhb/9780199694013.013.45.

Bogaard, A., Styring, A., Ater, M., et al. (2018) From traditional farming in Morocco to early urban agroecology in northern Mesopotamia: combining present-day arable weed surveys and crop isotope analysis to reconstruct past agrosystems in (semi-) arid regions. *Environmental Archaeology* 23, 303–22. DOI: 10.1080/14614103.2016.1261217.

Bogucki, P.I. (1984) Ceramic sieves of the Linear Pottery Culture and their economic implications. *Oxford Journal of Archaeology* 3(1), 15–30.

Boivin, N., Fuller, D.Q. and Crowther, A. (2012). Old World globalization and the Columbian exchange: Comparison and contrast. *World Archaeology* 44(3), 452–69.

Bökönyi, S. (1974) *History of Domestic Animals in Central and Eastern Europe*. Budapest: Akadémiai Kiadó.

Bollongino, R., Edwards, C.J., Alt, K.W., Burger, J. and Bradley D.G. (2006) Early history of European domestic cattle as revealed by ancient DNA. *Biology Letters* 2, 155–9.

Bollongino, R., Elsner, J., Vigne, J.-D. and Burger, J. (2008) Y-SNPs do not indicate hybridisation between European aurochs and domestic cattle. *PloS ONE* 3, e3418.

Bolton, L.S. (2007) An investigation into why a selection of Bronze Age pots from Kazakhstan have been repaired with bronze staples. Unpublished undergraduate dissertation, University of Exeter.

Boserup, E. (1965) *The Conditions of Agricultural Growth*. Woking and London: Unwin Brothers.

(1981) *Population and Technology*. Oxford: Blackwell.

Bouckaert, R., Lemey, P., Dunn, M., Greenhill, S.J., Alekseyenko, A.V., et al. (2012) Mapping the origins and expansion of the Indo-European language family. *Science* 337, 957–60.

Bowen, G.J. (2010) Isoscapes: spatial pattern in isotopic biogeochemistry. *Annual Review of Earth and Planetary Sciences* 38, 161–87.

Bowen, G.J. and Wilkinson, B. (2002) Spatial distribution of $\delta^{18}O$ in meteoric precipitation. *Geology* 30, 315–18.

Bradley, D.G. (2006) Documenting domestication: reading animal genetic texts. In: M.A. Zeder, D.G. Bradley, E. Emschwiller and B.D. Smith (eds), *Documenting Domestication: New Genetic and Archaeological Paradigms*. Berkeley: University of California Press, pp. 273–8.

Bradley, D.G., MacHugh, D.E., Cunningham, P. and Loftus, R.T. (1996) Mitochondrial diversity and the origins of African and European cattle. *Proceedings of the National Academy of Sciences* 93(10), 5131–5.

Bradley, R., Haselgrove, C., Vander Linden, M. and Webley, L. (2016) *The Later Prehistory of Western Europe: The Evidence of Development-Led Fieldwork*. Oxford: Oxford University Press.

Bramanti, B., Thomas, M.G., Haak, W., Unterländer, M., Jores, P., Tambets, K., et al. (2009) Genetic discontinuity between local hunter-gatherers and central Europe's first farmers. *Science* 326(5949), 137–40.

Brill, R.H. and Wampler, J.M. (1965) Isotope ratios in archaeological objects of lead. In: *Application of science in examination of works of art. Proceedings of the seminar: September 7–16, 1965*. Boston, MA: Museum of Fine Arts, pp. 155–66.

(1967) Isotope studies of ancient lead. *American Journal of Archaeology* 71(1), 63–77.

Britton, K., Grimes, V., Niven, L., Steele, T.E., McPherron, S., Soressi, M., et al. (2011) Strontium isotope evidence for migration in late Pleistocene Rangifer: implications for Neanderthal hunting strategies at the Middle Palaeolithic site of Jonzac, France. *Journal of Human Evolution* 61(2), 176–85.

Brochier, J.É. (2013) The use and abuse of culling profiles in recent zooarchaeological studies: some methodological comments on 'frequency correction' and its consequences. *Journal of Archaeological Science* 40(2), 1416–20.

Brombacher, C. (1997) Archaeobotanical investigations of Late Neolithic lakeshore settlements (Lake Biel, Switzerland). *Vegetation History and Archaeobotany* 6, 167–86.

Bronson, B. 1972. Farm labor and the evolution of food production. In: B. Spooner (ed.), *Population Growth: Anthropological Implications*. Cambridge, MA: MIT Press, pp. 190–218.

Brown, D. and Anthony, D. (1998) Bit wear, horseback riding and the Botai site in Kazakhstan. *Journal of Archaeological Science* 25(4), 331–47.

Brown, T.A. (2001) Ancient DNA. In: D.R. Brothwell and A.M. Pollard (eds), *Handbook of Archaeological Sciences*. Chichester: Wiley, pp. 301–12.

Brown, T. and Brown, K. (2011) *Biomolecular Archaeology: An Introduction*. Oxford: Wiley-Blackwell.

Buckland, P.C., Amorosi, T., Barlow, L.K., Dugmore, A.J., Mayewski, P.A., McGovern, T.H., et al. (1996) Bioarchaeological and climatological evidence for the fate of Norse farmers in medieval Greenland. *Antiquity* 70(267), 88–96.

Buckley, M., Fraser, S., Herman, J., Melton, N.D., Mulville, J. and Pálsdóttir, A.H. (2014) Species identification of archaeological marine mammals using collagen fingerprinting. *Journal of Archaeological Science* 41, 631–41.

Buckley, M., Kansa, S.W., Howard, S., Campbell, S., Thomas-Oates, J. and Collins, M. (2010) Distinguishing between archaeological sheep and goat bones using a single collagen peptide. *Journal of Archaeological Science* 37(1), 13–20.

Budd, P., Montgomery, J., Evans, J. and Barreiro, B. (2000) Human tooth enamel as a record of the comparative lead exposure of prehistoric and modern people. *Science of the Total Environment* 263(1–3), 1–10.

Bull, I.D., Simpson, I.A., van Bergen, P.F. and Evershed, R.P. (1999) Muck 'n' molecules: organic geochemical methods for detecting ancient manuring. *Antiquity* 73(279), 86–96.

Bunning, S.L., Jones, G. and Brown, T.A. (2012) Next generation sequencing of DNA in 3300-year-old charred cereal grains. *Journal of Archaeological Science* 39(8), 2780–4.

Burger, O., Hamilton, M.J. and Walker, R. (2005) The prey as patch model: optimal handling of resources with diminishing returns. *Journal of Archaeological Science* 32(8), 1147–58.

Burger, J., Kirchner, M., Bramanti, B., Haak, W. and Thomas, M.G. (2007) Absence of the lactase-persistence-associated allele in early Neolithic Europeans. *Proceedings of the National Academy of Sciences* 104, 3736–41.

Burton, J.H. and Hahn, R. (2016) Assessing the 'local' $^{87}Sr/^{86}Sr$ ratio for humans. In: G. Grupe and G.V. McGlynn (eds) *Isotopic Landscapes in Bioarchaeology*. Heidelberg: Springer, pp. 113–21.

Buttler, W. and Haberey, W. (1936) *Die Bandkeramische Ansiedlung bei Köln-Lindenthal*. Berlin: de Gruyter.

Buxó, R. (2007) Early agriculture in central and southern Spain. In: S. Colledge and J. Conolly (eds), *The Origins and Spread of Domestic Plants in Southwest Asia and Europe*. Walnut Creek, CA: Left Coast Press, pp. 155–71.

Campos, P.F., Willerslev, E., Sher, A., Orlando, L., Axelsson, E., Tikhonov, A., et al. (2010) Ancient DNA analyses exclude humans as the driving force behind late Pleistocene musk ox (*Ovibos moschatus*) population dynamics. *Proceedings of the National Academy of Sciences* 107(12), 5675–80.

Cannon, D.Y. (1987) *Marine Fish Osteology: A Manual for Archaeologists*. Burnaby: Simon Fraser University.

Cardini, A., Seetah, K. and Barker, G. (2015) How many specimens do I need? Sampling error in geometric morphometrics: Testing the sensitivity of means and variances in simple randomized selection experiments. *Zoomorphology* 134(2), 149–63.

Carniero, R.L. (1960) Slash-and-burn agriculture: a closer look at its implications for settlement patterns. In: A.F.C. Wallace (ed.), *Men and Cultures*. Philadelphia: University of Pennsylvania Press, pp. 229–34.

Carter, R.J. (1997) Age estimation of the roe deer (*Capreolus capreolus*) mandibles from the Mesolithic site of Star Carr, Yorkshire, based on radiographs of mandibular tooth development. *Journal of Zoology* 241(3), 495–502.

(1998) Reassessment of seasonality at the early Mesolithic site of Star Carr, Yorkshire based on radiographs of mandibular tooth development in red deer (*Cervus elaphus*). *Journal of Archaeological Science* 25(9), 851–6.

Casanova, E., Knowles, T.D., Williams, C., Crump, M.P. and Evershed, R.P. (2018) Practical considerations in high-precision compound-specific radiocarbon analyses: eliminating the effects of solvent and sample cross-contamination on accuracy and precision. *Analytical Chemistry* 90(18), 11025–32.

Cashdan, E. (1983a) Territoriality among human foragers: ecological models and an application to four Bushman groups. *Current Anthropology* 24(1), 47–55.

(1983b) Reply. *Current Anthropology* 24(1), 62–6.

Castillo, C. (2011) Rice in Thailand: the archaeobotanical contribution. *Rice* 4, 114–20.

Caulfield, S. (1978) Star Carr – an alternative view. *Irish Archaeological Research Forum* 5, 15–22.

Chang, C. (2006) The grass is greener on the other side: a study of pastoral mobility on the Eurasian steppe of southeastern Kazakhstan. In: F. Sellet, R. Greaves and P.-L. Yu (eds), *Archaeology and Ethnoarchaeology of Mobility*. Gainesville: University Press of Florida, pp. 184–200.

Chaplin, R.E. (1971) *The Study of Animal Bones from Archaeological Sites*. London: Seminar Press.

Charles, M., Bogaard, A., Jones, G., Hodgson, J. and Halstead, P. (2002) Ecological investigation of intensive cereal cultivation in the mountains of Asturias, NW Spain. *Vegetation History and Archaeobotany* 11, 133–42.

Charles, M., Forster, E., Wallace, M. and Jones, G. (2015) 'Nor ever lightning char thy grain': establishing archaeologically relevant charring conditions and their effect on glume wheat grain morphology. *Science and Technology of Archaeological Research* 1, DOI: 10.1179/2054892315Y.0000000008.

Charnov, E.L. (1976) Optimal foraging, the marginal value theorem. *Theoretical Population Biology* 9(2), 129–36.

Chen, Y.S., Torroni, A., Excoffier, L., Santachiara-Benerecetti, A.S. and Wallace, D.C. (1995) Analysis of mtDNA variation in African populations reveals the most ancient of all human continent-specific haplogroups. *American Journal of Human Genetics* 57(1), 133–49.

Childe, V.G. (1929) *The Danube in Prehistory*. Oxford: Clarendon Press.

(1954) *What Happened in History*. Harmsondsworth: Penguin.

(1957) *The Dawn of European Civilization*. London: Routledge.

Chisholm, M. (1962) *Rural Settlement and Land Use*. London: Hutchinson.

Clark, G. (1939) *Archaeology and Society: Reconstructing the Prehistoric Past*. London: Methuen.

Clark, G. (1957) *Archaeology and Society: Reconstructing the Prehistoric Past*, 3rd edn. London: Methuen.
Clark, J.D.G. (1942) Bees in antiquity. *Antiquity* 16, 208–15.
(1947a) Forest clearance and prehistoric farming. *Economic History Review*, 17, 45–51.
(1947b) Whales as an economic factor in prehistoric Europe. *Antiquity* 21, 84–104.
(1952) *Prehistoric Europe: The Economic Basis*. London: Methuen.
(1953) The economic approach to prehistory: Albert Reckitt Archaeological lecture 1953. *Proceedings of the British Academy* 39, 215–38.
(1954) *Excavations at Star Carr: An Early Mesolithic Site at Seamer Near Scarborough, Yorkshire*. Cambridge: Cambridge University Press.
(1961) *World Prehistory: An Outline*. Cambridge: Cambridge University Press.
(1972a) Foreword. In: E.S. Higgs (ed.), *Papers in Economic Prehistory: Studies by Members and Associates of the British Academy Major Research Project in the Early History of Agriculture*. Cambridge: Cambridge University Press, pp. vii–x.
(1972b) *Star Carr: A Case Study in Bioarchaeology*. Reading, MA: Addison-Wesley.
(1989) *Prehistory and Cambridge and Beyond*. Cambridge: Cambridge University Press.
Clarke, D. (1976) Mesolithic Europe: the economic basis. In: D. de G. Sieveking, I.H. Longworth and K.E. Wilson (eds), *Problems in Economic and Social Archaeology*. London: Duckworth, pp. 449–81.
Claßen, E. (2011) *Siedlungen der Bandkeramik bei Königshoven*. Rheinische Ausgrabungen 64.
Clayton, F., Sealy, J. and Pfeiffer, S. (2006) Weaning age among foragers at Matjes River Rock Shelter, South Africa, from stable nitrogen and carbon isotope analyses. *American Journal of Physical Anthropology* 129(2), 311–17.
Codding, B.F. and Bird, D.W. (2015) Behavioral ecology and the future of archaeological science. *Journal of Archaeological Science* 56, 9–20.
Cohen, A. and Serjeantson, D. (1986) *A Manual for the Identification of Bird Bones from Archaeological Sites*. London: Archetype.
Coles, J. (1973) *Archaeology by Experiment*. London: Hutchinson.
(1979) *Experimental Archaeology*. London: Academic Press.
Collins, M., Buckley, M., Grundy, H.H., Thomas-Oates, J., Wilson, J. and van Doorn, N. (2010) ZooMS: the collagen barcode and fingerprints. *Spectroscopy Europe* 22(2), 6.
Collins, M.J. and Copeland, L. (2011) Ancient starch: Cooked or just old? *Proceedings of the National Academy of Sciences* 108, E145.
Condamin, J., Formenti, F., Metais, M.O., Michel, M. and Blond, P. (1976) The application of gas chromatography to the tracing of oil in ancient amphorae. *Archaeometry* 18(2), 195–201.
Conklin, H.C. (1959) Population-land balance under systems of tropical forest agriculture. *Proceedings Pacific Science Congress* 7, 63.
Cook, W.R. (2011) Damage by the bit to the equine interdental space and second lower premolar. *Equine Veterinary Education* 23(7), 355–60.
Cooper, A. and Poinar, H.N. (2000) Ancient DNA: do it right or not at all. *Science* 5482(1139), 416.

Copley, M.S., Berstan, R., Dudd, S.N., Docherty, G., Mukherjee, A. J., Straker, V., Payne, S. and Evershed, R.P. (2003) Direct chemical evidence for widespread dairying in prehistoric Britain. *PNAS* 100, 1524–9.

Copley, M.S., Berstan, R., Mukherjee, A.J., Dudd, S.N., Straker, V., Payne, S. and Evershed, R.P. (2005a) Dairying in antiquity. III. Evidence from absorbed lipid residues dating to the British Neolithic. *Journal of Archaeological Science* 32, 523–46.

Copley, M.S., Berstan, R., Straker, V., Payne, S. and Evershed, R.P. (2005b) Dairying in antiquity. II. Evidence from absorbed lipid residues dating to the British Bronze Age. *Journal of Archaeological Science* 32, 505–21.

Copley, M.S., Berstan, R., Dudd, S. N., Straker, V., Payne, S. and Evershed, R.P. (2005c) Dairying in antiquity. I. Evidence from absorbed lipid residues dating to the British Iron Age. *Journal of Archaeological Science* 32, 485–503.

Copley, M.S., Evershed, R.P., Rose, P.J., Clapham, A., Edwards, D.N. and Horton, M.C. (2001) Processing palm fruits in the Nile Valley – biomolecular evidence from Qasr Ibrim. *Antiquity* 75, 538–42.

Corr, L.T., Richards, M.P., Jim, S., Ambrose, S.H., Mackie A. and Evershed, R.P. (2009) Probing dietary change of Kwäd̨ąy Dän Ts'ìnchį, an ancient glacier body from British Columbia: II. Deconvoluting whole skin and bone collagen δ^{13}C values via carbon isotope analysis of individual amino acids. *Journal of Archaeological Science* 36, 12–18.

Craig, H. (1953) The geochemistry of the stable carbon isotopes. *Geochimica et Cosmochimica Acta* 3(2–3), 53–92.

Craig, O.E., Chapman, J., Figler, A., Patay, P., Taylor, G. and Collins, M.J. (2003) 'Milk jugs' and other myths of the copper age of central Europe. *European Journal of Archaeology* 6(3), 251–65.

Craig, O.E., Forster, M., Andersen, S.H., Koch, E., Crombé, P., Milner, N.J., et al. (2007) Molecular and isotopic demonstration of the processing of aquatic products in northern European prehistoric pottery. *Archaeometry* 49(1), 135–52.

Craig, O.E., Love, G.D., Isaksson, S., Taylor, G. and Snape, C.E. (2004) Stable carbon isotopic characterisation of free and bound lipid constituents of archaeological ceramic vessels released by solvent extraction, alkaline hydrolysis and catalytic hydropyrolysis. *Journal of Analytical and Applied Pyrolysis* 71(2), 613–34.

Craig, O., Mulville, J., Pearson, M.P., Sokol, R., Gelsthorpe, K., Stacey, R. and Collins, M. (2000) Archaeology: detecting milk proteins in ancient pots. *Nature* 408(6810), 312.

Cramp, L.J.E. and Evershed, R.P. (2014) Reconstructing aquatic resource exploitation in human prehistory using lipid biomarkers and stable isotopes. In: H.D. Holland and K.K. Turekian (eds), *Treatise on Geochemistry: Archaeology and Anthropology*. Oxford and Amsterdam: Elsevier, pp. 319–39

Cramp, L.J., Jones, J., Sheridan, A., Smyth, J., Whelton, H., Mulville, J., et al. (2014) Immediate replacement of fishing with dairying by the earliest farmers of the northeast Atlantic archipelagos. *Proceedings of the Royal Society B: Biological Sciences* 281(1780), 20132372.

Crowther, A. (2012) The differential survival of native starch during cooking and implications for archaeological analyses: a review. *Archaeological and Anthropological Sciences* 4, 221–35.

Crowther, A., Haslam, M., Oakden, N., Walde, D. and Mercader, J. (2014) Documenting contamination in ancient starch laboratories. *Journal of Archaeological Science* 49, 90–104.

Cucchi, T., Mohaseb, A., Peigné, S., Debue, K., Orlando, L. and Mashkour, M. (2017) Detecting taxonomic and phylogenetic signals in equid cheek teeth: towards new palaeontological and archaeological proxies. *Royal Society Open Science* 4(4), 160997.

Cunliffe, B. (2015) *By Steppe, Desert, and Ocean: The Birth of Eurasia*. Oxford: Oxford University Press.

Currat, M. and Excoffier, L. (2004) Modern humans did not admix with Neanderthals during their range expansion into Europe. *PLoS Biology* 2(12), e421.

Dahm, R. (2008) Discovering DNA: Friedrich Miescher and the early years of nucleic acid research. *Human Genetics* 122(6), 565–81.

Damgaard, P.d.B., Marchi, N., Rasmussen, S., Peyrot, M., Renaud, G., Korneliussen, T., et al. (2018b) 137 ancient human genomes from across the Eurasian steppes. *Nature* 557(7705), 369–74.

Damgaard, P.d.B., Martiniano, R., Kamm, J., Moreno-Mayar, J.V., Kroonen, G., Peyrot, M., et al. (2018a) The first horse herders and the impact of Early Bronze Age steppe expansions into Asia. *Science*, DOI: 10.1126/science.aar7711.

Dansgaard, W. (1964) Stable isotopes in precipitation. *Tellus* 16(4), 436–68.

Davidson, I. (1981) Can we study prehistoric economy for fisher-gatherer-hunters? A historical approach to Cambridge 'palaeoeconomy'. In: A. Sheridan and G. Bailey (eds), *Economic Archaeology*. Oxford: British Archaeological Reports, pp. 17–33.

Davis, S.J. (1987) *The Archaeology of Animals*. London: Batsford.

Delhon, C., Martin, L., Argant, J. and Thiébault, S. (2008) Shepherds and plants in the Alps: multi-proxy archaeobotanical analysis of Neolithic dung from 'La Grande Rivoire' (Isère, France). *Journal of Archaeological Science* 35, 2937–52.

Denham, T.P., Haberle, S.G., Lentfer, C., Fullagar, R., Field, J., Therin, M., et al. (2003) Origins of agriculture at Kuk Swamp in the Highlands of New Guinea. *Science* 301, 189–93.

Denhardt, D. (2017) Effect of stress on human biology: epigenetics, adaptation, inheritance and social significance. *Journal of Cellular Physiology*. DOI: 10.1002/jcp.25837.

DeNiro, M.J. and Epstein, S. (1976) You are what you eat (plus a few ‰): the carbon isotope cycle in food chains. *Geological Society of America* 6, 834.

(1978) Influence of diet on the distribution of carbon isotopes in animals. *Geochimica et Cosmochimica Acta* 42(5), 495–506.

(1981) Influence of diet on the distribution of nitrogen isotopes in animals. *Geochimica et Cosmochimica Acta* 45(3), 341–51.

Dennell, R.W. (1972) The interpretation of plant remains: Bulgaria. In: E.S. Higgs (ed.), *Papers in Economic Prehistory: Studies by Members and Associates of the British Academy Major Research Project in the Early History of Agriculture*. Cambridge: Cambridge University Press, pp. 149–59.

(1976) The economic importance of plant resources represented on archaeological sites. *Journal of Archaeological Science* 3(3), 229–47.

(1983) *European Economic Prehistory: A New Approach*. London: Academic Press.

(1985) The hunter/gatherer/agricultural frontier in prehistoric temperate Europe. In: S. Green and S.M. Perlman (eds), *The Archaeology of Frontiers and Boundaries*. New York: Academic Press, pp. 113–40.

Dennell, R.W. and Webley, D. (1975) Prehistoric settlement and land use in southern Bulgaria. In: E.S. Higgs (ed.), *Palaeoeconomy: Being the Second Volume of Papers in Economic Prehistory by Members and Associates of the British Academy Major Research Project in the Early History of Agriculture*. Cambridge: Cambridge University Press, pp. 97–110.

Deschler-Erb, S. and Marti-Grädel, E. (2004) Viehhaltung und Jagd. Ergebnisse der Untersuchung der handaufgelesenen Tierknochen. In: S. Jacomet, U. Leuzinger and J. Schibler (eds), *Die jungsteinzeitliche Seeufersiedlung Arbon Bleiche 3: Umwelt und Wirtschaft*. Frauenfeld: Amt für Archäologie des Kantons Thurgau, pp. 158–252.

Deschler-Erb, S., Marti-Grädel, E. and Schibler, J. (2002) Bukranien in der jungsteinzeitlichen Siedlung Arbon-Bleiche 3: Status, Kult oder Zauber? *Archäologie der Schweiz* 25: 25–33.

Dickau, R., Bruno, M.C., Iriarte, J., Prümers, H., Betancourt, C.J., Holst, I. and Mayle, F.E. (2012) Diversity of cultivars and other plant resources used at habitation sites in the Llanos de Mojos, Beni, Bolivia: evidence from macrobotanical remains, starch and phytoliths. *Journal of Archaeological Science* 39, 357–70.

Dieckmann, B., Maier, U. and Vogt, R. (2001) Hornstaad – Zur inneren Dynamik einer jungneolithischen Dorfanlage am westlichen Bodensee. In: A. Lippert, M. Schultz, S. Shennan and M. Teschler-Nicola (eds) *Mensch und Umwelt während des Neolithikums und der Frühbronzezeit in Mitteleuropa*. Rahden: Verlag Marie-Leidorf GmbH, pp. 29–51.

Doebley, J. (2004) The genetics of maize evolution. *Annual Review of Genetics* 38, 37–59.

Döhle, H.-J. (1997). Zum Stand der Untersuchungen an neolithischen Tierknochen aus Mitteldeutschland. *Jahresschrift für mitteldeutsche Vorgeschichte* 79: 111–47.

Dole, M., Lane, G.A., Rudd, D.P. and Zaukelies, D.A. (1954) Isotopic composition of atmospheric oxygen and nitrogen. *Geochimica et Cosmochimica Acta* 6(2), 65–78.

Dong, Y., Li, C., Luan, F., Li, Z., Li, H., Cui, Y., et al. (2015) Low mitochondrial DNA diversity in an ancient population from China: insight into social organization at the Fujia site. *Human Biology* 87(1), 71–84.

Downs, E.F. and Lowenstein, J.M. (1995) Identification of archaeological blood proteins: A cautionary note. *Journal of Archaeological Science* 22(1), 11–16.

Dudd, S.N. and Evershed, R.P. (1998) Direct demonstration of milk as an element of archaeological economies. *Science* 282(5393), 1478–81.

Dudd, S.N., Evershed, R.P. and Gibson, A.M. (1999) Evidence for varying patterns of exploitation of animal products in different prehistoric pottery traditions based on lipids preserved in surface and absorbed residues. *Journal of Archaeological Science* 26(12), 1473–82.

Dungait, J.A.J., Doherty, G., Straker, V. and Evershed, R.P. (2010) Seasonal variations in bulk tissue, fatty acid and monosaccharide $\delta^{13}C$ values of leaves from mesotrophic grassland plant communities under different grazing managements. *Phytochemistry* 71, 415–28.

Dungait, J.A., Stear, N.A., van Dongen, B.E., Bol, R. and Evershed, R.P. (2008) Off-line pyrolysis and compound-specific stable carbon isotope analysis of lignin moieties: a new method for determining the fate of lignin residues in soil. *Rapid Communications in Mass Spectrometry* 22(11), 1631–9.

Dunne, J., Evershed, R.P., Salque, M., Cramp, L., Bruni, S., Ryan, K., et al. (2012) First dairying in green Saharan Africa in the fifth millennium BC. *Nature* 486(7403), 390–4.

Dunne, J., Mercuri, A.M., Evershed, R.P., Bruni, S. and di Lernia, S. (2016) Earliest direct evidence of plant processing in prehistoric Saharan pottery. *Nature Plants* 3(1), 16194.

Dupras, T.L. and Tocheri, M.W. (2007) Reconstructing infant weaning histories at Roman period Kellis, Egypt using stable isotope analysis of dentition. *American Journal of Physical Anthropology* 134(1), 63–74.

Dyson-Hudson, R. and Smith, E.A. (1978) Human territoriality: an ecological reassessment. *American Anthropologist* 80(1), 21–41.

Ebersbach, R. (2002) *Von Bauern und Rindern. Eine Ökosystemanalyse zur Bedeutung der Rinderhaltung in bäuerlichen Gesellschaften als Grundlage zur Modellbildung im Neolithikum.* Basler Beiträge zur Archäologie 15.

Ebersbach, R., Ruckstuhl, B. and Bleicher, N. (2015) *Zürich 'Mozartstrasse', Band 5. Die neolithischen Befunde und die Dendroarchäologie.* Zürich und Egg: Fotorotar.

Ebersbach, R. and Schade, C. (2004) Modelling the intensity of Linear Pottery land use – an example from the Mörlener Bucht in the Wetterau Basin, Hesse, Germany. In: S. Wien (ed.), *Enter the Past – the E-way into the Four Dimensions of Cultural Heritage.* Oxford: British Archaeological Reports, pp. 259–73.

Edwards, C.J., Bollongino, R., Scheu, A., Chamberlain, A., Tresset, A., Vigne, J.D., et al. (2007) Mitochondrial DNA analysis shows a Near Eastern Neolithic origin for domestic cattle and no indication of domestication of European aurochs. *Proceedings of the Royal Society of London B: Biological Sciences* 274(1616), 1377–85.

Eerkens, J.W. and Bartelink, E.J. (2013) Sex-biased weaning and early childhood diet among middle Holocene hunter-gatherers in Central California. *American Journal of Physical Anthropology* 152(4), 471–83.

Eerkens, J.W., Berget, A.G. and Bartelink, E.J. (2011) Estimating weaning and early childhood diet from serial micro-samples of dentin collagen. *Journal of Archaeological Science* 38(11), 3101–11.

Ellis, M.A., Merritt, C.W., Novak, S.A. and Dixon, K.J. (2011) The signature of starvation: a comparison of bone processing at a Chinese encampment in Montana and the Donner Party Camp in California. *Historical Archaeology* 45(2), 97–112.

Emlen, J.M. (1966) The role of time and energy in food preference. *American Naturalist* 100, 611–17.

Emswiller, E. (2006) Genetic data and plant domestication. In: M.A. Zeder, D.G. Bradley, E. Emschwiller and B.D. Smith (eds), *Documenting Domestication: New Genetic and Archaeological Paradigms.* Berkeley: University of California Press, pp. 99–122.

English Heritage (2008) *Management of Research Projects in the Historic Environment: PPN 3: Archaeological Excavation*. London: English Heritage.

Enk, J.M., Devault, A.M., Kuch, M., Murgha, Y.E., Rouillard, J.M. and Poinar, H.N. (2014) Ancient whole genome enrichment using baits built from modern DNA. *Molecular Biology and Evolution* 31(5), 1292–4.

Erasmus, U. (1986) *Fat and Oils: the Complete Guide to Fats and Oils in Health and Nutrition*. Vancouver: Alive Books.

Eren, M.I. and Outram, A.K. (2012) Preface to 'Faunal Extinctions and Introductions'. *World Archaeology* 44(1), 1–2.

Ericson, J.E. (1985) Strontium isotope characterization in the study of prehistoric human ecology. *Journal of Human Evolution* 14(5), 503–14.

Ervynck, A., Lentacker, A., Müldner, G., Richards, M. and Dobney, K. (2007) An investigation into the transition from forest dwelling pigs to farm animals in medieval Flanders, Belgium. In: U. Albarella, K. Dobney, A. Ervynck and P. Rowley-Conwy (eds), *Pigs and Humans, 10,000 Years of Interaction*. Oxford: Oxford University Press, pp. 171–93.

Evans, J.A., Pashley, V., Richards, G.J., Brereton, N. and Knowles, T.G. (2015) Geogenic lead isotope signatures from meat products in Great Britain: Potential for use in food authentication and supply chain traceability. *Science of the Total Environment* 537, 447–52.

Evershed, R.P. (2008a) Organic residue analysis in archaeology: the archaeological biomarker revolution. *Archaeometry* 50(6), 895–924.

(2008b) Experimental approaches to the interpretation of absorbed organic residues in archaeological ceramics. *World Archaeology* 40(1), 26–47.

Evershed, R.P., Arnot, K.I., Collister, J., Eglinton, G. and Charters, S. (1994) Application of isotope ratio monitoring gas chromatography–mass spectrometry to the analysis of organic residues of archaeological origin. *Analyst* 119(5), 909–14.

Evershed, R.P., Bethell, P.H., Reynolds, P.J. and Walsh, N.J. (1997b) 5β-Stigmastanol and related 5β-stanols as biomarkers of manuring: analysis of modern experimental material and assessment of the archaeological potential. *Journal of Archaeological Science* 24(6), 485–95.

Evershed, R.P., Dudd, S.N., Charters, S., Mottram, H.R., Stott, A.W., Raven, A., et al. (1999) Lipids as carriers of anthropogenic signals from prehistory. *Philosophical Transactions of the Royal Society* 354, 19–31.

Evershed, R.P., Dudd, S.N., Lockheart, M.J. and Jim, S. (2001) Lipids in archaeology. In: D.R. Brothwell and A.M. Pollard (eds), *Handbook of Archaeological Sciences*. Oxford: Wiley, pp. 331–49.

Evershed, R.P., Heron C. and Goad, L.J. (1991) Epicuticular wax components preserved in potsherds as chemical indicators of leafy vegetables in ancient diets. *Antiquity* 65, 540–4.

Evershed, R.P., Jerman, K. and Eglinton, G. (1985) Pine wood origin for pitch from the Mary Rose. *Nature* 314, 528–30.

Evershed, R.P., Payne, S., Sherratt, A.G., Copley, M.S., Coolidge, J., Urem-Kotsu, D., et al. (2008) Earliest date for milk use in the Near East and southeastern Europe linked to cattle herding. *Nature* 455, 528–31.

Evershed, R.P., Van Bergen, P.F., Peakman, T.M., Leigh-Firbank, E.C., Horton, M.C., Edwards, D., et al. (1997a) Archaeological frankincense. *Nature* 390(6661), 667–8.

Evershed, R.P., Vaughan, S.J., Dudd, S.N. and Soles, J.S. (1997c) Fuel for thought? Beeswax in lamps and conical cups from Late Minoan Crete. *Antiquity* 71, 979–85.

Ewbank, J.M., Phillipson, D.W., Whitehouse, R.D. and Higgs, E.S. (1964) Sheep in the Iron Age: a method of study. *Proceedings of the Prehistoric Society* 30, 423–6. Cambridge: Cambridge University Press.

Faegri, K. and Iversen, J. (1950) *Textbook of Modern Pollen Analysis*. Copenhagen: Einar Munksgaard.

Fagan, B. (2001) *Graham Clark: An Intellectual Biography of an Archaeologist*. Boulder, CO: Westview Press.

Farquhar, G.D., Ehleringer, J.R. and Hubick, K.T. (1989) Carbon isotope discrimination and photosynthesis. *Annual Review of Plant Physiology and Plant Molecular Biology* 40: 503–37.

Fernandes, R., Nadeau, M.J. and Grootes, P.M. (2012) Macronutrient-based model for dietary carbon routing in bone collagen and bioapatite. *Archaeological and Anthropological Sciences* 4(4), 291–301.

Ferrio, J.P., Araus, J.L., Buxó, R., Voltas, J. and Bort, J. (2005) Water management practices and climate in ancient agriculture: inferences from the stable isotope composition of archaeobotanical remains. *Vegetation History and Archaeobotany* 14(4), 510–17.

Feuerbach, L. (1850) Die Naturwissenschaft und die Revolution. *Ludwig Feuerbach. Werke. Bd. 4, Kritiken und Abhandlungen III*, pp. 243–65.

Feyerabend, P. (1975) *Against Method: An Outline of an Anarchist Theory of Knowledge*. London: NLB.

Fiedel, S. (1996) Blood from stones? Some methodological and interpretive problems in blood residue analysis. *Journal of Archaeological Science* 23(1), 139–47.

Flannery, K.V. (1969) Origins and ecological effects of early domestication in Iran and the Near East. In: P.J. Ucko and G.W. Dimbleby (eds), *The Domestication and Exploitation of Plants and Animals*. Chicago, IL: Aldine, pp. 73–100.

(1976a) Empirical determination of catchments in Oaxaca and Tehuacan. In: K.V. Flannery (ed.), *The Early Mesoamerican Village*. New York: Academic Press, pp. 103–17.

(1976b) The village and its catchment area. In: K.V. Flannery (ed.), *The Early Mesoamerican Village*. New York: Academic Press, pp. 163–87.

Foley, R. (1985) Optimality theory in anthropology. *Man* 20(2), 222–42.

Forbes, H. (1989) Of grandfathers and grand theories: the hierarchized ordering of responses to hazard in a Greek rural community. In: P. Halstead and J. O'Shea (eds), *Bad Year Economics: Cultural Responses to Risk and Uncertainty*. Cambridge: Cambridge University Press, pp. 87–97.

Forde, C.D. (1934) *Habitat, Economy and Society: A Geographical Introduction to Ethnology*. London: Methuen.

Fournié, G., Pfeiffer, D.U. and Bendrey, R. (2017) Early animal farming and zoonotic disease dynamics: modelling brucellosis transmission in Neolithic goat populations. *Open Science* 4(2), 160943.

Frachetti, M.D. (2008) *Pastoralist Landscapes and Social Interaction in Bronze Age Eurasia*. Berkeley: University of California Press.

(2009) Differentiated landscapes and non-uniform complexity among Bronze Age societies of the Eurasian steppe. In: B.K. Hanks, K.M. Linduff (eds),

Social Complexity in Prehistoric Eurasia. Cambridge: Cambridge University Press, pp. 19–46.

Frachetti, M. and Benecke, N. (2009) From sheep to (some) horses: 4500 years of herd structure at the pastoralist settlement of Begash (south-eastern Kazakhstan). *Antiquity* 83(322), 1023–37.

Frachetti, M.D., Spengler, R.N., Fritz, G.J. and Mar'yashev, A.N. (2010) Earliest direct evidence for broomcorn millet and wheat in the central Eurasian steppe region. *Antiquity* 84(326), 993–1010.

France, D.L. (2008) *Human and Nonhuman Bone Identification: A Color Atlas*. Boca Raton, FL: CRC Press.

Fraser, F.C. and King, J.E. (1954) Faunal remains. In J.D.G. Clark *Excavations at Star Carr: An Early Mesolithic Site at Seamer Near Scarborough, Yorkshire*. Cambridge: Cambridge University Press, pp. 70–95.

Fraser, R., Bogaard, A., Charles, M., Styring, A.K., Wallace, M., Jones, G., et al. Ditchfield (2013a) Assessing natural variation and the effects of charring, burial and pre-treatment on the stable carbon and nitrogen isotope values of archaeobotanical cereal and pulse remains. *Journal of Archaeological Science* 40: 4754–66.

Fraser, R.A., Bogaard, A., Heaton, T., Charles, M., Jones, G., Christensen, B.T., et al. (2011) Manuring and stable nitrogen isotope ratios in cereals and pulses: towards a new archaeobotanical approach to the inference of land use and dietary practices. *Journal of Archaeological Science* 38(10), 2790–804.

Fraser, R.A., Bogaard, A., Schäfer, M., Arbogast, R.-M. and Heaton, T.H.E.H. (2013b) Integrating botanical, faunal and human stable carbon and nitrogen isotope values to reconstruct land use and palaeodiet at LBK Vaihingen an der Enz, Baden-Württemberg. *World Archaeology* 45, 492–517.

Frei, K.M., Coutu, A.N., Smiarowski, K., Harrison, R., Madsen, C.K., Arneborg, J., et al. (2015). Was it for walrus? Viking Age settlement and medieval walrus ivory trade in Iceland and Greenland. *World Archaeology* 47(3), 439–466.

French, C. and Kousoulakou, M. (2003) Geomorphological and micromorphological investigations of palaeosols, valley sediments and a sunken floored dwelling at Botai, Kazakhstan. In: M.A. Levine, C. Renfrew and K.V. Boyle (eds), *Prehistoric Steppe Adaptation and the Horse*. Cambridge: McDonald Institute, pp. 105–14.

French, D.H., Hillman, G.C., Payne, S. and Payne, R.J. (1972) Excavations at Can Hasan III 1969–1970. In: E.S. Higgs (ed.), *Papers in Economic Prehistory: Studies by Members and Associates of the British Academy Major Research Project in the Early History of Agriculture*. Cambridge: Cambridge University Press, pp. 181–90.

Fridrich, C. (1994) Kulturgeschichtliche Betrachtungen zur Bandkeramik im Merzbachtal. In: J. Lüning and P. Stehli (eds), *Die Bandkeramik im Merzbachtal auf der Aldenhovener Platte*. Cologne: Rheinland-Verlag GmbH, pp. 207–393.

Frison, G.C. and Rehrer, C.A. (1970) Age determination of buffalo teeth eruption and wear. In: G.C. Frison (ed.), *Glenrock Buffalo Jump, 48CO304: Late Prehistoric Period Buffalo Procurement and Butchery*. Plains Anthropologist Memoirs 7, pp. 46–50.

Fry, E., Kim, S.K., Chigurapti, S., Mika, K.M., Ratan, A., Dammermann, A., et al. (2017) Accumulation and functional architecture of deleterious genetic variants during the extinction of Wrangel Island mammoths. *bioRxiv*, 137455.

Fullagar, R., Field, J., Denham, T. and Lentfer, C. (2006) Early and mid Holocene tool-use and processing of taro (Colocasia esculenta), yam (Dioscorea sp.) and other plants at Kuk Swamp in the highlands of Papua New Guinea. *Journal of Archaeological Science* 33(5), 595–614.

Fuller, B.T., Fuller, J.L., Sage, N.E., Harris, D.A., O'Connell, T.C. and Hedges, R.E. (2005) Nitrogen balance and $\delta^{15}N$: why you're not what you eat during nutritional stress. *Rapid Communications in Mass Spectrometry* 19(18), 2497–506.

Fuller, D.Q., Qin, L., Zheng, Y., Zhao, Z., Chen, X., Hosoya, L.A. and Sun, G.-P. (2009) The domestication process and domestication rate in rice: spikelet bases from the Lower Yangtze. *Science* 323, 1607–10.

Gallego Llorente, M.G., Jones, E.R., Eriksson, A., Siska, V., Arthur, K.W., Arthur, J.W., et al. (2015) Ancient Ethiopian genome reveals extensive Eurasian admixture in Eastern Africa. *Science* 350(6262), 820–2.

Gamba, C., Hanghøj, K., Gaunitz, C., Alfarhan, A.H., Alquraishi, S.A., Al-Rasheid, K.A., et al. (2015) Comparing the performance of three ancient DNA extraction methods for high-throughput sequencing. *Molecular Ecology Resources*. DOI: 10.1111/1755-0998.12470.

Gamble, C. (1979) Hunting strategies in the Central European Palaeolithic. In: *Proceedings of the Prehistoric Society* 45, 35–52.

Gamkrelidze T.V. and Ivanov V. (1995) *Indo-European and the Indo-Europeans: A Reconstruction and Historical Analysis of a Proto-Language and a Proto-Culture*, Vol. 1. Berlin: Mouton de Gruyter.

García-Granero, J.J. (2015) A tale of multi-proxies: integrating macro- and microbotanical remains to understand subsistence strategies. *Vegetation History and Archaeobotany* 24, 121–33.

Gaunitz, C., Fages, A., Hanghøj, K., Albrechtsen, A., Khan, N., Schubert, M., et al. (2018) Ancient genomes revisit the ancestry of domestic and Przewalski's horses. *Science* 360, 111–14.

Gerbault, P., Gillis, R., Vigne, J.-D., Tresset, A., Bréhard, S. and Thomas, M.G. (2016) Statistically robust representation and comparison of mortality profiles in archaeozoology. *Journal of Archaeological Science* 71, 24–32.

Gerbault, P., Liebert, A., Itan, Y., Powell, A., Currat, M., Burger, J., et al. (2011) Evolution of lactase persistence: an example of human niche construction. *Philosophical Transactions of the Royal Society of London B: Biological Sciences* 366(1566), 863–77.

Gerling, C., Doppler, T., Heyd, V., Knipper, C., Kuhn, T., Lehmann, M.F., et al. (2017) High-resolution isotopic evidence of specialised cattle dairying in the European Neolithic. *PLoS ONE* 12: e0180164.

Germanov, P.G. and Kosintsev, P.A. (1995) Kostnye ostatki poseleniia pozdney bronzy Druzhnyy 1 v Iuzhnom Zaural'e, konf., Rossiia i Vostok: problemy vzaimodeystviia, v. 5, N 2., Cheliabinsk, pp. 116–18.

Germonpré, M., Sablin, M.V., Stevens, R.E., Hedges, R.E., Hofreiter, M., Stiller, M. and Després, V.R. (2009) Fossil dogs and wolves from Palaeolithic sites in Belgium, the Ukraine and Russia: osteometry, ancient DNA and stable isotopes. *Journal of Archaeological Science* 36(2), 473–90.

Gernaey, A.M., Waite, E.R., Collins, M.J., Craig, O.E. and Sokol, R.J. (2001) Survival and interpretation of archaeological protein. In: D.R. Brothwell and A.M. Pollard (eds), *Handbook of Archaeological Sciences*. Chichester: Wiley, pp. 323–9.

Gilbert, B.M. (1990) *Mammalian Osteology*. Columbia: Missouri Archaeological Society.

Giles, R.J. and Brown, T.A. (2008) Improved methodology for extraction and amplification of DNA from single grains of charred wheat. *Journal of Archaeological Science* 35(9), 2585–8.

Gillis, R., Bréhard, S., Bălăşescu, A., Ughetto-Monfrin, J., Popovici, D., Vigne, J.D. and Balasse, M. (2013) Sophisticated cattle dairy husbandry at Borduşani-Popină (Romania, fifth millennium BC): the evidence from complementary analysis of mortality profiles and stable isotopes. *World Archaeology* 45(3), 447–72.

Gillis, R.E., Kovačiková, L., Bréhard, S., Guthmann, E., Vostrovská, I., Nohálová, H., et al. (2017). The evolution of dual meat and milk cattle husbandry in *Linearbandkeramik* societies. *Proceedings of the Royal Society B: Biological Sciences* 284, 20170905.

Glassow, M.A. (1978) The concept of carrying capacity in the study of cultural process. *Advances in Archaeological Method and Theory* 1, 31–48.

Gokhman, D., Lavi, E., Prüfer, K., Fraga, M.F., Riancho, J.A., Kelso, J., et al. (2014) Reconstructing the DNA methylation maps of the Neandertal and the Denisovan. *Science* 344(6183), 523–7.

Gokhman, D., Malul, A. and Carmel, L. (2017) Inferring past environments from ancient epigenomes. *Molecular Biology and Evolution*, p.msx211.

Gokhman, D., Meshorer, E. and Carmel, L. (2016) Epigenetics: it's getting old. Past meets future in paleoepigenetics. *Trends in Ecology & Evolution* 31(4), 290–300.

Gott, B., Barton, H., Samuel, D. and Torrence, R. (2006) Biology of starch. In: R. Torrence and H. Barton (eds), *Ancient Starch Research*. Walnut Creek, CA: Left Coast Press, pp. 35–45.

Graham, R.W., Belmecheri, S., Choy, K., Culleton, B.J., Davies, L.J., Froese, D., et al. (2016) Timing and causes of mid-Holocene mammoth extinction on St. Paul Island, Alaska. *Proceedings of the National Academy of Sciences* 113(33), 9310–14.

Green, R.E., Krause, J., Ptak, S.E., Briggs, A.W., Ronan, M.T., Simons, J.F., et al. (2006) Analysis of one million base pairs of Neanderthal DNA. *Nature* 444(7117), 330–6.

Green, R.E., Malaspinas, A.S., Krause, J., Briggs, A.W., Johnson, P.L., Uhler, C., et al. (2008) A complete Neandertal mitochondrial genome sequence determined by high-throughput sequencing. *Cell* 134(3), 416–26.

Greenfield, H.J. (1999) The origins of metallurgy: distinguishing stone from metal cut-marks on bones from archaeological sites. *Journal of Archaeological Science* 26(7), 797–808.

Gregoricka, L.A. and Judd, M.A. (2016) Isotopic evidence for diet among historic Bedouin of Khirbat al-Mudayna, Jordan. *International Journal of Osteoarchaeology* 26(4), 705–15.

Grigg, D. (1979) Ester Boserup's theory of agrarian change: a critical review. *Progress in Human Geography* 3, 64–84.
Grigson, C. (1981) Fauna. In: I. Simmons and M. Tooley (eds), *The Environment in British Prehistory*. London: Duckworth, pp. 110–24.
Gross, B.L. and Zhao, Z. (2014) Archaeological and genetic insights into the origins of domesticated rice. *Proceedings of the National Academy of Sciences* 111(17), 6190–7.
Grupe, G. and McGlynn, G.C. (2016) Preface. In: G. Grupe and G.C. McGlynn (eds), *Isotopic Landscapes in Bioarchaeology*. Heidleberg: Springer, pp. v–viii.
Gu, Y., Zhao, Z. and Pearsall, D.M. (2013) Phytolith morphology research on wild and domesticated rice species in East Asia. *Quaternary International* 287, 141–8.
Guiry, E.J., Hepburn, J.C. and Richards, M.P. (2016) High-resolution serial sampling for nitrogen stable isotope analysis of archaeological mammal teeth. *Journal of Archaeological Science* 69, 21–8.
Gunn, A. (2009). *Essential Forensic Biology*, 2nd edn. Chichester: John Wiley & Sons.
Haak, W., Brandt, G., de Jong, H.N., Meyer, C., Ganslmeier, R., Heyd, V., et al. (2008) Ancient DNA, Strontium isotopes, and osteological analyses shed light on social and kinship organization of the Later Stone Age. *Proceedings of the National Academy of Sciences* 105(47), 18226–31.
Haak, W., Forster, P., Bramanti, B., Matsumura, S., Brandt, G., Tänzer, M., et al. (2005) Ancient DNA from the first European farmers in 7500-year-old Neolithic sites. *Science* 310(5750), 1016–18.
Haak, W., Lazaridis, I., Patterson, N., Rohland, N., Mallick, S., Llamas, B., et al. (2015) Massive migration from the steppe was a source for Indo-European languages in Europe. *Nature* 522, 207–11.
Hachem, L. (1999) Apport de l'archéozoologie a la connaissance de l'organisation villageoise rubanée. In: F. Breamer, S. Cleuziou and A. Coudart (eds), *Habitat et société, XIXe Rencontres d'Archéologie et d'Histoire d'Antibes*. Antibes: APDCA, pp. 325–38.
(2000) New observations on the Bandkeramik house and social organization. *Antiquity* 74, 308–12.
Hafner, A. (2013) UNESCO World Heritage 'prehistoric pile-dwellings around the Alps': chances and challenges for management and research of cultural heritage under water. In Roio, M. (ed.), *The Changing Coastal and Maritime Culture. The 5th Baltic Sea Region Cultural Heritage Forum, Tallinn 18–20 September 2013*. Tallin: Estonian National Heritage Board.
Haile, J., Froese, D.G., MacPhee, R.D., Roberts, R.G., Arnold, L.J., Reyes, A.V., et al. (2009) Ancient DNA reveals late survival of mammoth and horse in interior Alaska. *Proceedings of the National Academy of Sciences* 106(52), 22352–7.
Hajdinjak, M., Fu, Q., Hübner, A., Petr, M., Mafessoni, F., Grote, S., et al. (2018) Reconstructing the genetic history of late Neanderthals. *Nature* 555(7698), 652–6.
Halstead, P. (1989a) Like rising damp? An ecological approach to the spread of farming in south east and central Europe. In: A. Milles, D. Williams and N. Gardner (eds), *The Beginnings of Agriculture*. Oxford: British Archaeological Reports, pp. 23–53.

(1989b) The economy has a normal surplus: economic stability and social change among early farming communities. In: P. Halstead and J. O'Shea (eds), *Bad Year Economics: Cultural Responses to Risk and Uncertainty*. Cambridge: Cambridge University Press, pp. 68–80.

(1992) From reciprocity to redistribution: modelling the exchange of livestock in Neolithic Greece. *Anthropozoologica* 16, 19–30.

(2003) Texts and bones: contrasting Linear B and archaeozoological evidence for animal exploitation in Mycenaean southern Greece. *British School at Athens Studies* 9, 257–61.

(2014) *Two Oxen Ahead: Pre-Mechanized Farming in the Mediterranean*. Chichester: Wiley Blackwell.

Halstead, P. and Isaakidou, V. (2011) A pig fed by hand is worth two in the bush: ethnoarchaeology of pig husbandry in Greece and its archaeological implications. In: U. Albarella (ed.), *Ethnozooarchaeology: the Present Past of Human–Animal Relationships*. Oxford: Oxbow, pp. 160–74.

Halstead, P. and O'Shea, J. (eds) (1989a) *Bad Year Economics: Cultural Responses to Risk and Uncertainty*. Cambridge: Cambridge University Press.

(1989b) Introduction: cultural responses to risk and uncertainty. In: P. Halstead and J. O'Shea (eds), *Bad Year Economics: Cultural Responses to Risk and Uncertainty*. Cambridge: Cambridge University Press, pp. 1–7.

Hamilton, J. and Thomas, R. (2012) Pannage, pulses and pigs: isotopic and zooarchaeological evidence for changing pig management practices in later medieval England. *Medieval Archaeology* 56(1), 234–59.

Hanghøj, K., Seguin-Orlando, A., Schubert, M., Madsen, T., Pedersen, J.S., Willerslev, E. and Orlando, L. (2016) Fast, accurate and automatic ancient nucleosome and methylation maps with epiPALEOMIX. *Molecular Biology and Evolution* 33(12), 3284–98.

Hanks, B.K. and Linduff, K.M. (2009) Reconsidering steppe social complexity within world prehistory. In: B.K. Hanks and K.M. Linduff (eds), *Social Complexity in Prehistoric Eurasia*. Cambridge: Cambridge University Press, pp. 1–7.

Hansel, F.A., Copley, M.S., Madureira, L.A. and Evershed, R.P. (2004) Thermally produced ω-(o-alkylphenyl) alkanoic acids provide evidence for the processing of marine products in archaeological pottery vessels. *Tetrahedron Letters* 45(14), 2999–3002.

Harcourt, R.A. (1971) Animal bones from Durrington Walls. In: G.J. Wainwright and I.H. Longworth (eds), *Durrington Walls Excavations 1966–1968*. London: Society of Antiquaries, pp. 338–50.

Harding, R.M., Fullerton, S.M., Griffiths, R.C., Bond, J., Cox, M.J., Schneider, J.A., et al. (1997) Archaic African and Asian lineages in the genetic ancestry of modern humans. *American Journal of Human Genetics* 60(4), 772–89.

Harris, D.R. and Hillman, G.C. (eds) (1989) *Foraging and Farming: The Evolution of Plant Exploitation*. London: Unwin Hyman.

Hart, J.P., Urquhart, G.R., Feranec, R.S. and Lovis, W.A. (2009) Non-linear relationship between bulk $\delta^{13}C$ and percent maize in carbonized cooking residues and the potential of false-negatives in detecting maize. *Journal of Archaeological Science* 36(10), 2206–12.

Hart, R.H. (2001) Where the buffalo roamed – or did they? *Great Plains Research* 11(1), 83–102.

Haruda, A.F. (2014) Central Asian economies and ecologies in the Late Bronze Age: geometric morphometrics of the caprid astragalus and zooarchaeological investigations of pastoralism. PhD thesis, University of Exeter. http://hdl.handle.net/10871/17496.

(2017) Separating sheep (*Ovis aries* L.) and goats (*Capra hircus* L.) using geometric morphometric methods: an investigation of astragalus morphology from late and final Bronze Age central Asian contexts. *International Journal of Osteoarchaeology* 27(4), 551–62.

Haslam, M. (2004) The decomposition of starch grains in soils: implications for archaeological residue analysis. *Journal of Archaeological Science* 31, 1715–34.

Hastorf, C.A. (2009) Rio Balsas most likely region for maize domestication. *Proceedings of the National Academy of Sciences* 106(13), 4957–8.

Hastorf, C.A. and Popper, V.S. (eds) (1988) *Current Paleoethnobotany: Analytical Methods and Cultural Interpretations of Archaeological Plant Remains*. Chicago, IL: University of Chicago Press.

Hayden, B. (1975) The carrying capacity dilemma: An alternate approach. *Memoirs of the Society for American Archaeology* 30, 11–21.

Healy, K. (2017) Fuck nuance. *Sociological Theory* 35(2), 118–27.

Heard, E. and Martienssen, R.A. (2014) Transgenerational epigenetic inheritance: myths and mechanisms. *Cell* 157(1), 95–109.

Heck, L., Wilson, L.A., Evin, A., Stange, M. and Sánchez-Villagra, M.R. (2018) Shape variation and modularity of skull and teeth in domesticated horses and wild equids. *Frontiers in Zoology* 15(1), 14.

Hedges, S.B. and Schweitzer, M.H. (1995) Detecting dinosaur DNA. *Science* 268(5214), 1191–2.

Helbaek, H. (1959) The domestication of food plants in the Old World. *Science* 130, 365–72.

Hendy, J., Colonese, A.C., Franz, I., Fernandes, R., Fischer, R., Orton, D., et al. (2018a) Ancient proteins from ceramic vessels at Çatalhöyük West reveal the hidden cuisine of early farmers. *Nature Communications* 9(1), 4064.

Hendy, J., Warinner, C., Bouwman, A., Collins, M.J., Fiddyment, S., Fischer, R., et al. (2018b) Proteomic evidence of dietary sources in ancient dental calculus. *Proceedings of the Royal Society B* 285(1883), 20180977.

Hendy, J., Welker, F., Demarchi, B., Speller, C., Warinner, C. and Collins, M.J. (2018c) A guide to ancient protein studies. *Nature Ecology and Evolution* 2, 791–9.

Henry, A.G., Hudson, H.F. and Piperno, D.R. (2009) Changes in starch grain morphologies from cooking. *Journal of Archaeological Science* 36, 915–22.

Henry, D.O. (1985) Preagricultural sedentism: the Natufian example. In: T.D. Price and J.A. Brown (eds), *Prehistoric Hunter-Gatherers: The Emergence of Cultural Complexity*. Orlando, FL: Academic Press, pp. 365–84.

(1989) *From Foraging to Agriculture*. Philadelphia: University of Pennsylvania Press.

Herring, D.A., Saunders, S.R. and Katzenberg, M.A. (1998) Investigating the weaning process in past populations. *American Journal of Physical Anthropology* 105(4), 425–39.

Hershkovitz, I., Donoghue, H.D., Minnikin, D.E., May, H., Lee, O.Y.C., Feldman, M., et al. (2015) Tuberculosis origin: the Neolithic scenario. *Tuberculosis* 95, S122–S126.

Higgs, E.S. (ed.) (1972) *Papers in Economic Prehistory: Studies by Members and Associates of the British Academy Major Research Project in the Early History of Agriculture*. Cambridge: Cambridge University Press.

(ed.) (1975) *Palaeoeconomy: Being the Second Volume of Papers in Economic Prehistory by Members and Associates of the British Academy Major Research Project in the Early History of Agriculture*. Cambridge: Cambridge University Press.

Higgs, E.S. and Jarman, M.R. (1975) Palaeoeconomy. In: E.S. Higgs (ed.), *Palaeoeconomy: Being the Second Volume of Papers in Economic Prehistory by Members and Associates of the British Academy Major Research Project in the Early History of Agriculture*. Cambridge: Cambridge University Press, pp. 1–8.

Higgs, E.S. and Vita-Finzi, C. (1972) Prehistoric economies: a territorial approach. In: E.S. Higgs (ed.), *Papers in Economic Prehistory: Studies by Members and Associates of the British Academy Major Research Project in the Early History of Agriculture*. Cambridge: Cambridge University Press, pp. 27–36.

Higham, C. (1966) Stock rearing in prehistoric Europe, with special reference to the Danish islands and the Alpine foreland. Unpublished thesis: University of Cambridge.

Higham, C.F. (1968a) Stock rearing as a cultural factor in prehistoric Europe. *Proceedings of the Prehistoric Society* 33, 84–106.

Higham, C.F.W. (1968b) Patterns of prehistoric economic exploitation on the Alpine Foreland. *Vierteljahrsschrift der Naturforschenden Gesellschaft in Zürich* 113, 41–92.

(1969) Towards an economic prehistory of Europe. *Current Anthropology* 10(2/3), 139–50.

Higham, C.F.W. and Message, M.A. (1969) An assessment of a prehistoric technique of bovine husbandry. In: D. Brothwell and E. Higgs (eds), *Science in Archaeology*. London: Thames & Hudson, pp. 315–30.

Higham, T.G., Jacobi, R.M. and Ramsey, C.B. (2006) AMS radiocarbon dating of ancient bone using ultrafiltration. *Radiocarbon* 48(2), 179–95.

Higuchi, R., Bowman, B., Freiberger, M., Ryder, O.A. and Wilson, A.C. (1984) DNA sequences from the quagga, an extinct member of the horse family. *Nature* 312, 282–4.

Hilditch, T.P. and Williams, P.N. (1964) *The Chemical Composition of Natural Fats*, 4th edn. New York: Wiley.

Hill, J.D. (1995) *Ritual and Rubbish in the Iron Age of Wessex*. Oxford: British Archaeological Reports.

Hillman, G. (1981) Reconstructing crop husbandry practices from charred remains of crops. In: R. Mercer (ed.), *Farming Practice in British Prehistory*. Edinburgh: Edinburgh University Press, pp. 123–62.

(1984) Interpretation of archaeological plant remains: the application of ethnographic models from Turkey. In: W. Van Zeist and W.A. Casperie (eds), *Plants and Ancient Man*. Rotterdam: Balkema, pp. 1–41.

(1996) Late Pleistocene changes in wild plant-foods available to hunter-gatherers of the northern Fertile Crescent: possible preludes to cereal cultivation. In: D.R. Harris (ed.), *The Origins and Spread of Agriculture and Pastoralism in Eurasia*. Washington, DC: Smithsonian Press.

Hillman, G.C. and Davies, M.S. (1990a) Measured domestication rates in wild wheats and barley under primitive cultivation, and their archaeological implications. *Journal of World Prehistory* 4(2), 157–222.

(1990b) Domestication rates in wild-type wheats and barley under primitive cultivation. *Biological Journal of the Linnean Society* 39(1), 39–78.

Hodder, I. (1986) *Reading the Past: Current Approaches to Interpretation in Archaeology*. Cambridge: Cambridge University Press.

(1990) *The Domestication of Europe*. Oxford: Blackwell.

(2012) Introduction: contemporary theoretical debate in archaeology. In I. Hodder (ed.) *Archaeological Theory Today*, 2nd edn. Cambridge: Polity Press, pp. 1–14.

Hodder, I. and Orton, C. (1976) *Spatial Analysis in Archaeology*. Cambridge: Cambridge University Press.

Hodgson, J.A. and Disotell, T.R. (2008) No evidence of a Neanderthal contribution to modern human diversity. *Genome Biology* 9(2), 206.

Hodson, M.J., Parker, A.G., Leng, M.J. and Sloane, H.J. (2008) Silicon, oxygen and carbon isotope composition of wheat (*Triticum aestivum* L.) phytoliths: implications for palaeoecology and archaeology. *Journal of Quaternary Science* 23, 331–9.

Holl, H.M., Brooks, S.A., Archer, S., Brown, K., Malvick, J., Penedo, M.C.T. and Bellone, R.R. (2016) Variant in the RFWD3 gene associated with PATN1, a modifier of leopard complex spotting. *Animal Genetics* 47(1), 91–101.

Hong, C., Jiang, H., Lü, E., Wu, Y., Guo, L., Xie, Y., et al. (2012) Identification of milk component in ancient food residue by proteomics. *PloS one* 7(5), e37053.

Hosch, S. and Jacomet, S. (2004) Ackerbau und Sammelwirtschaft. Ergebnisse der Untersuchung von Samen und Früchten. In: S. Jacomet, U. Leuzinger and J. Schibler (eds), *Die jungsteinzeitliche Seeufersiedlung Arbon Bleiche 3: Umwelt und Wirtschaft*. Frauenfeld: Amt für Archäologie des Kantons Thurgau, pp. 112–57.

Howland, M.R., Corr, L.T., Young, S.M., Jones, V., Jim, S., Van Der Merwe, N.J., et al. (2003) Expression of the dietary isotope signal in the compound-specific δ13C values of pig bone lipids and amino acids. *International Journal of Osteoarchaeology* 13(1–2), 54–65.

Hu, Y., Hu, S., Wang, W., Wu, X., Marshall, F. B., Chen, X., et al. (2014) Earliest evidence for commensal processes of cat domestication. *Proceedings of the National Academy of Sciences* 111(1), 116–20.

Hullar, M.A. and Fu, B.C. (2014) Diet, the gut microbiome, and epigenetics. *Cancer Journal* 20(3), 170–5.

Hunt, H.V., Vander Linden, M., Liu, X., Motuzaite-Matuzeviciute G. and Jones, M.K. (2008) Millets across Eurasia: chronology and context of early records of the genera *Panicum* and *Setaria* from archaeological sites in the Old World. *Vegetation History and Archaeobotany* 17, S5–S18.

Hurcombe, L.M. (2014) *Perishable Material Culture in Prehistory: Investigating the Missing Majority*. Abingdon: Routledge.

Ingold, T. (1980) *Hunter, Pastoralists and Ranchers*. Cambridge: Cambridge University Press.

Iriarte, J. (2003) Assessing the feasibility of identifying maize through the analysis of cross-shaped size and three-dimensional morphology of phytoliths in the grasslands of southeastern South America. *Journal of Archaeological Science* 30, 1085–94.

(2007) New perspectives on early plant domestication and the development of agriculture in the Americas. In: T. Denham, J. Iriarte and L. Vrydaghs (eds) *Rethinking Agriculture: Archaeological and Ethnoarchaeological Perspectives*, Walnut Creek, CA: Left Coast Press, pp. 167–88.

Iriarte, J., Holst, I., Marozzi, O., Listopad, C., Alonso, E., Rinderknecht, A. and Montaña, J. (2004) Evidence for cultivar adoption and emerging complexity during the mid-Holocene in the La Plata basin. *Nature* 432, 614–17.

Iriarte, J., Power, M.J., Rostain, S., Mayle, F.E., Jones, H., Watling, J., et al. (2012) Fire-free land use in pre-1492 Amazonian savannas. *Proceedings of the National Academy of Sciences* 109, 6473–8.

Isaakidou, V. (2006) Ploughing with cows: Knossos and the secondary products revolution. In: D. Serjeantson and D. Field (eds), *Animals in the Neolithic of Britain and Europe*. Oxford: Oxbow Books, pp. 95–112.

(2011) Farming regimes in Neolithic Europe: gardening with cows and other models. In: Hadjikoumis, A., Robinson, E. and Viner, S. (eds), *The Dynamics of Neolithisation in Europe: Studies in honour of Andrew Sherratt*. Oxford: Oxbow, pp. 90–112.

Itan, Y., Powell, A., Beaumont, M.A., Burger, J. and Thomas, M.G. (2009) The origins of lactase persistence in Europe. *PLoS Computational Biology* 5(8), p.e1000491.

Iversen, J. (1941) Landnam i Danmarks stenalder: En pollenanalytisk undersøgelse over det første landbrugs indvirkning paa vegetationsudviklingen. *Danmarks Geologiske Undersogelse, Series* 2, 66, 1–68.

(1949) The influence of prehistoric man on vegetation. *Danmarks Geologiske Undersogelse, Series* 4, 3, 1–25.

Jackson, R. (1972) A vicious circle? The consequences of Von Thünen in tropical Africa. *Area* 4(4), 258–61.

Jacomet, S. and Brombacher, C. (2005) Reconstructing intra-site patterns in Neolithic lakeshore settlements: the state of archaeobotanical research and future prospects. In: P. Della Casa and M. Trachsel (eds) *WES'04 – Wetland Economies and Societies. Proceedings of the International Conference in Zurich, 10–13 March 2004*. Zurich: Chronos, pp. 69–94.

Jacomet, S., Brombacher, C. and Dick, M. (1989) *Archäobotanik am Zürichsee. Ackerbau, Sammelwirtschaft und Umwelt von neolithischen und bronzezeitlichen Seeufersiedlungen im Raum Zürich*. Zurich: Orell Füssli Verlag.

Jacomet, S., Ebersbach, R., Akeret, Ö., Antolín, F., Baum, T., Bogaard, A., et al. (2016) On-site data cast doubts on the hypothesis of shifting cultivation in the late Neolithic (*c*. 4300–2400 cal BC): Landscape management as an alternative paradigm. *The Holocene* 26, 1858–74.

Jacomet, S., Leuzinger, U. and Schibler, J. (2004) *Die jungsteinzeitliche Seeufersiedlung Arbon Bleiche 3: Umwelt und Wirtschaft, Archäologie im Thurgau*. Frauenfeld: Amt für Archäologie des Kantons Thurgau.

Jaenicke-Despres, V., Buckler, E.S., Smith, B.D., Gilbert, M.T.P., Cooper, A., Doebley, J. and Pääbo, S. (2003) Early allelic selection in maize as revealed by ancient DNA. *Science* 302(5648), 1206–8.

Jakucs, J., Bánffy, E., Oross, K., Voicsek, V., Bronk Ramsey, C., Dunbar, E., et al. (2016) Between the Vinča and *Linearbandkeramik* worlds: the diversity of practices and identities in the 54th-53rd centuries cal BC in southwest Hungary and beyond. *Journal of World Prehistory* 29, 267–336.

Janowitz Koch, I., Clark, M.M., Thompson, M.J., Deere-Machemer, K.A., Wang, J., Duarte, L., et al. (2016) The concerted impact of domestication and transposon insertions on methylation patterns between dogs and grey wolves. *Molecular Ecology* 25(8), 1838–55.

Jansen, T., Forster, P., Levine, M.A., Oelke, H., Hurles, M., Renfrew, C., Weber, J. and Olek, K. (2002) Mitichondrial DNA and the origins of the domestic horse. *Proceedings of the National Academy of Sciences* 99(16), 10905–10.

Jarman, H.N. (1972) The origins of wheat and barley cultivation. In: E.S. Higgs (ed.), *Papers in Economic Prehistory: Studies by Members and Associates of the British Academy Major Research Project in the Early History of Agriculture*. Cambridge: Cambridge University Press, pp. 15–26.

Jarman, H.N., Legge, A.J. and Charles, J.A. (1972) Retrieval of plant remains from archaeological sites by froth flotation. In: E.S. Higgs (ed.), *Papers in Economic Prehistory: Studies by Members and Associates of the British Academy Major Research Project in the Early History of Agriculture*. Cambridge: Cambridge University Press, pp. 39–48.

Jarman, M.R., Bailey, G.N. and Jarman, H.N. (eds) (1982) *Early European Agriculture: Its Foundation and Development*. Cambridge: Cambridge University Press.

Jarman, M.R., Vita-Finzi, C. and Higgs, E.S. (1972) Site catchment analysis in archaeology. In: P.J. Ucko, R. Tringham and G.W. Dimbleby (eds), *Man, Settlement and Urbanism*. London: Duckworth, pp. 61–6.

Jarman, M.R. and Webley, D. (1975) Settlement and land use in Capitanata, Italy. In: E.S. Higgs (ed.), *Palaeoeconomy: Being the Second Volume of Papers in Economic Prehistory by Members and Associates of the British Academy Major Research Project in the Early History of Agriculture*. Cambridge: Cambridge University Press, pp. 177–222.

Jay, M., Fuller, B.T., Richards, M.P., Knüsel, C.J. and King, S.S. (2008) Iron Age breastfeeding practices in Britain: isotopic evidence from Wetwang Slack, East Yorkshire. *American Journal of Physical Anthropology* 136(3), 327–37.

Jenkins, E. (2009) Phytolith taphonomy: a comparison of dry ashing and acid extraction on the breakdown of conjoined phytoliths formed in *Triticum durum*. *Journal of Archaeological Science* 36, 2402–7.

Jenkins, E., Jamjoum, K., Nuimat, S., Stafford, R., Nortcliff, S. and Mithen, S. (2016) Identifying ancient water availability through phytolith analysis: an experimental approach. *Journal of Archaeological Science* 73, 82–93.

Jensen, P. (2014) Behaviour epigenetics–The connection between environment, stress and welfare. *Applied Animal Behaviour Science* 157, 1–7.

Jeong, C., Wilkin, S., Amgalantugs, T., Bouwman, A.S., Taylor, W.T.T., Hagan, R.W., et al. (2018) Bronze Age population dynamics and the rise of dairy pastoralism on the eastern Eurasian steppe. *Proceedings of the National Academy of Sciences* 115(48), E11248–E11255.

Johnson, E.V., Parmenter, P.C. and Outram, A.K. (2016) A new approach to profiling taphonomic history through bone fracture analysis, with an example application to the *Linearbandkeramik* site of Ludwinowo 7. *Journal of Archaeological Science: Reports* 9, 623–9.

Johnson, E.V., Timpson, A., Thomas, M.G. and Outram, A.K. (2018) Reduced intensity of bone fat exploitation correlates with increased potential access to dairy fats in early Neolithic Europe. *Journal of Archaeological Science* 94, 60–9.

Johnson, M. (1999) *Archaeological Theory: An Introduction*. Oxford: Blackwell.

Jones, B.A., Grace, D., Kock, R., Alonso, S., Rushton, J., Said, M.Y., et al. (2013) Zoonosis emergence linked to agricultural intensification and environmental change. *Proceedings of the National Academy of Sciences* 110(21), 8399–404.

Jones, E.R., Zarina, G., Moiseyev, V., Lightfoot, E., Nigst, P.R., Manica, A., et al. (2017) The Neolithic transition in the Baltic was not driven by admixture with early European farmers. *Current Biology* 27(4), 576–82.

Jones, G. (1984) Interpretation of archaeological plant remains: ethnographic models from Greece. In W. Van Zeist and W.A. Casperie (eds) *Plants and Ancient Man*. Rotterdam: Balkema, pp. 43–61.

Jones, G., Bogaard, A., Halstead, P., Charles, M. and Smith, H. (1999) Identifying the intensity of crop husbandry practices on the basis of weed floras. *Annals of the British School at Athens* 94, 167–89.

Jones, G., Bogaard, A., Charles, M. and Hodgson, J.G. (2000a) Distinguishing the effects of agricultural practices relating to fertility and disturbance: a functional ecological approach in archaeobotany. *Journal of Archaeological Science* 27, 1073–84.

Jones, G., Valamoti, S. and Charles, M. (2000b) Early crop diversity: a 'new' glume wheat from northern Greece. *Vegetation History and Archaeobotany* 9, 133–46.

Jones, M., Hunt, H., Lightfoot, E., Lister, D., Liu, X. and Motuzaite-Matuzeviciute, G. (2011) Food globalization in prehistory. *World Archaeology* 43(4), 665–75.

Judkins, G., Smith, M. and Keys, E. (2008) Determinism within human–environment research and the rediscovery of environmental causation. *The Geographical Journal* 174(1), 17–29.

Julien, M.A., Bocherens, H., Burke, A., Drucker, D.G., Patou-Mathis, M., Krotova, O. and Péan, S. (2012) Were European steppe bison migratory? ^{18}O, ^{13}C and Sr intra-tooth isotopic variations applied to a palaeoethological reconstruction. *Quaternary International* 271, 106–19.

Kadwell, M., Fernandez, M., Stanley, H.F., Baldi, R., Wheeler, J.C., Rosadio, R. and Bruford, M.W. (2001) Genetic analysis reveals the wild ancestors of the llama and the alpaca. *Proceedings of the Royal Society of London B: Biological Sciences* 268(1485), 2575–84.

Kafil, H.S., baha Hosseini, S., Sohrabi, M. and Asgharzadeh, M. (2014) Brucellosis: presence of zoonosis infection 3,500 years ago in north of Iran. *Asian Pacific Journal of Tropical Disease* 4, S684–S686.

Kalieva, S.S. and Logvin, V.N. (1997) *Skotovody Turgaya v Tret'em Tysyacheletii do Nashej Ehry*, Kustanai: Kustanai University.

Karr, L.P., Outram, A.K. and Hannus, L.A. (2010) A chronology of bone marrow and bone grease exploitation at the Mitchell Prehistoric Indian Village. *Plains Anthropologist* 55(215), 215–23.

Karr, L.P., Short, E.G., Hannus, L.A. and Outram, A.K. (2015) A bone grease processing station at the Mitchell Prehistoric Indian Village: Archaeological evidence for the exploitation of bone fats. *Environmental Archaeology* 20(1), 1–12

Kasparov A.K. and Outram, A.K. (2013) Nekotorye zamechaniia po povodu osteologicheskih materialov kompleksa Lisakovky (poselenie i mogil'niki epohi bronzy). In: E. Usmanova (ed.), *Pamiatniki Lisakovskoy okrugi: arheologicheskie siuzhety*. Karaganda: Tengri, pp. 230–9.

Katzenberg, M.A., Herring, D.A. and Saunders, S.R. (1996) Weaning and infant mortality: evaluating the skeletal evidence. *American Journal of Physical Anthropology* 101(S23), 177–99.

Kealhofer, L. (2002) Changing perceptions of risk: the development of agro-ecosystems in Southeast Asia. *American Anthropologist* 104, 178–94.

Keeley, L.H. (1988) Hunter-gatherer economic complexity and 'population pressure': A cross-cultural analysis. *Journal of Anthropological Archaeology* 7(4), 373–411.

(1991) Ethnographic models for Late Glacial hunter-gatherers. In: N. Barton, A.J. Roberts and D.A. Roe (eds), *The Late Glacial in North-West Europe: Human Adaptation and Environmental Change at the End of the Pleistocene*. York: Council for British Archaeology, pp. 179–90.

Keene, A. (1979) Economic optimization models and the study of hunter-gatherer subsistence settlement systems. In: C. Renfrew and K. Cooke (eds), *Transformations: Mathematical Approaches to Culture Change*. New York: Academic Press, pp. 369–404.

Kelekna, P. (2009) *The Horse in Human History*. Cambridge: Cambridge University Press.

Kelly, E.F., Amundson, R.G., Marino, B.D. and DeNiro, M.J. (1991) Stable isotope ratios of carbon in phytoliths as a quantitative method of monitoring vegetation and climate change. *Quaternary Research* 35, 222–33.

Kelly, R.L. (1995) *The Foraging Spectrum: Diversity in Hunter-Gatherer Lifeways*. Washington, DC: Smithsonian Institution Press.

(2013) *The Lifeways of Hunter-Gatherers: The Foraging Spectrum*. Cambridge: Cambridge University Press.

Kendall, I.P., Lee, M.R. and Evershed, R.P. (2017) The effect of trophic level on individual amino acid δ^{15}N values in a terrestrial ruminant food web. *STAR: Science & Technology of Archaeological Research* 3(1), 135–45.

Kim, J. (2017) Gut microbiome, a potent modulator of epigenetics in human diseases. *Journal of Bacteriology and Virology* 47(2), 75–86.

Kislenko, A. and Tatarintseva, N. (1999) The eastern Ural steppe at the end of the Stone Age. In: M. Levine, Y. Rassamakin, A. Kislenko and N. Tatarintseva (eds), *Late Prehistoric Exploitation of the Eurasian Steppe*. Cambridge: McDonald Institute, pp. 183–216.

Klein, R.G. and Cruz-Uribe, K. (1984) *The Analysis of Animal Bones from Archaeological Sites*. Chicago, IL: University of Chicago Press.

Knipper, C. (2011). *Die räumliche Organisation der linearbandkeramischen Rind erhaltung: naturwissenschaftliche und archäologische Untersuchungen*. BAR International Series 2035. Oxford: Archaeopress.

Knörzer, K.-H. (1971). Urgeschichtliche Unkräuter im Rheinland: ein Beitrag zur Entstehungsgeschichte der Segetalgesellschaften. *Vegetatio* 23, 89–111.

Knudson K.J., Williams H.M., Buikstra J.E., Tomczak P.D., Gordon G.W. and Anbar A.D. (2010) Introducing $\delta^{88}Sr/^{86}Sr$ analysis in archaeology: a demonstration of the utility of strontium isotope fractionation in paleodietary studies. *Journal of Archaeological Science* 37, 2352–64.

Koch, P.L., Fisher, D.C. and Dettman, D. (1989) Oxygen isotope variation in the tusks of extinct proboscideans: a measure of season of death and seasonality. *Geology* 17(6), 515–19.

Koch, P.L., Tuross, N. and Fogel, M.L. (1997) The effects of sample treatment and diagenesis on the isotopic integrity of carbonate in biogenic hydroxylapatite. *Journal of Archaeological Science* 24(5), 417–29.

Kohl, P.L. (2007) *The Making of Bronze Age Eurasia*. Cambridge: Cambridge University Press.

Kohler, T.A., Smith, M.E., Bogaard, A., Feinman, G.M., Peterson, C.E., Betzenhauser, A., et al. (2017) Greater post-Neolithic wealth disparities in Eurasia than in North America and Mesoamerica. *Nature* 551(7682), 619–22.

Kohn, M.J. (1999) You are what you eat. *Science* 283(5400), 335–6.

Kooyman, B., Newman, M. E. and Ceri, H. (1992) Verifying the reliability of blood residue analysis on archaeological tools. *Journal of Archaeological Science* 19(3), 265–9.

Koryakova, L. and Epimakhov, A. (2007) *The Urals and Western Siberia in the Bronze and Iron Ages*. Cambridge: Cambridge University Press.

Kosiba, S.B., Tykot, R.H. and Carlsson, D. (2007) Stable isotopes as indicators of change in the food procurement and food preference of Viking Age and Early Christian populations on Gotland (Sweden). *Journal of Anthropological Archaeology* 26(3), 394–411.

Kosintsev, P.A. (1989) Ohota i skotovodstvo u naseleniia lesostepnogo Zaural'ia v epohu bronzy, Stanovlenie i razvitie proizvodiashego hoziaystva na Urale, UrO AN SSSR, Sverdlovsk, pp. 84–108.

Krause-Kyora, B., Makarewicz, C., Evin, A., Flink, L.G., Dobney, K., Larson, G., et al. (2013) Use of domesticated pigs by Mesolithic hunter-gatherers in northwestern Europe. *Nature Communications* 4, 2348.

Kremenetski, C.V., Tarasov, P.E. and Cherkinsky, A.E. (1997) Postglacial development of Kazakhstan pine forests. *Geographie physique et Quaternaire* 51(3), 391–404.

Kreuz, A. (1990) *Die ersten Bauern Mitteleuropas – eine archäobotanische Untersuchung zur Umwelt und Landwirtschaft der Ältesten Bandkeramik*. Analecta Praehistorica Leidensia 23. Leiden: University of Leiden.

(2007) Archaeobotanical perspectives on the beginning of agriculture north of the Alps. In: S. Colledge and J. Conolly (eds), *The Origins and Spread of Domestic Plant in Southwest Asia and Europe*. Walnut Creek, CA: Left Coast Press, pp. 259–94.

(2012) Die Vertreibung aus dem Paradies? Archäobiologische Ergebnisse zum Frühneolithikum im westlichen Mitteleuropa. *Bericht der Römisch-Germanischen Kommission* 91, 23–196.

Kreuz, A and Marinova, E. (2017) Archaeobotanical evidence of crop growing and diet within the areas of the Karanovo and the Linear Pottery Cultures: a quantitative and qualitative approach. *Vegetation History and Archaeobotany* 26, 639–57.

Kreuz, A., Marinova, E.M., Schäfer, E. and Wiethold, J. (2005) A comparison of early Neolithic crop and weed assemblages from the *Linearbandkeramik* and the Bulgarian Neolithic cultures: differences and similarities. *Vegetation History and Archaeobotany* 14, 237–58.

Kruk, J. (1973) *Studia Osadnicze nad Neolitem Wyzyn Lessowych (Studies on the Neolithic Settlement of the Loess Uplands)*. Warsaw: Polska Akademia Nauk, Instytut Historii Kultury Materialnej.

Kuhn, S.L. and Miller, D.S. (2015) Artifacts as patches: the marginal value theorem and stone tool life histories. In: N. Goodale and W. Andrefsky, Jr (eds), *Lithic Technological Systems and Evolutionary Theory*. Cambridge: Cambridge University Press, pp. 172–97.

Kuhn, T.S. (1996) *The Structure of Scientific Revolutions*. 3rd edn. Chicago, IL: University of Chicago Press.

Kuzmina, I.E. (1997) *Horses of North Eurasia from the Pliocene Till the Present Time*. St. Petersburg: Zoological Institute of the Russian Academy of Sciences.

Laland, K.N. and O'Brien, M.J. (2010) Niche Construction Theory and archaeology. *Journal of Archaeological Method and Theory* 17(4), 303–22.

Lang, C., Peters, J., Pöllath, N., Schmidt, K. and Grupe, G. (2013) Gazelle behaviour and human presence at early Neolithic Göbekli Tepe, south-east Anatolia. *World Archaeology* 45(3), 410–29.

Lantos, I., Spangenberg, J.E., Giovannetti, M.A., Ratto, N. and Maier, M.S. (2015) Maize consumption in pre-Hispanic south-central Andes: chemical and microscopic evidence from organic residues in archaeological pottery from western Tinogasta (Catamarca, Argentina). *Journal of Archaeological Science* 55, 83–99.

Larson, G., Albarella, U., Dobney, K., Rowley-Conwy, P., Schibler, J., Tresset, A., et al. (2007) Ancient DNA, pig domestication, and the spread of the Neolithic into Europe. *Proceedings of the National Academy of Sciences* 104(39), 15276–81.

Larson, G. and Burger, J. (2013) A population genetics view of animal domestication. *Trends in Genetics* 29, 195–205.

Larson, G., Dobney, K., Albarella, U., Fang, M., Matisoo-Smith, E., Robins, J., Lowden, S., et al. (2005) Worldwide phylogeography of wild boar reveals multiple centers of pig domestication. *Science* 307(5715), 1618–21.

Larson, G. and Fuller, D.Q. (2014) The evolution of animal domestication. *Annual Review of Ecology, Evolution, and Systematics* 45, 115–36.

Lee, E.S., Song, E.J. and Nam, Y.D. (2017) Dysbiosis of gut microbiome and its impact on epigenetic regulation. *Journal of Clinical Epigenetics* 3(S1), 14.

Lee, R.B. and DeVore, I. (1968) Problems in the study of hunters and gatherers. In: R.B. Lee and I. DeVore (eds), *Man the Hunter*. Chicago, IL: Aldine, pp. 3–12.

Legge, A.J. (1972) Prehistoric exploitation on gazelle in Palestine. In: E.S. Higgs (ed.), *Palaeoeconomy: Being the Second Volume of Papers in Economic*

Prehistory by Members and Associates of the British Academy Major Research Project in the Early History of Agriculture. Cambridge: Cambridge University Press, pp. 119–24.

(1981) Aspects of cattle husbandry. In: R. Mercer (ed.), *Farming Practice in British Prehistory*. Edinburgh: Edinburgh University Press, pp. 169–81.

(2005) Milk use in prehistory: the osteological evidence. In: J. Mulville and A. K. Outram (eds), *The Zooarchaeology of Fats, Oils, Milk and Dairying*. Oxford: Oxbow, pp. 8–13.

Legge, A.J. and Rowley-Conwy, P.A. (1988) *Star Carr Revisited*. London: Centre for Extra Mural Studies.

Le Huray, J.D. and Schutkowski, H. (2005) Diet and social status during the La Tene period in Bohemia: carbon and nitrogen stable isotope analysis of bone collagen from Kutná Hora-Karlov and Radovesice. *Journal of Anthropological Archaeology* 24(2), 135–47.

Leonardi, M., Boschin, F., Giampoudakis, K., Beyer, R.M., Krapp, M., Bendrey, R., et al. (2018) Late Quaternary horses in Eurasia in the face of climate and vegetation change. *Science Advances* 4(7), eaar5589.

Leonardi, M., Gerbault, P., Thomas, M.G. and Burger, J. (2012) The evolution of lactase persistence in Europe. A synthesis of archaeological and genetic evidence. *International Dairy Journal* 22(2), pp. 88–97.

Leonardi, M., Librado, P., Der Sarkissian, C., Schubert, M., Alfarhan, A.H., Alquraishi, S.A., et al. (2017) Evolutionary patterns and processes: lessons from ancient DNA. *Systematic Biology* 66(1), e1–e29.

Lepetz, S. (2013) Horse sacrifice in a Pazyryk culture kurgan: the princely tomb of Berel' (Kazakhstan). Selection criteria and slaughter procedures. *Anthropozoologica* 48(2), 309–21.

Leuzinger, U. (2002) Holzartefakte. In: A. de Capitani, S. Deschler-Erb, U. Leuzinger, E. Marti-Grädel and J. Schibler (eds), *Die jungsteinzeitliche Siedlung Arbon Bleiche 3: Funde*. Frauenfeld: Amt für Archäologie des Kantons Thurgau, pp. 76–114.

Levine, M. (1999) The origins of horse husbandry on the Eurasian steppe. In: M. Levine, Y. Rassamakin, A. Kislenko and N. Tatarintseva (eds), *Late Prehistoric Exploitation of the Eurasian Steppe*. Cambridge: McDonald Institute. pp. 5–58.

(2004) Exploring the criteria for early horse domestication. In: M. Jones (ed.), *Traces of Ancestry: Studies in Honour of Colin Renfrew*. Cambridge: McDonald Institute. pp. 115–26.

Levine, M.A. (2005) Domestication and early history of the horse. In: D. Mills and S. McDonnell (eds), *The Domestic Horse: The Origins, Development and Management of its Behavior*. Cambridge: Cambridge University Press, pp. 5–22.

Levine, M.A., Bailey, G.N., Whitwell, K.E. and Jeffcott, L.B. (2000) Palaeopathology and horse domestication. In: G. Bailey, R. Charles and N. Winder (eds), *Human Ecodynamics and Environmental Archaeology*. Oxford: Oxbow, pp. 123–33.

Levine, M. and Kislenko, A.M. (1997) New Eneolithic and Early Bronze Age radiocarbon dates for north Kazakhstan and south Siberia. *Cambridge Archaeological Journal* 7(2), 297–300.

Levine, M.A., Whitwell, K.E. and Jeffcott, L.B. (2002) A Romano-British horse burial from Icklingham, Suffolk. *Archaeofauna* 11, 63–102.

(2005) Abnormal thoracic vertebrae and the evolution of horse husbandry. *Archaeofauna: International Journal of Archaeozoology* 14, 93–109.

Lewis, J., Pike, A.W.G., Coath, C.D. and Evershed, R.P. (2017) Strontium concentration, radiogenic ($^{87}Sr/^{86}Sr$) and stable ($\delta^{88}Sr$) strontium isotope systematics in a controlled feeding study. *Science and Technology of Archaeological Research* 3(1), 53–65.

Lewontin, R.C. (1982) Organism and environment. In: H.C. Plotkin (ed.), *Learning, Development and Culture*. New York: Wiley, pp. 151–70.

(1983) Gene, organism and environment. In: D.S. Bendall (ed.), *Evolution from Molecules to Men*. Cambridge: Cambridge University Press, pp. 273–85.

Liamputtong, P. (2007) *Childrearing and Infant Care Issues: A cross-cultural perspective*. New York: Nova Publishers.

Libby, W.F. (1946) Atmospheric helium three and radiocarbon from cosmic radiation. *Physical Review* 69(11–12), 671.

Librado, P., Der Sarkissian, C., Ermini, L., Schubert, M., Jónsson, H., Albrechtsen, A., et al. (2015) Tracking the origins of Yakutian horses and the genetic basis for their fast adaptation to subarctic environments. *Proceedings of the National Academy of Sciences* 112(50), E6889–E6897.

Librado, P., Gamba, C., Gaunitz, C., Der Sarkissian, C., Pruvost, M., Albrechtsen, A., et al. (2017) Ancient genomic changes associated with domestication of the horse. *Science* 356(6336), 442–5.

Lidén, K., Eriksson, G., Nordqvist, B., Götherström, A. and Bendixen, E. (2004) 'The wet and the wild followed by the dry and the tame'–or did they occur at the same time? Diet in Mesolithic–Neolithic southern Sweden. *Antiquity* 78(299), 23–33.

Liebert, A., Lopez, S., Jones, B.L., Montalva, N., Gerbault, P., Lau, W., et al. (2017) World-wide distributions of lactase persistence alleles and the complex effects of recombination and selection. *Human Genetics* 136, 1445–53.

Lightfoot, E., Liu, X. and Jones, M.K. (2013) Why move starchy cereals? A review of the isotopic evidence for prehistoric millet consumption across Eurasia. *World Archaeology* 45(4), 574–623.

Lightfoot, E., Motuzaite-Matuzeviciute, G., O'Connell, T.C., Kukushkin, I.A., Loman, V., Varfolomeev, V., et al. (2015) How 'pastoral' is pastoralism? Dietary diversity in Bronze Age communities in the Central Kazakhstan Steppes. *Archaeometry* 57 (Suppl. 1), 232–49.

Lipson, M. et al. (2017) Parallel palaeogenomic trancests reveal complex genetic history of early European farmers. *Nature* 551, 368–72.

Linderholm, A. (2015) Ancient DNA: the next generation–chapter and verse. *Biological Journal of the Linnean Society* 117(1), 150–60.

Linderholm, A., Jonson, C. H., Svensk, O. and Lidén, K. (2008) Diet and status in Birka: stable isotopes and grave goods compared. *Antiquity* 82(316), 446–61.

Linderholm, A. and Larson, G. (2013) The role of humans in facilitating and sustaining coat colour variation in domestic animals. *Seminars in Cell & Developmental Biology* 24(6), 587–93.

Lindgren, G., Backström, N., Swinburne, J., Hellborg, L., Einarsson, A., Sandberg, K., Cothran, G., et al. (2004) Limited number of patrilines in horse domestication. *Nature Genetics* 36(4), 335–6.

Lindqvist, C. and Possnert, G. (1997) The subsistence economy and diet at Jakobs/Ajvide, Eksta parish and other prehistoric dwelling and burial sites on Gotland in long-term perspective. In: G. Burenhult (ed.), *Remote sensing 1*, Stockholm: Stockholm University, pp. 29–90.

Llamas, B., Valverde, G., Fehren-Schmitz, L., Weyrich, L.S., Cooper, A. and Haak, W. (2017) From the field to the laboratory: Controlling DNA contamination in human ancient DNA research in the high-throughput sequencing era. *STAR: Science & Technology of Archaeological Research* 3(1), 1–14.

Longinelli, A. (1984) Oxygen isotopes in mammal bone phosphate: a new tool for paleohydrological and paleoclimatological research? *Geochimica et Cosmochimica Acta* 48(2), 385–90.

Loy, T.H. (1983) Prehistoric blood residues: detection on tool surfaces and identification of species of origin. *Science* 220, 1269–71.

Lubell, D., Jackes, M., Schwarcz, H., Knyf, M. and Meiklejohn, C. (1994) The Mesolithic–Neolithic transition in Portugal: isotopic and dental evidence of diet. *Journal of Archaeological Science* 21(2), 201–16.

Ludwig, A., Pruvost, M., Reissmann, M., Benecke, N., Brockmann, G. A., Castaños, P., et al. (2009) Coat color variation at the beginning of horse domestication. *Science* 324(5926), 485.

Ludwig, A., Reissmann, M., Benecke, N., Bellone, R., Sandoval-Castellanos, E., Cieslak, M., et al. (2015) Twenty-five thousand years of fluctuating selection on leopard complex spotting and congenital night blindness in horses. *Philosophical Transactions of the Royal Society B* 370(1660), 20130386.

Lüning, J. (2000) *Steinzeitliche Bauern in Deutschland – die Landwirtschaft im Neolithikum*. Universitätsforschungen zur prähistorischen Archäologie aus dem Seminar für Vor- und Frühgeschichte der Universität Frankfurt/M, vol 58. Bonn: Dr. Rudolf Habelt GmbH.

(2006) Missionare aus dem Western bekehren und belehren. *Archäologie in Deutschland* 2006(3), 28–31.

Lyman, R.L. (1994) *Vertebrate Taphonomy*. Cambridge: Cambridge University Press.

(2008) *Quantitative Paleozoology*. Cambridge: Cambridge University Press.

Lyotard, J.-F. (1984) *The Postmodern Condition: A Report on Knowledge*. Manchester: Manchester University Press.

MacArthur, R.H. and Pianka, E.R. (1966) On optimal use of a patchy environment. *American Naturalist* 100, 603–9.

MacHugh, D.E., Larson, G. and Orlando, L. (2017) Taming the past: ancient DNA and the study of animal domestication. *Annual Review of Animal Biosciences* 5, 329–51.

MacHugh, D.E., Shriver, M.D., Loftus, R.T., Cunningham, P. and Bradley, D.G. (1997) Microsatellite DNA variation and the evolution, domestication and phylogeography of taurine and zebu cattle (*Bos taurus* and *Bos indicus*). *Genetics* 146(3), 1071–86.

MacNeish, R.S. and Eubanks, M.W. (2000) Comparative analysis of the Río Balsas and Tehuacán models for the origin of maize. *Latin American Antiquity* 11, 3–20.
Madella, M. and Lancelotti, C. (2012) Taphonomy and phytoliths: A user manual. *Quaternary International* 275, 76–83.
Madella, M., García-Granero, J.J., Out, W.A., Ryan, P. and Usai, D. (2014) Microbotanical evidence of domestic cereals in Africa 7000 years ago. *PLoS One* 9(10), e110177.
Madella, M., Jones, M.K., Echlin, P., Powers-Jones, A. and Moore, M. (2009) Plant water availability and analytical microscope of phytoliths: Implications for ancient irrigation in arid zones. *Quaternary International* 193, 32–40.
Madsen, D.B. and Schmitt, D.N. (1998) Mass collecting and the diet breadth model: A Great Basin example. *Journal of Archaeological Science* 25(5), 445–55.
Mallory, J.P. (1996) *In Search of the Indo-Europeans: Language, Archaeology and Myth*. London: Thames & Hudson.
Maier, U. and Vogt, R. (2001) *Botanische und pedologische Untersuchungen zur Ufersiedlung Hornstaad-Hörnle IA*. Stuttgart: Konrad Theiss Verlag.
Makarewicz, C.A. (2018) Stable isotopes in pastoralist archaeology as indicators of diet, mobility, and animal husbandry practices. In: A.R. Ventresca Miller and C.A. Makarewicz (eds), *Isotopic Investigations of Pastoralism in Prehistory*. Abingdon: Routledge, pp. 141–58.
Makarewicz, C.A. and Sealy, J. (2015) Dietary reconstruction, mobility, and the analysis of ancient skeletal tissues: expanding the prospects of stable isotope research in archaeology. *Journal of Archaeological Science* 56, 146–58.
Makarova L.A. (1976) Harakteristika kostnogo materiala iz poseleniia Sargary, Proshloe Kazakhstana po arkheologicheskim istochnikam, Almaty, pp. 211–26.
(1977) Zhivotnye Atasu i drugih poseleniy Central'nogo Kazakhstana, Arkheologicheskie isledovaniia v Otrare, Almaty, pp. 124–31.
(1980) Kosti zhivotnyh iz dvuh poseleniy epohi bronzy v Severnom Kazakhstane, Arkheologicheskie isledovaniia drevnego i srednevekovogo Kazakhstana, Almaty, pp. 141–51.
Marciniak, A. (2005) *Placing Animals in the Neolithic: Social Zooarchaeology of Prehistoric Communities*. London: UCL Press.
Marom, N. and Bar-Oz, G. (2009) Culling profiles: the indeterminacy of archaeozoological data to survivorship curve modelling of sheep and goat herd maintenance strategies. *Journal of Archaeological Science* 36(5), 1184–7.
Matisoo-Smith, E. and Horsbugh, K.A. (2012) *DNA for Archaeologists*. Walnut Creek, CA: Left Coast Press.
Matlova, V., Roffet-Salque, M., Pavlu, I., Kyselka, J., Sedlarova, I., Filip, V. and Evershed, R.P. (2017) Defining pottery use and animal management at the Neolithic site of Bylany (Czech Republic). *Journal of Archaeological Science: Reports* 14, 262–74.
Matsui, A. (2008) *Fundamentals of Zooarchaeology in Japan*. Kyoto: Kyoto University Press.
Matsuoka, Y., Vigouroux, Y., Goodman, M.M., Sanchez, J., Buckler, E. and Doebley, J. (2002) A single domestication for maize shown by multilocus

microsatellite genotyping. *Proceedings of the National Academy of Sciences* 99(9), 6080–4.

Matuzeviciute, G.M., Lightfoot, E., O'Connell, T.C., Voyakin, D., Liu, X., Loman, V., et al. (2015) The extent of cereal cultivation among the Bronze Age to Turkic period societies of Kazakhstan determined using stable isotope analysis of bone collagen. *Journal of Archaeological Science* 59, 23–34.

Mayr, C., Grupe, G., Toncala, A. and Lihl, C.M. (2016) Linking oxygen isotopes of animal phosphate with altimetry, results from archaeological finds from a transect in the Alps. In: G. Grupe and G.V. McGlynn (eds), *Isotopic Landscapes in Bioarchaeology*. Heidelberg: Springer, pp. 157–72.

McClaran, M.P. and Umlauf, M. (2000) Desert grassland dynamics estimated from carbon isotopes in grass phytoliths and soil organic matter. *Journal of Vegetation Science* 11, 71–6.

McCorriston, J. and Hole, F. (1991) The ecology of seasonal stress and the origins of agriculture in the Near East. *American Anthropologist* 93(1), 46–69.

Mercader, J., Abtosway, M., Baquedano, E., Bird, R.W., Díez-Martín, F., Domínguez-Rodrigo, M., et al. (2017) Starch contamination landscapes in field archaeology: Olduvai Gorge, Tanzania. *Boreas*, DOI: 10.1111/bor.12241.

Mertz, I.V. and Mertz, V.K. (2013) Novye materialy rannego bronzovogo veka iz Zapadnoj chasti Kulundinskoj ravniny. In: G.A. Kubareva and V.P. Semibratov (eds), *Sohranenie i izuchenie kul'turnogo nasledija Altajskogo kraja: materialy XVIII XIX regional'nyh nauchno-prakticheskih konferencij*. Barnaul: AZBUKA, pp. 207–15.

Metcalfe, D. and Jones, K.T. (1988) A reconsideration of animal body part utility indices. *American Antiquity* 59(1), 486–504.

Mileto, S., Kaiser, E., Rassamakin, Y. and Evershed, R.P. (2017) New insights into the subsistence economy of the Eneolithic Dereivka culture of the Ukrainian North-Pontic region through lipid residues analysis of pottery vessels. *Journal of Archaeological Science: Reports* 13, 67–74.

Miller, G.L. (2015) Ritual economy and craft production in small-scale societies: evidence from microwear analysis of Hopewell bladelets. *Journal of Anthropological Archaeology* 39, 124–38.

Miller, N.F., Spengler, R.N. and Frachetti, M. (2016) Millet cultivation across Eurasia: origins, spread, and the influence of seasonal climate. *The Holocene* 26(10), 1566–75.

Milner, N., Craig, O.E., Bailey, G.N., Pedersen, K. and Andersen, S.H. (2004) Something fishy in the Neolithic? A re-evaluation of stable isotope analysis of Mesolithic and Neolithic coastal populations. *Antiquity* 78(299), 9–22.

Minagawa, M. and Wada, E. (1984) Stepwise enrichment of ^{15}N along food chains: further evidence and the relation between $\delta^{15}N$ and animal age. *Geochimica et Cosmochimica Acta* 48(5), 1135–40.

Miyake, Y. and Wada, E. (1967) The abundance ratio of $^{15}N/^{14}N$ in marine environments. *Records of Oceanographic Works in Japan* 9(1), 37–53.

Molleson, T. and Blondiaux, J. (1994) Riders' bones from Kish, Iraq. *Cambridge Archaeological Journal* 4(2), 312–16.

Montgomery, J., Beaumont, J., Jay, M., Keefe, K., Gledhill, A.R., Cook, G.T., et al. (2013a) Strategic and sporadic marine consumption at the onset of the

Neolithic: increasing temporal resolution in the isotope evidence. *Antiquity* 87(338), 1060–72.

Montgomery, J., Budd, P. and Evans, J. (2000) Reconstructing the lifetime movements of ancient people: a Neolithic case study from southern England. *European Journal of Archaeology* 3(3), 370–85.

Montgomery, J., Evans, J.A., Chenery, S.R., Pashley, V. and Killgrove, K. (2010) 'Gleaming, white and deadly': using lead to track human exposure and geographic origins in the Roman period in Britain. *Journal of Roman Archaeology; supplementary series* 78, 199–226.

Montgomery, J., Evans, J.A. and Horstwood, M.S. (2013b) Evidence for long-term averaging of strontium in bovine enamel using TIMS and LA-MC-ICP-MS strontium isotope intra-molar profiles. *Environmental Archaeology* 15(1), 32–42.

Moore, A.M.T. and Hillman, G.C. (1992) The Pleistocene to Holocene transition and human economy in Southwest Asia: The impact of the Younger Dryas. *American Antiquity*, 482–94.

Moore, A.M.T., Hillman, G.C. and Legge, A.J. (1975) The excavation of Tell Abu Hureyra in Syria: a preliminary report. *Proceedings of the Prehistoric Society* 41, 50–77.

(2000) *Village on the Euphrates: From Foraging to Farming at Abu Hureyra*. Oxford: Oxford University Press.

Morgan, E.D., Titus, L., Small, R.J. and Edwards, C. (1984) Gas-chromatographic analysis of fatty material from a Thule midden. *Archaeometry* 26, 43–8.

Morris, J. (2008) Re-examining associated bone groups from southern England and Yorkshire *c.* 4000 BC to AD 1550. Unpublished PhD thesis, University of Bournemouth.

Motuzaite-Matuzeviciute, G., Staff, R.A., Hunt, H.V., Liu, X. and Jones, M.K. (2013) The early chronology of broomcorn millet (*Panicum miliaceum*) in Europe. *Antiquity* 87(338), 1073–85.

Mukherjee, A.J., Copley, M.S., Berstan, R., Clark, K.A. and Evershed, R.P. (2005) Interpretation of $\delta^{13}C$ values of fatty acids in relation to animal husbandry, food processing and consumption in prehistory. In: J. Mulville and A.K. Outram (eds), *The Zooarchaeology of Fats, Oils, Milk and Dairying*. Oxford: Oxbow, pp. 77–93.

Mukherjee, A.J., Gibson, A.M. and Evershed, R.P. (2008) Trends in pig product processing at British Neolithic Grooved Ware sites traced through organic residues in potsherds. *Journal of Archaeological Science* 35(7), 2059–73.

Mullis, K.B. and Faloona, F.A. (1987) Specific synthesis of DNA in vitro via a polymerase-catalyzed chain reaction. *Methods in Enzymology* 155, 335–50.

Mullis, K., Faloona, F., Scharf, S., Saiki, R.K., Horn, G.T. and Erlich, H. (1986) Specific enzymatic amplification of DNA in vitro: the polymerase chain reaction. *Cold Spring Harbor Symposia on Quantitative Biology* 51, 263–73.

Murray, D.C., Haile, J., Dortch, J., White, N.E., Haouchar, D., Bellgard, M.I., et al. (2013) Scrapheap Challenge: A novel bulk-bone metabarcoding method to investigate ancient DNA in faunal assemblages. *Scientific Reports* 3, 337.

Mutolo, M.J., Jenny, L.L., Buszek, A.R., Fenton, T.W. and Foran, D.R. (2012) Osteological and molecular identification of brucellosis in ancient Butrint, Albania. *American Journal of Physical Anthropology* 147(2), 254–63.

Nagel, M.C. (1982) Frederick Soddy: From Alchemy to Isotopes. *Journal of Chemical Education* 59(9), 739–40.

Nätt, D., Rubin, C.J., Wright, D., Johnsson, M., Beltéky, J., Andersson, L. and Jensen, P. (2012) Heritable genome-wide variation of gene expression and promoter methylation between wild and domesticated chickens. *BMC Genomics* 13, 59.

Nehlich, O. (2015) The application of sulphur isotope analyses in archaeological research: a review. *Earth-Science Reviews* 142, 1–17.

Nelson, B.K., DeNiro, M.J., Schoeninger, M.J., De Paolo, D.J. and Hare, P.E. (1986) Effects of diagenesis on strontium, carbon, nitrogen and oxygen concentration and isotopic composition of bone. *Geochimica et Cosmochimica Acta* 50(9), 1941–9.

Nenquin, J. (1961) *Salt: A Study in Economic Prehistory*. Brugge: De Tempel.

Neil, S., Evans, J., Montgomery, J. and Scarre, C. (2016) Isotopic evidence for residential mobility of farming communities during the transition to agriculture in Britain. *Royal Society Open Science* 3(1), 150522.

Nistelberger, H.M., Smith, O., Wales, N., Star, B. and Boessenkool, S. (2016) The efficacy of high-throughput sequencing and target enrichment on charred archaeobotanical remains. *Scientific Reports* 6, 37347.

Nitsch, E., Andreou, S., Creuzieux, A., Gardeisen, A., Halstead, P., Isaakidou, V., et al. (2017) A bottom-up view of food surplus: using stable carbon and nitrogen isotope analysis to investigate agricultural strategies and diet at Bronze Age Archontiko and Thessaloniki Toumba, northern Greece. *World Archaeology* 49, 105–37.

Nitsch, E.K., Charles, M. and Bogaard, A. (2015) Calculating a statistically robust $\delta^{13}C$ and $\delta^{15}N$ offset for charred cereal and pulse seeds. *STAR: Science & Technology of Archaeological Research* 1(1), 1–8.

Nitsch, E.K., Humphrey, L.T. and Hedges, R.E. (2011) Using stable isotope analysis to examine the effect of economic change on breastfeeding practices in Spitalfields, London, UK. *American Journal of Physical Anthropology* 146(4), 619–28.

Noonan, J.P., Coop, G., Kudaravalli, S., Smith, D., Krause, J., Alessi, J., et al. (2006) Sequencing and analysis of Neanderthal genomic DNA. *Science* 314(5802), 1113–18.

O'Connell, T., Levine, M. and Hedges, R. (2003) The importance of fish in the diet of Central Eurasian peoples from the Mesolithic to the Early Iron Age. In: M. Levine, C. Renfrew and K. Boyle (eds), *Prehistoric Steppe Adaptation and the Horse*. Cambridge: McDonald Institute for Archaeological Research, pp. 253–68.

O'Connor, T. (2013) *Animals as Neighbours: The Past and Present of Commensal Species*. East Lansing: Michigan State University Press.

O'Day, S.J., van Neer, W. and Ervynck, A. (eds) (2004) *Behaviour Behind Bones: The Zooarchaeology of Ritual, Religion, Status and Identity*. Oxford: Oxbow Books.

Odum, E.P. (1959) *Fundamentals of Ecology*. London: Saunders.

Olsen, S.J. (1964) *Mammal Remains from Archaeological Sites, Part 1: Southeastern and Southwestern United States*. Cambridge, MA: Harvard University Press.

Olsen, S.L. (1989) Solutré: a theoretical approach to the reconstruction of upper Palaeolithic hunting strategies. *Journal of Human Evolution* 18(4), 295–327.

Olsen, S. L. (1996) Horse hunters of the Ice Age. In: S. Olsen (ed.), *Horses through Time*. Boulder, CO: Roberts Rinehart, pp. 35–56.

Olsen, S.L. (2003) The exploitation of horses at Botai, Kazakhstan. In: M. Levine, C. Renfrew and K. Boyle (eds), *Prehistoric Steppe Adaptation and the Horse*. Cambridge: McDonald Institute. pp. 83–104.

Olsen, S.A. (2006a) Early horse domestication on the Eurasian Steppe. In: M.A. Zeder, D.G. Bradley, E. Emschwiller and B.D. Smith (eds), *Documenting Domestication: New Genetic and Archaeological Paradigms*, Berkeley: University of California Press, pp. 245–69.

(2006b) Early horse domestication: weighing the evidence. In: S.L. Olsen, S. Grant, A.M. Choyke and L. Bartosiewicz (eds), *Horses and Humans: The Evolution of Human–Equine Relationships*. Oxford: Archaeopress, pp. 81–113.

Olsen, S.A., Bradley, B., Maki, D. and Outram, A. (2006) Community organization among Copper Age sedentary horse pastoralists of Kazakhstan. In: D.L. Peterson, L.M. Popova and A.T. Smith (eds), *Beyond the Steppe and the Sown: Proceedings of the 2002 University of Chicago Conference on Eurasian Archaeology*. Leiden: Brill. pp. 89–111.

Orlando, L. (2015) The first aurochs genome reveals the breeding history of British and European cattle. *Genome Biology* 16(1), 225.

Orlando, L., Ginolhac, A., Zhang, G., Froese, D., Albrechtsen, A., Stiller, M., et al. (2013) Recalibrating *Equus* evolution using the genome sequence of an early Middle Pleistocene horse. *Nature* 499(7456), 74–8.

Orlando, L. and Willerslev, E. (2014) An epigenetic window into the past? *Science* 345(6196), 511–12.

Ottoni, C., Girdland Flink, L., Evin, A., Geörg, C., De Cupere, B., Van Neer, W., et al. (2013) Pig domestication and human-mediated dispersal in western Eurasia revealed through ancient DNA and geometric morphometrics. *Molecular Biology and Evolution* 30(4), 824–32.

Outram, A.K. (1998) The identification and Palaeoeconomic context of prehistoric bone marrow and grease exploitation. Unpublished PhD Thesis. University of Durham, England.

(1999) A comparison of Paleo-Eskimo and medieval Norse bone fat exploitation in western Greenland. *Arctic Anthropology* 103–17.

(2001) A new approach to identifying bone marrow and grease exploitation: why the indeterminate fragments should not be ignored. *Journal of Archaeological Science* 28(4), 401–10.

(2002) Bone fracture and within-bone nutrients: an experimentally based method for investigating levels of marrow extraction. In: P. Miracle and N. Milner (eds), *Consuming Passions and Patterns of Consumption*, Cambridge: McDonald Institute for Archaeological Research, pp. 51–64.

(2003) Comparing levels of subsistence stress amongst Norse settlers in Iceland and Greenland using levels of bone fat exploitation as an indicator. *Environmental Archaeology* 8(2), 119–28.

(2004a) Applied models and indices vs. high-resolution, observed data: detailed fracture and fragmentation analyses for the investigation of skeletal part abundance patterns. *Journal of Taphonomy* 2(3), 167–84.

(2004b) Identifying dietary stress in marginal environments: bone fats, optimal foraging theory and the seasonal round. In: M. Mondini, S. Munoz and S. Wickler (eds), *Colonisation, Migration and Marginal Areas: A Zooarchaeological Approach*. Oxford: Oxbow, pp. 74–85.

(2006) Juggling with indices: a review of the evidence and interpretations regarding upper Palaeolithic horse skeletal part abundances. In: S.L. Olsen, S. Grant, A.M. Choyke and L. Bartosiewicz (eds), *Horses and Humans: The Evolution of Human–Equine Relationships*. Oxford: Archaeopress, pp. 49–60.

(2014) Animal domestications. In: V. Cumming, P. Jordan and M. Zvelebil (eds), *Oxford Handbook of the Archaeology and Anthropology of Hunter-Gatherers*. Oxford: Oxford University Press, pp. 749–63.

(2015) Pastoralism. In: G. Barker and C. Goucher (eds), *The Cambridge World History, Volume II: A World with Agriculture, 12,000* BCE *– 500* CE. Cambridge: Cambridge University Press, pp. 161–85.

(2017) Answering zooarchaeological questions from the analysis of animal bones and organic pottery residues: a critical comparison. In: P.A. Rowley-Conwy, D. Serjeantson and P. Halstead (eds), *Economic Zooarchaeology Studies in Hunting, Herding and Early Agriculture*. Oxford: Oxbow Books, pp. 148–56.

Outram, A.K., Kasparov, A., Stear, N.A., Varfolomeev, V., Usmanova, E. and Evershed, R.P. (2012) Patterns of pastoralism in later Bronze Age Kazakhstan: new evidence from faunal and lipid residue analyses. *Journal of Archaeological Science* 39, 2424–35.

Outram, A. and Rowley-Conwy, P. (1998) Meat and marrow utility indices for horse (*Equus*). *Journal of Archaeological Science* 25, 839–49.

Outram, A.K., Stear, N.A., Bendrey, R., Olsen, S., Kasparov, A., Zaibert, V., et al. (2009) The earliest horse harnessing and milking. *Science* 323(5919), 1332–5.

Outram, A.K., Stear, N.A., Kasparov, A., Usmanova, E., Varfolomeev, V. and Evershed, R.P. (2011) Horses for the dead: funerary foodways in Bronze Age Kazakhstan. *Antiquity* 85, 116–28.

Overton, N.J. and Hamilakis, Y. (2013) A manifesto for a social zooarchaeology. Swans and other beings in the Mesolithic. *Archaeological Dialogues* 20(2), 111–36.

Pääbo, S. (1985) Molecular cloning of ancient Egyptian mummy DNA. *Nature* 314, 644–5.

(1989) Ancient DNA: extraction, characterization, molecular cloning, and enzymatic amplification. *Proceedings of the National Academy of Sciences* 86(6), 1939–43.

Palmer, C. and Van der Veen, M. (2002) Archaeobotany and the social context of food. *Acta Palaeobotanica* 42(2), 195–202.

Paludan-Müller, C. (1978) High Atlantic food gathering in northwestern Zealand, ecological conditions and spatial representation. In: K. Kristiansen and C. Paludan-Müller (eds), *New Directions in Scandinavian Archaeology*. Copenhagen: National Museum of Denmark, pp. 120–57.

Park, S.D., Magee, D.A., McGettigan, P.A., Teasdale, M.D., Edwards, C.J., Lohan, A.J., et al. (2015) Genome sequencing of the extinct Eurasian wild aurochs,

Bos primigenius, illuminates the phylogeography and evolution of cattle. *Genome Biology* 16(1), 234.

Parmenter, P.C.R. (2015) A reassessment of the role of animals at the Etton Causewayed Enclosure. PhD Thesis. University of Exeter, England. http://hdl.handle.net/10871/18013.

Parmenter, P.C.R., Johnson, E.V. and Outram, A.K. (2015) Inventing the Neolithic? Putting evidence-based interpretation back into the study of faunal remains from causewayed enclosures. *World Archaeology* 57(5), 819–33.

Payne, S. (1969) A metrical distinction between sheep and goat metacarpals. In: P.J. Ucko and G.W. Dimbleby (eds), *The Domestication and Exploitation of Plants and Animals*. London: Duckworth, pp. 295–305.

(1972a) Partial recover and sample bias: the results of some sieving experiments. In: E.S. Higgs (ed.), *Papers in Economic Prehistory: Studies by Members and Associates of the British Academy Major Research Project in the Early History of Agriculture*. Cambridge: Cambridge University Press, pp. 49–64.

(1972b) On the interpretation of bone samples from archaeological sites. In: E.S. Higgs (ed.), *Papers in Economic Prehistory: Studies by Members and Associates of the British Academy Major Research Project in the Early History of Agriculture*. Cambridge: Cambridge University Press, pp. 27–36.

(1973) Kill off patterns in sheep and goats: the mandibles from Asvan Kale. *Anatolian Studies* 23, 281–303.

Pearsall, D.M. (2000) *Palaeoethnobotany: A Handbook of Procedures*, 2nd edn. San Diego, CA: Academic Press.

Pearsall, D.M., Chandler-Ezell, K. and Chandler-Ezell, A. (2003) Identifying maize in Neotropical sediments and soils using cob phytoliths. *Journal of Archaeological Science* 30, 611–27.

Pedersen, M.W., Overballe-Petersen, S., Ermini, L., Der Sarkissian, C., Haile, J., Hellstrom, M., et al. (2015) Ancient and modern environmental DNA. *Philosphical Transactions of the Royal Society B* 370(1660), 20130383.

Pedersen, J.S., Valen, E., Velazquez, A.M.V., Parker, B.J., Rasmussen, M., Lindgreen, S., et al. (2014) Genome-wide nucleosome map and cytosine methylation levels of an ancient human genome. *Genome Research* 24(3), 454–66.

Peleg, Z., Fahima, T., Korol, A.B., Abbo, S. and Saranga, Y. (2011) Genetic analysis of wheat domestication and evolution under domestication. *Journal of Experimental Botany* 62(14), 5051–61.

Peña-Chocarro, L. (2007) Early agriculture in central and southern Spain. In: S. Colledge and J. Conolly (eds), *The origins of domestic plants in Southwest Asia and Europe*. Walnut Creek, CA: Left Coast Press, pp. 173–87.

Peng, J.H., Sun, D. and Nevo, E. (2011) Domestication evolution, genetics and genomics in wheat. *Molecular Breeding* 28(3), 281.

Peukert, S., Bol, R., Roberts, W., Macleod, C.J.A., Murray, P.J., Dixon, E.R. and Brazier R.E. (2012). Understanding spatial variability of soil properties: a key step in establishing field- to farm-scale agro-ecosystem experiments. *Rapid Communications in Mass Spectrometry* 26, 2413–21.

Piggott, S. (1992) *Wagon, Chariot and Carriage*. London: Thames & Hudson.

Piperno, D. (2006) *Phytoliths. A Comprehensive Guide for Archaeologists and Palaeoecologists*. Lanham, MD, New York, Toronto and Oxford: Altamira.

Piperno, D.R. (2017) Assessing elements of an extended evolutionary synthesis for plant domestication and agricultural origin research. *Proceedings of the National Academy of Sciences* 114(25), 6429–37.

Piperno, D.R. and Holst, I. (1998) The presence of starch grains on prehistoric stone tools from the humid neotropics: indications of early tuber use and agriculture in Panama. *Journal of Archaeological Science* 25(8), 765–76.

Piperno, D.R., Ranere, A.J., Holst, I., Iriarte, J. and Dickau, R. (2009) Starch grain and phytolith evidence for early ninth millennium B.P. maize from the Central Balsas River valley, Mexico. *Proceedings of the National Academy of Sciences* 106, 5019–24.

Pitts, M. (1979) Hides and antlers: a new look at the hunter-gatherer site of Star Carr, North Yorksire, England. *World Archaeology* 11, 32–42.

Popper, K. (1959) *The Logic of Scientific Discovery*. London: Hutchinson.

Privat, K., O'Connell, T., Neal, K. and Hedges, R. (2005) Fermented dairy product analysis and palaeodietary repercussions: is stable isotope analysis not cheesy enough? In: J. Mulville and A.K. Outram (eds), *The Zooarchaeology of Fats, Oils, Milk and Dairying*. Oxford: Oxbow, pp. 60–6.

Quinlan, R.J. (2007) Human parental effort and environmental risk. *Proceedings of the Royal Society of London B: Biological Sciences* 274(1606), 121–5.

Quintelier, K., Ervynck, A., Müldner, G., Neer, W., Richards, M.P. and Fuller, B.T. (2014) Isotopic examination of links between diet, social differentiation, and DISH at the post-medieval Carmelite Friary of Aalst, Belgium. *American Journal of Physical Anthropology* 153(2), 203–13.

Ramos-Madrigal, J., Smith, B.D., Moreno-Mayar, J.V., Gopalakrishnan, S., Ross-Ibarra, J., Gilbert, M.T.P. and Wales, N. (2016) Genome sequence of a 5,310-year-old maize cob provides insights into the early stages of maize domestication. *Current Biology* 26(23), 3195–201.

Ranere, A.J., Piperno, D.R., Holst, I., Dickau, R. and Iriarte, J. (2009) The cultural and chronological context of early Holocene maize and squash domestication in the Central Balsas River Valley. *Proceedings of the National Academy of Sciences* 106, 5014–18.

Rasmussen, M., Anzick, S.L., Waters, M.R., Skoglund, P., DeGiorgio, M., Stafford Jr, T.W., et al. (2014) The genome of a Late Pleistocene human from a Clovis burial site in western Montana. *Nature* 506(7487), 225–9.

Rasmussen, M., Li, Y., Lindgreen, S., Pedersen, J.S., Albrechtsen, A., Moltke, I., et al. (2010) Ancient human genome sequence of an extinct Palaeo-Eskimo. *Nature* 463(7282), 757–62.

Reber, E., Baumann, T.E., Monaghan, G. W. and Myers, K.N. (2015) Absorbed Residue Analysis of a Mississippi Plain Jar from Angel Mounds (12Vg1) Lipid Distribution Revisited. *Advances in Archaeological Practice* 3(1), 29–49.

Reber, E.A., Dudd, S.N., Van der Merwe, N.J. and Evershed, R.P. (2004) Direct detection of maize in pottery residues via compound specific stable carbon isotope analysis. *Antiquity* 78(301), 682–91.

Reber, E. A. and Evershed, R. P. (2004a) How Did Mississippians Prepare Maize? The Application of Compound-Specific Carbon Isotope Analysis to Absorbed Pottery Residues From Several Mississippi Valley Sites. *Archaeometry* 46(1), 19–33.

Reber, E. A. and Evershed, R.P. (2004b) Identification of maize in absorbed organic residues: a cautionary tale. *Journal of Archaeological Science* 31(4), 399–410.

Reidhead, V. (1979) Linear programming models in archaeology. *Annual Review of Anthropology* 8, 543–78.

Reitmaier, T., Doppler, T., Pike, A.W., Deschler-Erb, S., Hajdas, I., Walser, C. and Gerling, C. (2018) Alpine cattle management during the bronze age at Ramosch-Mottata, Switzerland. *Quaternary International* 484, 19–31.

Reitsema, L.J. (2013) Beyond diet reconstruction: stable isotope applications to human physiology, health, and nutrition. *American Journal of Human Biology* 25(4), 445–56.

Reitz, E.J. and Wing, E.A. (2008) *Zooarchaeology, 2nd ed.* Cambridge: Cambridge University Press.

Renfrew, C. (1982) Polity and power: interaction, intensification and exploitation. In: C. Renfrew and M. Wagstaff (eds), *An Island Polity: the Archaeology of Exploitation on Melos*. Cambridge: Cambridge University Press, pp. 264–90.

Renfrew C. (1987) *Archaeology and Language: The Puzzle of Indo-European Origins*. London: Jonathan Cape.

(2002a) The emerging synthesis: the archaeogenetics of farming/language dispersals and other spread zones. In: P. Bellwood and C. Renfrew (eds), *Examining the Farming/Language Dispersal Hypothesis*. Cambridge: McDonald Institute, pp. 3–16.

Renfrew, C. (2002b) Pastoralism and interaction: Some introductory questions. In: K. Boyle, C. Renfrew and M. Levine (eds), *Ancient interactions: East and west in Eurasia*. Cambridge: McDonald Institute, pp. 1–10.

Renfrew, C. and Bahn, B. (2012) *Archaeology: Theories, Methods and Practice. 6th Edition*. London: Thames & Hudson.

Renfrew, J. (ed.) (1991) *New Light on Early Farming: Recent Developments in Palaeoethnobotany*. Edinburgh: Edinburgh University Press.

Reuther, J.D., Lowenstein, J.M., Gerlach, S.C., Hood, D., Scheuenstuhl, G. and Ubelaker, D.H. (2006) The use of an improved pRIA technique in the identification of protein residues. *Journal of Archaeological Science* 33(4), 531–7.

Reynolds, P. (1978) *Iron Age Farm: The Butser Experiment*. London: British Museum.

(1981) Deadstock and Livestock. In: R. Mercer (ed.), *Farming Practice in British Prehistory*. Edinburgh: Edinburgh University Press, pp. 97–122.

Richards, M.P. and Hedges, R.E.M. (1999) A Neolithic revolution? New evidence of diet in the British Neolithic. *Antiquity* 73(282), 891–7.

Richards, M.P. and Montgomery, J. (2012) Isotope analysis and palaeopathology: a short review and future developments. In: J. Buikstra and C. Roberts (eds), *The Global History of Paleopathology: Pioneers and Prospects*. Oxford: OUP, pp. 718–31.

Richards, M.P. and Schulting, R.J. (2006) Touch not the fish: the Mesolithic-Neolithic change of diet and its significance. *Antiquity* 80(308), 444–56.

Richards, T.W. and Lembert, M.E. (1914) The atomic weight of lead of radioactive origin. *Journal of the American Chemical Society* 36(7), 1329–44.

Riehl, S., Bryson, R. and Pustovoytov, K. (2008) Changing growing conditions for crops during the Near Eastern Bronze Age (3000–1200 BC): the stable carbon isotope evidence. *Journal of Archaeological Science* 35(4), 1011–22.

Ringrose, T.J. (1993) Bone counts and statistics: a critique. *Journal of Archaeological Science* 20, 121–57.

Rival, A., Beulé, T., Bertossi, F.A., Tregear, J. and Jaligot, E. (2010) Plant epigenetics: from genomes to epigenomes. *Notulae Botanicae Horti Agrobotanici Cluj-Napoca* 38(2), 9–15.

Robb, J. and Miracle, P. (2007) Beyond 'migration' versus 'acculturation': new models for the spread of agriculture. In: Whittle and V. Cummings (eds), *Going Over: the Mesolithic-Neolithic Transition in North-west Europe*. London: British Academy, pp. 99–115.

Robinson, N., Evershed, R.P., Higgs, W.J., Jerman, K. and Eglinton, G. (1987) Proof of a pine wood origin for pitch from Tudor (Mary Rose) and Etruscan shipwrecks: application of analytical organic chemistry in archaeology. *Analyst* 112(5), 637–44.

Roffet-Salque, M., Lee, M.R., Timpson, A. and Evershed, R.P. (2017) Impact of modern cattle feeding practices on milk fatty acid stable carbon isotope compositions emphasise the need for caution in selecting reference animal tissues and products for archaeological investigations. *Archaeological and Anthropological Sciences* 9(7), 1343–8.

Roffet-Salque, M., Marciniak, A., Valdes, P.J., Pawłowska, K., Pyzel, J., Czerniak, L., Krüger, M., Roberts, C.N., Pitter, S. and Evershed, R.P. (2018) Evidence for the impact of the 8.2-kyBP climate event on Near Eastern early farmers. *Proceedings of the National Academy of Sciences* 115(35), 8705–9.

Roffet-Salque, M., Regert, M., Evershed, R.P., Outram, A.K., Cramp, L.J., Decavallas, O., et al. (2015) Widespread exploitation of the honeybee by early Neolithic farmers. *Nature* 527(7577), 226–30.

Roper, D.C. (1979) The method and theory of site catchment analysis: a review. *Advances in Archaeological Method and Theory* 2, 119–40.

Rösch, M., Kleinmann, A., Lechterbeck, J. and Wick, L. (2014) Botanical off-site and on-site data as indicators of different land use systems: A discussion with examples from Southwest Germany. *Vegetation History and Archaeobotany* 23, 121–33.

Rosen, A. and Weiner, S. (1994) Identifying ancient irrigation: a new method using opaline phytoliths from emmer wheat. *Journal of Archaeological Science* 21, 125–32.

Rossman, D.L. (1976) A site catchment analysis of San Lorenzo, Veracruz. In: K.V. Flannery (ed.), *The Early Mesoamerican Village*. New York: Academic Press, pp. 95–103.

Rottoli, M. and Pessina, A. (2007) Early agriculture in central and southern Spain. In: S. Colledge and J. Conolly (eds), *The Origins and Spread of Domestic Plants in Southwest Asia and Europe*. Walnut Creek, CA: Left Coast Press, pp. 141–53.

Rowley-Conwy, P.A. (1981a) Mesolithic Danish bacon: permanent and temporary sites in the Danish Mesolithic. In: G. Bailey and A. Sheridan (eds), *Economic Archaeology*. Oxford: British Archaeological Reports, pp. 51–8.

(1981b) Slash and burn in the temperate European Neolithic. In: R. Mercer (ed.), *Farming Practice in British Prehistory*. Edinburgh: Edinburgh University Press, pp. 85–96.

(1983) Sedentary hunters: the Ertebølle example. In: G. Bailey (ed.), *Hunter-Gatherer Economy in Prehistory: A European Perspective*. Cambridge: Cambridge University Press, pp. 111–26.

(1986) Between cave painters and crop planters: aspects of the temperate European Mesolithic. In: M. Zvelebil (ed.), *Hunters in Transition: Mesolithic Societies of Temperate Eurasia and their Transition to Farming*. Cambridge: Cambridge University Press, pp. 17–32.

(1987) Animal bones in mesolithic studies: recent progress and hopes for the future. In: P. Rowley-Conwy, M. Zvelebil and H.P. Blankholm (eds.), *Mesolithic Northwest Europe – Recent Trends*. Sheffield: Department of Archaeology and Prehistory, pp. 74–81.

(1994) Dung, dirt and deposits: site formation under conditions of near-perfect preservation at Qasr Ibrim, Egyptian Nubia. In: R. Luff and P.A. Rowley-Conwy (eds), *Whither Environmental Archaeology?* Oxford: Oxbow, pp. 25–32.

(1998a) Meat, furs and skins: Mesolithic animal bones from Ringkloster, a seasonal hunting camp in Jutland. *Journal of Danish Archaeology* v.12 1994–95, 87–98.

(1998b) Cemeteries, seasonality and complexity in the Ertebølle of Southern Scandinavia. In: M. Zvelebil, R. Dennell and L. Domańska (eds), *Harvesting the Sea, Farming the Forest: The Emergence of Neolithic Societies in the Baltic region*. Sheffield: Sheffield Academic Press, pp. 193–202.

(1999) Economic prehistory in Southern Scandinavia. In: J. Coles, R. Bewley and P. Mellars (eds), *World Prehistory: Studies in Memory of Grahame Clark*. Oxford: Oxford University Press, pp. 125–59.

(2001) Time, change and the archaeology of hunter-gatherers: how original is the 'Original Affluent Society'? In: C. Panter-Brick, R.H. Layton and P. Rowley-Conwy (eds), *Hunter-Gatherers: An Interdisciplinary Perspective*. Cambridge: Cambridge University Press, pp. 39–72.

Rowley-Conwy, P., Halstead, P. and Collins, P. (2002) Derivation and application of a food utility index (FUI) for European wild boar (*Sus scrofa* L.). *Environmental Archaeology* 7(1), 77–88.

Rowley-Conwy, P. and Layton, R. (2011) Foraging and farming as niche construction: stable and unstable adaptations. *Philosophical Transactions of the Royal Society B: Biological Sciences* 366(1566), 849–62.

Rowley-Conwy, P. and Storå, J. (1997) Pitted Ware seals and pigs from Ajvide, Gotland: methods of study and first results. In: G. Burenhult (ed.), *Remote Sensing 1*, Stockholm: Stockholm University, pp. 113–25.

Russell, N. (2012) *Social Zooarchaeology: Humans and Animals in Prehistory*. Cambridge: Cambridge University Press.

Rutgers, L.V., Van Strydonck, M., Boudin, M. and Van der Linde, C. (2009) Stable isotope data from the early Christian catacombs of ancient Rome: new insights into the dietary habits of Rome's early Christians. *Journal of Archaeological Science* 36(5), 1127–34.

Saag, L., Varul, L., Scheib, C.L., Stenderup, J., Allentoft, M.E., Saag, L., Pagani, L., Reidla, M., Tambets, K., Metspalu, E., Kriiska, A., Willerslev, E., Kivisild, T. and Metspalu, M. (2017) Extensive farming in Estonia started through a sex-biased migration from the Steppe. *Current Biology* 27(14), 2185–93.

Sahlins, M. (1974) *Stone Age Economics*. London: Tavistock.

Salque, M., Bogucki, P.I., Pyzel, J., Sobkowiak-Tabaka, I., Grygiel, R., Szmyt, M. and Evershed, R.P. (2013). Earliest evidence for cheese making in the sixth millennium BC in northern Europe. *Nature* 493(7433), 522–5.

Samuel, D. (2006) Modified starch. In: R. Torrence and H. Barton (eds), *Ancient Starch Research*. Walnut Creek, CA: Left Coast Press, pp. 205–16.

Sanger, F. and Coulson, A.R. (1975). A rapid method for determining sequences in DNA by primed synthesis with DNA polymerase. *Journal of Molecular Biology* 94(3), 441IN19447–446IN20448.

Sanger, F., Nicklen, S. and Coulson, A.R. (1977) DNA sequencing with chain-terminating inhibitors. *Proceedings of the National Academy of Sciences* 74(12), 5463–7.

Sano, K. (2012) Functional variability in the Magdalenian of north-western Europe: A lithic microwear analysis of the Gönnersdorf K-II assemblage. *Quaternary International* 272, 264–74.

Savelle, J.M. and Friesen, M.T. (1996) An Odontocete (Cetacea) meat utility index. *Journal of Archaeological Science* 23(5), 713–21.

Schäfer, M. (2010). *Archäozoologische Untersuchung der Tierknochen aus der linearbandkeramischen Siedlung Vaihingen/Enz (Kreis Ludwigsburg D) und ihre Interpretation*. Unpublished PhD, Basel University.

Schaefer, N.K., Shapiro, B. and Green, R.E. (2016) Detecting hybridization using ancient DNA. *Molecular Ecology* 25(11), 2398–412.

Schibler, J. (2001). Methodische Überlegungen zum Problem der Einschätzung der Bedeutung von Jagd und Viehwirtschaft im schweizerischen Neolithikum. In: R.-M. Arbogast, C. Jeunesse and J. Schibler (eds), *Premières rencontres danubiennes, Strasbourg 20 et 21 novembre 1996, Actes de la première table-ronde; Rôle et statut de la chasse dans le Néolithique ancien danubien (5500–4900 av. J.-C.)*. Rahden: Verlag Marie Leidorf, pp. 153–70.

Schibler, J., Hüster-Plogmann, H., Jacomet, S., Brombacher, C., Gross-Klee, E. and Rast-Eicher, A. (1997) *Ökonomie und Ökologie neolithischer und bronzezeitlicher Ufersiedlungen am Zürichsee*. Zurich: Zürich und Egg.

Schier, W. (2009) Extensiver Brandfeldbau und die Ausbreitung der neolithischen Wirtschaftsweise in Mitteleuropa und Südskandinavien am Ende der 5. Jahrtausends v. Chr. *Praehistorische Zeitschrift* 84, 15–43.

Schmaus, T.M., Chang, C. and Tourtellotte, P.A. (2018) A model for pastoral mobility in Iron Age Kazakhstan. *Journal of Archaeological Science: Reports* 17, 137–43.

Schmid, E. (1972) *Atlas of Animal Bones: For Prehistorians, Archaeologists, and Quaternary Geologists*. Amsterdam: Elsevier.

Schoeninger, M.J. and DeNiro, M.J. (1984) Nitrogen and carbon isotopic composition of bone collagen from marine and terrestrial animals. *Geochimica et Cosmochimica Acta* 48(4), 625–39.

Schoville, B.J. and Otárola-Castillo, E. (2014) A model of hunter-gatherer skeletal element transport: the effect of prey body size, carriers, and distance. *Journal of Human Evolution* 73, 1–14.

Schurr, M.R. (1998) Using stable nitrogen-isotopes to study weaning behavior in past populations. *World Archaeology* 30(2), 327–42.

Schutkowski, H. (2006) *Human Ecology: Biocultural Adaptations in Human Communities*. Heidelberg: Springer.

Sealy, J. (2001) Body tissue chemistry and palaeodiet. In: D.R. Brothwell and A.M. Pollard (eds), *Handbook of Archaeological Sciences*. Chichester: Wiley, pp. 269–79.

Seetah, K. (2008) Modern analogy, cultural theory and experimental replication: a merging point at the cutting edge of archaeology. *World Archaeology* 40(1), 135–50.

Seetah, K., Cucchi, T., Dobney, K. and Barker, G. (2014) A geometric morphometric re-evaluation of the use of dental form to explore population differences in horses (*Equus caballus*) and its potential zooarchaeological application. *Journal of Archaeological Science* 41, 904–10.

Ségurel, L. and Bon, C. (2017) On the Evolution of Lactase Persistence in Humans. *Annual Review of Genomics and Human Genetics* 18(8.1), 8.23

Seguin-Orlando, A., Gamba, C., Der Sarkissian, C., Ermini, L., Louvel, G., Boulygina, E., et al. (2015) Pros and cons of methylation-based enrichment methods for ancient DNA. *Scientific Reports* 5, 11826.

Seinfeld, D.M., von Nagy, C. and Pohl, M.D. (2009) Determining Olmec maize use through bulk stable carbon isotope analysis. *Journal of Archaeological Science* 36(11), 2560–5.

Service, E.R. (1962) *Primitive Social Organization: An Evolutionary Perspective*. New York: Random House.

(1966) *The Hunters*. Englewood Cliffs: Prentice-Hall.

Sharp, Z.D., Atudorei, V., Panarello, H.O., Fernández, J. and Douthitt, C. (2003) Hydrogen isotope systematics of hair: archeological and forensic applications. *Journal of Archaeological Science* 30(12), 1709–16.

Shaw, H., Montgomery, J., Redfern, R., Gowland, R. and Evans, J. (2016) Identifying migrants in Roman London using lead and strontium stable isotopes. *Journal of Archaeological Science* 66, 57–68.

Sherratt, A. (1980). Water, soil and seasonality in early cereal cultivation. *World Archaeology* 2, 313–30.

Sherratt, A.G. (1981) Plough and pastoralism, aspects of the secondary products revolution, In: I. Hodder, G. Isaac and N. Hammond (eds.), *Patterns of the Past*. Cambridge: Cambridge University Press, pp. 261–306.

(1983) The secondary products revolution of animals in the Old World, *World Archaeology* 15, 90–104.

Sherratt, A. (2006) The Trans-Eurasian exchange: the prehistory of Chinese relations with the West. In: Mair, V. (ed.), *Contact and Exchange in the Ancient World*. Honolulu: Hawaii University Press, pp. 32–53.

Shillito, L.M. and Ryan, P. (2013) Surfaces and streets: Phytoliths, micromorphology and changing use of space at neolithic Çatalhöyük (Turkey). *Antiquity* 87(337), 684–700.

Shishlina, N. (2003) Yamnaya culture pastoral exploitation: a local sequence. In: M. Levine, C. Renfrew and K. Boyle (eds), *Prehistoric Steppe Adaptation and the Horse*. Cambridge: McDonald Institute, pp. 353–65.

Sielmann, B. (1971) Der Einfluß der Umwelt auf die neolithische Besiedlung Südwestdeutschlands unter besonderer Berücksichtigung der Verhältnisse am nördlichen Oberrhein. *Acta praehistorica et Archaeologica* 2, 65–197.

Silver, I.A. (1969) The ageing of domestic animals. In: D. Brothwell and E. Higgs (eds), *Science in Archaeology*. London: Thames & Hudson, pp. 283–302.

Sluyter, A. (2003) Neo-Environmental Determinism, Intellectual Damage Control, and Nature/Society Science. *Antipode* 35(4), 813–17.

Smith, B.D. (2007) Niche construction and the behavioral context of plant and animal domestication. *Evolutionary Anthropology: Issues, News, and Reviews* 16(5), 188–99.

(2009) Core conceptual flaws in human behavioral ecology. *Communicative and Integrative Biology* 2(6), 533–4.

(2011) A cultural Niche Construction Theory of initial domestication. *Biological Theory* 6(3), 260–71.

Smith, B.D. and Zeder, M.A. (2013) The onset of the anthropocene. *Anthropocene* 4, 8–13.

Smith, E.A. (1983) Comment on: Territoriality among human foragers: ecological models and an application to four Bushman groups. *Current Anthropology* 24(1), 61.

Smith, P.R. and Wilson, M.T. (2001) Blood residues in archaeology. In: D.R. Brothwell and A.M. Pollard (eds), *Handbook of Archaeological Sciences*. Chichester: Wiley, pp. 313–22.

Sobolik, K.D. and Steele, D.G. (1996) *A Turtle Atlas to Facilitate Archaeological Identifications*. Rapid City: Mammoth Site of Hot Springs and Kristin Sobolik.

Soddy, F. (1913) Intra-atomic charge. *Nature* 92(2301), 399–400.

Spangenberg, J.E., Matuschik, I., Jacomet, S. and Schibler, J. (2008) Direct evidence for the existence of dairying farms in prehistoric Central Europe (4th millennium BC). *Isotopes in Environmental and Health Studies* 44, 189–200.

Speth, J.D. (1983) *Bison Kills and Bone Counts: Decision Making by Ancient Hunters*. Chicago: University of Chicago Press.

Speth, J.D. and Spielmann, K.A. (1983) Energy source, protein metabolism, and hunter-gatherer subsistence strategies. *Journal of Anthropological Archaeology* 2, 1–31.

Spigelman, M., Donoghue, H.D., Abdeen, Z., Ereqat, S., Sarie, I., Greenblatt, C.L., et al. (2015) Evolutionary changes in the genome of Mycobacterium tuberculosis and the human genome from 9000 years BP until modern times. *Tuberculosis* 95, S145–S149.

Stear, N.A. (2008) *Changing patterns of animal exploitation in the prehistoric Eurasian steppe: an integrated molecular, stable isotope and archaeological approach*, Unpublished Thesis, University of Bristol.

Stewart, N.A., Gerlach, R.F., Gowland, R.L., Gron, K.J. and Montgomery, J. (2017) Sex determination of human remains from peptides in tooth enamel. *Proceedings of the National Academy of Sciences* 114(52), 13649–54.

Stiner, M.C. (2001) Thirty years on the 'Broad Spectrum Revolution' and Palaeolithic demography. *Proceedings of the National Academy of Sciences* 98(13), 6993–6.

Stott, A.W., Berstan, R., Evershed, R.P., Bronk-Ramsey, C., Hedges, R.E. and Humm, M.J. (2003) Direct dating of archaeological pottery by compound-specific ^{14}C analysis of preserved lipids. *Analytical Chemistry* 75(19), 5037–45.

Stott, A., Berstan, R., Evershed, P., Hedges, R., Ramsey, C. B. and Humm, M. (2001) Radiocarbon dating of single compounds isolated from pottery cooking vessel residues. *Radiocarbon* 43(2A), 191–7.

Street, J. (1969) An evaluation of the concept of carrying capacity. *Professional Geographer* 21, 104–7.

Strien, H.-C. (2005) Familientraditionen in der bandkeramischen Siedlung bei Vaihingen/Enz. In: J. Lüning, C. Fridrich and A. Zimmerman (eds), *Die Bandkeramik im 21. Jahrhundert: Symposium in der Abtei Brauweiler bei Köln vom 16.9.-19.9.2002*. Rahden: Verlag Marie Leidorf, pp. 189–97.

(2011) Chronological and social interpretation of the artefactual assemblage. In: A. Bogaard, *Plant Use and Crop Husbandry in an Early Neolithic Village: Vaihingen an der Enz, Baden-Württemberg*. Bonn: Habelt, pp. 19–23.

(2014) Eine neue Seriation der ältesten Linienbandkeramik: Zeitliche und räumliche Differenzierung. In: H.-J. Beier, R. Einicke and E. Biermann (eds), *Material – Werkzeug: Werkzeug – Material & Klinge, Messer, Schwert und Co. – Neues aus der Schneidenwelt. Aktuelles aus der Neolithforschung. Beiträge der Tagungen der Arbeitsgemeinschaft Werkzeuge und Waffen Pottenstein (Fränkische Schweiz) 2011 & Herxheim bei Landau in der Pfalz 2012 sowie Aktuelles*. Varia neolithica VIII, pp. 141–61.

Sturdy, D.A. (1975) Some reindeer economies in prehistoric Europe. In: E.S. Higgs (ed.), *Palaeoeconomy: Being the Second Volume of Papers in Economic Prehistory by Members and Associates of the British Academy Major Research Project in the Early History of Agriculture*. Cambridge: Cambridge University Press, pp. 55–96.

Styring, A.K., Ater, M., Hmimsa, Y., Fraser, R., Miller, H., Neef, R., et al. (2016a). Disentangling the effect of farming practice from aridity on crop stable isotope values: A present-day model from Morocco and its application to early farming sites in the eastern Mediterranean. *The Anthropocene Review* 3: 2–22

Styring, A.K., Charles, M., Fantone, F., Hald, M.M., McMahon, A., Meadow, R.H., et al. (2017a) Isotope evidence for agricultural extensification reveals how the world's first cities were fed. *Nature Plants* 3(6), 17076.

Styring, A.K., Fraser, R.A., Arbogast, R.M., Halstead, P., Isaakidou, V., Pearson, J.A., et al. (2015) Refining human palaeodietary reconstruction using amino acid δ^{15}N values of plants, animals and humans. *Journal of Archaeological Science* 53, 504–15.

Styring, A.K., Fraser, R.A., Bogaard, A. and Evershed, R.P. (2014a) The effect of manuring on cereal and pulse amino acid delta N-15 values. *Phytochemistry* 102, 40–5.

Styring, A.K., Fraser, R.A., Bogaard A. and Evershed, R.P. (2014b) Cereal grain, rachis and pulse seed amino acid delta N-15 values as indicators of plant nitrogen metabolism. *Phytochemistry* 97, 20–9.

Styring, A., Maier, U., Stephan, E., Schlichtherle, H. and Bogaard, A. (2016) Cultivation of choice: new insights into farming practices at Neolithic lakeshore sites. *Antiquity* 90, 95–110.

Styring, A., Manning, H., Fraser, R., Wallace, M., Jones, G., Charles, M., et al. (2013) The effect of charring and burial on the biochemical composition of cereal grains: investigating the integrity of archaeological plant material. *Journal of Archaeological Science* 40, 4767–79.

Styring, A., Rösch, M., Stephan, E., Stika, H.-P., Fischer, E., Sillmann, M. and Bogaard, A. (2017b) Centralisation and long-term change in farming regimes: comparing agricultural practice in Neolithic and Iron Age south-west Germany. *Proceedings of the Prehistoric Society* 83, 357–81.

Sykes, N. (2004) The introduction of fallow deer to Britain: a zooarchaeological perspective. *Environmental Archaeology* 9(1), 75–83.

(2014) *Beastly Questions: Animal Answers to Archaeological Issues*. London: Bloomsbury.

Sykes, N.J., White, J., Hayes, T.E. and Palmer, M.R. (2006) Tracking animals using strontium isotopes in teeth: the role of fallow deer (*Dama dama*) in Roman Britain. *Antiquity* 80(310), 948–59.

Taché, K. and Craig, O.E. (2015) Cooperative harvesting of aquatic resources and the beginning of pottery production in north-eastern North America. *Antiquity* 89(343), 177–90.

Tarasov, P.E., Jolly, D. and Kaplan, J.O. (1997) A continuous Late Glacial and Holocene record of vegetation changes in Kazakhstan. *Palaeogeography, Palaeoclimatology, Palaeoecology* 136(1–4), 281–92.

Tauber, H. (1981) ^{13}C evidence for dietary habits of prehistoric man in Denmark. *Nature* 292, 332–3.

Taylor, W.T.T., Bayarsaikhan, J. and Tuvshinjargal, T. (2015) Equine cranial morphology and the identification of riding and chariotry in late Bronze Age Mongolia. *Antiquity* 89(346), 854–71.

Thomas, J. (1991) *Rethinking the Neolithic*. Cambridge: Cambridge University Press.

(1999) *Understanding the Neolithic*. London: Routledge.

(2003) Thoughts on the 'repacked' Neolithic revolution. *Antiquity* 77(295), 67–74.

Thomson, J.J. (1913) Bakerian lecture: Rays of positive electricity. *Proceedings of the Royal Society of London. Series A, Containing Papers of a Mathematical and Physical Character* 89(607), 1–20.

Tilley, C. (1981) Economy and society: what relationship? In: G. Bailey and A. Sheridan (eds), *Economic Archaeology*. Oxford: British Archaeological Reports, pp. 131–48.

Tito, R.Y., Knights, D., Metcalf, J., Obregon-Tito, A.J., Cleeland, L., Najar, F., et al. (2012) Insights from characterizing extinct human gut microbiomes. *PloS One* 7(12), e51146.

Tito, R.Y., Macmil, S., Wiley, G., Najar, F., Cleeland, L., Qu, C., et al. (2008) Phylotyping and functional analysis of two ancient human microbiomes. *PLoS One* 3(11), e3703.

Torrence, R. (2006) Starch and archaeology. In: R. Torrence and H. Barton (eds), *Ancient Starch Research*, Walnut Creek, CA: Left Coast Press, pp. 17–33.

Towers, J., Gledhill, A., Bond, J. and Montgomery, J. (2014) An investigation of cattle birth seasonality using δ^{13}C and δ^{18}O profiles within first molar enamel. *Archaeometry* 56(S1), 208–36.

Tresset, A. and Vigne, J.-D. (2001) La chasse, principal élément structurant la diversité des faunes archéologiques du Néolithique ancien, en Europe tempérée at en Méditerranée: tentative d'interpretation fonctionelle. In: R.-M. Arbogast, C. Jeunesse and J. Schibler (eds), *Premières rencontres danubiennes, Strasbourg 20 et 21 novembre 1996, Actes de la première table-ronde; Rôle et statut de la chasse dans le Néolithique ancien danubien (5500–4900 av. J.-C.)*. Rahden: Verlag Marie Leidorf, pp. 129–51.

Trigger, B.G. (1989) *A History of Archaeological Thought*. Cambridge: Cambridge University Press.

Troy, C.S., MacHugh, D.E., Bailey, J.F. and Magee, D.A. (2001) Genetic evidence for Near-Eastern origins of European cattle. *Nature* 410(6832), 1088–91.

Tsalkin V.I. (1972) Fauna iz raskopok andronovskih pamiatnikov v Priural'e, Osnovnye problemy teriologii. *Proceedings of MOIP* 48, 66–81.

Turner, B.L., Kamenov, G.D., Kingston, J.D. and Armelagos, G.J. (2009) Insights into immigration and social class at Machu Picchu, Peru based on oxygen, strontium, and lead isotopic analysis. *Journal of Archaeological Science* 36(2), 317–32.

Tuross, N., Barnes, I. and Potts, R. (1996) Protein identification of blood residues on experimental stone tools. *Journal of Archaeological Science* 23(2), 289–96.

Tykot, R.H. (2004) Stable Isotopes and Diet: You Are What You Eat. In: M. Martini, M. Milazzo and M. Piacentini (eds), *Physics Methods in Archaeometry. Proceedings of the International School of Physics 'Enrico Fermi' Course CLIV*, Bologna, Italy: Società Italiana di Fisica, pp. 433–44.

Ugent, D., Pozorski, S. and Pozorski, T. (1981) Prehistoric remains of the sweet potato from the Casma Valley of Peru. *Phytologia* 49, 401–15.

Usmanova, E (2005) *Mogilnik Lisakovskij: Fakty i Parallyeli*. Lisakovsk: Lisakovsk Museum.

Vaiglova, P., Snoeck, C., Nitsch, E., Bogaard, A. and Lee-Thorp, J. (2014) Impact of contamination and pre-treatment on stable carbon and nitrogen isotopic composition of charred plant remains. *Rapid Communications in Mass Spectrometry* 28, 2497–510.

Valamoti, S., Samuel, D., Bayram, M. and Marinova, E. (2008) Prehistoric cereal foods from Greece and Bulgaria: investigation of starch microstructure in experimental and archaeological charred remains. *Vegetation History and Archaeobotany* 17 (Suppl 1), S265–S276.

Vallebueno-Estrada, M., Rodríguez-Arévalo, I., Rougon-Cardoso, A., González, J.M., Cook, A.G., Montiel, R. and Vielle-Calzada, J.-P. (2017) The earliest maize from San Marcos Tehuacan is a partial domesticate with genomic evidence of inbreeding. *Proceedings of the National Academy of Sciences* 113, 14151–6.

van der Merwe, N.J. and Vogel, J.C. (1978) ^{13}C content of human collagen as a measure of prehistoric diet in woodland North America. *Nature* 276, 815–16.

van Zeist, W. (1969) Reflections on prehistoric environment in the Near East. In: P.J. Ucko and G.W. Dimbleby (eds), *The Domestication and Exploitation of Plants and Animals*. London: Duckworth, pp. 35–46.

van Zeist, W. and Casperie, W.A. (eds) (1984) *Plants and Ancient Man: Studies in Palaeoethnobotany*. Rotterdam: Balkema.

Ventresca Miller, A.R., Winter-Schuh, C., Usmanova, E.R., Logvin, A., Shevnina, I. and Makarewicz, C.A. (2017) Pastoralist Mobility in Bronze Age Landscapes of Northern Kazakhstan: $^{87}Sr/^{86}Sr$ and $\delta^{18}O$ Analyses of Human Dentition from Bestamak and Lisakovsk. *Environmental Archaeology*, DOI: 10.1080/14614103.2017.1390031.

Verbricky-Todd, E. (1984) *Communal Buffalo Hunting among the Plains Indians*. Edmonton: Archaeological Survey of Alberta.

Vigne, J-D. and Helmer, D. (2007) Was milk a 'secondary product' in the Old World neolithisation process? Its role in the domestication of cattle, sheep and goats. *Anthropozoologica* 42, 9–40.

Vilà, C., Leonard, J.A. and Beja-Pereira, A. (2006) Genetic documentation of horse and donkey domestication. In: M.A. Zeder, D.G. Bradley, E. Emschwiller and B.D. Smith (eds), *Documenting domestication: new genetic and archaeological paradigms*, Berkeley: University of California Press, pp. 342–53.

Vilà, C., Leonard, A., Götherström, S., Marklund, J., Sandberg, K., Lidén, R., et al. (2001) Widespread origins of domestic horse lineages. *Science* 291, 474–7.

Vita-Finzi, C. and Higgs, E.S. (1970) Prehistoric economy in the Mount Carmel area of Palestine: site catchment analysis. *Proceedings on the Prehistoric Society* 36, 1–37.

Vogel, J.C. and Van der Merwe, N.J. (1977) Isotopic evidence for early maize cultivation in New York State. *American Antiquity* 42, 238–42.

von den Driesch, A.E. (1976) *A Guide to the Measurement of Animal Bones from Archaeological Sites*. Cambridge, MA: Peabody Museum.

von Holstein, I.C., Rogers, P.W., Craig, O.E., Penkman, K.E., Newton, J. and Collins, M.J. (2016) Provenancing Archaeological Wool Textiles from Medieval Northern Europe by Light Stable Isotope Analysis ($\delta^{13}C$, $\delta^{15}N$, $\delta^{2}H$). *PloS one* 11(10), p.e0162330.

Wada, E., Mizutani, H. and Minagawa, M. (1991) The use of stable isotopes for food web analysis. *Critical Reviews in Food Science & Nutrition* 30(4), 361–71.

Wall, J.D. and Kim, S.K. (2007) Inconsistencies in Neanderthal genomic DNA sequences. *PLoS Genetics* 3(10), p.e175.

Wallace, M., Jones, G., Charles, M., Fraser, R., Halstead, P., Heaton, T.H. and Bogaard, A. (2013) Stable carbon isotope analysis as a direct means of inferring crop water status and water management practices. *World Archaeology* 45(3), 388–409.

Wang, C.C., Farina, S.E. and Li, H. (2013) Neanderthal DNA and modern human origins. *Quaternary International* 295, 126–9.

Warinner, C., Hendy, J., Speller, C., Cappellini, E., Fischer, R., Trachsel, C., et al. (2014) Direct evidence of milk consumption from ancient human dental calculus. *Scientific Reports* 4, 7104.

Warinner, C., Speller, C. and Collins, M.J. (2015a) A new era in palaeomicrobiology: prospects for ancient dental calculus as a long-term record of the human oral microbiome. *Philosophical Transactions of the Royal Society B* 370(1660), 20130376.

Warinner, C., Speller, C., Collins, M.J. and Lewis, C.M. (2015b) Ancient human microbiomes. *Journal of Human Evolution* 79, 125–36.

Watson, J.D. and Crick, F.H. (1953) Molecular structure of nucleic acids. *Nature* 171(4356), 737–8.

Warmuth, V., Eriksson, A., Bower, M.A., Barker, G., Barrett, E., Hanks, B.K., et al. (2012) Reconstructing the origin and spread of horse domestication in the Eurasian steppe *Proceedings from the National Academy of Sciences* 109(21), 8202–6.

Webb, E.A. and Longstaffe, F.J. (2000) The oxygen isotopic compositions of silica phytoliths and plant water in grasses: Implications for the study of paleoclimate. *Geochemica et Cosmochimica* 64, 767–80.

Webb, E.C., Lewis, J., Shain, A., Kastrisianaki-Guyton, E., Honch, H.V., Stewart, A., et al. (2017) The influence of varying proportions of terrestrial and marine dietary protein on the stable carbon-isotope compositions of pig tissues from a controlled feeding experiment. *Science and Technology of Archaeological Research* 3(1), 36–52.

Webb, E.C., Honch, N.V., Dunn, P.J., Linderholm, A., Eriksson, G., Lidén, K. and Evershed, R.P. (2018) Compound-specific amino acid isotopic proxies for distinguishing between terrestrial and aquatic resource consumption. *Archaeological and Anthropological Sciences* 10(1), 1–18.

Webb, S.D. and Hemmings, C.A. (2006) Last horses and first humans in North America. In: S.L. Olsen, S. Grant, A.M. Choyke and L. Bartosiewicz (eds), *Horses and humans: the evolution of human-equine relationships*. Oxford: Archaeopress, pp. 11–23.

Webley, D. (1972) Soils and site location in prehistoric Palestine. In: E.S. Higgs (ed.), *Papers in Economic Prehistory: Studies by Members and Associates of the British Academy Major Research Project in the Early History of Agriculture*. Cambridge: Cambridge University Press, pp. 169–80.

Weisskopf, A., Harvey, E., Kingwell-Banham, E., Kajale, M., Mohanty, R. and Fuller, D.Q. (2014) Archaeobotanical implications of phytolith assemblages from cultivated rice systems, wild rice stands and macro-regional patterns. *Journal of Archaeological Science* 51, 43–53.

Weisskopf, A.R. and Lee, G.A. (2016) Phytolith identification criteria for foxtail and broomcorn millets: a new approach to calculating crop ratios. *Archaeological and Anthropological Sciences* 8(1), 29–42.

Weisskopf, A., Qin, L., Ding, J., Ding, P., Sun, G. and Fuller, D.Q. (2015) Phytoliths and rice: from wet to dry and back again in the Neolithic Lower Yangtze. *Antiquity* 89, 1051–63.

Wendrich, W. and Barnard, H. (2008) The archaeology of mobility: definitions and research approaches. In: H. Barnard and W. Wendrich (eds), *The Archaeology of Mobility: Old World and New World Nomadism*. Los Angeles: Cotsen Institute, University of California, pp. 1–24.

West, D. (2006) Horse hunting in Central Europe at the end of the Pleistocene. In: S.L. Olsen, S. Grant, A.M. Choyke and L. Bartosiewicz (eds), *Horses and Humans: The Evolution of Human-equine Relationships*. Oxford: Archaeopress, pp. 25–47.

West, J.A. and Louys, J. (2007) Differentiating bamboo from stone tool cut marks in the zooarchaeological record, with a discussion on the use of bamboo knives. *Journal of Archaeological Science* 34(4), 512–18.

White, T.D. (1992) *Prehistoric Cannibalism at Mancos 5MTUMR-2346*. Princeton: Princeton University Press.

White, T.E. (1952) Animal bone and plains archaeology. *Plains Archaeological Conference Newsletter* 4, 46–8.

(1953) Observations on the butchering technique of some aboriginal peoples. *American Antiquity* 19, 160–4.

Whittle, A. (1996) *Europe in the Neolithic*. Cambridge: Cambridge University Press.

(1997) Moving on and moving around: Neolithic settlement mobility. In: P. Topping (ed.), *Neolithic Landscapes*. Oxford: Oxbow, pp. 15–22.

Widga, C., Walker, J.D. and Stockli, L.D. (2010) Middle Holocene Bison diet and mobility in the eastern Great Plains (USA) based on $\delta^{13}C$, $\delta^{18}O$, and $^{87}Sr/^{86}Sr$ analyses of tooth enamel carbonate. *Quaternary Research* 73(3), 449–63.

Wilkinson, P.F. (1972) Current experimental domestication and its relevance to prehistory. In: E.S. Higgs (ed.), *Papers in Economic Prehistory: Studies by Members and Associates of the British Academy Major Research Project in the Early History of Agriculture*. Cambridge: Cambridge University Press, pp. 107–18.

Willerslev, R., Vitebsky, P. and Alekseyev, A. (2015) Sacrifice as the ideal hunt: a cosmological explanation for the origin of reindeer domestication. *Journal of the Royal Anthropological Institute* 21(1), 1–23.

Winterhalder, B. (1986) Diet choice, risk, and food sharing in a stochastic environment. *Journal of Anthropological Archaeology* 5(4), 369–92.

Woodward, S.R., Weyand, N.J. and Bunnell, M. (1994) DNA sequence from Cretaceous period bone fragments. *Science* 266(5188), 1229–32.

Wu, Y., Jiang, L., Zheng, Y., Wang, C. and Zhao, Z. (2014) Morphological trend analysis of rice phytolith during the early Neolithic in the Lower Yangtze. *Journal of Archaeological Science* 49, 326–31.

Xie, S., Nott, C.J., Avsejs, L. A., Maddy, D., Chambers, F.M. and Evershed, R.P. (2004) Molecular and isotopic stratigraphy in an ombrotrophic mire for paleoclimate reconstruction. *Geochimica et Cosmochimica Acta* 68(13), 2849–62.

Yevdokimov, V.V. and Varfolomeev, V.V. (2002) *Ehpoxa Bronzy Central'novo i Cevernovo Kazaxstana*, Karaganda: E.A. Bukatov Karaganda State University.

Yohe, R.M. and Bamforth, D.B. (2013) Late Pleistocene protein residues from the Mahaffy cache, Colorado. *Journal of Archaeological Science* 40(5), 2337–43.

Young, D.L., Huyen, Y. and Allard, M.W. (1995) Testing the validity of the cytochrome b sequence from Cretaceous period bone fragments as dinosaur DNA. *Cladistics* 11(2), 199–209.

Zaibert, V.F. (2009) *Botaiskaya Kultura*. Almaty: KazAkparat.

Zaibert, V.F., Tyulevaev, A., Zadorozhnyj, A.V. and Kulakov, U. (2007) *Tajny Drevnyej Stepi: Issledovaniya Poseleniya Botaj (2004–2006)*. Kokshetau: Kokshetau University.

Zarky, A. (1976) Statistical analysis of site catchments at Ocos, Guatemala. In: K.V. Flannery (ed.), *The Early Mesoamerican Village*. New York: Academic Press, pp. 117–28.

Zazzo, A., Bendrey, R., Vella, D., Moloney, A.P., Monahan, F.J. and Schmidt, O. (2012) A refined sampling strategy for intra-tooth stable isotope analysis of mammalian enamel. *Geochimica et Cosmochimica Acta* 84, 1–13.

Zazzo, A., Cerling, T.E., Ehleringer, J.R., Moloney, A.P., Monahan, F.J. and Schmidt, O. (2015) Isotopic composition of sheep wool records seasonality of climate and diet. *Rapid Communications in Mass Spectrometry* 29(15), 1357–69.

Zeder, M.A. (2012a) The broad spectrum revolution at 40: resource diversity, intensification, and an alternative to optimal foraging explanations. *Journal of Anthropological Archaeology* 31(3), 241–64.

(2012b). The domestication of animals. *Journal of Anthropological Research* 68(2), 161–90.

Zeder, M.A. and Lapham, H.A. (2010) Assessing the reliability of criteria used to identify postcranial bones in sheep, *Ovis*, and goats, *Capra*. *Journal of Archaeological Science* 37(11), 2887–905.

Zhao, Z., Pearsall, D.M., Benfer, R.A. Jr. and Piperno, D. (1998) Distinguishing rice (*Oryza sativa* Poaceae) from wild *Oryza* species through phytolith analysis, II: finalised method. *Economic Botany* 52, 134–45.

Ziesemer, K.A., Mann, A.E., Sankaranarayanan, K., Schroeder, H., Ozga, A.T., Brandt, B.W., et al. (2015) Intrinsic challenges in ancient microbiome reconstruction using 16S rRNA gene amplification. *Scientific Reports* 5, 16498.

Zischler, H., Hoss, M., Handt, O., von Haeseler, A., van der Kuyl, A.C., Goudsmit, J. and Pääbo, S. (1995) Detecting dinosaur DNA. *Science* 268 (5214), 1192–3.

Zohary, D. and Hopf, M. (1988) *Domestication of Plants in the Old World*. Oxford: Clarendon.

Zvelebil, M. (1986) Mesolithic prelude and Neolithic revolution. In: M. Zvelebil (ed.), *Hunters in Transition: Mesolithic Societies of Temperate Eurasia and their Transition to Farming*. Cambridge: Cambridge University Press, pp. 5–16.

(1995) Hunting, gathering and husbandry? Management and food resources by the late Mesolithic communities of temperate Europe. In: D.V. Campana (ed.), *Before Farming: Hunter-Gatherer Society and Subsistence*. Philadelphia, PA: MASCA, pp. 79–104.

(1998) Agricultural frontiers, Neolithic origins, and the transition to farming in the Baltic Basin. In: M. Zvelebil, R. Dennell and L. Domańska (eds), *Harvesting the Sea, Farming the Forest: The Emergence of Neolithic Societies in the Baltic region*. Sheffield: Sheffield Academic Press, pp. 9–28.

Zvelebil, M. and Rowley-Conwy, P. (1984) Transition to farming in northern Europe: a hunter-gatherer perspective. *Norwegian Archaeological Review* 17, 104–28.

(1986) Foragers and farmers in Atlantic Europe. In: M. Zvelebil (ed.), *Hunters in Transition: Mesolithic Societies of Temperate Eurasia and their Transition to Farming*. Cambridge: Cambridge University Press, pp. 67–93.

Index

For EU product safety concerns, contact us at Calle de José Abascal, 56–1°,
28003 Madrid, Spain or eugpsr@cambridge.org.

www.ingramcontent.com/pod-product-compliance
Lightning Source LLC
LaVergne TN
LVHW011810200926
848484LV00005B/1127

* 9 7 8 1 1 0 7 1 2 8 7 7 4 *